Praise for *Reimagining Buddhism: Understanding Sangharakshita and His Teachings*

This book sensitively and critically examines one of the most important figures in Buddhism's twentieth-century transmission to Britain. It throws light on Sangharakshita as poet, mystic, creative spiritual thinker, innovator, and the architect of what is now the Triratna Buddhist Community. It is also unafraid to ask difficult questions about Sangharakshita's complex character. This should be essential reading for anyone interested in Buddhism's presence in the west. – **Elizabeth J. Harris**, University of Birmingham, President of the UK Association for Buddhist Studies

Vishvapani has discovered a golden thread running through Sangharakshita's work, which is the image of organic growth, common to Buddhism and Romantic poetry. *Reimagining Buddhism* uses that thread to explore Sangharakshita's whole approach to the Dharma and to founding a new movement. This is a breakthrough work of study, reflection, and synthesis. – **Dhivan Thomas Jones**, author of *This Being, That Becomes*

A thoroughly enjoyable, stimulating look at one of the West's principle Buddhist teachers. Vishvapani views the life of Sangharakshita through the prism of Sangharakshita's use of images, exploring his poems and personal writings as well as his teachings. I personally knew Sangharakshita for over forty years and yet I still found new treasures here. Vishvapani doesn't shy away from the criticisms and controversies but puts these in the context of the whole personality of Sangharakshita. – **Dharmacharini Anagarika Parami**, senior teacher in Triratna, Chair of the Glasgow Buddhist Centre, and member of the College of Public Preceptors

Following the publication of Sangharakshita's *Complete Works* this is a book many of us have been waiting for, and it will become an essential text for all interested in the development of Buddhism in its engagement with Western culture. Vishvapani brings intellectual rigour, beautiful writing, and incisive thought alongside his personal devotion to and practice of the Dharma. – **The Rev'd Canon Richard Peers,** former Dean of Llandaff Cathedral

Self-confessedly a complex man, it seemed impossible even for those of us who worked closely with Sangharakshita to encompass his remarkable depth as well as his human personality, at times arguably flawed. This book successfully reveals something of the inner force that moved him. It will certainly help both his disciples and his critics understand better who he really is. – **Subhuti**, President London Buddhist Centre and Adhisthana, author of *Sangharakshita: A New Voice in the Buddhist Tradition* and *Mind in Harmony*

Vishvapani opens the door to the rich treasury of Sangharakshita's legacy, revealing previously obscure gems and shedding fresh light on familiar facets of Sangharakshita's teaching. A book to which I will keep returning! – **Prajnaketu**, author of *Cyberloka: A Buddhist Guide to Digital Life*

In a clear, accessible, and detailed exploration, Vishvapani offers a thought-provoking account of how the diverse expressions of Buddhism in the East came alive in the imagination of Sangharakshita, resulting in a new international Buddhist movement. Without shying away from the documented challenges, Vishvapani guides us to a deeper understanding of Sangharakshita's formidable spirit, as well as the breadth of his approach to sharing the truth. – **Suryagupta**, Chair of the London Buddhist Centre

With a rare combination of careful reading, meticulous research, and generous imagination, Vishvapani invites us to understand his subject in entirely new ways. I have been familiar with Sangharakshita's life and writings for more than forty years, but I was surprised, delighted, and sometimes troubled by the fresh perspectives and insights of this accessible yet profound, lively yet substantial book. – **Vidyadevi**, editor of Sangharakshita's *Complete Works*

REIMAGINING BUDDHISM
Understanding Sangharakshita and his teachings

VISHVAPANI BLOMFIELD

Windhorse Publications
38 Newmarket Road
Cambridge CB5 8DT
info@windhorsepublications.com
windhorsepublications.com

© Vishvapani Blomfield, 2025

The right of Vishvapani Blomfield to be identified as the author of this work has been asserted by him in accordance with the Copyright, Designs and Patents Act 1988.

No portion of this book may be utilized in any form for the training, development, enhancement, or operation of any artificial intelligence technologies. This prohibition includes all forms of AI, including generative models, neural networks, and any other types of computational intelligence. This restriction extends to all methods of obtaining or utilizing data, including but not limited to data scraping, data mining, direct or indirect observation, manual entry, or any innovative data sourcing techniques that might be developed in the future.

Cover design: Dhammarati
Cover image: Photograph of Sangharakshita by J.O. Mallander, 1993, courtesy of Urgyen Sangharakshita Trust.
Typesetting by Tarajyoti

British Library Cataloguing in Publication Data:
A catalogue record for this book is available from the British Library.

ISBN 978-1-915342-45-4

All quotations from Windhorse Publications titles are reprinted by permission of Windhorse Publications.

Contents

About the Author   vii
Author's Acknowledgements   viii
Publisher's Acknowledgements   ix
A Note on Terminology   x

Introduction: Meeting Sangharakshita   1

Part One   **Living in the Stream**   23
Chapter One   Meeting the Guru   25
Chapter Two   Western Buddhism   51
Chapter Three   Actions and Consequences   77

Part Two   **Imagining the Path**   91
Chapter Four   Consciousness and the Path   93
Chapter Five   The Illumined Path   111
Chapter Six   Love and Beauty   127
Chapter Seven   Imagination and the Path   143
Chapter Eight   Sangharakshita's Imagination   155

Part Three   **Tracing the Path**   167
Chapter Nine   The Unity of Buddhism   169
Chapter Ten   Conditionality and the Path   199
Chapter Eleven   The Path in Practice   217
Chapter Twelve   Growth and Development   231
Chapter Thirteen   Wider Contexts   249
Chapter Fourteen   Imagining the Buddha   261

Part Four	**Creating a Movement**	273
Chapter Fifteen	Sangharakshita's Roles	275
Chapter Sixteen	Spiritual Community	287
Chapter Seventeen	Alternative Traditions	319
Chapter Eighteen	Seeds and Flowers	335

Notes 341

Bibliography 367

Index 373

About the Author

Vishvapani is the author of *Gautama Buddha: The Life and Teachings of the Awakened One* (Quercus, 2011) and the editor of *Challenging Times: Stories of Buddhist Practice When Things Get Tough* (Windhorse Publications, 2006). Since 2006 he has been the Buddhist contributor to BBC Radio 4's 'Thought for the Day'.

He lives in Cardiff with his wife and son, and his work over the years has included mindfulness teaching, writing, broadcasting, leading pilgrimages to the Buddhist holy places, and holding central positions within the Triratna Buddhist Community. He became a Buddhist as a teenager and was ordained into the Triratna Buddhist Order in 1992.

Author's Acknowledgements

I am grateful to everyone involved in producing *The Complete Works of Sangharakshita*, especially the principal editors: Vidyadevi, Kalyanaprabha, and Pabodhana. The project is a huge achievement that makes Sangharakshita's work far more easily available. The vast *Concordance* that is volume 27, compiled by Vidyadevi, appeared a few weeks before I finished writing, and helped me on the final stretch. Satyalila's indexes were also very helpful. I must also thank everyone at Windhorse Publications who worked both on the *Complete Works* project and on this book.

I am indebted to Nagabodhi and Dhivan for their insightful comments on the text at various stages of development, for their own work on the topics I cover, and for conversations over many years. I am also indebted to Dhammamegha for her comments from a publisher's perspective. Subhuti was extraordinarily generous with both his time and his attention. I thank him for that, and for everything I have learned from him over the years.

I thank Jayaraja, who organized a fundraising campaign to help me complete the book, and everyone who contributed to that campaign, including the community at Adhiṣṭhāna. Special thanks go to Dhivati, who established a fund administered by the Triratna Order convenors that made a grant, which also helped me write.

Finally, I thank my wife Kamalagita, my son, and my Order chapter, who had to put up with me through the writing process.

Publisher's Acknowledgements

We would like to thank the individuals who supported this book through our 'Sponsor-a-book' campaign (www.windhorsepublications.com/sponsor) and the Friends of Windhorse Publications initiative (www.windhorsepublications.com/friends).

Windhorse Publications wish to gratefully acknowledge a grant from Future Dharma and the Triratna European Chairs' Assembly Fund towards the production of this book.

A Note on Terminology

Names change, and in the course of his life Dennis Lingwood became Anagārika Dharmapriya, Bhikkhu Sangharakshita, and Urgyen Sangharakshita. For simplicity, this book calls him Sangharakshita throughout his life.

The name of the movement he founded also changed from Friends of the Western Sangha to Friends of the Western Buddhist Order (or 'FWBO'), and then the Triratna Buddhist Community (or 'Triratna'). I use the name that was current in the period I discuss, and 'the FWBO/Triratna' when both names apply.

The early Buddhist texts are often referred to as 'the Pāli Canon', but they exist in languages other than Pāli, and the Chinese *Āgama*s are increasingly recognized as an important recension of these texts, along with the Pāli *Nikāya*s. Following scholarly practice, this book refers to these early sources as 'the Discourses'. Strictly speaking, 'the Pāli Canon' includes the Vinaya and Abhidhamma as well as the suttas, but 'the Discourses' refers to the suttas and their Chinese equivalents.

Spirit and letter are interdependent. Divorced from the living spirit of the Master's teaching, the letter of the Dharma, however faithfully transmitted, is dead, a thing of idle words and empty concepts: separated from its concrete embodiment in the letter, the spirit of the Dharma, however exalted, lacking a medium of communication is rendered inoperative. In writing about Buddhism one should therefore be careful to pay equal attention to both aspects. The ideal account would in fact show spiritual experiences crystallizing into concrete doctrinal and disciplinary forms and these resolving themselves back into spiritual experiences. Full justice would then be done both to the letter and to the spirit of the tradition.

Sangharakshita, *The Three Jewels*[1]

Introduction

Meeting Sangharakshita

Last words

On 10 November 2018 I travelled from my home in Cardiff to Adhiṣṭhāna – the retreat centre complex in Herefordshire where Sangharakshita spent his final years. He had died eleven days earlier, aged ninety-three, and his body was laid out in a shrine room beside the Sangharakshita Library building – home to the thousands of books he accumulated in a life of studying, teaching, and practising Buddhism.

The room was kept cool, which meant there was no need to embalm Sangharakshita's body. It was gaunt and the skin was stretched tight, but, in most respects, he was remarkably unchanged. People quietly entered the room to sit with him and left just as quietly. The atmosphere was calm with a hint of solemnity, and, sitting beside his body, I was moved by the fullness of Sangharakshita's life and the many ways it had influenced my own. Through his teachings I had learned to practise Buddhism and, though I could have learned this from another teacher, his way of expressing Buddhism spoke to me as no other version did. I was happy he seemed to be resting so peacefully and sensed (or maybe I simply imagined) a benign and tranquil presence filling the room. I knew the people around me would also be reflecting on what they had gained in meetings with Sangharakshita or through his books, lectures, and the Triratna movement that he founded.

Later in the day, over 1,000 people, including representatives of numerous Buddhist traditions, attended the funeral ceremony while many others watched on video links. A rainbow shimmered in the sky as his body was interred – buried, not cremated – in a space that would be surmounted by a mound recalling the earliest Buddhist stupas. Visitors reported double rainbows as they headed home.

◦ ◦ ◦

I offer this vignette as a partial explanation for this book. It isn't a work of discipleship in a simple sense, and it offers appraisal along with approval; but it is, nonetheless, the product of a lifetime's engagement with the Friends of the Western Buddhist Order (FWBO), the Buddhist movement that changed its name in 2010 to the Triratna Buddhist Community. I was ordained into the Triratna Buddhist Order in 1992 and have been active as an Order member ever since. Throughout that time, I have read, studied, and reflected on Sangharakshita, and for seven years, from 1999 to 2005, I lived at Madhyamaloka community, a large house in suburban Birmingham that, for two decades, was a sort of headquarters for the FWBO. Sangharakshita lived in an annex to the main building, either alone or with a companion, and, for the first three years I lived there, he joined the community for an evening meal.

Another incident from the day of the funeral suggests the complexity involved in taking Sangharakshita as a subject – at least for me. I travelled to Adhiṣṭhāna by way of a BBC radio studio where I was interviewed for an obituary programme called 'Last Word' that was featuring Sangharakshita.[1] Having discussed his qualities and achievements, the conversation turned to the subject that dogged his reputation: the period between 1968 and the mid-1980s when he was sexually active with male students. I told the interviewer I thought his behaviour had been ill-judged, painful for some of his sexual partners (at least in the long term), and disastrous for his wider standing. It was hard to balance appreciation and criticism and give an accurate sense of this remarkable but complicated man.

◦ ◦ ◦

Many of those drawn to a religious movement seek guidance from a wise and compassionate teacher but, for better or worse, I am more sceptical and cautious. I want to think for myself, but am also drawn by a feeling for spiritual experience and the knowledge that I can't navigate it alone. I encountered the FWBO as a teenager and quickly felt it was my spiritual home. That has never left me. I've witnessed mistakes and ethical breaches, but never doubted the movement's basic integrity.

The same is true of Sangharakshita, whom I got to know personally when I lived at Madhyamaloka. Our shared cultural interests made a connection between us, and conversations after dinner could range through reflections, poems, sutras, ideas, and memories, drawing out Sangharakshita's knowledge and showing its aliveness for him. But the conversations revolved around him and, especially when visitors were present, they could be painfully stilted.

A personal meeting with Sangharakshita was different. He sat in his upstairs room at Madhyamaloka, books overflowing their shelves, surrounded by buddha images, curios, and the semi-precious gemstones he enjoyed for their colour and symbolism. He was kindly and interested, speaking with care, weighing each word and measuring each thought. I felt my thoughts slow to his pace and, if I challenged him, my arguments sometimes seemed superficial when set within the large space of his awareness.

In 2005 I left Madhyamaloka, devoted myself to writing, and then became a mindfulness teacher. I also married and became a father. I was no less a Buddhist, but I felt distanced from Sangharakshita mainly because of my experience as a spokesman for the FWBO when criticisms of his sexual behaviour surfaced in 1997 and 2003. I knew a straightforward response should include an element of apology, but found it impossible to speak straightforwardly when Sangharakshita himself was unwilling to respond.

The criticisms revived in the UK media in 2016, prompting another round of soul-searching within the Order. I supported a group of senior Order members who investigated what had happened and addressed it as fully as possible.[2] I also started writing an account of Triratna that, rather than focusing on Sangharakshita himself, outlined the tenets of 'Triratna Buddhism'. It was an impossible task. I recognized that his thought grew from his lived experience rather than abstract principles and often addressed matters of spiritual life that could scarcely be formulated at all. I saw that what drew me to his teaching wasn't his interpretation of the Buddhist tradition, ethical guidance, meditation instruction, or even the project of 'western Buddhism'. It was his imagination.

Thinking in images

The first time I heard Sangharakshita speak was in November 1980. I was two weeks away from my sixteenth birthday and had been a mitra (literally 'friend') within the Friends of the Western Buddhist Order for four months. A year earlier I had started attending meditation classes in an FWBO centre close to my home in the South London suburb of Croydon. The energetic and idealistic people I met spoke about 'growth and development' – the same language I had learned from my psychotherapist parents – and their enthusiastic talk of building a 'New Society' echoed my parents' socialism.

On my way home from school I often dropped in to the Buddhist centre to help in the restaurant and perhaps attend a class. The name 'Bhante' – referring to Sangharakshita – was on everyone's lips, often spoken with hushed respect, and the phrase 'Bhante says ...' peppered the conversation.[3] At classes we sometimes listened to a recording of one of his lectures, and I became familiar with his distinctive and rather odd way of speaking: methodical, precise, and at the same time insistent, his London vowels inflected by some other rhythm – perhaps the product of the two decades he spent in India, or perhaps a more individual idiosyncrasy.

This evening was special. Sangharakshita, aged fifty-five, was giving a talk with the intriguing title 'The Taste of Freedom', so I travelled with others to Caxton Hall in Central London. Since 1975 Sangharakshita had lived in a country retreat centre in Norfolk called Padmaloka while Order members led activities at FWBO centres like the one I attended. Each year, he gave one or more public talks, and the themes he introduced prompted earnest discussions across the movement.

By 1980 Sangharakshita's period of intensive teaching was ending, and he hadn't given a public talk like this for over a year. Men and women in their twenties and thirties filled the lobby at Caxton Hall, having travelled from FWBO sanghas across the UK: up from Brighton, down from Glasgow and Norwich, and across

London from the imposing new London Buddhist Centre that had opened two years earlier. They hugged old friends, shared news of their projects, and spoke excitedly about the lecture.

Sangharakshita took the stage, a bespectacled middle-aged man with a slightly bulbous nose, wearing a brown woollen jacket over a beige turtle-neck. A golden band hung around his neck – a version of the *kesa*s all Order members wore. He spoke vigorously and with precision, starting characteristically with a question: 'What is Buddhism?' Historically, he said, Buddhism was known as the Dharma, and the Buddha's best definition was not a concept but an image. His text was the *Uposatha Sutta*, a discourse given by the Buddha, set down in the Pāli language and included in a collection known as the *Udāna*.[4] The Buddha and a group of monks are sitting together deep into the night, until an incident prompts the Buddha to speak. He describes the ocean, identifying eight characteristics, each of which he then applies to the Dharma. Sangharakshita's subject was the sixth: just as the ocean has a single, distinctive taste – the taste of salt – the Dharma is marked by the taste of freedom.

The rest of the lecture concerned freedom as it is discussed in the Buddhist tradition, touching on Buddhist ideas and Sangharakshita's expressions of them. Its centre was a series of images, and images within images, the first being the ocean itself. In the *Uposatha Sutta* the Buddha says the ocean is strange and wonderful. It invites us to swim in it, but the fetters of fixed self-view, doubt, and attachment to rites and rituals hold us back. All the same, Sangharakshita declared, it was within our capacity to free ourselves from these bonds: 'If you practise the *Dharma-Vinaya* you will yourself become free.'[5]

The talk culminated in an image of liberation drawn from the Buddhist Tantra:

> If we were then to visualize an image of that quintessential spirit, we would begin with the image of space or the image of the usual way we perceive space: the sky, infinite in extent, deep blue in colour, and perfectly pure. In the midst of this image there would be another image: a figure flying through the sky. It is a naked, red figure, a female figure. Her long

black hair is streaming out behind her, her face is uplifted in ecstasy, and there is a smile on her lips. She is what is known in Buddhist tradition as the *ḍākinī* or 'lady of space', the embodiment of the spiritual energy of the Buddha. She is absolutely free: free to fly in any direction – north, south, east, west, the zenith, and the nadir. She is free, even, to remain still. Hers is the liberty of infinite space. She enjoys the Taste of Freedom.[6]

Sangharakshita seemed to know what he was describing and to be telling me I could experience this freedom for myself. I just needed to engage in the steady work of Buddhist practice and open myself to a dimension of experience the images expressed. By the talk's conclusion I felt I had entered the world he described.

Seeking Sangharakshita

'The Taste of Freedom' introduced me to Buddhism as an act of the imagination. This was a distinctive part of Sangharakshita's presentation, and this book explores it as a key to understanding Sangharakshita himself. 'The Taste of Freedom' is a helpful starting point because the purpose of its imagery is to evoke a more primary reality. Like the ocean, he says, the Dharma is strange:

> It is something of which we have only heard. It is foreign to us; it is not our native element. Indeed, the Buddha himself is strange to us. He is a stranger in an ultimate sense. He comes from another world, another dimension, as it were. He stands at our door, perhaps, but we do not recognize him.

The Dharma is also wonderful:

> continually speaking to us, singing to us, playing its own inimitable music to us, in its own indescribably appealing and fascinating way. It is no dull religious monument; it is alive with all sorts of brilliant and tender lights, all sorts of vivid and delicate colours.[7]

Throughout his work Sangharakshita keeps returning to the Dharma's beauty, aliveness, and indefinability. He frequently describes how, as a bespectacled teenager seeking esoteric wisdom in wartime London, he stumbled into the 'aloof, reserved, almost mysterious'[8] Watkins bookshop, just off Charing Cross Road in Central London, where an aged man in thick spectacles sat beneath a large portrait of Mme Blavatsky, the founder of theosophy. He bought a volume including translations of the *Diamond Sutra* and the *Platform Sutra*. It was filled with 'bad grammar, faulty syntax, and wrong use of words', but shining through its pages he sensed 'a light which is not of this world'.[9] Nothing he had previously encountered remotely approached the *Diamond Sutra*:

> The truth was here, not in the sense of a particular set of words, teachings, or doctrines, but in the sense of some metaphysical or transcendental dimension suggested by the words, hinted at by the thoughts and ideas and teachings, which was essentially beyond them all but nevertheless in some way communicated or mediated by them.[10]

In one place he says the sutra's impact is 'like a thunderbolt, crushing and destroying you'[11] but, judging by the account in his memoirs, he could encompass its message:

> Though this book epitomizes a teaching of such rarified sublimity that even *arhants*, saints who have attained individual Nirvāṇa, are said to become confused and afraid when they hear of it for the first time, I at once joyfully embraced it with an unqualified acceptance and assent.[12]

While Sangharakshita never claimed to be enlightened, to say that one has joyfully embraced a truth that confuses *arahants* is to say a great deal – and not just that one has an affinity with the path of the bodhisattva rather than that of the *arahant*.[13] These works offered Sangharakshita his 'first direct insight into the true nature of reality'[14] – the essential truth, beyond concepts, to which all Buddhist teachings refer. From that point on, he 'had no doubts about Buddhism, or about the spiritual path'.[15] He commented on the *Diamond Sutra* in 1970: 'It is as though the Dharma touches some spring in you, opens something up that was hitherto blocked, melts something that was congealed, frees up energy that was imprisoned.'[16] From this point he was 'drawn forward, never doubting the direction'.[17]

The *Diamond Sutra* gave Sangharakshita an enduring sense of the 'metaphysical or transcendental dimension' and the 'spiritual or transcendental experience'[18] that are embodied in the Buddha, Dharma, and Sangha – collectively known as 'the Three Jewels'. Everything that followed in Sangharakshita's life rested on this foundation, and his thought, as it developed over the following seventy-six years, explored its implications. From his earliest writings to his final papers, he returned to the same fundamental concerns.

Sangharakshita's most important expression of his outlook as a Buddhist is the 1988 paper *The History of My Going for Refuge*. It traces how he found an understanding of Buddhism that placed the transcendental perspective he glimpsed through reading the *Diamond Sutra* at the heart of his life. Like most Buddhists, he was introduced to going for refuge to the Three Jewels as a relatively insignificant preliminary practice, but came to regard it as 'the central and definitive act of the Buddhist life'.[19]

Several things follow that are relevant to the present book. Firstly, going for refuge is an *act* rather than a principle or a doctrine. Sangharakshita often used concepts and abstractions, but he was alert to the danger that,

> forgetting that the concepts of the mind are simply instruments for the realization of certain purposes, we begin endowing them with a life of their own, and treat them as though they possessed independent existence and inherent validity.[20]

The closest Sangharakshita came to defining his fundamental philosophical position was to say that he stressed 'the primacy of experience over thoughts' – a position he identified with Madhyamaka philosophy.[21] The meaning of the Three Jewels can only be discovered by an individual through their spiritual experience, and *The History* takes the form of a narrative, rather than a doctrinal exposition, because that conveys his understanding of Buddhism as he had come by it – through concrete experience rather than abstract reasoning.

Secondly, Sangharakshita's focus on the essential elements of Buddhism implies a critical perspective on the Buddhist tradition. He kept insisting that, however sophisticated they may be, Buddhist teachings and practices were merely methods for realizing buddhahood. They were metaphors rather than definitive truths, fingers pointing towards the moon rather than the moon itself, or a raft whose purpose is to let travellers cross a river. All Buddhist schools would accept this principle, but Sangharakshita felt it intuitively and pursued its implications rigorously. He thought everything through for himself, weighing the Buddhist schools to distinguish when their teachings truly pointed towards a transcendental experience and when their attention was fixed on the finger. The rest of his views follow from that.

This makes engagement with metaphor and symbolism particularly important within the Buddhist path. Sangharakshita's 1961 book *The Three Jewels* discusses four ways in which Buddhist sources express nirvāṇa. The predominant method in the early sources is 'negative' (i.e. calling it the 'unborn', 'uncompounded', 'unbecome', and so on), but this seemingly suggests that nirvāṇa is simply a negation of ordinary experience. A second approach expresses it positively, as a form of knowledge, liberation, energy, or feeling, personifying it as 'an absolute person', or presenting it in terms of consciousness. Sangharakshita was drawn to positive expressions like these but recognized that they risk presenting nirvāṇa as a 'thing'. A third alternative is the esoteric method of defining the spiritual goal in paradoxical terms that make no rational sense. The final approach is using 'the language not of abstractions but of concrete images'. The merit of this approach is that images declare their non-literal character and encourage an expansive understanding:

> While negative descriptions of absolute whiteness tell us
> it is not black, positive ones that it is like milk or snow
> only whiter, and paradoxical ones that it is in reality a

non-whiteness, symbolical or poetical descriptions exhibit before us all the magic colours of the rainbow.[22]

Sangharakshita often used symbols in this way. 'The Taste of Freedom' shows him at his most characteristic, exploring the unique capacity of images to evoke something beyond their literal meaning, and it is just one of hundreds of talks and seminars he gave in the two decades following his return to the UK in 1964 that form the centre of his work. They often establish a rational framework of understanding before drawing listeners into a non-conceptual, image-based mode. Some talks explore the imagery of Buddhist teachings and texts to distil their essential message – 'Archetypal Symbolism in the Biography of the Buddha', 'Parables, Myths, and Symbols of Mahāyāna Buddhism in the *White Lotus Sutra*', or 'Creative Symbols of the Tantric Path to Enlightenment'.[23] In part, this is a stylistic choice, and many of his talks and writings have a different emphasis; in part, it was a way of introducing his audience to a subtler form of understanding than concepts, one that was better suited to addressing spiritual experience:

> The language of symbolism is a language that we too have to learn to speak. We may be ready, even glib, with the language of ideas and concepts – we may discuss Buddhist philosophy endlessly – but this must be complemented by the language of images. This dimension of communication may be comparatively unfamiliar to us, but by immersing ourselves in legends, myths, and symbols, we can learn to understand and even speak that language.[24]

• • •

Sangharakshita resists easy categorization. He was a thinker but not a philosopher; he commented on many Buddhist scriptures but didn't pass on the teachings of a particular school; as a Dharma teacher he drew extensively on Buddhist scholarship but considered it merely a tool for understanding Buddhism's outer expressions. The object of both devotion and controversy, his innovations could exasperate conservatives while his conservative temperament dissatisfied modernizers. He was part of a generation of westerners who studied with spiritual teachers in Asia after the Second World War and a unique figure whose contribution to western Buddhism fits none of its usual categories.

This book approaches Sangharakshita as a symbolic, or imaginative, thinker. He was as much a poet as a prose writer until he was thirty, and his developing consciousness was influenced by Blake, Shelley, Yeats, and others in the extended Romantic tradition. From them, he learned to recognize what Coleridge calls 'the danger of thinking without images'[25] and to master the alternative, which is thinking with images, or even thinking *in* images. The faculty that enables this has no obvious Buddhist name, and Sangharakshita drew on western sources in speaking of it as intuition, or imagination.

Whether or not these are always necessary to achieving the wisdom Buddhism describes, they were Sangharakshita's way of doing so, at least on the level of his fundamental orientation. As a Dharma teacher he was sensitive to the range of his students' temperaments, but his teaching is inseparable from his distinctive 'spiritual temperament'. My intention is not to suggest that his teaching expressed merely his subjective biases: his overriding concerns were distinguishing the true meaning of the Dharma and communicating it to others, and, if he was an imaginative thinker, he was also a very careful one. Nonetheless, this book is based on the premise that we see those teachings more clearly if we recognize the character that shaped them and its interaction with the needs to which Sangharakshita responded.

Characterizing that temperament involves a degree of interpretation, but Sangharakshita was unusually able to characterize himself. At the start of *The History*, he says he must explain why he has approached his subject through a narrative, and offers an anecdote:

> Some years ago an astrologer friend drew my birth chart, and according to this chart I had most of my planets below the horizon, which apparently meant that the influences which these planets represented were operating not in the field of consciousness but below it.

Leaving aside the merits of astrology, Sangharakshita says this accurately described how he experienced the world. Intuition guided his actions, and the course of his life – including his work as a teacher and the founder of a Buddhist movement – had been determined 'by impulse and intuition rather than by reason and logic'.[26]

The epigraph that prefaces *The History* suggests what 'intuition' meant to Sangharakshita. It is a quotation from a book by a favourite writer, John Middleton Murry, that describes Murry's spiritual crisis after the death of his wife, the short-story writer Katherine Mansfield. Guided by his literary heroes, Shakespeare and the English Romantic poets, Murry discovered what it meant to follow his intuition or 'instinct', and the passage Sangharakshita quotes sums up his understanding:

> To discover that within myself which I *must* obey, to gain some awareness of the law which operates in the organic whole of the internal world, to feel this internal world as an organic whole working out its own destiny according to some secret vital principle, to know which acts and utterances are a liberation from obstacles and an accession of strength, to acknowledge secret loyalties which one cannot deny without impoverishment and starvation – this is to possess one's soul indeed, and it is not easy either to do or to explain.[27]

The passage presents intuition as a guiding faculty that connects a deeply felt understanding with a reality that cannot be grasped in any other way, and in quoting it Sangharakshita implied that a 'secret vital principle' guided his own life, and that he experienced his own 'internal world' as an 'organic whole'. In Sangharakshita's life as *The History* recounts it, this principle was 'going for refuge to the Three Jewels', or perhaps the impulse to realize what these Three Jewels represent. Being intuitive, Sangharakshita says, he came to this realization through a meandering progression, which he likens to the butterfly in Yeats's poem 'Tom O'Roughley'. The butterfly zigzags from flower to flower and symbolizes the psyche or soul, unlike the hawk, which 'hurls itself straight on its prey, and symbolizes the logical mind'.[28] Consequently, Sangharakshita explains in *The History*:

I shall not simply be tracing a series of logical deductions from – or even of more and more extensive practical applications of – a concept or principle comprehended in its fullness, and in all its bearings, from the very beginning.[29]

The progress he describes is guided by intuition in Murry's sense, or what Sangharakshita called in 1950 'a purely spiritual perception of spiritual realities by the inner spiritual sense'.[30]

• • •

It is possible to overstate the extent to which Sangharakshita was intuitive as opposed to rational, and both aspects were important to him. His memoirs describe the tension he felt as a newly ordained bhikkhu between two sides of his character, which he called Sangharakshita I and Sangharakshita II:

Sangharakshita I wanted to enjoy the beauty of nature, to read and write poetry, to listen to music, to look at paintings and sculpture, to experience emotion, to lie in bed and dream, to see places, to meet people. Sangharakshita II wanted to realize the truth, to read and write philosophy, to observe the precepts, to get up early and meditate, to mortify the flesh, to fast and pray.[31]

If Sangharakshita I represented emotion and intuition, Sangharakshita II combined rigorous rationality with will. The tension resolved itself quickly, at least on one level, and before long he was composing versified translations from Pāli, writing serious-minded poems, and producing essays like *The Religion of Art*, which triumphantly declares: 'Art and religion overlap.'[32] But the psychological conflict between the two Sangharakshitas points to a deeper tension that is evident throughout his life.

In his compendious *Book of Enlightened Masters*, the religious scholar Andrew Rawlinson discusses Sangharakshita along with many other western teachers of Asian spiritual traditions. Placing him in this context, Rawlinson says Sangharakshita's approach is 'structured' because it depends on an underlying belief in an inherent order.[33] In other words, Sangharakshita understood reality to be governed by the regular pattern of actions and consequences, or 'conditionality', and his teachings mainly express this patterned understanding. We see this in his emphasis on following a path of regular steps, a graded approach to meditation, concern with the conditions that support effective Dharma practice and the methodical training for ordination. But Rawlinson also identifies a visionary, non-rational aspect of Sangharakshita's makeup that situates the patterning of reality within a sense of its mystery. He valued reason but considered it a tool that had inherent limitations: 'one penetrates beyond the rational by exhausting the resources of the rational mind.'[34] And *The Three Jewels* suggests:

> Concepts had therefore better be treated as symbols, the value of which lies not in their literal meaning so much as in their suggestiveness. They should be handled in the spirit not of logic but of poetry; not pushed hither and thither with grim calculation like pieces on a chessboard, but tossed lightly, playfully in the air like a juggler's multicoloured balls.[35]

The heart of this book is the discussion of Sangharakshita's teachings in Parts Two and Three, which traces what it meant for him to approach the profound issues that underlie the Buddhist path while doing justice to both structure and mystery. We shall see this combination in every aspect of his work.

The organic whole

This book will not subject Sangharakshita to sociological or psychoanalytic analysis, nor will it attempt to distil a philosophical system from his work. By his own testimony, Sangharakshita was a 'rather messy thinker'[36] and, for all his self-descriptions, he reflected, 'I am a rather complex person [...] [and] a mystery to myself, even if not to others.'[37] Presumably, he found himself a mystery because he was intuitive and the forces driving him were, to some degree, unconscious. He sometimes suggested that people might approach his work as they would approach that of a poet or novelist, and a paper entitled *Criticism East and West*, written in 1988 for a conference on 'Criticism in Crisis', indicates what he meant.[38] Having acknowledged his unfamiliarity with contemporary literary criticism, Sangharakshita quotes another essay by Murry that describes how he engaged with a writer. He read and absorbed their work until he sensed 'the central golden thread of a poet's being'. Then he entered a mystery:

> There is a wall, as it were, of dense, warm darkness before me – a darkness that is secretly alive and thrilling to the sense. This, I like to believe, is the reflection in myself of the darkness which broods over the poet's creative mind. It forms slowly and gradually gathers while I read his work. The sense of mystery deepens and deepens, but the quality of the mystery becomes more plain. There is a moment when, as though unconsciously and out of my control, the deeper rhythm of a poet's work, the rise and fall of the great moods that determined what he was and what he wrote, enter into me also. I feel his presence, I am obedient to it, and it seems to me as though the breathing of my spirit is at one with his.[39]

This is reading as discipleship. It asks us to enter a writer's imaginative world by using our own imagination. This emotional or experiential approach to reading is closer to the aesthetic criticism of Walter Pater or Oscar Wilde than to most academic literary criticism, but the Harvard critic Helen Vendler describes a similar approach in her book *Poets Thinking*:

> In justice to the poets, we must call what they do, in conceiving and completing the finished poem, an intricate form of thinking, even if that means expanding our idea of what thinking is. And if we are to understand a poem, we must reconstruct the anterior thinking that generated its surface, its 'visible core'. That thinking is always in process, always active. And it issues not in axioms, but in pictures of the human mind at work, recalling, evaluating and structuring experience. The evolving discoveries of a poem [...] can only be grasped by our participating in the process they unfold.[40]

Vendler also uses the phrases 'thinking in images' and 'image thinking' (which have much older antecedents) to account for what a poet does.[41]

Approaching Sangharakshita in the manner of Murry or Vendler means recognizing the golden thread at the core of his being and the anterior thinking linking it to his work. It means tracing how he finds the coherence of Buddhist teachings and practice by treating them as a living organism rather than a system or a mechanism. It means understanding his meaning through his images as well as his ideas, and tracing the patterns of image thinking that give his work its organic unity. And it means understanding that he saw Buddhist texts and teachings as ways of imagining reality that enable people to achieve the goals of the Buddhist life.

• • •

In one sense we cannot know the mind of another person, let alone trace their imagination, and this is especially true if that person possesses an inner life as deep as Sangharakshita's. He refers in his memoirs to the Tibetan tradition of distinguishing the outer, inner, and secret levels of biography, and observes that he lived on different levels:

> Though neither a saint nor a great teacher, I too had an outer, an inner, and a secret life (secret in the Tibetan Buddhist sense) and had, therefore, in principle, not only an outer and an inner biography but a secret one as well.[42]

He reflects that, for all their extent, his memoirs had a good deal to say about his outer life, rather less about his inner life, and very little about his secret life. To some degree it eluded even Sangharakshita himself, manifesting only in his dreams and his strongest poems.

Yet, from another perspective, we express our inner, and maybe even our secret, lives in everything we do. W.B. Yeats remarks in an essay on Shakespeare: 'I have often had the fancy that there is one myth for every man, which, if we but knew it, would make us understand all he did and thought.'⁴³ This is what we have come to call an archetypal way of viewing human consciousness, and the archetypal psychologist James Hillman says:

> It is as if consciousness rests upon a self-sustaining and imagining substrate – an inner place or deeper person or ongoing presence – that is simply there even when all our subjectivity, ego, and consciousness go into eclipse.⁴⁴

In this sense, we understand a person best when we recognize that mythic substrate, whether or not the person is wholly conscious of it.

Reading the *Diamond Sutra* and the *Platform Sutra* was the central transformative experience of Sangharakshita's life, not just because of what he learned from the texts but because they reminded him of something he *already knew*. That gave his experience a deep centre around which other experiences constellated. In his understanding, awareness develops on many levels from present-moment experience to a deep pattern one may only recognize retrospectively:

> In the end, looking back through all the strange twists and turns of a lifetime, a noble pattern emerges of a life integrating itself, sometimes apparently against all the odds, around that ideal. The message is that if you have cultivated a strong will to follow the transcendental path, you will be impelled, seemingly inevitably, towards spiritual attainment. [...] [J]ust as the flower is implicit in the seed, the goal of spiritual growth is implicit in human consciousness.⁴⁵

Sangharakshita expands these reflections in his commentary on the *Songs of Milarepa*. Behind our character, he says, we each have an implicit gestalt: 'something that guides you or pushes you from behind, or which is immanent in your activity'.⁴⁶ Sangharakshita was wary of the idea that we possess buddha nature, but he believed something deep within us is attuned to life's purpose:

> [I]t is as though our gestalt is us, already completed, in a manner of speaking, outside time, and our life consists in the living out of that in time. That's not just a metaphysical abstraction. It's something you actually feel, a power motivating you through life.[47]

• • •

An adequate account of Sangharakshita must locate this deep centre, noble pattern, and motivating power. That is the aim of this book and perhaps any accurate account of his work. When Vidyadevi, his principal editor, compiled a selection of representative excerpts from his writing entitled *The Essential Sangharakshita*, she says:

> I found myself surrounded by a glittering but muddled heap of words. All my attempts to organize them seemed just to shift the heap into another heap; and the words, taken from their contexts, kept losing their lustre.[48]

In place of a conceptual schema, the organizing principle she found was the mandala of the five buddhas: a symbolic pattern akin to the organic coherence of a plant or a body.

A mandala arranges its contents in space, and it won't suffice for a book that also traces Sangharakshita's development over time. This book uses a combination of narrative and exposition to identify how Sangharakshita's imagination influenced his life and shaped his thought.

Part One is an account of Sangharakshita's life that relates outward events to his spiritual experience, particularly his sense of a source of inspiration beyond his conscious will.

The subject of Parts Two and Three is the nature of the Buddhist path and what it means to practise it. Part Two relates the elements of the path as Sangharakshita envisaged it to his understanding of such fundamental issues as the nature of consciousness and its relation to the path, conditionality, and nirvāṇa. This also means exploring what the imagination meant for him, including his view of art, the importance for him of love and beauty, how he combined

Platonic and Romantic thinking with Buddhist conceptions, and his own archetypal experience.

Part Three traces Sangharakshita's presentation of the Buddhist path and the Buddhist tradition as it developed through his career, beginning with *A Survey of Buddhism* – the most important book he wrote in his formative period. The Dharma, as he imagines it, is alive, so it can be understood as a process of growth and development, or even the 'path of the Higher Evolution'. But this occurs in relation to the transcendent qualities of the Three Jewels, and the nature of the path depends on the relation between the two. What that means for the individual is best expressed in the act of going for refuge to the Three Jewels.

The subject of Part Four is the FWBO/Triratna – the community Sangharakshita founded, within which his ideas continue to be lived out by his disciples. His understanding of the movement and his own role as a leader were as distinctive as his teachings and reflected the same outlook.

Like any other book, this one has certain limitations. It is principally a study of Sangharakshita's published writing, and its main source material is the *Complete Works*, whose twenty-seven hefty volumes were published while the book was being written. For many of Sangharakshita's direct disciples, his teaching came through his personal communication rather than his writing, and they may feel the Sangharakshita I describe is a literary figure rather than the person they knew. Some of the published works are based on the lectures and seminars he gave after 1964, and something is lost when they are rendered in print. More seminars have not become books, and this work makes only limited use of their transcripts. It includes a section on the FWBO/Triratna, but it cannot do justice to what happened when hundreds and then thousands of people tried to put Sangharakshita's teachings into practice. That subject would require another book written in a different way. This one also has little to say about Triratna in India and what Sangharakshita's teaching means for the country's new Buddhists. That would also require a separate study, and I apologize to my Indian friends for this very considerable limitation. The greatest limitation of all concerns the scope and richness of Sangharakshita's life, thought, and writing, which include much that eludes these pages.

• • •

Sangharakshita's career as a writer and teacher spanned seven decades. His first essay was published when he was eighteen, and he kept composing pieces of writing even when he was too frail to write them down himself, until a month before he died aged ninety-three. It will help to distinguish the phases of that career and introduce how I will refer to each:

1. 1944–64: a *foundational period* when Sangharakshita was living in India. In this time, he worked out his basic approach to Buddhism, culminating in *A Survey of Buddhism*, written between 1954 and 1957. He wrote most of his best poetry in his twenties, including *The Veil of Stars*, which he wrote between 1951 and 1954.
2. 1964–87: the *central period* of Sangharakshita's career, which began with his return to the West. In the first of these decades, he taught at the Hampstead Buddhist Vihara and developed the FWBO. From the mid-1970s, when he was in his fifties and the FWBO had become an established movement, his lifestyle, teaching, and role in the movement all changed.
3. 1987–2009: when Sangharakshita was in his sixties, his writing entered a largely *retrospective period*. He stopped leading seminars, gave far fewer lectures, and gradually withdrew from organizational leadership. He mainly wrote memoirs and autobiographically based accounts of his thought. The major change in this period came in 2002 when he fell ill.
4. 2009–18: a *late period* following his illness in which Sangharakshita had less capacity. His output includes several late papers, written by Subhuti following conversations with Sangharakshita, which bring together the elements of his thinking and clarify its underlying shape. He kept composing a sequence of short reflective pieces right up to his death.

Sangharakshita was both an abstract and a concrete thinker who continually related his ideas about spiritual life to his experience of practising it. For this reason, this book begins with an account of his life. However, as he remarked:

> Even the fullest and frankest autobiography is no more than a thin cross-section, a narrow segment, of the whole which is the man himself as, for a certain length of time, he moves about in space, and wakes and sleeps and dreams.[49]

The story of Sangharakshita's life can be told in many ways and occurred on many levels. His memoirs approach it through his memories, and *The History of My Going for Refuge* does so by tracing his engagement with a central aspect of the Buddhist path. The account in Part One sketches its overall outline but focuses particularly on his experience of forces that he identified sometimes with deeper strata of his psyche, and sometimes with powerful universal or transcendental energies that seemed to originate beyond him. It centres on Sangharakshita's experience of tantric initiation and particularly his connection with Padmasambhava. This is intended to illustrate a much larger process, not to suggest that he understood this dimension of experience in specifically tantric terms or that his connection to Padmasambhava was more significant than his connection to other figures. It is also a context for exploring his sexual life, and the controversy it produced.

Part One

Living in the Stream

Not I, not I, but the wind that blows through me!
A fine wind is blowing the new direction of Time.
If only I let it bear me, carry me, if only it carry me

D.H. Lawrence, 'Song of a Man Who Has Come Through'

Chapter One
Meeting the Guru

Kalimpong, 1962

The Triyana Vardhana Vihara, Sangharakshita's monastery on the outskirts of Kalimpong, comprised a stone cottage in four acres of land perched on a rocky spur above a steep, terraced hillside. It faced due west onto a deep valley and

> fields of autumn rice descending in a succession of narrow, sinuous terraces of emerald green to where, more than a thousand feet below, the river winds like a silver ribbon through the purple shadows of the hills.[1]

The blueness of the autumn sky, Sangharakshita said, had an 'unimaginable depth and delicacy',[2] and reaching into it, beyond the 'haze-softened foothills',[3] were the jagged Himalayan peaks, brilliant in the sunlight. The great peak of Mount Kanchenjunga rose above them all, and at dawn Sangharakshita would watch as the sunrise flushed its peaks a fiery pink, and then 'Pink would change to crimson, crimson to apricot, apricot to the purest, brightest gold.'[4]

But, if Kalimpong was peaceful, the wider world was not, and Asian Buddhism faced many enemies. War raged in Vietnam where Buddhists were caught between the Communist North and the Catholic-led South. Chinese forces had recently taken over Tibet, and many Tibetan refugees had fled to Kalimpong and the surrounding district. The Chinese opposed Tibet's ancient Buddhist culture, and Sangharakshita's friend Dhardo Rimpoche wrote the following year:

> Dark clouds have arisen from all quarters and the brilliance of the sun of religion and culture has been overcast. Especially from the East, the demon of eclipse has, it seems, greedily devoured the sun.[5]

On 20 October 1962 Chinese troops crossed into Indian territory both in Ladakh and along the McMahon Line east of Bhutan, just 250 miles from Kalimpong.[6] Meanwhile, on the other side of the world, the Cuban Missile Crisis was at its height. On 22 October President Kennedy made his famous broadcast declaring the US navy would prevent Soviet ships from supplying military equipment to Cuba and threatening a full nuclear strike.

• • •

On 21 October 1962 the thirty-seven-year-old Sangharakshita spent two days in the Vihara's shrine room with his friend and teacher Kachu Rimpoche.[7] They sat opposite one another, a table piled with *torma*s (offerings) and ritual implements between them. A gangly English novice, born Laurence Mills and known in later years as Bhikkhu Khantipalo, describes the shrine room in *Noble Friendship*, his memoir of his time at the Vihara and his association with Sangharakshita:

> When we closed the door to the veranda, few sounds could be heard, maybe muted birdsong, if it was light enough, or sounds of foot-travellers to the nearest village. But within the room there was an indescribable natural silence. And though it was an ordinary enough small room, within it was a presence, a sort of 'shiningness' hard to put into words.[8]

In 1963 Sangharakshita offered his own description:

> As the sun sets behind the blue Darjeeling hills, its last rays, slanting down across the valley and in at the shrine door, set ablaze the silver and brass alter utensils and softly light up the smiling gilded face of the standing Buddha-image occupying the place of honour on the topmost tier.[9]

Kachu Rimpoche had come to the Vihara to perform a strictly private ritual, called an *abhiṣeka* in Sanskrit or a *wang* in Tibetan, which would create a spiritual connection between Sangharakshita and the mysterious figure of Padmasambhava, the subduer of demons. The *abhiṣeka* deepened Sangharakshita's engagement with Tibetan Buddhism, and, in combination with other tantric practices, seems to have touched something powerful within him.

Life at the Vihara
In 1962 Sangharakshita was thirty-seven and mid-way through his life journey. Photos show a gaunt, bespectacled figure with a wide smile, his hair cut short, bhikkhu-style, and his bearing conveys vigorous resolution. *Noble Friendship* recalls Khantipalo's impression of Sangharakshita on their first meeting.

> As we turned the corner onto its veranda we saw a monk in dark orange robes, smiling as we approached. I noticed he had a certain poise, a certain authority, combined with obvious pleasure at our arrival. He appeared to be about ten years older than I was, shorter in stature and slender in build. His movements were graceful and his greeting [...] warm-hearted.[10]

According to the account of life at the Vihara in *Noble Friendship*, the two monks rose early and meditated together. Khantipalo's practice focused on the mindfulness of breathing and the variations on loving-kindness meditation known as the *brahmavihāra*s. Sangharakshita practised these himself, but his practice focused on the *sādhana*s – meditation practices on various buddha figures – he had received in the preceding years. They also performed puja, a devotional ceremony that combined verses from different branches of the Buddhist tradition, including the Pāli *Ratana Sutta* and the Sanskrit *Bodhicaryāvatāra* and *Heart Sutra*.

After breakfast Sangharakshita wrote on his typewriter, becoming concentrated as soon as he sat down at his desk. He found writing pleasurable, and it was so large a part of his identity, he later reflected, that he sometimes found it difficult to say whether he was 'a Buddhist who writes or a writer who was a Buddhist'.[11]

If he grew stiff or a difficulty puzzled him, he left his desk and walked up and down the veranda in front of the cottage until it was resolved. He particularly enjoyed writing during the rainy season, when the world was hushed by rain 'falling peacefully on the roofs, on the leaves of the trees, and on the crops in the fields'.[12]

Sangharakshita was working on an ambitious multi-volume project called *The Heritage of Buddhism*, which began when he was asked to write entries on Buddhism for the *Oriya Encyclopaedia*. His articles far exceeded what had been commissioned, and he developed some of them into the 'introduction to Buddhism' later published as *The Three Jewels*. A further set of articles became the account of Buddhist canonical literature that was published as *The Eternal Legacy*. A third series on Buddhist schools was intended to form part of a book on 'The Pattern of Development in Buddhism', and he planned a fourth volume on 'Forms and Functions of Buddhist Art' and a fifth on 'Meditation in the Three Yanas'.[13] Although the third volume was not completed and the fourth and fifth were never even started, the project engaged Sangharakshita deeply. *The Eternal Legacy* required him to read or reread many canonical works, and they so gripped his imagination that he felt himself transported to the worlds they evoked. At lunchtime, Khantipalo recalls, Sangharakshita would sometimes spend the entire meal in silence, his thoughts still absorbed in his writing.

Although Sangharakshita was just seven years older than Khantipalo, the younger monk believed he had found an ideal Dharma teacher and spiritual friend. Khantipalo was impressed by how intensely Sangharakshita could apply himself, whether at work on his typewriter or, later, on a teaching tour among Ambedkarite Buddhists. The two men often discussed Buddhist teachings, and Khantipalo pairs his account of the older man with passages in the Buddhist scriptures describing how an ideal monk would comport himself, noting Sangharakshita's combination of mindfulness and spontaneity, the kindness in his personal relations, his sense of humour, and his equanimity.

The Vihara's lifestyle was one of 'relaxed asceticism' which 'had no grimness attached to it'[14] and, partly because of the stretched finances, meals might include no more than soupy rice. When

Sangharakshita eventually weighed himself two years later in England, he was only 8.5 stone.[15] Often, though, there were vegetables grown in the four acres of terraced hillside below the Vihara, which Sangharakshita developed into a market garden with buckwheat, maize, bananas, and bamboo, along with orchids, zinnias, and roses for the shrine. He would take breaks from writing to supervise the gardening work, and at the height of the season he sold fruit from the Vihara's hundred orange trees at the Kalimpong market.

Sangharakshita had constructed a four-roomed thatched guesthouse in the Vihara's grounds that usually housed several visitors. In the spring of 1963, for example, he told a friend that five young Tibetans, including the young Sogyal Rimpoche, were staying there to improve their English.[16] A steady stream of Buddhist monks, and one or two nuns, of all traditions passed through the Vihara, along with other visitors. Christmas Humphreys, president of the London Buddhist Society, had travelled to Kalimpong that Easter and 'made a round of high-ranking lamas with Bhante [Sangharakshita] as my interpreter and guide'.[17] Other westerners lived in the town, a colonial hill station where officials had adjourned to escape the hot season, and Sangharakshita's circle included a group of somewhat eccentric spiritual seekers and scholars for whom it was 'a quiet, inexpensive place conducive to their pursuits'.[18] Younger travellers also came through, precursors of the hippies who flooded India a few years later; in June 1962 the 'slouching, dirty, dishevelled, hirsute' figure of the Beat poet Allen Ginsberg appeared on the Vihara's veranda intent on finding someone who could give him tantric initiation, especially if this involved sexual practices.[19] Ginsberg left Kalimpong having met several of Sangharakshita's friends and teachers, but was otherwise disappointed.

Sangharakshita's work
Notwithstanding the Vihara's modest size and remote location, Sangharakshita's ambitions were large. The 1963 report reviewing the Vihara's first five years described it as a centre for Buddhist studies, meditation, and the ordination and training of monks and others to meet what Sangharakshita sensed was a growing

interest in Buddhism around the world.[20] Throughout his time in Kalimpong, Sangharakshita also taught the local Newar Buddhist community, regularly lectured in nearby Sikkhim, and organized Buddhist festival celebrations that brought together Buddhists from the various traditions.

In addition to *The Heritage of Buddhism*, many other literary projects occupied Sangharakshita. He helped friends with their writing and translations, and edited the volumes of *The Buddhist Library* series for a Bombay publisher. He was also, effectively, the editor of *The Mahabodhi Journal*, which was published monthly by the Mahabodhi Society of India. Sangharakshita's hero Anagārika Dharmapāla had founded the Society in 1891 to revive Buddhism in India. Sangharakshita had visited its Ceylonese headquarters as a young conscript in the Second World War but discovered, with deep disappointment, that the Society was riven by internal conflicts and effectively moribund. But he found Dharmapāla himself an inspiring figure, shared the Society's non-sectarian stance, and embraced its mission to revive Buddhism. Formally, the Vihara was a branch of the Society, though Sangharakshita always stressed its independence.[21]

The Mahabodhi Journal appeared each month with articles on all schools of Buddhism. It was widely read far beyond India, and Sangharakshita's editorials discussed such topics as Buddhism's relevance to the modern world and the need for a Buddhist revival. He urged Buddhists to make a greater effort to overcome their differences, and he criticized sectarianism, especially Theravādin. Elsewhere, he argued, more radically, that, if Buddhism was to meet the needs of the modern world, new kinds of bhikkhus and upāsakas (lay followers) were needed.[22]

The Buddhist revival in India had taken a huge step forward in 1956 when Dr Ambedkar, the country's former law minister and principal author or drafter of the Constitution of the Indian Republic, converted to Buddhism. Hundreds of thousands – eventually millions – of his followers followed his example, almost all of them members of the community considered 'untouchable' in the Hindu caste system and later referred to as 'Dalits'. Sangharakshita arrived in Nagpur the day Dr Ambedkar died, just six weeks after their conversion, and he played a decisive part in rallying his supporters.

He threw himself into the new Buddhist movement and estimated that he personally officiated at the conversion ceremonies of around 200,000 people. Each year in the cool season he embarked on a teaching tour, 'criss-crossing the northern and central parts of India by train, bus, and bullock cart'.[23] Arriving at an 'ex-Untouchable' village, Sangharakshita wrote, he would be greeted by large crowds, garlanded and taken on a bullock cart, amid 'a seething, struggling mass of humanity which slowly surges forward and pours through the narrow streets of the village'.[24] In villages he would give a talk and administer the refuges and precepts to up to 1,000 people at a time, and in cities the numbers could be much larger. These events moved him profoundly:

> I could see from the light in their eyes and the rapturous look on their faces, in repeating the words of the ancient Pāli formula the ex-Untouchables, far from just 'taking *pansil*', were in fact giving expression to their heartfelt conviction that Buddhism was their only hope, their only salvation.[25]

The longest of these tours, lasting nearly eight months from October 1960 to April 1961, included hundreds of talks and meetings. Sangharakshita didn't tour the following winter, but Khantipalo travelled with him in late 1962. 'People were usually very quiet and most of them really tried to understand what was being explained. The whole atmosphere was very impressive, though without the heaviness of solemnity.' Whatever happened, Khantipalo observed, Sangharakshita consistently displayed 'a stoic acceptance of unexpected obstacles and the ability to make light of them in a humorous way'.[26]

Through the various strands of his work, Sangharakshita's name had spread. His poems were published in Indian periodicals, his articles were read and republished, and his major book, *A Survey of Buddhism*, was widely acclaimed on its publication in 1957. He was loved and celebrated by many in the Ambedkarite communities, and his editing work brought him into contact with a wide circle of scholars and writers, some of whom lived in Kalimpong or passed through it. He corresponded with other writers, bhikkhus across Asia, Indian friends of all sorts, and Buddhists in the West, and by 1963 his correspondence had grown so voluminous that he told a friend who complained he had neglected her: 'for every one letter I write I receive six.'[27] His friend the German Buddhist Lama Govinda was more forgiving: 'I sometimes wonder how you find the time to write letters at all. I certainly would have collapsed with a programme like yours.'[28]

Beneath the surface

What was happening *within* Sangharakshita, beneath the self-assured and accomplished outward character that so impressed Khantipalo? It is possible, of course, that there was no inner tension, just a steady mindful practice and a growing understanding. His memoirs say relatively little about the deeper strata of his emotional life. Unlike an autobiography, he observed, a volume of memoirs is merely an account of 'what one remembers of one's life as one looks back on it',[29] and the steady narrative reflects the seemingly unflappable demeanour he displayed. He writes in *The Rainbow Road* that his engagement with Buddhism changed in his early twenties when he lived as a wandering ascetic:

> From being a quasi-instinctive attraction, a sort of spiritual falling-in-love, it became more of the nature of a reasoned conviction that included understanding as well as emotion, clarity as well as passion.[30]

But we should distinguish Sangharakshita's undemonstrative appearance from his character as a whole. The final volume of his memoirs, *Moving against the Stream*, recalls that, having moved to England just a couple of years after the Padmasambhava *abhiṣeka*, he wondered why he didn't miss his Indian friends more, and concludes that, while he was neither lacking in concern for other people nor lacking in emotion generally, thanks to his English stiff upper lip, restricted childhood, and the constraints of being a bhikkhu, his feelings were 'buried beneath layers of reticence and reserve through which it was difficult for them to break'.[31]

It is hard to trace emotions that are so deeply buried, but he said in 1978:

> The forces at work in my personality when I was young were so powerful, so complex, even contradictory, that had I not discovered something as worthy of my commitment and devotion as the Three Jewels I believe they would have ripped me apart. I honestly think I would have gone mad.[32]

Sangharakshita's memoirs betray little evidence of incipient insanity, but a clue is in the painful and confusing tension between the intuitive Sangharakshita I and the ascetic Sangharakshita II. For a while, the two 'remained separate and distinct, even mutually antagonistic', and would alternate, 'sometimes even within the space of a single day, with now one now the other predominating'.[33] While Sangharakshita was training as a Theravādin bhikkhu in 1949/50 the tension led to disaster:

> Angered by the encroachments of Sangharakshita I, who was reading more poetry than ever, and who had written a long poem which, though it had a Buddhist theme, was still a poem, Sangharakshita II suddenly burned the two notebooks in which his rival had written all the poems he had composed from the time of their departure from England right down to about the middle of their sojourn in Singapore.[34]

The split suggested two approaches to spiritual life. One included Sangharakshita's love of beauty, especially the beauty of poetry; the other valued rigour and discipline. He later reflected: 'My spiritual life seemed to derive nourishment from both streams of inspiration',[35] and spoke of reconciliation rather than resolution between these aspects of his character:

> [I]t isn't possible for Sangharakshita I to get rid of Sangharakshita II, and it isn't possible for Sangharakshita II to get rid of Sangharakshita I. They have to co-exist. There has to be, it seems, a sort of fruitful tension, or even a fruitful conflict, between the two, as they interact with each other.[36]

His developed understanding of integration went much further. He spoke of integrating the heights and depths of the psyche, and associated the process with dreams, symbols, and myth. Returning to the figure of Padmasambhava offers a way to trace these processes in Sangharakshita.

Padmasambhava

Padmasambhava is, at the same time, a historical person, a legendary hero, an archetype, and an embodiment of buddhahood. The legends present him as a tantric guru, familiarly known to Tibetans as Guru Rimpoche ('Precious Teacher'), who possessed the powers of a wizard or shaman along with the attainments of a buddha. In later years, when Sangharakshita wrote or spoke about Padmasambhava, he dwelled principally on the legend of Padmasambhava's arrival in Tibet in the wake of Śāntarakṣita, a scholarly Indian pandit who tells the Tibetan king that his doctrine is 'whatever is proved correct after examining it by reason and to avoid all that does not agree with reason'.[37] According to the legend, when Śāntarakṣita started to build the great Samye monastery, the Tibetan demons and spirits grew angry, perhaps believing they were being displaced, and they destroyed at night the work that had been done in the day. To deal with them, the king summoned Padmasambhava, hearing him to be a master of deep meditation who had dwelled in cremation grounds in the company of *ḍākinī*s – the semi-wrathful female embodiments of unbounded energy who hold the key to spiritual liberation.

Sangharakshita first visited the Himalayas in 1945, while still a soldier in the British army, to see his Uncle Dick, who was living in Darjeeling. He visited the Yi-gah Cho-ling monastery in Ghoom, not far from Kalimpong, where the 'stillness and vibrancy' of its atmosphere set off reverberations at 'unfathomable depths', stirring a sense that he should dedicate his life to the Dharma.[38] In 1951, now a young bhikkhu based in Kalimpong, Sangharakshita visited the Tamang Buddhist Temple in nearby Darjeeling. Stepping into a darkened shrine, illuminated only by the light that came from the opened door, he made out the outline of an image that seemed to fill the chamber. '[T]he most remarkable and impressive thing about this great figure was his face', he recalled.

His features were half Indian, half Tibetan, he had a thin black
moustache, and his brows were slightly knitted, almost as
though in anger. His expression was extremely intelligent and
penetrating, powerful and commanding, even fierce.[39]

The image of Padmasambhava seemed to activate something in
Sangharakshita:

Having taken it in, I felt that it had always been there, and
that in seeing the figure of Padmasambhava I had become
conscious of a spiritual presence that had in fact been with
me all the time. Though I had never seen the figure of
Padmasambhava before, it was familiar to me as no other
figure on earth was familiar: familiar and fascinating. It
was familiar as my own self, yet at the same time infinitely
mysterious, infinitely wonderful, and infinitely inspiring.[40]

From this time, he says, 'the precious guru' occupied an important
place in his inner spiritual world.

Later in the same year Sangharakshita visited Yi-gah Cho-
ling with Lama Govinda and his partner Li Gotami, and noticed
the devotion with which his companions gazed on the images
of Śākyamuni and Padmasambhava, as if they sensed 'the living
spiritual presence' of which the images were merely representations.
Once again, the impact was uncanny. The mantras they recited 'not
only sounded strangely familiar but also set up reverberations
that made themselves felt in the remotest corners of my being'.[41]

Padmasambhava exists liminally, between the human realm, the
spirit realm, and the realm of Buddhahood, and symbols, which
are important in all Vajrayāna contexts, are especially important
in representations of Padmasambhava. The most important of the
implements he holds is a vajra: a diamond that is also a thunderbolt,
which represents the indestructible strength and irresistible power
of the Enlightened mind:

It destroys our intellectual assumptions, usually adopted so
unthinkingly. It destroys the psychological conditionings in
which we are enmeshed. It destroys the emotional hang-ups

to which we are so attached. It destroys, in short, ourselves as we are at present. [...] The experience of reality in what the Tantras call its 'nakedness' can be a shattering experience.[42]

The symbol is far older than Padmasambhava or the Vajrayāna Buddhism that he practised – the 'Diamond Vehicle' now mainly associated with Tibetan Buddhism – and that provides the name of the *Diamond Sutra* (the *Vajracchedikā Sūtra*, or 'sutra that cuts like a vajra or diamond'). Aged twenty-two, six years after his first, transformative reading of this text, Sangharakshita wrote an article that calls the sutra 'an attempt to elucidate the content of a bodhisattva's consciousness'. It says we must regard the bodhisattva not as an individual being but as 'a supra-personal cosmic force making toward Enlightenment'.[43] The implication is that, in reading the sutra, Sangharakshita had glimpsed, or experienced, a mode of being that was powerful and dynamic as well as transcendent and mysterious. He found many other expressions of this, including the figure of Padmasambhava, and a poem from 1954, entitled 'The Stream of Stars', suggests how he experienced it:

> The stream of my desire no more
> Rolls through the muddy fields of earth;
> Between the azure banks of heaven
> A stream of stars has come to birth.
>
> No more on my soul's current float
> Dead leaves from wind-dishevelled trees;
> But swanlike, many a shining boat
> Bends low before the heavenly breeze.
>
> The fountains of my heart no more
> Ooze slow into some stagnant place,
> But in great tranquil rivers pour
> Into the boundless sea of space.[44]

The poem echoes 'The Song of Asia' from Shelley's *Prometheus Unbound*:

My soul is an enchanted boat,
Which, like a sleeping swan, doth float
Upon the silver waves of thy sweet singing.⁴⁵

Shelley's soul drifts passively on the stream, but in Sangharakshita's poem the current has force and direction, and we can scarcely miss the Buddhist significance of entering the stream like a *sotāpanna*, a 'stream entrant' who is henceforth destined for nirvāṇa. While early Buddhism offers various definitions of a *sotāpanna*, it says relatively little about the stream itself, though the image is important in later Buddhism. For Sangharakshita it meant a current or force beyond his individual will that carried him forward. At the end of his life, Sangharakshita returned to the phrase 'a suprapersonal force' as he brought his teachings together in a final form and gave a central place to the current of Dharmic energy, both within and beyond him.

The outsider
In 2015 and nearing the end of his life, Sangharakshita recalled that, around the time of the Padmasambhava *abhiṣeka*, he had read Colin Wilson's book *The Outsider*.⁴⁶ Influenced by existentialism, Wilson is sometimes bracketed with the playwright John Osborne as an 'Angry Young Man' – a description that could scarcely be applied to the ardent but equanimous English monk who read it in Kalimpong. Sangharakshita says he found the book interesting, even though he didn't consider himself an outsider at the time, but, with the perspective afforded by old age, he saw things differently. He wasn't an outsider as a small child, having been 'born into a family of which I was a fully accepted member'.⁴⁷ But, aged nine, he was diagnosed with valvular heart disease, and confined to bed with strict orders that he should be kept absolutely quiet and receive no visitors – not even his sister Joan, who lived in the same house. For another child this might have been an irreparable trauma, but for the nine-year-old Dennis Lingwood it was a liberation. He discovered he was a reader, and books, especially *The Children's Encyclopaedia*, were gateways to an unimaginably exciting *inner* world. His reading was voracious and miscellaneous.⁴⁸

Returning to school aged eleven, he was treated as an invalid and set apart from the other children. His education was largely self-directed, 'for neither before nor after my illness was I able to learn at school anything that could be considered either useful or interesting'.[49] Then came the war and the dislocating experience of evacuation. His refuge, once again, was the burgeoning literary and spiritual interests that brought more self-discovery. 'The Awakening of the Heart', a long autobiographical poem written in 1949, relates how he felt, as a teenager, that literature offered 'a lush wonderland of thought' so overwhelming in beauty that he dreamed of spending 1,000 years immersed in it. The idyll shattered, the poem says, when a bomb struck his house, leaving just '[t]he bomb-struck rubble of my room'. Skipping over his discovery of Buddhism, his parents' divorce, and conscription into the British army (a life to which he thought he was particularly ill-suited), it declares:

> Thereafter it was mine to roam
> Without a friend, without a home,
> For many a year, with unquiet breast,
> Perplexed between the East and West.[50]

No doubt this is hyperbolic, but in 'going forth' he separated himself from mainstream society. His role as a Buddhist monk in non-Buddhist India set him apart from ordinary social life, and, for Indians who thought in terms of caste, he was a white *mleccha*, or barbarian. He was even an outsider within the monastic community as, notwithstanding his Theravādin ordination, he never thought of himself as a Theravādin. Other Buddhists had not impressed him, and even Lama Govinda, whom he greatly admired, was a 'kindred spirit' rather than a teacher. He responded wholeheartedly to the then uneducated and reviled Ambedkarite new Buddhist population, and they embraced him in return. But he reflected: 'It was because I was an Outsider that the new Buddhists trusted me. Like them, I was outside the Hindu caste system. We were Outsiders together.'[51]

Sometimes, Sangharakshita felt a deeper, existential estrangement. One day in 1953 he wrote in a diary:

> When I went out [I] experienced deeply the unreality of all things. People seemed like ghosts and shadows. My body seemed to float along the road. Was half out of my normal consciousness. The mind was poised, steady, and without desires, though not very clear.[52]

If we set this beside the equally existential connection to the natural world he expresses in his essays and poetry, we begin to approach the complexity of this intense, observant young English monk.

Sexual feelings

Looking back, it seemed to Sangharakshita that his sense of being an outsider had a straightforward origin:

> I was not an Outsider because I loved the poetry of Robert Herrick, or was exhilarated by Nietzsche's *Thus Spake Zarathustra*, or even because I regarded myself as a Buddhist. I was an Outsider for deeper and darker reasons. I was an Outsider because I was sexually attracted to men, not to women, and I had been aware of this since the age of 14.[53]

Sangharakshita never felt guilty about his homosexual feelings, but from an early age he knew 'it was something of which society disapproved and that I should not speak about it to anyone'.[54] Homosexuality was illegal in both India and England, and he imagined late in his life what might have happened had he been passed unfit for military service and remained in England:

> Had I simply repressed my feelings I might not have fallen foul of the law, but my whole sexual and emotional life would have been stultified. On the other hand, had I ventured to act upon them, even to a limited extent, I would have had to do so furtively, even secretly, with the consciousness that I was not only breaking the law but leading a double life. I would have been always anxious, afraid of being found out, and unable to be fully open even with those with whom I broke the law.[55]

Colin Wilson Revisited tallies the emotional cost:

> Keeping my feelings to myself became a habit, especially
> when those feelings were very strong and directed to another
> man. Many years were to pass before I was able to give
> expression to such feelings even to a limited extent.[56]

Poetry offered an outlet, at least while Sangharakshita was in his twenties. He called his poetry 'a sort of spiritual autobiography, sketchy perhaps but perhaps revealing, or at least suggesting, aspects of my life that would not otherwise be known'.[57] 'Goldfish', written in 1950 when he was twenty-four or twenty-five, likens his feelings to goldfish swimming among the weeds at the bottom of a pond:

> In the dim green stillness of the pool
> There is a redness as of gold
> Flashing among the dark brown weeds,
> Glimmer on glimmer, bright but cold,
> Of the black-finned goldfish beautiful
> That breathe down there where the lotus breeds.
>
> Deep in the ocean of my soul
> Flickers an anguish red as fire,
> Twining among my oozy thoughts,
> Glimmer on glimmer of hot desire
> Leaping and sparkling beyond control
> In the darkness there where the heart contorts.[58]

There is no mistaking the 'hot desire' the second stanza acknowledges, and the third declares a 'fierce red love that racks me sore' and cannot be expressed outwardly. If a goldfish rises to the surface, it will be caught, so it chooses to hide among the weeds, and Sangharakshita's sexual feelings must likewise be concealed in 'the dark green depths of my innermost soul'.

Sangharakshita's major poetic achievement is *The Veil of Stars* (1954). It describes falling in love, the bitterness the Lover feels when his love isn't reciprocated, and the painful process of transcendence that concludes with the poet absorbed in sublimity and compassion. The poem is clearly based in personal experience, but it doesn't follow that Sangharakshita had transcended sexual desire. Looking back in 2009, he said that as a monk he had maintained his vows, but it had sometimes been a struggle; he describes his life from 1950 to the mid-1960s as a period of 'somewhat unhealthy celibacy',[59] and a poem from 1957 calls celibacy 'harsh abstinence'.[60] People hostile to Sangharakshita have passed on rumours that he breached his vows during his time in India, and it is true that he was often in the company of young men. But the rumours have never been specific, and our sole firsthand witness, Khantipalo, who was well aware of them, insisted Sangharakshita 'led a pure and blameless life morally'.[61]

That purity didn't come easily, and a sonnet from 1955 expresses Sangharakshita's incredulity at the idea that Buddhist practice could be considered a straightforward process. There is no reason to think it refers to sexuality alone, but there is no mistaking the intensity of the struggle it describes:

> But those who read their own hearts, inly wise,
> Know that the Way's a hacked path, roughly made
> Through densest jungle, deep in the Unknown...
> And that, though burn a thousand baleful eyes
> Like death-lamps round, serene and unafraid,
> Man through the hideous dark must plunge alone.[62]

• • •

As the years went by, Sangharakshita's engagement with Tibetan Buddhists became increasingly important to him. Kalimpong is close to Sikkim and Bhutan, on the edge of the vast Himalayan region where Buddhism was still practised as it had been for 1,000 years, and it was an important staging post in wool exports from eastern Tibet to India. It was home to Nepalis, many of them Buddhist, as well as Sikkimese, Indians, and Bhutanese. Monks and long-established Vajrayāna temples were part of Kalimpong society, and Kalimpong had long been a centre for opponents of the old Tibetan government. Throughout the 1950s senior Tibetan Buddhist lamas crossed the border from Tibet to India, and after the failed 1959 uprising the Dalai Lama himself joined them.

The Vajrayāna initially seemed to Sangharakshita like 'a jungle in which one could very easily get lost',[63] and his 'rather methodical and tidy mind' balked at tantric imagery, which presented 'heaps of unorganized material that didn't seem to fit together in any neat fashion'.[64] In time, Tibetans would become skilled in communicating their traditions to westerners (though cultural differences remained problematic), but in the 1950s that had barely started. In studying the Pāli suttas Sangharakshita could draw on almost a century of scholarship in English, but western understanding of Tibetan Buddhist traditions, and especially the shamanic aspects that are particularly associated with Padmasambhava and the Nyingma tradition, was rudimentary and often hostile. Helmut Hoffmann's influential *Religions of Tibet*, published in German in 1956 and in English translation in 1961, declared that the religion of the Nyingmapas was not Buddhism at all but 'Padmaism' and had been created by 'a strange holy man and sorcerer' named Padmasambhava.[65]

Sangharakshita's circle in Kalimpong included people like George Roerich, Marco Pallis, and Prince Peter of Greece, as well as Lama Govinda (who lived in another part of the Himalayas), for whom Tibet was a symbol of all that was lacking in western culture. They made it their business to elicit accurate information about Tibetan Buddhism, but they continued to idealize it. For Pallis, the country symbolized something western countries had lost or forgotten under the assault of 'the all-devouring monster of modernism'.[66] Govinda writes in his memoir *The Way of the White Clouds*:

> Tibet has become the symbol of all that present-day humanity is longing for, either because it has been lost or not yet been realized or because it is in danger of disappearing from human sight: the stability of a tradition, which has its roots not only in a historical or cultural past, but within the innermost being of man, in whose depth this past is enshrined as an ever-present source of inspiration.[67]

Sangharakshita was wary of these romantic accounts and later remarked: 'The West is no more materialistic than the East. One might say that the West is simply more "successful" in its pursuit of materialism.'[68] Nonetheless, with the help of his European friends and Tibetan lamas, Sangharakshita gradually found his way through the tantric jungle. By the time of the *Survey* he recognized that it was really a garden, and the proliferating imagery formed 'an enormously complicated, but remarkably logical, system' that extended Mahāyāna teachings.[69]

Sangharakshita's growing interest in the Vajrayāna coincided with the challenge he had long felt in his spiritual life of going beyond his limiting ego while relying on his own efforts. It seemed impossible to do both: 'Like an unwanted but faithful dog, [the ego] is kicked out of the front door only to creep in at the back.'[70] His Bombay friend Dr Mehta convinced him, at least in principle, that the only way to escape the trap was to submit himself to a higher source of guidance. Mehta's teachings owed more to spiritualism and theosophy than Buddhism, but his advice chimed with a dream featuring two ashrams that recurred throughout Sangharakshita's time in India. The first ashram was at the base of a mountain, open to all and busy with religious activities, but it had a small door that opened to a long flight of steps leading upwards. At the top of the stairs was a secret ashram, known to a very few, and standing before a Tibetan-style case containing golden buddha figures to greet Sangharakshita was the Hindu figure Rishi Agastya. When the dream occurred, Sangharakshita later recalled, 'I had a strong sense of transmission, of energy being transmitted.'[71]

Sangharakshita's intuitive connection with this 'higher level' became dramatically real when he followed a strong instinct that he should travel on 6 December 1956 to Nagpur, where Dr Ambedkar's conversion had taken place. Just an hour after his arrival, news broke that Dr Ambedkar had died in Bombay. Sangharakshita asked that a meeting be arranged, and later that night he arrived at a huge assembly of Dr Ambedkar's inconsolable followers. As he spoke, he sensed that '[a]bove the crowd there hung an enormous Presence',[72] as real to him as the people he was addressing, though whether it represented Dr Ambedkar's presence or the faith of his followers, he couldn't say. Sangharakshita addressed dozens of meetings in the following days, and found his experience was heightened in a distinctive way:

I felt that I was not a person but an impersonal force. At one
stage I was working quite literally without any thought,
just as one is in samādhi. Also, I felt hardly any tiredness –
certainly not at all what one would have expected from such a
tremendous strain.[73]

Dr Ambedkar's followers believed that through his presence in Nagpur at this critical time Sangharakshita had 'saved Nagpur for Buddhism'.

Moved, in part, by the sense of being an impersonal force, Sangharakshita felt the time was right to request tantric initiation into the *sādhana* (visualization practice) of a buddha or bodhisattva figure. Since 1945 or 1946 Sangharakshita had been practising the *ānāpāna-sati*, or mindfulness of breathing, which he had learned from the Theravādin Bhikkhu Soma in Singapore, later adding the *mettābhāvanā*, or development of loving-kindness practice.[74] Vajrayāna practice includes visualization and much else that connects the practitioner to buddha figures, or divine and wrathful beings, and the energies and qualities they embody. The practices are passed on orally, 'from heart to ear', in the context of ritual transmission or initiation by a qualified lama with whom the practitioner makes a spiritual connection.

Back in Kalimpong four months after the seismic events in Nagpur, Sangharakshita heard a renowned Nyingma lama named Sangye Dorje had arrived in the district. The lama had spent many years meditating in Eastern Tibet, and now wandered freely from place to place, widely respected as a spiritual master with magical powers. He was known by the epithet 'Chattrul' (or Chetul), which meant 'without affairs', because of his complete indifference to rank, position, and ecclesiastical matters. The Catholic contemplative Thomas Merton met Chattrul Rimpoche in 1968 and thought him a great man, 'marked by complete simplicity and freedom'.[75]

Sangharakshita met Chattrul in a village outside Kalimpong. Merton said he looked like 'a vigorous old peasant',[76] and Sangharakshita writes that his face was 'coarse and unrefined almost to the point of brutality'. But the Tibetan's 'rock-like strength' impressed Sangharakshita,[77] and he asked him the identity of his *yidam* or *iṣṭa-devatā* (tutelary deity). Chattrul said it was Green Tārā, adding that she had been the *yidam* of many great Indian and Tibetan pandits. He gave Sangharakshita the initiation and, the next day, he instructed him in practising the *sādhana* of Green Tārā. For Sangharakshita, this meant 'she was the transcendental counterpart of my own mundane nature', and the initiation fulfilled his need for guidance. From this point on, he later said, 'my whole spiritual life was guided from that dimension.'[78]

By 1962, when the Padmasambhava *abhiṣeka* took place, Sangharakshita had studied Tibetan philosophy with the aid of friends and teachers including Kachu Rimpoche, Dhardo Rimpoche, and Yogi Chen. This was personal dialogue rather than formal instruction in a Tibetan textual syllabus, and an important element for him was the quality of the communication:

> This is communication in the context of going for refuge: a shared exploration of the spiritual world between people who are in a relationship of complete honesty and harmony. The communication is the exploration and the exploration is the communication; in this way spiritual progress takes place.[79]

Sangharakshita filtered the intricate patterns of tantric imagery through his own sensibility, treating them as a kind of hermetic poetry that opened another dimension of experience. Perhaps this was akin to his sense of being 'reminded' by his encounters with figures like Padmasambhava of a level of experience that was accessible, yet beyond time, mysterious but strangely familiar, like something he had once known, then forgotten, and now recalled. It is only partly accurate to contrast this with the Tibetans' more literal traditional understanding, as even ordinary Buddhists understand that Padmasambhava and the other buddhas and bodhisattvas represent an archetypal realm beyond historical existence.

The most revered of the lamas Sangharakshita met was Jamyang Khyentse Rimpoche – a legendary figure in modern Tibetan Buddhism whom he happened to meet soon after the Rimpoche arrived in Kalimpong. Sangharakshita didn't want to be like 'those Tibetan Buddhists who collected *wongkurs* [empowerments] in much the same way as English schoolboys collected postage stamps',[80] but Kachu Rimpoche told Sangharakshita he should request an initiation.

In October 1957, five years before the Padmasambhava *abhiṣeka*, Jamyang Khyentse initiated Sangharakshita into a connection with Mañjughoṣa, Avalokiteśvara, Vajrapāṇi, and Tārā (once again). He also commissioned a thangka showing the buddha figures and two yellow-robed figures in caves, one meditating and one teaching, explaining that they represented Sangharakshita himself. Through these initiations, Jamyang Khyentse told Sangharakshita, he had 'transmitted to me the essence of the teachings of the great masters who were depicted in it. I was now their spiritual heir and successor.'[81]

Initiation

Jamyang Khyentse was too old to take on new students, so he asked Kachu Rimpoche to supervise Sangharakshita's progress and initiate him into the Padmasambhava *sādhana*. The 1962 *abhiṣeka* fulfilled this intention. By convention, the details of what occurs in such a ceremony are secret, and even at the time they were somewhat obscure to Sangharakshita himself. He recalled that Kachu chanted hoarsely in classical Tibetan for hour upon hour while Sangharakshita breathed in the sharply scented Tibetan incense and absorbed the atmosphere. But throughout the ceremony he sensed the lama's devotion to Padmasambhava and the Nyingma lineage.

After verses creating the symbolic ritual space came stages of purification, invocation, and blessing, followed by instructions on practising the Padmasambhava *sādhana*. The general pattern of such practices is well known. The early stages recapitulate the stages of the Mahāyāna Buddhist path, starting with faith in the buddhas and going for refuge to the Three Jewels. Then comes the bodhisattva vow – dedication to attaining Enlightenment for the sake of all beings – followed by meditation on the void nature of existence. The centre of the practice is a more direct engagement with the *yidam*, in this case Padmasambhava, who is imagined or visualized:

Drawing gradually nearer to the visualized image, and thus to those qualities, we feel as if the visualized image was drawing nearer to us. We feel that we are absorbing within ourselves the Buddha's own qualities.[82]

What one does, Sangharakshita said in a lecture seven years later,

> is to see this visualized form more and more brightly, more and more vividly, more and more gloriously, and then gradually feel oneself merging with it, one's heart merging with the heart of the Buddha or Bodhisattva, the heart of Enlightenment. In this way one contemplates, one assimilates, one becomes one with, the virtues of the Tathāgatas.[83]

In 1972 Sangharakshita gave a series of lectures on the 'Creative Symbols of Tantric Buddhism', which described two other practices connected to Padmasambhava that he took up at this time: the going for refuge and prostration practice,[84] and the *guru-yoga*.

At the start of the *guru-yoga*, he says, 'you feel, you imagine, that you are nothing but light, that your body – your bones, flesh, blood, marrow, skin, heart – and your mind, your thoughts, are transmuted into pure, brilliant, blazing light.' Eventually, this light emanating from the guru – one's immediate teacher – or from Padmasambhava, the archetypal guru, who is seated above one's head, pours into one's own body. 'You experience the compassion of the guru and feel his blessing, his *adhiṣṭhāna*, as it is called, descending upon you.' A white *oṃ* syllable appears on his forehead, a red *āḥ* syllable at his throat, and a deep blue *hūṃ* at his heart, and light flows to the equivalent places in the disciple's body, and a sense of Padmasambhava's essence descends into the disciple's heart:

> [Y]ou feel, coming down through your body – or rather through your whole psychophysical organism – a flood of what is called knowledge nectar. You feel as though you have absorbed transcendental wisdom, as though you are becoming filled with nectar, until it fills your whole body, your whole being. As that happens, the guru in your heart is transformed

into the light of great bliss, overwhelming ecstasy, and you feel your body, speech, and mind becoming one with the body, speech, and mind of the guru.[85]

Sangharakshita said that, when he received the Vajrasattva initiation from Dudjom Rimpoche in 1959, he experienced energy coming 'like a ray of light from him to me'.[86] This was the only time he had such an experience, and he warned it was a mistake to think this was a 'transmission of power' or a literal substance you could hand on in your turn. He preferred to say that the guru's 'energy-full personality' activated something in the disciple who could then foster it:

> At the time of initiation, the guru plants a seed in the soil of the disciple's heart. The seed comes from outside, from the guru, but as a disciple you yourself have to tend it, cultivate it, water it, give it light and warmth. If you do this [...] the plant will blossom into a magnificent lotus [...] [and] the disciple will become [...] Vajrasattva, the *vajra*-being [...]: the disciple himself or herself will become a guru.[87]

Along with the Padmasambhava *sādhana* and the *mūla-yoga*s, Kachu Rimpoche introduced Sangharakshita to the *sādhana* of Amitayus, the buddha of long life, and gave him the Dharma name 'Urgyen' or 'Orgyen', the Tibetan form of 'Uḍḍiyāna', the semi-mythical country where Padmasambhava was born. Sangharakshita tells us he enjoyed the suggestion that 'my true home was in the mysterious land of Uḍḍiyāna',[88] and in 1985 he asked to be called Urgyen Sangharakshita. The name connected him to the legacies of both Indian and Tibetan Buddhism, and recognized Padmasambhava's importance in his life.

Changing conditions

Sangharakshita's discussions of Padmasambhava in the years after the *abhiṣeka* associate Padmasambhava with the transformation of the psychic depths, symbolized by his converting the Tibetan demons to the Dharma. He associates Padmasambhava with the path of transformation that must follow any transformative spiritual vision, and with the stream or current of spiritual energy that Sangharakshita sensed at the heart of the Buddhist tradition. These themes give a sense of the currents of Sangharakshita's spiritual life that accompanied outer changes in later years.

In the following months, the problems Sangharakshita faced in India became clearer. Following Dr Ambedkar's death in 1956, the Ambedkarite movement had divided into a dozen factions, all vying for prominence. If Sangharakshita accepted an invitation from one organization, they claimed he supported them exclusively, so, where possible, he stayed with non-Ambedkarite friends and sometimes spoke under the auspices of a women's association that was unaffiliated to any of the factions. But, however many talks he gave, he couldn't follow up the interest they generated, and feared that starting his own activities would invite hostility.[89]

The war between India and China changed life in Kalimpong. Chinese troops advanced deep into Indian territory, and Sangharakshita's aristocratic friends made plans to flee the town. He wrote an editorial declaring 'the terrible day of awakening and reckoning has come', and warned that Buddhists who had a connection with Communism were 'using the sacred name of Buddhism as a cloak for their subversive and anti-national activities'.[90] One day, the authorities arrested the town's entire Chinese community, barring the hermit Yogi Chen. The Chinese declared a ceasefire after a few weeks, and several months later India and China agreed a peace treaty. But tensions continued, Indian soldiers still appeared on Kalimpong streets, and heavy artillery regularly moved through the region. Young Tibetan friends were recruited to fight as guerrillas inside Tibet, reportedly by the CIA, and the authorities were growing wary of non-Indian citizens in the region. In 1959, Communist-sympathizing Indian newspapers had run a story alleging that Sangharakshita was an imperialist agent who had helped smuggle the young Dalai Lama out of Tibet.[91] In the nationalist mood that followed the war, stories spread that he was a Chinese spy or perhaps a CIA operative.[92]

In late 1963 the English Sangha Trust, an organization dedicated to establishing a monastic sangha in Britain, invited Sangharakshita to stay at the Hampstead Buddhist Vihara in the hope that he might help resolve difficulties there and ease tensions with the multi-denominational Buddhist Society. Sangharakshita's initial inclination was to decline. He was settled at the Vihara, valued his teachers, and knew the followers of Dr Ambedkar needed his help. It was a 'deeply, richly satisfying' existence.[93] But Khantipalo insisted it was his duty to help: 'it was my duty to help spread the Dharma in England, inasmuch as I had been born and brought up there.'[94] Dhardo Rimpoche agreed, and Sangharakshita recognized the force of their arguments. Besides, it meant he could visit his parents and his sister after an absence of twenty years.

Sangharakshita accepted the Trust's invitation, and thought he would spend six months in England before returning to India. As things turned out, the visit extended, and a new phase of his life began.

Chapter Two

Western Buddhism

The Hampstead Buddhist Vihara

Sangharakshita took a flight from India, sent off by a small group of well-wishers, and, after a stopover in Paris, arrived at Heathrow on 12 August 1964. Christmas Humphreys drove him from the airport to the Hampstead Buddhist Vihara in St John's Wood, North London. As they approached the Vihara, Humphreys told Sangharakshita he hoped he would see himself as 'the Buddhist vicar of Hampstead'.[1] It wasn't a promising start. Worse followed at the Vihara, where he found a more poisonous 'psychic atmosphere' than any he had previously encountered. The Buddhist Society and the Sangha Association were 'at each other's throats', and he heard 'the most alarming rumours' about 'almost everybody of prominence'.[2]

But, if the start of Sangharakshita's stay was inauspicious and the end was what he called a debacle, the intervening period was one of the most inspired and creative periods of his life. He sometimes delivered talks at three different London venues in a week – all fresh material – as well as speaking at many regional Buddhist societies. He continued to lecture prolifically after he left the Vihara, and many of these talks were recorded and later transcribed, edited, and published.

Most of the people attending the Vihara and the Society had staid middle-class lives, focused on family and profession, and Sangharakshita challenged them. As Stephen Batchelor writes:

> Sangharakshita recognized that there was tremendous potential for the Dharma in Britain. The English Sangha Trust,

however, believed that the only acceptable form of *sangha* was the kind of traditional Theravāda monasticism of which he had been so critical in India, while the Buddhist Society seemed to promote Buddhism as a kind of spiritual pastime rather than a fully committed engagement with the Dharma.[3]

Sangharakshita was told 'English Buddhists were not able to practise more than five minutes meditation at a time, and that I was on no account to try to give them more!'[4] He later described a culture of reading books, following purely theoretical interests in Zen or Tantra, and picking up a jumble of ideas, without being truly affected.[5] When they did take up meditation, especially the vipassanā practices favoured by some at the Vihara, the result could be 'a strange pseudo-spirituality', which he termed 'alienated awareness'.[6] In talk after talk, he challenged his listeners to find emotional equivalents of their intellectual understanding, and insisted that Buddhist practice meant engaging the whole of one's being, right down to the unconscious psychic depths:

> The problem that faces us is how to know not just in the heights, mentally, but emotionally, in the profoundest places of our being, so that we know from the top to the bottom of ourselves wholly and totally. We can't ignore the depths. Out of the depths come our energies of instinct, emotion, and will, and somehow they have to be harnessed to the chariot of the spiritual life; otherwise they will drag us in some other direction. They've got to be harnessed, they've got to be integrated.[7]

His message was that Buddhist practice means embracing these unconscious energies, infusing them with awareness and integrating them, both psychologically and in the terms of the Dharma. He introduced puja and loving-kindness practice to the Vihara, spoke of engaging with myth and symbol, and emphasized the need for complete engagement. He kept returning to the theme of engaging the depths when he left the Vihara, notably in the 1967 series 'Aspects of Buddhist Psychology', which includes lectures on 'The Psycho-Spiritual Symbolism of the Tibetan Book of the

Dead', 'The Mandala: Tantric Symbol of Integration', and 'The Depth Psychology of the Yogācāra'.

Sangharakshita understood transformation in terms of the distinction between the twin paths of 'vision' and 'transformation'. His own moments of vision began with reading the *Diamond Sutra*, but, as he explained in 1966:

> The path of vision represents the realization of truth by the conscious mind, and the path of transformation represents the penetration of that truth into the depths of the unconscious. The path of transformation is much more difficult, because the unconscious mind is much more difficult to transform than the conscious mind.[8]

It is easy to think this message was aimed at the middle-class men and women whom Sangharakshita wanted to rouse from their complacent conventionality, or countercultural young people hungry for a message of radical transformation. But he was also speaking about himself and describing his own experience of Buddhist practice.

* * *

Sangharakshita reflected that in writing *Moving against the Stream*, his memoir of this period, he noticed ways he was changing that he hadn't recognized. He was 'moving in the direction of something like the FWBO, even though I didn't see that at the time'.[9] And something, it seems, was stirring emotionally. He had always felt a need for companionship and, when a thirty-year-old photographer named Terry Delamere attended some of his classes at the Vihara, an intense bond developed between the two men. Sangharakshita often stayed overnight at Terry's flat, and they would speak late into the night.[10] It's hardly surprising that others, especially the prurient and those unfavourably disposed towards Sangharakshita, concluded their connection was sexual, but he always denied this: 'There was never any question of sex between Terry and I. He would simply not have been interested, and that was not the nature of our friendship.'[11]

The crucial experience in Terry's life had been seeing 'the pure white light' under the influence of ether administered to address his recurrent depression. It left him 'standing *in* pure knowledge' and was 'a moment of total comprehension that represented a human being's perfect and total development'.[12] The parallel with Sangharakshita's experience when he first read the *Diamond Sutra* meant he felt 'a spiritual, even a transcendental' affinity with Terry:

> Neither Terry nor I had been able to remain permanently on that higher level. Both of us had been forced to descend and devote ourselves to the task of what he called dispelling the clouds obscuring the pure light of the mind and what I, more Buddhistically, thought of as self- and world-transformation in accordance with Perfect Vision. But though both had descended, it was as though we had descended on either side of a veil, a veil that was sufficiently transparent for us to be able to communicate with each other through it without too much difficulty.[13]

The affinity between the men wasn't *only* transcendental. Nagabodhi calls it 'a strong, intimate friendship, an instant and mutual attraction and a meeting of emotional needs', and its lasting significance for Sangharakshita was the range of those needs. Nagabodhi writes:

> Considering his life up to that point as a child, as a young man in India, and now in the stifling atmosphere of the Vihara, it must have been liberating to feel able to share himself in his native language with someone interested in him as a person, a 'kindred spirit', rather than as 'the monk'. He might have felt in Terry's burning hunger to be united with 'the clear white light' something that resonated with his own hunger for the truth. And, as Terry talked about his issues with sex, it's hard not to imagine Sangharakshita's relief, finally, to talk to someone about his own.[14]

• • •

This was a time of heightened experience. Sangharakshita's diary entry for 6 December 1965 reads:

> Slept very little. Feverish most of the night. Mental state very clear. Extraordinary experience of Transcendental, such as have not had since leaving Kalimpong. Terry had experience of intensely heightened state of awareness.[15]

He dreamed again of the two monasteries, one an ordinary house and the other hidden away, whose existence he had forgotten: 'It was as though I was living, on another level, a secret life that normally had no point of direct contact with my outer or even with my inner life.'[16] But that secret existence was bursting into his waking experience. In breach of the minor monastic rules, he let his hair grow longer than the regulation finger's breadth, sometimes ate after midday, and occasionally ventured out of his London flat wearing ordinary clothes. In 1966 he travelled with Terry through France to Italy and Greece, immersing himself in the high culture that filled the galleries, churches, and ancient sites. He read voraciously, sensing on an archetypal level of his experience the possibility of a new synthesis between Buddhism and western culture.[17]

Sangharakshita's Sunday afternoon talks at the Vihara attracted a sizeable following of mostly young people, some of whom regarded him as their teacher, and a lively group transformed the Vihara's atmosphere. One man, who was later ordained as Vangisa, recalled the impact of meeting Sangharakshita there:

> He was *real*. I had met one or two remarkable people in my life, but nobody who was quite so incontrovertibly, ineluctably real. Meeting him brought me into more direct contact with myself and my hidden problems. It also activated positive emotions. The chaos was there but it was a happy and at times inspired chaos.[18]

Sangharakshita sensed the possibility of developing something that went beyond what he had achieved in India. He decided to pay a farewell visit to India and, in September 1966, he flew with Terry to Bombay. They travelled, met his old friends, and addressed large gatherings of Dr Ambedkar's new Buddhist followers. At the Kalimpong Vihara he found a letter from the English Sangha Trust announcing they wouldn't renew their invitation on the grounds that 'I had not comported myself in a manner fitting the religious office that I held in the Order.' He turned to Terry and declared, '[This] means a new Buddhist movement!'[19]

• • •

Sangharakshita's opponents never publicly stated their accusations, but an editorial by Maurice Walshe, the chairman of the English Sangha Trust, in the January 1968 issue of *The Western Buddhist* probably gives a sense of his position:

> There are far too many spurious 'Buddhists' about, whose self-invented teachings at best spread confusion and at worst, when combined with drug-taking and other practices, lead to moral degradation and personal tragedy. It is not only the right but the duty of true Buddhists to proclaim the genuine teaching and denounce imposters and spiritual demagogues.[20]

It is reasonable to assume that Sangharakshita was the principal morally degraded imposter that Walshe had in mind.[21] For his part, Sangharakshita later spoke of 'Pāli fundamentalists' who 'adopted towards the Pāli scriptures the same sort of attitude that Christian, especially Protestant, fundamentalists adopt towards the Bible'.[22] He also thought Walshe had a Machiavellian side to his character.

There is little merit in re-litigating the dispute, but two themes have lasting relevance. The first is the assumption that Sangharakshita's relationship with Terry was sexual. There is no evidence for this. Only the two people directly involved knew the truth, and Terry never commented while Sangharakshita always insisted that he remained celibate. At the same time, Sangharakshita made little effort to act in ways his critics would have considered fitting for a 'respectable' bhikkhu. Some people clearly believed that, having veered away from their idea of how a bhikkhu should behave, he felt free to do what he liked. Christmas Humphreys wrote to Sangharakshita in Kalimpong:

> It is the image you have created which is the real cause of the present crisis, even though no 'offence' has been committed by you or anyone at any time. It is your public image that is in question. You have to face the depth and power of the English middle-class mind, and its abhorrence of homosexuality.[23]

Sangharakshita responded with an indignant telegram declaring: 'NO INTENTION BEING SACRIFICED COMBINATION HINAYANA BRITISH RESPECTABILITY STOP.'[24] He wrote to one of his supporters that Humphreys was 'burning incense at the shrine of the British Middle-Class Mind',[25] and later commented that the responses showed that, at least in England,

> it was difficult for men to develop more than ordinarily close friendships without incurring the suspicion of homosexuality and, in some cases, the unpleasant and even painful consequences of such suspicion.[26]

But, even if we discount accusations of sexual activity, Sangharakshita's position at the Vihara was fundamentally untenable, and both parties bear some responsibility for the clash. Walshe insisted, following Sangharakshita's departure, that Hampstead was 'a Buddhist Vihara in the Theravādin tradition'[27] whose purpose was 'to lay the foundations of a Buddhist branch of the Bhikkhu Sangha, having unquestioned validity of ordination and the full force of the ancient tradition'.[28] Sangharakshita was a well-known critic of the Theravāda, and the Vihara's magazine introduced him as someone who 'envisaged Buddhism as one teaching, though split by history into different *yānas*'.[29] If it really was a Theravādin Vihara, the trustees should never have invited Sangharakshita. Perhaps they thought that, as the most senior British monk[30] and with a foot in both the Theravāda and pan-Buddhist camps, he would mediate between the Vihara and the Buddhist Society. He tried to do so, but, if they also thought he would quietly support Theravāda-style activities at the Vihara, they completely misjudged him.

Sangharakshita must also bear some responsibility. He may have thought that, as the senior-most British-born monk, he would be able to shape the Vihara as he thought best, and it is possible that some at the Vihara didn't agree with Walshe that it should be exclusively Theravādin. But Sangharakshita's teaching at the Vihara didn't just diverge from a Theravādin presentation: it innovated in entirely new ways, and he established a community around the Vihara whose members had no interest in the Theravāda. He later recognized 'it would have been hard to avoid conflict because I did not believe the whole truth was contained in the Theravāda.'[31] Walshe's ambition to create an English Theravādin bhikkhu sangha depended on the Vihara's resources, and he realized his goal in 1977 when the Trust's assets enabled a group of western monks led by Ajahn Sumedho to establish Chithurst Priory in Sussex, the first in a network of linked monasteries across western countries.

The false accusations, homophobia, and committee-room politics gave the falling out at Hampstead an unpleasantness that lingered for many years. It freed Sangharakshita to operate in a new way, and I once asked him if perhaps the debacle was a blessing in disguise. 'Perhaps', he replied. 'Though the disguise was very heavy.'[32]

In the wilderness, 1967

The dispute that ended Sangharakshita's time at the Hampstead Buddhist Vihara was the pivot on which his Buddhist career turned. In India he was celebrated for his writing and respected for his work with the followers of Dr Ambedkar. Henceforth, he was a more isolated figure, but he comments in *Moving against the Stream* that the Trust's letter, 'coming as it did like a flash of lightning, had suddenly revealed possibilities that had hitherto been shrouded in darkness or perceived only dimly'.[33] He began teaching independently with the aid of a group of supporters, an organization was formed to promote his activities, and in April 1967 a small centre opened in Monmouth Street, in Central London, beneath a shop called Sakura.³⁴ A year later, in April 1968, he conducted ordinations into the Western Buddhist Order, and his supporters formed a charity called the Friends of the Western Buddhist Order, or FWBO.

Sangharakshita's accounts of the period following his departure from the Hampstead Vihara often mention his sense of being 'in the wilderness', and sometimes evoke the image of the biblical scapegoat:

> How did it feel
> To be left alone in the desert
> Loaded down with the sins
> Of a whole people?³⁵

The established Buddhist world had rejected him, and, though that was clearly painful, it was also a liberation:

> I felt free to strike out in an entirely new direction, even if this meant sometimes flying in the face of accepted 'tradition'. Thus, I experimented not only with sex but with drugs, alcohol and dress, as well as in a hundred other ways. At the same time, I read, meditated, and lectured intensively. My overall purpose in all this was to create a new, radical Buddhist movement that was both genuinely Buddhist and genuinely Western.³⁶

The 1967 poem 'Fourth Metamorphosis' describes a wish to renounce every ascribed identity:

> Too long have I been a camel
> Ship of the Desert
> Too long knelt to be laden
> With other men's merchandise.
>
> Too long have I been a lion
> Lord of the Jungle
> Too long fought
> Paper-and-tinsel dragons

Too long have I been a child
Parent of the Future

Now it is time to be
Myself.[37]

Sangharakshita had been cast out because he didn't act as people expected a monk to act. Meanwhile, all around him, young people were embarking on a sexual revolution and, in July 1967, the Sexual Offences Act removed the legal penalty for sex between men over the age of twenty-one. He was a forty-two-year-old virgin who had been struggling with sexual feelings: 'everything seemed to be in the melting pot. I was, in a sense, free to do what I wanted, free to do whatever I felt was best.'[38] A 1968 poem declares:

I want to break out,
Batter down the door,
Go tramping black heather all day
On the windy moor.

Escape from physical bounds became an apocalyptic impulse to '[s]hatter time and space'.[39]

In the same year a young American named Carter visited the Monmouth Street centre and needed somewhere to stay for the night. 'Shall I make you up a bed on the floor, or will you sleep with me?' asked Sangharakshita. Carter replied, 'I'll sleep with you.' Sangharakshita later described the young American as 'six feet or more in height, and twenty-one years old, he had tousled, sun-bleached hair and blue eyes, and his well-proportioned body seemed made of gold rather than flesh.' Sangharakshita called what happened next 'my initiation into the world of erotic bliss'.[40] It began a period in which he was sexually active that lasted up to the mid-1980s.

In doing this, Sangharakshita later said, he was following his intuition. He never presented sex as a tantric connection in the manner of Chögyam Trungpa, who slept with many of his female disciples and said he was 'having a love affair with all his students'.[41] There is also no indication that he idealized sex as many others did at this time, especially in the counterculture. He said his principal motivation was 'a desire for deeper and more authentic human communication':

> In the late 'sixties and early 'seventies 'communication' was very much in the air and it was widely believed [...] that the sexual relation is the highest form of human communication. Though I did not really share this belief, I was conscious that my experience of this aspect of life had been very limited, and therefore decided to ascertain the truth of the matter for myself.[42]

Sangharakshita wrote this in 1992, in a 'Letter to a Friend' (later made public) who had questioned his behaviour. A poem from 1969, entitled 'The Great Reader', suggests what communication meant to him at the time:

> Night after night, I read
> The Book of You, turning
> Page after illuminated
> Page, dazzled
> By the gold, lost
> Among red and blue traceries,
> [...] all the while
> Desperately
> Seeking to spell out the subtleties
> Of a smile, the meaning
> Of your life for mine
> Maybe.

Communication held the same fascination he had felt as a boy lying on his elbow 'in yellow light'[43] and immersing himself in the magical world of literature. Sangharakshita brought this quality of openness, warmth, and honesty to his interactions with the people who were gathering around the FWBO, and encouraged them to do the same. He led 'communication exercises' on retreats, and emphasized 'the value of friendship to one's spiritual life'.[44]

In later years it became clear that some of Sangharakshita's sexual activity had been problematic for some of his partners, and we shall come to the problems in Chapter Three. But we understand them better by setting his behaviour in the context of his life on all its levels. James Hillman observed in 1968 that more was at stake in the sexual revolution than sex alone:

> The real revolution going on in the individual soul is not so much sexual as it is psychic and symbolic, a struggle for a wholly new (yet most ancient and religious) experience of reality which only happens to be carried for us in its nascence by a sexual fantasy of this psychic reality.[45]

Hillman thought the transcendence people sought in sex was realized only if those feelings were internalized, rather than acted out, and that required moral constraint. This is, broadly, the Buddhist view, and it was Sangharakshita's basic understanding, but after almost two decades as a monk he no longer saw celibacy as the solution.

Sangharakshita often spoke in this period of the need to be whole and integrated on every level, and said that meant opening to deep psychic forces. He spoke for instance of integrating unconscious energies until they were completely absorbed within conscious awareness, like light banishing darkness, 'so that there is one illumination from top to bottom, not just a little sunlight on the peaks and the rest below in total darkness'.[46] Practice was messier, in both Sangharakshita's life and psychoanalytic understanding, but he insisted these energies must somehow be engaged if Enlightenment was to be more than a fantasy. '[T]ranscendental Reality', he said in 1969, 'is to be experienced by the *whole man*, functioning with the utmost intensity at the height of his unified being.'[47]

Padmasambhava's taming of the Tibetan spirits was an important image for Sangharakshita of integrating the depths of experience, but there were others, and the integration he sought wasn't just a matter of personal psychology. In the Italian churches he visited in 1966 he was drawn to the image of St Jerome, the translator of the Bible into Latin, who is depicted sometimes in the wilderness and sometimes in a cave or a study. For Sangharakshita, Jerome embodied the archetype of the translator who must plumb the depths of their understanding to render the meaning of a text in another language. He saw himself as a translator in that sense:

> I was trying to communicate the spirit of the Dharma in terms of Western rather than in terms of Eastern culture. I was thus a translator, with all that that implies in the way of seeking to fathom the uttermost depths of what one is trying to translate so that one may translate it faithfully.[48]

This is only possible by fathoming one's own utmost depths and then 'translating what one has experienced on one level of consciousness into terms appropriate to another level of consciousness'. That level of consciousness is elusive, but images such as the figure of St Jerome mediated it for Sangharakshita. The 1984 paper 'St Jerome Revisited' (which surveys the saint's rich associations) concludes:

> St Jerome is therefore not only the translator and interpreter but also the creator and artist, and because he is the creator and artist he is the true individual; for the corollary of the fact that all knowledge is, in a sense, identical with its object, and that what one translates is one level of one's own being into another, is that all translation is essentially an individual and even a solitary activity.[49]

The best testimony to what was happening within Sangharakshita in this period is his teaching, which was at its most innovative and brilliant, and many of his lectures remain influential five decades later. He was finding new ways to express old truths. Nietzsche's Zarathustra cries, 'like all creators, I have grown weary of the old tongues',[50] and the 1969 poem 'New' declares Sangharakshita's desire for fresh expression:

> I should like to speak
> With a new voice, speak
> Like Adam in the Garden

> [...]
> I should like to use
> New words, use
> Words pristine, primeval, words
> Pure and bright as snow-crystals, words
> Resonant, expressive, creative,
> Such as, breathed to music, built Ilion.
> (The old words
> Are too tired soiled stale lifeless.)[51]

* * *

Sangharakshita knew his lifestyle and teaching prompted disapproval in some quarters. On what authority had he founded a new order? Who had authorized him to combine Mahāyāna and Theravāda teachings or speak of Buddhism as the 'path of the Higher Evolution'? Who said he could have sex? He reflected in the 1993 work *Forty-Three Years Ago: Reflections on My Bhikkhu Ordination*:

> The wilderness is a wonderful place. In it many things become clear to one. What became clear to me was not the absolute centrality, in the Buddhist life, of the act of Going for Refuge to the Three Jewels (this had been clear to me for some time), so much as the need for the fact of that centrality to find 'collective' embodiment in a new Buddhist movement, and it was because this had become clear to me that I was led to found the Western Buddhist Order.[52]

He still devoted most of his time to studying, writing, and teaching, and felt more engaged than ever with the Dharma. Ceasing to be a monk didn't mean he was becoming a layperson, in the traditional sense. He remained 'Sangharakshita' rather than reverting to 'Dennis', for some years continued to wear monk's robes when he taught (albeit over civilian clothes), and published as the 'Venerable Maha Sthavira Sangharakshita'.[53] For his critics this showed his hypocrisy, or – worse – that he was using the prestige of monasticism to win disciples and find sex, but in his view it simply reflected the gap between an old form of Buddhist commitment and something new.

Sangharakshita's sexual activity also raised questions among some of his students in the FWBO. Not everyone knew about it, but most did, and most of those accepted it. Nagabodhi writes of the early 1970s:

> Sangharakshita was such a radical character and so obviously a genuine Buddhist, that whether or not he was living as a monk wasn't an issue. If anything, the development made him a more interesting character and more in tune with the times.[54]

A memoir by an Order member named Buddhadasa describes what happened when, in the same period, a friend heard that Sangharakshita had made a sexual approach to one of his fellow community members. Buddhadasa suggested they raise it with Sangharakshita directly:

> Sitting at ease on the carpet of his living room floor, leaning against his armchair, he listened to what we had to say. When he came to speak, he neither denied, defended or justified his behaviour. He simply said, in effect, that he would like us both to know that he was completely happy with his conduct and living as he chose to live. Whether this statement, spoken so pleasantly and naturally, completely satisfied Malcolm, I had my doubts, but it satisfied me. I felt that Sangharakshita was being utterly authentic and sincere about his sexuality.[55]

Perhaps a model for Sangharakshita was 'the artist', whom he celebrated in this period, in the Romantic way, as someone who was 'independent in spirit, and to a large extent free from group conditioning'. Society might condemn such a person, but that was a secondary matter:

> The real question is not whether the artist is immoral, but whether flouting conventional morality is wrong. Only too often it is clear that conventional morality itself is at fault, and

that the artist's rejection of it is simply an expression of his or her own healthier and more balanced mental attitude.[56]

That's an attractive image, though it's perhaps also worth recalling the mess that often attends artists' personal lives and their (perhaps unwitting) impact on others.

• • •

Sangharakshita's heightened consciousness in this period included pain as well as inspiration. One day, he reflected on the Buddhist legend in which intense anguish overwhelms Avalokiteśvara, the bodhisattva of compassion, as he contemplates the sufferings of sentient beings. His head splits into 1,000 pieces, and Sangharakshita recalls in his memoirs:

> When I reached this point in the story I was very deeply affected. I started sobbing uncontrollably. In between my sobs I kept crying out to the friend who was with me, 'His head split into a thousand pieces! His head split into a thousand pieces!' This sobbing and crying out must have lasted for up to half an hour. I am not a person who sheds tears easily, and the experience has not been repeated, though the impression it made on me persists.[57]

In April 1968, after many late nights discussing Terry's growing despair, and just a few days after the first ordinations into the Western Buddhist Order, Terry committed suicide. *Moving against the Stream* concludes:

> But though I missed Terry, and wept every day for six months, what he had called 'this event' was not an unrelieved tragedy. The day after his death I took the classes at Sakura as usual. While meditating I heard these words:
>
> Pain shall be transmuted into joy, suffering into ecstasy,
> When to the eternal life of Buddhahood
> We all awake.[58]

For all the difficulties, Sangharakshita felt something else was at work. 'There are times', he later reflected, 'when I am dimly aware of a vast, overshadowing Consciousness that has, through me, founded the Order and set in motion our whole Movement.'[59]

Pundarika, 1972

18 May 1972. Sangharakshita stood in the first-floor shrine room of Pundarika, the FWBO's main centre, housed in a former piano factory in Archway, North London. The neighbourhood was scheduled for redevelopment and largely derelict. Students, artists, junkies, and dropouts squatted disused houses in the surrounding streets along with the 'embattled and suspicious' remnants of the former community.[60] A grammar-free poem printed in the *FWBO Newsletter* evokes both the surroundings and the experience of people attending the centre:

like a lotus in the mud
    surrounded by demolition sites
  burnt out cars
  paint pots
      rusty brass beds
    milk crates
    and corrugated fences
  some dirty children
      pull a dog along
          on a piece of tatty rope
[...]
        cracked windows
          first-floor meditation hall
            white walls and sacred air
      bodhisattvas sit
          like mountains
              and concentrate
          someone in the street
            slams a car door
              nothing moves
                  except for a little dust[61]

The event was billed as 'Padmasambhava Day', and seventy people had come to hear Sangharakshita's talk and participate in a puja featuring mantras, gongs, and cymbals. A few in the audience had the Pāli or Sanskrit names of members of the Western Buddhist Order that Sangharakshita had established four years earlier, but active Order members were scarce. On discovering the FWBO in 1970, Buddhadasa found 'the number of active and dedicated Order members was in fact pitifully small, maybe no more than three or four from the two dozen or so that had been previously ordained in 1968 and 1969.'[62] Sangharakshita himself said the following year: 'the majority of members are lukewarm in their commitment [...] and lax in their practice of the Path.'[63]

But something was changing. Around 1970, Ananda noticed, 'a new kind of energy and thought came into existence, born perhaps out of a greater awareness of a need for the Dharma in the West.'[64] Visiting the FWBO in London in 1971 Abhaya sensed 'a gathering of momentum in preparation for a breakthrough'.[65] Members of a newer group who weren't yet ordained were eager to put Sangharakshita's talk of a 'New Society' into practice. Some had squatted houses around the centre, forming the first FWBO communities, all of which initially included both men and women. Nagabodhi was one of these young people and recalled Sangharakshita in this period:

> To be around him was like being in the company of a bigger presence in a bigger universe. Despite, or perhaps because of, the extreme mindfulness of his movements and diction, his knowledge, refinement, and wisdom, there was something almost unnervingly different about him, something deliberate, conscious, but quietly untamed.[66]

As this was a public talk, Sangharakshita wore bhikkhu robes over western clothes, his lank and greasy hair hanging down to his shoulders. His speaking voice, which can still be heard on a muddy tape recording, is steady and deliberate, with an emphatic cadence somewhat lightened by amusement. The title of his talk was 'Padmasambhava: Tantric Guru of Tibet'.

Sangharakshita often spoke about Padmasambhava, but this is one of only two lectures entirely devoted to him. It begins with the encounter in the Darjeeling gompa, the legends surrounding Padmasambhava's life, and a sketch of what can be said about him historically. The main subject is Padmasambhava's subjugation of the Tibetan gods, whom Sangharakshita interprets as embodiments of the non-rational forces of 'the Tibetan collective unconscious'. In subduing them, he says, Padmasambhava integrated these forces into 'the great current of the spiritual life of Tibetan Buddhism'. Likewise, for the Dharma to take root in western countries, it must engage the deep cultural energies of western culture. First, individuals must engage their own psyches:

> It's not enough just to read books on Buddhism, to listen to lectures. One must also meditate, one must plumb the depths within oneself. One must chant, perform pujas, engage in symbolical ritual. It's not enough just to think, even to think about Buddhism; one must feel. One must respond with one's whole being.

Individual transformation was just the start. If enough people made that change, '[we will] have a genuine authentic Buddhist spiritual movement in this country'. The FWBO was the vehicle and, notwithstanding Pundarika's insalubrious setting, Sangharakshita thought the germinal movement had the potential to become a new 'spiritual tradition' that far surpassed the 'little wave of intellectual interest' he had encountered on his return to England.[67] Writing in the *FWBO Newsletter* the following year he said:

> The handful of people who, six years ago, met and meditated together for the first time in a tiny basement in Monmouth Street started something – or were started by something – the vast potential of which is only just now beginning to be realized. I am convinced that, whatever its present limitations may be, the FWBO is not only the most important factor in all our lives, but *one of the main growing points of the Higher Evolution in the western hemisphere.*[68]

The London Buddhist Centre, 1979

It is Padmasambhava Day, 10 September 1979. Sangharakshita, aged fifty-four and cutting a substantial middle-aged figure, stands in the shrine room of the London Buddhist Centre in Bethnal Green – the LBC. In just a few years, the FWBO had grown significantly, with the opening of several urban centres and retreat centres in the UK and other centres overseas. Some in the audience were seeing 'Bhante' in the flesh for the first time, though, of course, they had listened to recordings of his lectures at Dharma classes and on retreats, perhaps read some of his books and heard him quoted in deferential tones.

The LBC had opened a year earlier after an epic building programme that converted a derelict Victorian fire station into what FWBO publications declared to be the largest urban Buddhist centre in Europe. The shrine room was in the space from which fire engines had raced onto Roman Road with bells ringing and horses straining, but now it was triple-glazed and insulated, and a giant, gold-painted Buddha, owing as much to Greek statuary as to Indian *rūpa*s, dominated the room.

The LBC wasn't just a place to teach and practise Buddhism – it declared Buddhism's arrival in the modern world. This wasn't eastern Buddhism in the West, or western life with a Buddhist dimension; it was 'western Buddhism' made concrete. The Dharma might be timeless, and the Buddhist tradition filled with riches, but the building declared they had been reborn. The LBC was a bridge to 'a new and total way of life based upon the growth and development of individuals'.[69] Dozens of men and women, mostly in their twenties and thirties, lived in single-sex residential communities in and around the building, and many worked together in the co-operative businesses that were springing up in the neighbourhood: a café, a wholefood shop, a building company, a typesetting business, and more. Over a hundred Order members ran FWBO centres or branches in other British cities, many with their own residential communities and right-livelihood projects.[70] Uniquely for a British Buddhist movement at this time, FWBO activities had spread overseas. Activities had started in Holland, Finland, and New Zealand, and a dynamic

Order member called Lokamitra had recently moved to India with two companions to pick up Sangharakshita's work among the followers of Dr Ambedkar.

By then Sangharakshita's base was a country house turned retreat centre in Norfolk, which he had named Padmaloka (meaning 'Lotus Realm').[71] One visitor in this period recalled the 'old-fashioned garden, the serene shrine-room, Sangharakshita's study and books, the strange forest, the river, the pungent smell of the fields'.[72] Sangharakshita sometimes wryly described himself as a 'Norfolk country gentleman',[73] and in later years he still loved the 'ancient oak trees overspread with foliage', the 'lawn molehill-pitted with flower beds', and the woodland visited by 'small shy deer'.[74]

Was there more beneath the surface of Sangharakshita's life in 1979, as there had been in 1962 – more than was evident to the students and disciples? A poem written the previous year entitled 'Before Dawn' evokes another Sangharakshita who woke early with an anxious, attenuated sense of unreality:

> Cut off from what I really think and feel,
> The substance of my life becomes ideal.
>
> A whited sepulchre, a plaster saint,
> Is not much use, however bright its paint.
>
> Dreaming, awake, I must do all I can
> To join the inward and the outward man.
>
> Death stares me in the face: I watch and pray.
> So near the goal, and yet so far away![75]

But, if Sangharakshita sensed a distance between his inward self – the self of his dreams – and his waking experience and outward persona, he said little else about it, despite publishing a detailed account of his activities in 1979.[76]

In the months before the Padmasambhava Day talk, Sangharakshita had travelled to India and then New Zealand. In India large crowds and former students eager to renew their contact had greeted Sangharakshita. His past activities had acquired an almost legendary status, and now he could offer his Ambedkarite listeners a modern Buddhist movement that, he believed, exactly suited their needs. Lokamitra, the leader of the Order team, was an accomplished teacher and organizer in his own right, and Sangharakshita was confident the team were conveying the spirit of the movement. Through them, he said, 'something very clear and very pure had started flowing through the stagnant wastes of Maharashtrian Buddhism'.[77]

From India Sangharakshita travelled to New Zealand, where FWBO activities were well established, and gave a series of talks with the title 'A New Buddhist Movement – the Meaning of the FWBO'. As he described it, the FWBO was much more that an organization. He called it 'a "current" of positive emotional and spiritual energy', and warned 'it will give you a shock.'[78]

To express the movement's meaning, Sangharakshita had increasingly been using images and symbols. He called the Order a manifestation of the 1,000-armed Avalokiteśvara, the bodhisattva of compassion, and said the movement was the windhorse, a winged horse carrying on its back the Three Jewels, emblems of Buddhism. A windhorse mural had been painted in the LBC's courtyard entrance, evoking 'all the aroused energies, all the aroused positive mental states that are capable of being the bearer of the Three Jewels'.[79] Ian Oliver travelled to many FWBO centres to write a book on *Buddhism in Britain,* published in 1979, and testified to the 'intensity of energy' that was palpable throughout the movement.[80]

Fifteen years after Sangharakshita's return to England, eleven years after the first ordinations into the Western Buddhist Order, and just seven years after his talk in the modest surroundings of Pundarika, what he had achieved was astonishing.

* * *

Sangharakshita arrived at the LBC at the end of a daylong festival that included readings from the newly published translation of *The Life and Liberation of Padmasambhava.* He was greeted by 'eager, expectant faces',[81] and a buoyant, enthusiastic atmosphere. He had had no time to prepare a talk, but was at the peak of his speaking powers and addressing his audience without notes seemed to release something in him. Reading *The Life and Liberation* earlier in the year had been 'a major imaginative and spiritual experience' for him and, reviewing the book for the *FWBO Newsletter*, he described Padmasambhava's mission in a way that perhaps echoed his own sense of channelling something larger than his conscious self.

> One gets the impression not only of a vivid and powerful spiritual 'personality' heroically battling with the forces of evil but also of a stream of impersonal spiritual energy which is coterminous with historical Buddhism itself and which, intervening in the course of events age after age, and assuming a variety of forms, brings under its control all the swirling emotional-psychic energies which at one or another level of mundane existence obstruct the liberating influence of the Dharma.[82]

The LBC talk describes four archetypal Buddhist figures: the *manu*, the Buddha, the guru, and the *tertön*. The *manu* is the lawgiver, and in this context represents the need for an ethical society that is necessary for the Dharma to flourish. The Buddha discovers and proclaims the Dharma but, Sangharakshita comments, the Buddha of history 'had time to proclaim the teaching only in a general way, and he addressed it mainly to the conscious, rational part of humanity'.[83] This is where the figure of the guru comes in, and Padmasambhava is its archetypal embodiment: '[H]e is concerned with the transformation of the depths, and this is why he figures as the subduer of gods and demons.' The Buddhist practitioner must do the same: 'You've got to descend into the flames, as Blake would have said, and transform them.' These deep energies can then be integrated with 'the purer, clearer energies of the spiritual life, so that our spiritual life pulses with life and energy'. Sangharakshita also connects Padmasambhava's role with the paths of vision and transformation:

> If we take the Buddha as the personification of the path of vision, Padmasambhava is the personification of the path of

transformation [...] Padmasambhava represents that powerful principle of transformation.[84]

The last figure is the *tertön*, who discovers hidden teachings, or *terma*s. As Sangharakshita says: 'Circumstances change, and new versions of the teachings need to be adapted to new circumstances.' For that reason, Padmasambhava, representing the principle of transformation, concealed teachings that would be rediscovered when the time was right. The *terma*s are 'inspirations which come to us for our guidance in accordance with the general principles of the teaching in both its visionary and its transforming aspects'.

Although Sangharakshita doesn't say so explicitly, the figure of the *tertön* echoed his own role. Perhaps, like Padmasambhava, Sangharakshita believed he had travelled deep into his own psyche and, like a *tertön*, discovered there hidden or forgotten teachings that renewed the Dharma's relevance. These were lessons of the depths rather than inspirations from above:

> You don't have to go outside the world to find the transcendental. You go very deeply into it. You utilize all its forces, all its energies, integrate them with yourself, and that is your spiritual life.

Accessed and integrated, these energies constitute a mighty force:

> Let the demons come! Let all the gods and demons of the City of London and the West, and the whole world, come and be transformed. One shouldn't be afraid of the gods and demons, or of the *ḍākinīs*, even if they do ride upon buffaloes. Let them come! But let them be transformed, and let them contribute their energy to the spiritual life.[85]

The talk implies a further parallel. If Sangharakshita was the *tertön*, the FWBO was the *terma*: the tangible, outward product of this inner transformation. And if the FWBO was true to his inspiration, it could transform not just the inner demons of individuals but the demonic forces that were alive in the world. 'There are economic demons, sociological demons, political demons, even religious demons and philosophical demons, all of which need to be brought under control.' This was the FWBO's inner meaning and true purpose:

> It's not simply a Buddhist movement in the narrow sense [...] It's a stream of spiritual energy that deeply transforms and transfigures everything and everyone with which and with whom it comes into contact. Padmasambhava encountered gods, demons, and *ḍākinīs*, and transformed them, and this is what we must do, if we're strong enough. We should not flee from these energies but allow ourselves to be in contact with them within our own selves, transform them, and go forward along the path with renewed energy, strength, and inspiration.[86]

Chapter Three
Actions and Consequences

Transition

The Sierra de Aitana mountains rise inland above the crowded beaches of the Spanish Costa Blanca, and one of the valleys snaking through their upper reaches is particularly secluded. Bounded by high limestone cliffs, scarcely a sound enters from the outside world, and Sangharakshita renamed it Guhyaloka, meaning 'the hidden world'. Below the cliffs are scree slopes, then gorse and wild rosemary followed by terraces filled with almond and olive trees. The weathered cliffs make a gap-toothed skyline, and rocky outcrops prod upwards in the valley's centre.

Guhyaloka was bought in 1985 as a birthday present when Sangharakshita turned sixty. His home was a bungalow on the main slope, halfway down the valley, facing south and surrounded by pines and holly oak. If Padmaloka was 'romantic pastoral', Guhyaloka was 'gothic sublime', like Kalimpong, and the terrain matched his mood. He wanted to withdraw gradually from institutional responsibilities, spending the winters in the milder climate and devoting himself to writing.

But events moved at their own pace. On Christmas Eve 1986 Sangharakshita found he couldn't urinate, and discomfort quickly spread through his body. The support team fetched a doctor from the nearest village, but on examining Sangharakshita the doctor realized he needed a catheter to relieve the stoppage. In the time it took the doctor to go back to the village and return with the correct equipment, Sangharakshita's pain grew almost unbearable. He repeatedly blacked out and thought he might die. He returned to England and arranged to see a specialist who said he needed an operation on his prostate. Cancer couldn't be ruled out: 'Make no mistake about it', the doctor told him. 'This is major surgery.'[1] He was sixty-one years old and had a premonition that he might die under anaesthetic.

Reflection on death had always been a part of Sangharakshita's Buddhist practice, but in the preceding years he had contemplated his own mortality with a new intensity. He placed a skull on the desk at Padmaloka and pondered St Jerome, who is depicted in his cell with a lion, a skull representing death, and an hourglass representing the rapid passage of time. The 1984 paper *St Jerome Revisited* dwells at length on mortality, quoting Marvell's lines: 'But at my back I always hear Time's wingèd chariot hurrying near.'[2]

The prostate operation and the prospect of dying sharpened these reflections and focused Sangharakshita's attention on changes that would allow the FWBO to continue without him. He had never seen the movement as an organization or viewed himself as its leader in an organizational sense. It was structured as a network of autonomous charities directed by Order members, and responsibility lay with the people who were directly involved. But he was the head of the Order, with responsibility for conducting ordinations.

Sangharakshita didn't die under the surgeon's knife, and set about handing on his responsibilities. He wrote *The History of My Going for Refuge* and presented it to a gathering of Order members in April 1988, explaining how he had come to consider going for refuge the central act of the Buddhist life and how the Order embodied it. The text also explained his understanding of the Buddhist path through his personal experience and as a practice. Some Order members had already started to conduct ordinations on Sangharakshita's behalf, and he now appointed a small group as 'public preceptors'. They were to make final decisions on readiness for ordination and conduct ordinations, and over the next few years they developed 'ordination processes' to help men and women prepare for ordination. In later years, the public preceptors were formed into a college that developed an elaborate system for ordinations around the world.

A second health scare in 1988[3] sharpened Sangharakshita's desire to move on:

> I did not want to function mainly as the head and, so to speak, administrator of the WBO and FWBO or to devote the greater part of my time and energy to organizational matters, as has been increasingly the case in recent years. If it was at all possible, I wanted to make a further creative contribution to the development of the movement rather than to confine myself to helping with the running of the movement as it already existed.[4]

He never stopped feeling the weight of his responsibility to the movement or the mission that had led him to found it, and as late as 1996 he felt it was 'incumbent upon me, during such time as I have left, to do whatever I can to ensure the continuity, well-being, and growth of the Movement after my departure from the scene'.[5] But he stopped leading seminars, gave fewer public lectures, and devoted himself to writing. He continued to distil his understanding of the Order and movement in papers and lectures, but much of his writing looked back over his life. He had begun his memoirs while he was in Kalimpong and completed the first volume in 1973. Now he produced two more substantial volumes and later completed a fourth. Along with the shorter volume *Precious Teachers* (which covered the gap between the third and fourth volumes), they offered a detailed account of his life up to 1967. The only other full-length works he wrote were *The FWBO and 'Protestant Buddhism'* (1992), which engaged polemically with an academic critique of the FWBO, and *From Genesis to the Diamond Sutra* (2005), another retrospective work that explored his engagement with Christianity. He also wrote occasional pieces and checked the many volumes that were edited from his earlier teachings. His steady temperament produced a steady life increasingly centred on memory, writing, reading and reflection, personal meetings, and a few important friendships.

But Sangharakshita's life was not one of unalloyed peace. In 1997 *The Guardian* published a long article criticizing his sexual activity and highlighting other difficulties in the FWBO. A poem, written in 1998, described his feelings on arriving at Guhyaloka in its wake. The pine trees welcomed him, his soul was expanded, and he communed with the 'giant shapes of stone' that dominated it. But the valley was a refuge from 'the venom-dripping tongue / And the shafts that fly in darkness'. Its 'grey, ancient forms' told him:

> Though the 'worldly winds' assail me,
> Though friends my cause abjure,
> Far from the magic valley
> The word will be: Endure.[6]

In 1999, on his seventy-fifth birthday, he handed on the headship of the Order to the public preceptors with the comment: 'I have done what I can.'[7] He then went straight to Guhyaloka where he wrote a poem expressing satisfaction and perhaps relief:

> Drenched in silence, drenched in starlight,
> With peace my thoughts are crowned
> And I sense within this 'being'
> A 'not-being' more profound.[8]

He later said that in handing on the headship he sensed that something had passed from him.[9]

But more difficulties would follow. In 2002 a combination of high blood pressure, insomnia, and palpitations precipitated a period of sleep deprivation that continued for over a year. On a good night he might have a few hours' sleep, but it was broken and usually unsatisfying. He had little energy, and often felt on the verge of collapse. He recalled, in a short piece written a decade later entitled *A Season in Hell*, that '[t]iredness was piled on tiredness, suffering on suffering, torture on torture.'[10] The friends who supported him, and others in the Madhyamaloka community, observed that, under the pressure of his insomnia, character traits came to the fore that his mindfulness and self-possession had hitherto contained. He had always been 'a worrier'[11] and now his insomnia, and the side-effects of the drugs he took to treat it, produced an intense anxiety that could make him peevish and demanding.

Sangharakshita was complex and contradictory, even *in extremis*. Sometimes, in a snatched period of sleep, he dreamed that he sat among yellow-robed monks, saw 'diamonds strewn across a dark background like stars across the midnight sky', or found himself 'walking down a broad tunnel that led into the depths of the earth'.[12] He slowly recovered, but he had become an old man.

Sex and controversy

The ethics of Sangharakshita's sexual activity in the years between 1967 and the mid-1980s (when he returned to celibacy) have been the subject of intense, prolonged, and often critical discussion – internally within Triratna, in the wider Buddhist world, and in the British media. For all this, it remains a difficult subject to discuss. The evidence for what happened takes the form of personal testimonies, and Sangharakshita's sexual partners have expressed a range of responses to what happened, while he had his own account of events. Reporting on his most prominent critic's testimony has taken it at face value but disregarded the account Sangharakshita offered in 2017.[13]

The discussion is further complicated by changing attitudes to sex. Conventional sexual morality, including the middle-class abhorrence of homosexuality Christmas Humphreys described, was normal in the 1960s and 1970s. The counterculture rebelled against those attitudes and enjoyed the freedom afforded by the sexual revolution, while gay culture embraced the possibilities that followed the legalization of homosexuality. Things looked different in the late 1980s – the era of feminism, AIDS, and *Sex in the Forbidden Zone* – and different again in the 2000s – the period of sexual-abuse scandals in different churches and the trends that became the 'Me Too' movement. Should we judge Sangharakshita by the standards of the time in which he was sexually active or those of a later period?

In 1987 one of Sangharakshita's former partners started to speak out against him, first within the FWBO and then to the media. In 1997 a Buddhist from outside the FWBO combined the testimony of Sangharakshita's critics at the Hampstead Vihara with that of former members of the FWBO, and compiled a dossier that he sent to the UK media. An article appeared in *The Guardian* that included criticisms of Sangharakshita and accounts of unethical behaviour at an FWBO centre a decade earlier.[14] A fuller version of the dossier, entitled *The FWBO Files*, was published anonymously online in 1998. In 2003 another former partner (who carried more credibility with people who knew the individuals concerned) shared his own account of sexual contact with Sangharakshita and its impact. Two similar testimonies followed in later years, and even Sangharakshita's longest-standing partner, who lived with him for most of the 1980s, resigned from the Order stating his unhappiness.

Conversations with Bhante

In August 2009 Sangharakshita met three senior Order members – Nagabodhi, Mahamati, and Subhuti – at Madhyamaloka, the large Victorian house in Birmingham that had been his home since 1995. He was eighty-four, and prolonged illness had weakened him. He walked slowly with the support of a stick, and macular degeneration meant he saw only a distorted image of what was in front of him. But, though his energy was limited, his mind remained clear.

Earlier in the year, Sangharakshita had met a group of Order members to address issues in the movement. The result was an interview published as 'What is the Western Buddhist Order?', which we will come to at the end of this book. The main subject for the second round of discussions was his sexual activity. His interlocutors understood the issues it had raised and knew Sangharakshita hadn't fully answered his critics, so they pressed him to say more about the motivations behind his behaviour and its impact. The discussion was later published as *Conversations with Bhante*.[15]

Sangharakshita told the three that, while he had never made a secret of his sexual behaviour, he had been reluctant to talk about it. That reflected his general reticence and the effect of spending much of his life in societies where homosexuality was illegal and deemed shameful. Looking back at his sexual experiences, he said: 'I certainly enjoyed it, in what I think was a healthy way. For me, you could say, sex was something very pleasant and enjoyable, but no big deal.' It wasn't a spiritual path, 'just a normal, healthy human activity, which should not be depreciated on its own level'. That matched his view that 'the reason sexual relationships were so difficult, and sometimes ended so disastrously, was that people were investing far too much in them.' He thought that, for someone who was serious about Dharma practice, 'sex has a legitimate place somewhere near the periphery of the personal mandala' (i.e. at the edge of their life, rather than at its centre).[16] He had been interested in sex as a means to communicate more deeply, but had concluded:

> With intimacy you have a physical experience of the other person that is unique to the sexual situation. You know the other person better, in certain respects, and there is also an emotional exchange, but that emotional exchange is very rarely a form of communication, because it is almost always mixed up with projection and craving.[17]

He presented his sexual activity as what we might term consenting sex between adults, and said he had only initiated it when he felt a 'sexual frisson' or 'mutual chemistry':

> I did not feel I was forcing anybody and would have regarded that as a quite wrong thing to do. Perhaps in a very few cases they were not as willing as I had supposed at the time – that is possible. It is not always easy to find out what is going on in someone else's mind, especially if you don't know them very well.[18]

The *Conversations* are candid, but they don't fully address the testimonies of Sangharakshita's disaffected former partners. He said little about the power imbalance, though he later acknowledged to Subhuti that the intensity of his energy may have made it difficult for people to resist his advances.

The criticisms continued and, in 2016 and 2017, another campaign prompted a piece on regional BBC TV and an article in *The Observer*.[19] More articles followed that characterized Sangharakshita in increasingly negative terms, prompting further rounds of soul-searching in the Order in which criticisms of his sexual activity often mixed with disagreements over his teachings. Partly in response, a group of senior Order members, calling itself the Adhiṣṭhāna Kula, contacted the twenty-four men with whom Sangharakshita had been sexually involved. Their report, published in 2020, recognized the difficulty of drawing conclusions about a person's behaviour, 'especially when the person involved is one's Buddhist teacher'.

Nonetheless, it candidly acknowledged the negative impact of Sangharakshita's behaviour on some of his partners:

> Sangharakshita did not adequately recognize the power imbalance between teacher and student, did not see how this might compromise the junior party's ability to refuse a sexual advance, and did not sufficiently understand the emotional impact that sexual relations were liable to have on the student.[20]

What's more, it said, 'Sangharakshita was sometimes unwilling or unable to have meaningful dialogue after the sexual involvement ended.'

• • •

There is no doubt in my mind that Sangharakshita was a thoughtful and considerate person who was sensitive to the feelings of others. I don't believe he used his prestige and position to gain sex, or that he had any sense that he was coercing others. However, I find it hard to understand how he failed to anticipate that his sexual encounters would have powerful and unpredictable effects on at least some of his partners. No doubt, Sangharakshita's thinking was affected by attitudes to sex in the counterculture and the gay community, which typically set such considerations aside. He says in the *Conversations* that he considered himself sexually inexperienced, not the one who was 'older, more experienced, the teacher'.[21] But there's the difficulty: he *was* the teacher. Other problems largely followed from that: his partners' sense of being overwhelmed by his presence or rejected when he moved on, their loss of initiative in the face of his overtures, and their confusion in subsequently relating to Sangharakshita as both a teacher and a lover. In some cases, these feelings took decades to surface, but it isn't surprising that they did.

Like others who admire Sangharakshita but are critical of his sexual behaviour, I have struggled with these issues, but in writing this book I have come to situate them in a larger context. Some will regard any attempt to understand Sangharakshita's motivations as a distraction from the people who say they suffered through his actions. My own view is that, in any ethical reckoning, it is important to consider both motivations and consequences. That means situating Sangharakshita's sexual behaviour within the broad themes of his life, especially the ones explored in this part of the present volume.

A supra-personal force
After *What Is the Western Buddhist Order?* and *Conversations with Bhante*, Sangharakshita realized he had more to say about his understanding of the Dharma. Lacking the capacity to write this himself, he asked Subhuti to join him for more conversations, which Subhuti turned into a series of papers. We shall come to several of these in later chapters, but one is particularly relevant to the aspects of Sangharakshita's life drawn out here. It is entitled *'A Supra-Personal Force or Energy Working through Me': The Triratna Buddhist Community and the Stream of the Dharma*.

In 2009 a poem entitled 'The Wind' came fully formed into Sangharakshita's mind:

> A wind was in my sails. It blew
> Stronger and fiercer by the hour.
> I do not know from whence it came,
> Or why. I only knew its power.
>
> Sometimes it dashed me on the rocks,
> Sometimes it spun me round and round.
> Sometimes I laughed aloud for joy,
> Sometimes I felt a peace profound.
>
> It drove me on, that manic wind,
> When I was young. It drives me still
> Now I am old. It lives in me,
> Its breath my breath, its will my will.[22]

The poem is a mini-autobiography, presenting Sangharakshita's life solely through his connection with a powerful force that is beyond and within him. At first sight, it is hard to reconcile his methodical character and regular habits with the description of being spun around and dashed on the rocks. But the poem chimes with his suggestion in *The History of My Going for Refuge* that 'the course of my life had been determined by impulse and intuition rather than by reason and logic.'[23]

'The Wind' represents something Sangharakshita was reluctant to explain: as the poem says, he didn't know 'from whence it came, or why'. However, it echoes Shelley's 'Ode to the West Wind', which also presents the wind as a universal force. Shelley's wind is both 'destroyer' and 'preserver', and drives through the natural world while signifying something more than nature. Awakened from his 'summer dreams', the poet recognizes something in himself that, like the wind, is 'tameless, and swift, and proud'. He surrenders to it, content to be blown like a leaf or a cloud, but also implores it to join with him:

> Be thou, Spirit fierce,
> My spirit! Be thou me, impetuous one!
> Drive my dead thoughts over the universe
> Like wither'd leaves to quicken a new birth![24]

In Sangharakshita's poem the prayer has been answered, and by the end he is one with the wind: 'Its breath my breath, its will my will'.

The preceding chapters have noted this wind or power throughout Sangharakshita's life. It is there in his formative encounter with the *Diamond Sutra* and his sense, in the wake of Dr Ambedkar's death, that he was 'not a person but an impersonal force'.[25] It is present in his commitment to spreading Buddhist teachings and his wish to devote himself to an influence beyond his ego. It is relevant to the importance he placed in the late 1960s on integrating deep psychic forces and the depths he plumbed to re-express Buddhism in a new culture. It is explicitly present in his desire to open himself to the influence of the Buddha, Tārā, and other figures, and Padmasambhava represented it in an especially vivid form. It is also the context for his creativity as he established the FWBO, re-expressed Buddhist teachings, and discovered new ways to live a Buddhist life. He wrote to Subhuti:

I may also say that in recent years, on looking back over the history of the FWBO/Triratna, I have been amazed at what has been accomplished. At the same time, I have felt, or rather seen very clearly, that it has not been accomplished just by me. It was as though a supra-personal energy or force was working through me, an energy or force for which, in a way, I was not responsible.[26]

Sangharakshita's reluctance to define this force suggests a concern that any definition would be taken to suggest an eternal absolute reality such as the Christian Holy Spirit. Subhuti writes that Sangharakshita was simply 'getting at the way a Dharmic motivation feels and especially the difference in the experience from our normal sense of willing and wanting'.[27] Sangharakshita concurred: Dharmic motivation *felt like* a force that was beyond him and worked through him, or even 'a consciousness beyond his own'.[28]

This is also a context for understanding Sangharakshita's sexual behaviour. It isn't an excuse, and it doesn't diminish the sometimes harmful consequences of his actions, but it helps explain how he spoke about it. He often said his sexual activity was part of the same creative exploration that produced his Dharma teaching. He couldn't separate them, as he thought his critics wanted him to:

> They want a good Sangharakshita and a bad Sangharakshita. They can't square that there seem to be two Sangharakshitas – one of which they are very critical of and the other that they admire. They'd like to have one half of me without the other, but obviously that is impossible. People in the movement need to see me as a whole person – they can't divide me up into separate bits.[29]

For all this, a problem remains. The issue for at least some of Sangharakshita's questioners isn't squaring a good Sangharakshita with one they criticized, but reconciling the good intentions he described with their painful effects.

There is more to say about the wind, stream, or force that Sangharakshita describes, but that relies on an understanding of spiritual experience, and therefore the nature of consciousness, as Buddhism describes it and Sangharakshita presents it. As consciousness is conditioned, it also requires an understanding of conditionality – the question of *how things happen* that is the central concern of Buddhist thought. The following chapters will explore these subjects through Sangharakshita's writings, talks, and seminars and the experiences from which they grew.

● ● ●

In the main, Sangharakshita's final years were happy ones, even though he couldn't see and could barely walk unassisted. In 2013 he settled at Adhiṣṭhāna in the Herefordshire countryside, close to the library he had long wanted to establish, amid the activities of the movement he founded and with the companionship of his old friend Paramartha and others. The two men studied sutras together and made occasional visits, and Sangharakshita dictated a stream of short essays. They include many reminiscences of family, friends, psychic experiences, and a variety of encounters, and some returned to the Buddhist themes he had pondered for many years. The final piece, written two weeks before his death on 30 October 2018, expressed his continuing interest in the magical element of Dharma practice through a reflection on mantra as 'the locus of a power or energy which is unknown to science and cannot be measured by ordinary means'.[30]

In December 2016, having almost died, Sangharakshita shared a *Statement of Apology and Regret*:

> I being its founder, Triratna sometimes bears the mark not of the Dharma but of my own particular personality. That personality is a complex one and in certain respects I did not act in accordance with what my position in the movement demanded or even as a true Buddhist. I am thinking in particular of the times when I have hurt, harmed or upset fellow Buddhists, whether within Triratna or out of it.[31]

A little later, he clarified that his confession 'covered a wide field, as my unskilfulness had done, from being disrespectful to my father as a teenager to some of my sexual activity with Order members and Mitras'.[32] His regret for the harmful aspects of his sexual behaviour was no doubt genuine, but he couldn't isolate it.

Sangharakshita's experience was always multi-layered. One of his final reminiscences describes his dreams in the years he lived at Adhiṣṭhāna. In one, he was travelling in space:

> The craft in which I travelled was white, and I was surrounded by the same blue sky as in other dreams. Sometimes I experienced a sense of expansion, of unknown possibilities, and even of freedom from cares.[33]

A poem called 'Argosies', written in 1952, recalls his experience as a boy of sailing a white boat in a green pool and the expansive possibilities its short journey evoked:

> Was to his infant soul obscurely given,
> Beneath the brown shade of the willow trees,
> Foreknowledge of those argosies which now
> Loom white-winged o'er him from the deeps of life?[34]

In other dreams, he seemed to pass through a solemn and mysterious initiation, another *abhiṣeka* or ordination:

> I very much wanted this ordination and I received it thanks to the intervention of someone I knew, who approached the giver of the initiation on my behalf. At one point the latter was standing beside me and squeezed my arm as a sign that he would be giving me the initiation, whereupon I burst into tears.[35]

This has an added poignancy as the medication Sangharakshita was receiving left him feeling detached. His emotional reticence in any case meant that he had rarely shed tears at any point in his life, with all its intensity and its many dimensions.

Part Two

Imagining the Path

Ah, need I say, dear friend, that to the brim
My heart was full? I made no vows, but vows
Were then made for me: bond unknown to me
Was given, that I should be – else sinning greatly –
A dedicated spirit. On I walked
In blessedness, which even yet remains.

William Wordsworth, The Prelude

Chapter Four

Consciousness and the Path

The path to buddhahood

The overarching subject of Sangharakshita's work, and the great concern of his life, was the nature of the Dharma – the Buddha's teaching, and particularly the path to Enlightenment. He worked out his basic understanding in the writing he produced in India, though he continued to refine that understanding throughout his life. Returning to the West, he described it in many ways and developed a practical version that responded to his students' spiritual needs. But, as we will see in the following chapters, the outline of his thinking is visible in his formative spiritual experiences, and his memoirs and poems are particularly helpful in recognizing its imaginative underpinnings.

To understand Sangharakshita's presentation we must also locate it within the Buddhist tradition – a complex matter, as the tradition is divided into many schools that offer numerous versions of the Buddhist path. However, all schools share the basic Buddhist account of existence that distinguishes *saṃsāra* (the domain of unenlightened, conditioned experience), *nirvāṇa* (an entirely different, unconditioned state), and the path that leads from one to the other. From the outset, Buddhism held that the meaning of these terms was provisional, and nirvāṇa is 'beyond the reach of the rational mind'. It can be neither described nor even thought about because attaining it means abandoning the most basic categories of existence, such as the distinction between 'self' and 'not self', and Mahāyāna thought emphasizes that this means the path and ordinary experience are therefore also 'empty' and unknowable. Sangharakshita's experience of reading the *Diamond*

Sutra seems to have included a sense of this unknowability, and that awareness was ingrained, deeply felt, and personal:

> contact with Buddhism was, at the same time, contact with the depths of my own being [...] [I]n knowing Buddhism I was knowing myself, and [...] in knowing myself I was knowing Buddhism.[1]

Nonetheless, to follow the path and realize nirvāṇa we must have some conception of them, and Sangharakshita liked to quote Aśvaghoṣa's dictum: 'We use words to get free from words until we reach the pure wordless essence.'[2] Early Buddhism, he observes, tends to present nirvāṇa as a *transcendent* goal located at the end of the path, meaning that *saṃsāra* and *nirvāṇa* are largely conceived as 'mutually exclusive realities'.[3] Mahāyāna sources extend the transcendental orientation by envisaging the Buddha as a universal figure who exists outside time and space, but this also suggests that buddhahood is *immanently* present within ordinary existence as 'suchness' or buddha nature. The terms 'immanence' and 'transcendence' come from Christian theology, where they describe God's relation to the world, but Sangharakshita found them useful because they named aspects of his experience as a Buddhist.

These differences inevitably prompt questions about how we conceive the path. If *saṃsāra* and *nirvāṇa* are separate realities, how can we move from one to the other? As Sangharakshita asked late in his life: 'How, then, shall a mortal attain the Immortal State, or a conditioned being achieve the Unconditioned?'[4] If *saṃsāra* and *nirvāṇa* are not different and we are, in some sense, already enlightened, what is the meaning of the path and why should we make the effort to follow it? If they mingle, how does this mingling occur, and can nirvāṇa, or at least an intimation of it, be available to us before we reach it? The accounts of the path vary according to the schools' responses to these questions. If we envisage a transcendent goal, we will think it means moving along a path towards an objective, or perhaps surrendering ourselves devotionally to a higher power. If we think buddhahood is immanent within our experience, we need only uncover it, and the path is likely to be a matter of openness and receptivity.

How should we choose between these alternatives? Most Buddhists follow the answers of the school in which they practise, but from the start Sangharakshita was inspired by the whole tradition. His awareness of the provisionality of Buddhist concepts sufficed up to a point. As a poet he was sensitive to the irreducibility of experience, and valued images for their capacity to express an unconceptualized understanding. But as a philosopher he knew that, unless a meaning is spelled out, made consistent, and distinguished from other interpretations, it is likely to be misunderstood. As a young man he consequently wrote both poetry and philosophy, but experienced the tension between them in the contest between Sangharakshita I, the poet and dreamer, and Sangharakshita II, the philosopher and ascetic. He needed a coherent understanding of the path that was intellectually consistent, illuminated the teachings, and matched his experience.

For guidance, Sangharakshita turned to Buddhist scriptures and the modern Buddhist traditions that followed them, but the scriptures contradicted one another, and the schools (or, at least, the Theravāda) understood Buddhism in ways he thought misrepresented the texts. Throughout his twenties, these contradictions preoccupied him, and *A Survey of Buddhism* (1957) expressed his resolution. As well as seeking a coherent basis for his own practice, he thought Buddhism had answers to the problems facing the world. He wanted to restore its meaning for people who were already Buddhists, and recognized that he lived in a era of Buddhist history in which the whole Buddhist tradition was available. He also wanted to show its relevance to those who weren't Buddhists and draw out its meaning in a very different culture from the one in which it had developed.

These are large ambitions, but within Buddhism 'spiritual life' means the development of consciousness. We may therefore start with the question: what is consciousness?

The vertical dimension

Consciousness

The Buddha said a great deal about the mind, but he didn't offer a comprehensive theory of consciousness or pronounce definitively on the relationship between mind and body. As a result, Buddhists have understood consciousness in various ways that have produced differing accounts of the path. However, two elements are consistent. Firstly, Buddhism rejects the idea that the mind is reducible to the body. As Sangharakshita writes in an early essay, 'the body is neither the centre nor circumference of our experience, but only a small and temporary segment of it.'[5] This is fundamental because, as he insists in *A Survey of Buddhism*, willingness 'to admit the possibility of a spiritual experience which would transcend the physical senses and the rational mind' is a prerequisite for serious engagement with Buddhism.[6]

Secondly, Buddhism rejects the existence of a timeless, eternal *ātman* (a 'self' or 'soul'). This means that consciousness, like all phenomena, is impermanent. That is a negative formulation, but impermanence can also be expressed positively. As Sangharakshita wrote in 1949:

> Buddhism envisages the universe not as static but as dynamic, not as being or not-being but as becoming, flux, or *anicca*.
> This process of becoming should not be understood as a
> mere succession of discrete states, events, or things, but as an uninterrupted flow, a pure continuum.[7]

All Buddhists explain the process of change in terms of conditionality, or 'conditioned arising', which, as we shall see, is a central theme in Sangharakshita's thought. A second issue, which is harder to define but implicit in everything he wrote, is what we might call the context within which change occurs.

The 1956 essay *The Meaning of Buddhism and the Value of Art* includes one of Sangharakshita's clearest explanations. Being dynamic, he says, consciousness can move in two ways: contracting from a wider to a narrower state or expanding from a narrower to a wider one. The expansive movement is the purpose of all Buddhist practices:

> If they lead to an expansion of consciousness, to an illumination of mind and purification of heart, to a higher degree of spiritual sharp-sightedness, to emancipation from the fetters of egoism, then they may be considered as the teaching of the Master himself.[8]

In later years, Sangharakshita explained the movements as cyclic and progressive conditionality or, more experientially, as reactivity and creativity.

All these descriptions make abstract for the sake of clarity what was more fundamentally a matter of feeling, and Sangharakshita conveys the meaning of the vertical dimension as much through imagery as through concepts. One of his most vivid metaphors comes in his 1971 commentary on the *White Lotus Sutra*'s 'Parable of the Return Journey'. A rich man helps a poor man who doesn't know the rich man is his father, but the father recognizes the son and finds a way to pass on to him the wealth that is his birthright. For Sangharakshita, the father represents the 'higher self', while the son is the 'lower self', and he expands the spatial metaphor into an image of the potential for consciousness to expand:

> Imagine an enormous subterranean chamber all lit up from within. We are living in a tiny chamber next to – indeed part of – the larger one. A pane of glass which is transparent from only one side separates the two chambers, so that although someone in the large, illuminated chamber could see everything going on in the little chamber, from the little chamber we can see nothing at all of what is going on in the large chamber. In fact, we have no idea that there is a large chamber. But although cramped in our little chamber we may forget, indeed be oblivious to, the existence of the large chamber, the large chamber always has a window onto the little chamber.[9]

The image of confinement in a little chamber recalls the cave in Plato's parable where prisoners think the shadows on the wall are real substances, or perhaps William Blake's saying: 'For man has closed himself up, till he sees all things through narrow chinks of his cavern.'[10] The large chamber is an image of the full scope of consciousness.

A further qualification in *The Meaning of Buddhism and the Value of Art* defines the distinctive 'shape' of Sangharakshita's thought. The expansive movement can be understood on a vertical or a horizontal plane:

> By an upward or downward movement of expansion in consciousness is meant a heightening or deepening (the two expressions come to much the same thing) of experience, an increase of insight, or augmentation of understanding; by a movement of expansion outwards is meant a constant multiplication of our points of contact with the external world, a ceaseless enlargement and elaboration of that delicate network of sympathy and affection by which we are connected in a thousand ways not only with all other human beings, but with every other form of life.

Buddhism's full expression, he says, is found in 'the expansion of consciousness through the development of wisdom and compassion'.[11]

This model meant Sangharakshita viewed Dharma practice as an ascent through a vertical dimension of being, which also had an altruistic dimension that was expressed in different ways at different levels. The main organizing principle is the ascending path. In the early 2000s Wisdom Publications proposed a *Sangharakshita Reader* or *Pocket Sangharakshita*. The volume eventually produced by the editor Vidyadevi ran to over 800 pages, and clearly wouldn't fit into a pocket. Its published title, *The Essential Sangharakshita*, prompted him to ask: 'If this represents the essence of my teachings [...] what is the essence of this essence?' He answered:

> I eventually decided [it] had to be that of human spiritual development, a process that I see proceeding by way of a series of stages. The Buddhist scriptures describe the stages of spiritual development in many places and in many ways, but they all represent different stages on a single path of spiritual development.[12]

This meant more than a purely personal experience: it also correlated with an understanding of existence.

Cosmos

To speak of consciousness and its dimensions is to use psychological language, but, within Buddhist thought, psychology is inseparable from cosmology. As Sangharakshita writes in *The Three Jewels*:

> The 'objective' world we perceive, with all its seas and mountains, trees, houses, and human beings, is in reality a state of mind. Contrariwise, what is in reality a state of mind can appear as an objectively existing world which those who inhabit it or, more precisely, those who have been or who are in the mental state correlative to it, can actually experience and perceive.[13]

In the tradition shared by all schools, an ordinary state of consciousness means we experience the world as a domain termed the *kāmaloka*, or 'realm of desire for sensuous experience' (as Sangharakshita translates it).[14] The *kāmaloka* also includes the lower spirit realms, among whose inhabitants are the ghosts and nature spirits that appear in every premodern culture. Above the *kāmaloka* is the *rūpaloka*, or 'realm of archetypal form', which is said to be peopled by angelic figures; and above this is the *arūpaloka*, or 'realm of no archetypal form' or 'extremely subtle archetypal form', whose inhabitants (if such they can be termed) are extremely subtle divine beings. Together, the *kāmaloka*, *rūpaloka*, and *arūpaloka* comprise the 'three worlds' (*triloka*) that make up *saṃsāra*, or mundane and conditioned existence. This gives us an image of a cosmos extending not just in physical space, but on a vertical, spiritual axis that is invisible to astronomers. '[W]hereas the universe of science exists only in space and time', writes Sangharakshita, 'that of Buddhism exists also in depth.'[15]

This picture matched Sangharakshita's experience far more than most of his contemporaries'. Aged twelve or thirteen, he suddenly felt 'the complete absurdity of the mind being tied down to a single physical body' that left him with a sense of being imprisoned.[16] At other times in this period, he recalled that 'everything around me suddenly retreated as though to a great distance and became strangely ghostlike, all sounds were hushed, and I walked or rather floated through a great void.'[17] Such experiences recurred. Shortly after his arrival in India, a figure appeared to him:

> I was meditating one night when there suddenly appeared before me, as it were suspended in mid-air, the head of an old man [...] 'You're wasting your time,' he exclaimed [...] 'There's nothing in the universe but matter! Nothing but matter!' 'There is something higher than matter,' I promptly retorted. I know it, because I am experiencing it now.'[18]

Sangharakshita considered his visionary experiences modest and infrequent by comparison with those of the Kalimpong lamas, but occult experiences pepper his memoirs and recurred throughout his life.[19] The possibility of non-physical experience they demonstrated aligned him with a premodern outlook that differed, for example, from the viewpoint of western translators of Buddhist texts who often portrayed the Buddha as a rational sage. Where they minimized the role of divine beings in the Discourses, he embraced them:

> [T]he gods and goddesses [...] are not there simply as ornamentation. Their presence is itself part of the teaching. They provide glimpses of an ancient mode of human consciousness fully integrated into a universe of value, meaning, and purpose. To miss them is to miss the poetry, and the heart of the Buddha's message.[20]

The vertical dimension that is higher than merely physical existence implies an attitude towards what is above us. Sangharakshita's 1965 lecture 'The Lamas of Tibet' has a particularly clear account:

> [W]e have to understand the concept of degrees of reality, the idea that the level of experience we usually occupy – waking experience, the experience that comes through the five senses and the lower mind – is just one level of the experience of reality. Above this there are other, higher levels

of consciousness. The whole of existence is like a great ladder on which we occupy the lowest rung, speaking in terms of human understanding and experience and consciousness.[21]

A ladder implies a series of steps – a spiritual *hierarchy*. Sangharakshita knew the word was problematic for many of his listeners, but he insisted on using it throughout his teaching career:

> [O]bjectively one has a hierarchy of degrees of reality and subjectively one has the hierarchy of degrees of experience or even levels of Enlightenment. This being the case, we have also a hierarchy of being: there are beings occupying the lower reaches of the hierarchy and others who are on the higher levels and thus occupy a higher place in the hierarchy of beings.[22]

Sangharakshita thought the hierarchical was inherent in a Buddhist outlook:

> Buddhism is traditionally saturated in [hierarchy], to the extent that Buddhists are almost unable to step aside and see Buddhism as hierarchical. The very fact that the spiritual path consists of a series of steps or stages shows how deeply the hierarchical principle is embedded within Buddhism. In fact, the spiritual life itself is inseparable from the hierarchical principle.[23]

Sangharakshita distinguished this spiritual hierarchy from a social hierarchy based on 'earthly power and worldly position',[24] but thought it had social implications. Within Tibetan culture, as he observed it in Kalimpong, people naturally thought in terms of what he called 'a living chain of spiritual beings',[25] some more advanced and some less. Currents of influence ran through the hierarchy: 'a transmuting force or power' in the form of teachings and blessings descending from above, and 'a current of reverence, devotion, even worship' rising towards it. If the scale of spirit is in a sense fixed, he said in 1993, we are not fixed to that scale, and it's possible for us to rise from lower to the higher positions or degrees. It's in this upward movement, this progression, that the spiritual life consists.[26]

Sangharakshita reflected late in life that an attitude of 'looking up' with reverence and devotion came naturally to him, and that he had 'an affinity with Buddhism inasmuch as the path taught by the Buddha led to higher and ever higher states of being and consciousness'. He insisted this was more than a personal predilection, and that

> [a]ny attempt to minimize the importance of devotion in the spiritual life, or to limit it to a particular personality type, is a betrayal of the Buddha's teaching and does less than justice to human nature.[27]

The world as poetry

An episode from Sangharakshita's later life suggests how he experienced the vertical dimension. In late 1979 he was temporarily free of demands and found himself in a state of intense creativity. A letter to Order members gave his most detailed account of such a state:

> First of all came a period of 'silence', both internal and external, during which there were no objective demands made upon me and no 'needs' to meet. This meant that I could allow the responses that usually arise in connection with such demands and needs to die down, so that whatever mental processes then went on were, on the whole, self-originating. Next, out of the silence, which was also a kind of creative rest, there arose a certain rhythm, or a poem without words – a poem that went on and on, without interruption. This rhythm, or wordless poem, seemed to blend with whatever I saw, or rather, with whatever it was to which I directed my attention, or on which I allowed my mind to dwell. It could blend with it because, whether it was a natural object like a tree, a realm

of existence, or a figure from ancient Egyptian mythology, its
rhythm was the same as the rhythm that had arisen out of my
own silence, my own creative rest. As they blended, the two
rhythms gave birth to words, words which were descriptive of
the particular object on which I had allowed my mind to dwell
and which formed, in some cases, complete poems, in others,
only fragments of poems – perhaps a line or a couplet.

The state signified more than simply composing poems.
Sangharakshita experienced inspiration in various ways at different
times: as contact with a supra-personal force, as an encounter with
beauty, as uplift, or, as here, as a melting of selfhood that echoes
Murry's engagement with the 'deeper rhythm' of a poet's work:

At one stage it was as though the rhythm that arose within me
was the same as, or at least in accordance with, the rhythm
that arose within the depths of external nature and found
expression in trees, flowers, houses, and human beings – in
the whole objective order of existence. Whatever I allowed
my mind to rest on became a poem, just as whatever Midas
touched turned to gold. The whole world was material for
poetry. In fact, the whole world was a poem. It was a poem, to
the extent that the 'observer' was a poet.[28]

Sangharakshita recalls that, for months on end as a teenager,
'it was far easier for me to write poetry than not write it.'[29]
Something similar happened in his mid-twenties following his
arrival in Kalimpong, when poems poured from him describing
the enchantment of the natural environment, the richness of his
spiritual experience, and the blending of the two. Over the next few
years, he wrote a series of essays exploring the connection between
Buddhism and art, which dwell particularly on what happens
when ego-bound experience opens into an expansive region:

The Religion of Art may therefore be defined as conscious
surrender to the Beautiful, especially as manifested in
poetry, music, and the visual arts, as a means of breaking up
established egocentric patterns of behaviour and protracting

one's experience along the line of egolessness into the starry depths of Reality.³⁰

The 1979 letter picks up the same themes:

[T]he 'poetic' state of mind is, as I had sometimes felt before, a state in which the subject assimilates the object in such a way that the duality between them is to some extent mitigated and that this mitigated duality finds expression in the 'poem', or work of art generally, which is both subject and object, or in which the subject–object duality finds expression on a higher, more refined level.³¹

The resulting poems show the same interest in what lies beyond the ego:

My mind's a silver awning,
My heart a golden throne,
But none to sit beneath it,
Or rule from it alone.

[...]

My life's a rainbow tower,
My death a diamond well,
But none to scale or fathom
In heaven or in hell.³²

Nirvāṇa and the path

Merging with the goal

Sangharakshita remarked that the Buddha was reluctant to discuss nirvāṇa and focused instead on describing the path. His own teachings sometimes displayed the same reticence, and he wryly reflected in the 1965 lecture 'What Is Nirvāṇa?' that whenever he spoke about this subject, either in India and in England, his talks were popular, but his listeners' attitudes and behaviour were untouched. Instead, he suggests, we should 'get to know our unhappiness in all its comings and goings'. He concludes, no doubt with a touch of irony: 'Nirvāṇa consists in the full and complete understanding of why you want to reach Nirvāṇa.'[33]

Most Buddhist schools believe nirvāṇa is more readily accessible from the higher reaches of mundane existence. That is why many Buddhists (especially laypeople) seek rebirth in one of the higher heavenly realms, and meditators cultivate the states of profound absorption called *dhyānas*. Sangharakshita often described the path as an ascent through the three worlds, or a journey through increasingly positive and refined states of consciousness, and the 1983 paper 'The Bodhisattva Principle' sums up the relationship between these perspectives:

> Subjectively the spiritual life consists in an ascent through mental factors and mental states, i.e., consists in the actual development of such factors or states. Objectively, it consists in an ascent through worlds or realms or planes.[34]

It follows that the upper reaches of *saṃsāra* merge into *nirvāṇa*, and, ranging through the Buddhist tradition, Sangharakshita found many expressions of their blurred boundary. Discussing the higher reaches of the bodhisattva path, he says:

> [A]ccording to tradition, contact with ultimate reality, from the heights of the mundane, is made whenever the mind in the *dhyāna* state, whether higher or lower, turns with awareness from the mundane to the transcendental, when it begins to contemplate reality. It is then that the mundane *dhyāna* state becomes insight into the transcendental.[35]

The Three Jewels introduces the commentarial teaching of the three doors of liberation (*vimokṣamukhas*), which was particularly important for Sangharakshita. The three doors are the marks of existence, and contemplating them makes them doorways to states known as *samādhis* that belong to both the conditioned and the unconditioned. This suggests that, 'From a point of view somewhat deeper than that of their duality, conditioned and Unconditioned are not discrete but as it were continuous.'[36]

Sangharakshita sometimes speaks of this continuity as if it was his own experience. Discussing prayer in his commentary on the *Songs* of Milarepa, for example, he says:

> As your experience deepens, you experience it less and less as an object as opposed to a subject. The line of demarcation between you and it, so to speak, becomes finer and finer. You as it were merge into it, or it merges into you.[37]

The following chapters will explore the many ways in which Sangharakshita described the path as a journey through the vertical dimension, but this wasn't the whole of his account. From the start of his career, he recognized that it coexisted, in principle and in his experience, with other ways of understanding Buddhist practice.

The scent of nirvāṇa

Thinking in terms of a path leading towards a distant goal means viewing it from the practitioner's perspective. But Sangharakshita sometimes switches perspective and describes it from the viewpoint of buddhahood. The 1972 lecture 'The Word of the Buddha' describes the Dharma as a communication from 'buddha mind'. He imagines the highest level on which a buddha manifests, as 'one continuous "mass" of spiritual luminosity' or 'a vast and shoreless ocean in which millions of universes are just one tiny wave – or even just a fleck of foam – in the midst of that boundless ocean'.[38] In the 1980 lecture 'The Taste of Freedom' he says this ocean 'is singing to us, it's playing its own inimitable music to us in its own indescribably appealing and fascinating way.'[39] According to 'The Word of the Buddha', 'a sort of tremor, a sort of vibration [...] passes between the Enlightened mind and the mind that is just a little short of Enlightenment.' With great mental refinement one may become attuned to this vibration and hear it coming from all things because 'the Buddha-mind is, as it were, behind them all.'[40] To receive this message requires an intuitive receptivity to something that 'cannot be comprehended abstractly, but only by way of an actual experience akin to an aesthetic experience'.[41]

Sangharakshita found an explanation in *The Awakening of Faith in the Mahāyāna*, which he read while he was staying at Ramana

Maharshi's ashram in 1949. It told him, 'a man is able to renounce saṃsāra and realize nirvāṇa primarily because his deluded mind is permeated by the perfume of Suchness.'[42] This gives us 'an inner kinship' with nirvāṇa:

> The gaining of insight into the transcendental is not an irruption of something which is totally alien to us, but a manifestation at the level of our conscious mental activity of something which, in a much deeper sense, we *are*.[43]

The Awakening of Faith and the Buddhist traditions deriving from it use the image of a hall of mirrors to express the reflection of *nirvāṇa* in *saṃsāra*. Our ordinary experience may be 'deluded' or relative, but it reflects our non-dual, perfected nature (in the language of the Yogācāra school). Another version is a reflection in water:

> That which is reflected is upside down, so that, if a mountain is reflected in a lake, the peak of the mountain appears to be in the depths of the lake. It is in that way, you might say, that there is a reflection – in this case, let us say, of the *ālaya* – in us. The *ālaya*, one might say, represents the highest level, but it is lowest or deepest in us in the sense that it is the most hidden and most obscured.[44]

Elsewhere in Mahāyāna tradition the famous net of jewels associated with the god Indra, each of which reflects every other jewel, is an image for the interconnectedness of phenomena and the presence within them of the jewel of Awakening.

If nirvāṇa can express itself through sound, it can also be expressed through scent, and Sangharakshita's keen sense of smell made this particularly important for him. In a late reflection entitled *The Language of Scents* he recalls the coffee smells of South India, the gardenias of Kalimpong, and incense-burning parties with art students in Highgate: 'Each odour communicated something.'[45] In the same way, the mind has the potential to experience phenomena as a buddha does because 'everything is perfumed with the fragrance of True Suchness.'[46]

This is also the theme of a lecture in Sangharakshita's 1978 series on the *Vimalakīrti Nirdeśa* in which the great lay bodhisattva Vimalakīrti requests *amṛta*, or sweet-smelling nectar, because it represents 'a transcendental emanation of reality'. Sangharakshita refers again to *The Awakening of Faith*:

> This ultimate reality is spoken of [...] as 'perfuming' conditioned existence. Something of reality 'rubs off', so to speak, onto conditioned existence. A few infinitesimally tiny 'particles' are 'transmitted', and we can therefore perceive ultimate reality, however faintly, in the midst of conditioned existence. And, perceiving it, we can strive towards it.[47]

In this way of thinking, 'ultimate reality' both transcends the phenomenal world and is immanently present within it, meaning we can look for intimations of Enlightenment in our immediate experience. By Sangharakshita's own testimony, this was his experience:

> Practising meditation gives one at least a limited sense of this kind of influence. A time comes when you begin to sense something which you cannot describe or define. It doesn't come under any mundane category, yet at the same time there is nothing vague or cloudy about it. It is intensely vivid, intensely real, like the perfume of some unknown flower.

This sense can be refined and developed, he says, 'to the extent that eventually it can tell us where the perfume is coming from and which direction we have to take to find its source'.[48]

But how are we able to sense nirvāṇa in this way if it is unconditioned and transcendent? Sangharakshita believed the answer told us something important about human nature:

> we can perceive the subtle perfume of ultimate reality only because we have within us a kind of transcendental sense, something that has an affinity with the transcendental, something to which the 'particles' of the transcendental can be transmitted.[49]

'Faith' is the principal term Sangharakshita uses to describe the 'intuitive, emotional, even mystical' response of 'what is ultimate in us to what is ultimate in the universe.'[50] He thought something stirs when we encounter an image of the Buddha because 'there is that within us which resonates with that grandeur.'[51] The *Survey* uses yet another image:

> When the devotee hears the music of Enlightenment, when he stands in the very presence of the Buddha, his own Element of Buddhahood starts vibrating. Hence he knows that the great being before him is striking upon the strings of his own heart the mighty chord of supreme Enlightenment.[52]

* * *

Understanding Sangharakshita's spiritual character means recognizing that, when he writes in this way, he is describing his own experience as well as offering a theoretical understanding. What emerges includes a vivid sense of nirvāṇa as both a transcendent goal and an immanent presence. As a young man, he recognized the tension between them. Though he doesn't make the connections explicitly, we see its reflections in the tensions between Sangharakshita I and Sangharakshita II, and his response to Mahāyāna sutras and the early Buddhist Discourses. But perhaps the most distinctive feature of Sangharakshita's character as both a spiritual practitioner and a Buddhist teacher is that the two coexist, and his teaching explores the creative possibilities their combination enables. The following chapters will trace how he integrated this with a coherent understanding of the Buddhist tradition, reimagined the Buddhist path in these terms, and developed a Buddhist movement based on it. But we should start with their sources in Sangharakshita's experience and his understanding of the imagination.

Chapter Five

The Illumined Path

Unifying visions

If Sangharakshita's 1942 experience of reading the *Diamond Sutra* challenged every formulation or conception of the path, his poetry and memoirs describe how the different ways of conceiving it came together in the following years. The fragmentary poem 'Above Me Broods...', written in 1947, describes this as fully as anything Sangharakshita wrote, albeit in a condensed and elliptical form:

> Above me broods
> A world of mysteries and magnitudes.
> I see, I hear,
> More than what strikes the eye or meets the ear.
>
> Within me sleep
> Potencies deep, unfathomably deep,
> Which, when awake,
> The bonds of life, death, time and space will break.
>
> Infinity
> Above me like the blue sky do I see.
> Below, in me,
> Lies the reflection of infinity.[1]

Each of the poem's images expresses the poet's experience in terms of space. The first section is an apprehension of sublimity – the vast and mysterious 'world of mysteries and magnitudes' that broods above the poet. This suggests a transcendent reality that can be intuited but not defined, which he perceived viscerally but not through the normal senses. In the second section the poet recognizes his own unfathomably deep, but as yet unawakened, potencies, immanently present within him, and the apocalyptic power their awaking will unleash. In the third, he senses a correspondence between the sky-like infinity above him and its reflection in his own unfathomable depths. Transcendence, immanent potentiality, and the correspondence between them coexist within the poem as different aspects of a single apprehension. Its halting rhythms encourage us to read it slowly, as if it were spoken from a state of profound absorption and expressed a mystery that exceeds all formulations.

Also in 1947, having burned his British passport, Sangharakshita took up a homeless life according to the ancient pattern of the wandering ascetic:

> As we left Kausali it was raining, but, as in the course of our descent we emerged from the clouds into the bright sunshine below, we saw arching the road, at intervals of a few dozen yards, not only a single but double and triple rainbows. Every time we turned a bend we found more rainbows waiting for us. We passed through them as though through the multicoloured arcades of some celestial palace. Against the background of bright sunshine, jewel-like glittering raindrops, and hills of the freshest and most vivid green, this plethora of delicate seven-hued bows seemed like the epiphany of another world.[2]

The experience was emblematic for Sangharakshita. When the first volume of his memoirs was published in the UK by Heinemann, the editors cut the opening chapters describing his childhood and chose the evocative title *The Thousand Petalled Lotus*, perhaps hoping to repeat the success of Govinda's bestselling *The Way of the White Clouds*. His own choice was *The Rainbow Road*, and he restored the title when Windhorse Publications, the FWBO publisher, produced a second edition.[3] He reflected in old age that, for him, the rainbow was 'a symbol of the spiritual path, the track of which I have followed, in one way or another, all my life'. It represented his profound desire to inhabit a world transfigured by 'spirituality itself, especially when that spirituality reflected or was touched by something even higher'.[4]

A sense of enchantment hovers over the memoirs' account of the years that followed Sangharakshita's going forth, and another poem from 1947 captures his mood as he started to find his way as a Dharma practitioner and a poet:

> The dim sun sinks to rest
> In a west of watery gold.
> The young stars climb the sky
> And there like flowers unfold,
> In the forest vast of night,
> Petals of purest light.

The world's enchantment matches the profound wish that guided Sangharakshita in later years:

> So may my heart unfold,
> When the suns of the world have set,
> In the forest vast of the Void,
> Wisdom with Mercy met
> In that tranquil, silent hour,
> Like a flower and the scent of a flower.[5]

• • •

When Sangharakshita formulated his understanding of the path, he looked for ways to link immediate experience with transcendental sources of enchantment: an illumined path. He sometimes spoke of the path in two phases, as a path of vision and a path of transformation. By vision, or Perfect Vision, he meant an intuitive apprehension of the truth, which he likened to glimpsing a mountain in the distance, while transformation meant the long journey that leads one towards it. At other times Sangharakshita spoke of vision as intrinsic knowledge. One day in 1979 he placed a crystal in the lap of a bronze figure of Avalokiteśvara, the bodhisattva of compassion, and gazed at the shifting light it reflected:

'Look,' Avalokiteśvara seemed to be saying, 'the jewel in the lotus,' the potentiality that is at the heart of all sentient beings – and at one's own heart. Whatever one does, wherever one goes, one must never take one's eyes off that jewel.[6]

In a similar vein, the 1986 essay *The Priceless Jewel* discusses the Gnostic *Hymn of the Pearl*, which tells the story of a prince who enters a land of sorcery to find the One Pearl, which lies at the bottom of the sea. But the prince is drugged and forgets his purpose. Sangharakshita pairs this with the 'Parable of the Return Journey' in the *White Lotus Sutra*, in which a destitute traveller learns that, through all his wanderings, he has carried a jewel that a friend had sewn into his garment in case of such an eventuality. In both stories the protagonist learns that what he sought had been present all along. '[T]he jewel', Sangharakshita comments, 'signifies our own true nature', which is 'self-luminous [...] pure transparent consciousness, with no distinction between subject and object'.[7]

Amitābha's flower

The mountain peak is a distant but inspiring goal; the jewel in one's heart is an eternally present source of wisdom. These are different ways of envisaging the goal of Buddhism and the path leading to it, but each shares the other's qualities to some degree. The versions of the path Sangharakshita presents are neither wholly transcendent nor immanent, and the qualities of the mountain and the jewel come together in an image of the lotus flower.

In 1949, while Sangharakshita was still a wandering ascetic, he spent several weeks close to the ashram of Ramana Maharshi in Tamil Nadu, South India. It was a stirring time, in part because of the deeply impressive example of the maharshi himself, who sat in the meditation hall before his disciples and seemed to emanate 'a stream of purity' that filled the hall.[8] Sangharakshita and his travelling companion were staying in a cave overlooking a temple whose bell sounded day and night throughout his stay: 'Hour after hour it seemed to toll, incessant and insistent, wave after wave of brazen sound breaking upon me like the repeated thunder of surf on the sea shore.' The sound seemed to be beating him into some new shape, and he chanted the mantra of Avalokiteśvara, the bodhisattva of compassion – *oṃ maṇi padme hūṃ* – which is often translated as 'homage to the jewel in the lotus'.

One night, Sangharakshita felt his consciousness leaving his body. Before him appeared Amitābha, the buddha of infinite light, seated cross-legged on a red lotus above a sea, his right hand holding up a red lotus flower. He saw the vision 'as clearly as I had ever seen anything under the ordinary circumstances of my life, indeed far more clearly and vividly':

> The rich red colour of Amitābha himself, as well as of the two lotuses, and the setting sun, made a particularly deep impression on me. It was more wonderful, more appealing, than any earthly red: it was like red light, but so soft and, at the same time, so vivid, as to be altogether without parallel. …. a deep, rich, luminous red, like that of rubies, though at the same time soft and glowing, like the light of the setting sun.[9]

Amitābha embodies a transcendent reality that differs fundamentally from ordinary human consciousness. For the Mahāyāna, Sangharakshita wrote, archetypal buddhas like Amitābha are

> living images of Enlightenment, abstracted or prescinded from history, having, in a sense, nothing to do with history, existing outside space and time, the living embodiment of the ideal of Enlightenment itself.[10]

At the same time, Amitābha communicates his enlightened qualities through the light pouring from him and the lotus he holds up.

In standard representations Amitābha's hands are folded in his lap, indicating that he is absorbed in meditation. It is unconventional to see him holding a flower, but the lotus is an important symbol throughout Buddhism and the vision of Amitābha sealed its importance for Sangharakshita. Often in his writing the lotus represents the culmination of growth, but the vision most clearly echoes the foundation story of Ch'an and Zen

Buddhism, according to which the Buddha sat before an assembly of listeners and held up a golden flower. Only Mahakasyapa, one of his oldest disciples, understood the meaning and, to show his understanding, he smiled. The 'golden flower, in whose petals all the wisdom of the Buddhas was to be discerned',[11] represented what the Buddha knew, and Sangharakshita called the episode 'a direct communication of truth from one mind to another'.[12]

Growing like a lotus

The lotus in the mud

Sangharakshita's vision of Amitābha convinced him it was time to end his life as a freelance wanderer and receive ordination as a *śrāmaṇera*, or novice monk. In parallel, he wrote a series of poems exploring the image of the lotus as an emblem of Enlightenment and compassion. These culminate in 'The Lotus of Compassion' (1949), which describes another enchanted journey:

> The Lotus blooms tonight,
> The great golden Lotus of the Lord's Compassion.
> With white roots deep in the slime of this sad world,
> [...]
> O leave the crowded shore where men buy and sell,
> Shake off the soft detaining fingers of your friends,
> And in a little boat,
> At midnight, when the moon is full,
> And glitters at you from the water,
> Row swiftly to the quiet Heart of the Lake where the Lotus
>   blooms,
> The great golden Lotus of the Lord's Compassion;
> And you will feel the sweetness ineffable of its heart-fragrance
> Coming on a breeze which ripples the face of the silent waters
> To meet you beneath the stars.[13]

The *śrāmaṇera*, or novice, ordination took place at Kusinara, the place of the Buddha's Parinirvāṇa, on 12 May 1949,[14] and Sangharakshita spent the following months with the scholarly Bhikkhu Kashyap in Benares. The two men travelled to Kalimpong where Kashyap instructed Sangharakshita to 'stay and work for the good of Buddhism'.[15] Within a few months the young monk had started a small magazine called *Stepping Stones*, which he intended to be 'a journal of living Buddhism [...] imbued with the all-embracing spirit of the Mahāyāna'.[16] It would include his poems and essays along with articles by Buddhist writers based locally. The July 1950 issue contained a short essay by Sangharakshita entitled *The Awakening of the Heart*, which draws on the same stream of inspiration his poetry was exploring.

The essay begins with a parable that is worth quoting in full because it contains, through the image of a growing lotus, the basic elements of Sangharakshita's understanding of the path:

> Deep in the mud and slime of the river bed lodges the lotus seed. In the cold green darkness of that nether world of waters it dwells unseen and unsuspected. Age after age it seems to lurk there under layers of rotted vegetation and soft black mud, while the abysmal silence broods mother-like above it and all round, holding it tenderly in the soft darkness of her womb. Then, one day, a shaft of light comes plunging down through the watery gloom like a sword of emerald fire. The darkness seems to heave, shudder, and thrill beneath its touch. That twilight world glows a pale and delicate green, then a misty amber, and at last a clear bright translucent gold. With the light comes fire. And the seed, the lotus seed down there in its dark bed of death, feels the light and the warmth of that inflowing life and struggles to respond. Slowly, slowly come forth the thin white filaments, the pale green stem, the tiny tender leaves, and at last, just as the plant thrusts itself up from the chill green water into the warm sunlit air, comes forth all virgin-hard and tightly wrapped up within itself a little bud. But as the heat of the sun waxes stronger the bud swells and slowly unfolds until its pure white petals and golden heart are wide open to receive the kiss of benediction from its Lord.[17]

Most accounts of the Buddha's teaching, especially Theravādin ones, start with the four noble truths and the eightfold path, but

Sangharakshita also reports two earlier episodes in the traditional account. Firstly, the Buddha formulates his understanding as a process of conditioned arising; then, according to the *Ariyapariyesena Sutta*, he wonders whether anyone will be able to grasp what this means. He considers not teaching but sees a vision of beings in which they appear as lotuses:

> Some, born and growing in the water, might flourish while immersed in the water; some might stand at an even level with the water; while some might rise up from it.[18]

He realizes that our capacity to grow like lotuses aligns us with his insight, and he decides to teach.

This episode and its message of growth were central to how Sangharakshita envisaged the Buddhist path. The parable in *The Awakening of the Heart* derives from this, varying the canonical account by presenting it from the lotus's perspective. It suggests that, like seeds, human beings fulfil their nature through growing towards buddhahood.

Organic understanding

The perception of the world as a living entity is as old as human understanding itself, and we find it in all cultures.[19] In western cultural history it became self-conscious through the Romantic movement, which is usually said to have begun in the decades that followed the French Revolution, though its legacy continued in the arts and religion of the century that followed. Both the founding generation of 'High Romantics' and their successors were important for Sangharakshita in offering a language for his intuitions.

Romanticism is best understood as a reaction to the European Enlightenment, the Industrial Revolution, and the rationalist understanding that, critics said, treated the world as a machine. The German pioneers of Romanticism, especially Schlegel, Schelling, and Hegel, developed *Naturphilosophie*, a philosophical outlook that saw the world as a living organism. The first generation of English Romantics either came to similar conclusions independently or learned from their German contemporaries.

Samuel Taylor Coleridge, who assimilated German Romantic ideas into his own organic thinking, was one of Sangharakshita's five literary heroes, along with Samuel Johnson, William Blake, Oscar Wilde, and D.H. Lawrence.[20] Four of the five were opponents of Enlightenment reductionism while the fifth, Samuel Johnson, was an English pragmatist who opposed what he considered the excessive rationalism of the French Enlightenment.

In his classic 1953 study of Romantic aesthetics *The Mirror and the Lamp*, the American literary critic M.H. Abrams suggests, in terms that might equally apply to Sangharakshita, that Coleridge's thought possesses a distinctive consistency:

> it consists in a fidelity to the archetype, or founding image, to which he has committed himself. This is the root analogy between atomistic and organic, mechanic and vital – ultimately, between the root analogies of the machine and the growing plant.[21]

Calling this perception an analogy suggests a literary trope or a way of *describing* the world, but behind Coleridge's archetype is the feeling that the world is alive as we are, and that to live properly is to attune ourselves to that aliveness.

Sangharakshita felt this keenly, and echoed the Romantic critique of modern culture. He said in one lecture:

> The view we have inherited from late nineteenth-century science is that the universe is dead, more like a motor-car than a human body. But, at least metaphorically, one can usefully think of the universe as being much more like a living being.[22]

The mechanistic mind-set estranged modern people from an organic understanding that was natural to humanity and had only recently been lost. Aged twenty-two Sangharakshita wrote of the culture he had left:

> There is no central point whence our ideals issue and into which our activities return. Consequently, all that we do, however far its effects may be protracted into space far

distant and time yet to come, is essentially devoid of meaning, purpose, and value. We think, we feel, we act; but we know not why. A dark and inscrutable force seems to be sweeping our frailty before it as the wind drives the dead leaves along the ground.[23]

For 'modern man', he wrote a decade later in *A Survey of Buddhism*, 'there falls, like moonlight upon shifting leaves, no steady radiance of the Eternal upon the flickerings of his days.'[24] Buddhism gave a way back because it offered a coherent account of the universe as a spiritual domain and a path enabling the individual to join with it. Sangharakshita says in the *Survey*:

> The quest for holiness, which the study of the Dharma subserves, is a quest for spiritual wholeness, for complete integration of the 'personality' not with any subjective principle merely, but with Reality.[25]

On his return to the West he set out to create an alternative culture that allowed people to discover more authentic sources of meaning in the form of a Buddhist movement whose mission, he said in 1969, 'must be to replace a mechanistic universe with one that has meaning, that carries throughout its fabric intimations of spiritual values'.[26]

● ● ●

Organic understanding, whether Coleridge's or Sangharakshita's, develops around the metaphor of a plant's development of the sort the parable in *The Awakening of the Heart* describes. Its implications become visible if we distinguish its phases.

Firstly, the adult plant depends upon the 'antecedent power or principle in the seed',[27] as Coleridge says, and the mysterious connection between a seed and a flower, or an acorn and an oak tree, is a potent metaphor in many spiritual traditions. Within Mahāyāna Buddhism consciousness is sometimes said to contain 'buddha seeds' that stir into life when the light of the Dharma shines upon them. The whole process is both natural and miraculous because it involves the meeting of two orders of reality. '[T]he gradual awakening of Wisdom and Compassion within the human heart', writes Sangharakshita in *The Awakening of the Heart*, is possible only because it has been there all the time, 'however deeply and darkly it may be hidden away beneath layer on layer of greed, hatred, and delusion'.[28] *Nirvāṇa* is present within *saṃsāra*, and, in practising the Dharma, we align ourselves with a truth greater than our individual consciousness:

> Religion and the spiritual life are therefore built into the very structure of Reality – if such a stiff and architectural metaphor is permissible with reference to That which is essentially dynamic. They are no mere grafts on to the Tree of Life but spring from it as its fairest blossom and ripest fruit.[29]

For all Sangharakshita's later wariness of the misuse of buddha-nature language, the sense of something 'spiritual' that is available to us because it is built into the structure of reality is never absent from his teaching.

The second feature of a plant is that it grows, and growth, for Coleridge, is 'the first power of all living things'.[30] Sangharakshita's sense of spiritual life as a process of growth will run through the account of his work in the following chapters, and his work depends on the equation between the metaphor of growth and its abstract expression in the principle of conditionality.

Thirdly, a plant requires supportive conditions. In a 1994 talk entitled 'The Rain of the Dharma', Sangharakshita says: 'For the growth of a plant, five things are needed. First of all there needs to be a seed, and then the seed needs soil, warmth, light, and rain.' The seed is our potential for Enlightenment; the soil is 'circumstances that are favourable to spiritual growth'.[31] He adds that warmth comes from spiritual friendship, light from intellectual clarity, and rain from the Dharma. His emphasis on establishing supportive conditions gave his teachings a practicality and breadth that were important when he came to guide a Buddhist movement.

Next, a plant develops from its own source of energy and 'effectuates its own secret growth',[32] as Coleridge puts it. The

Buddha's vision of the lotuses suggests a similar capacity within human experience, and it is an important part of Sangharakshita's presentation of the path. He says in *The Three Jewels* (1961) that 'the urge to Enlightenment is immanent in all forms and spheres of life, from the humblest to the highest, and manifests whenever a kind and intelligent action is performed.'[33] In this sense, he says in one lecture,

> [Buddhism] is very broadly 'vitalist' in that it recognizes a will to Enlightenment somehow present in all forms of life and manifesting in any gesture of consideration or act of intelligent good will.[34]

Sangharakshita pondered these issues over many years, but only formulated how the elements related to one another in the final phase of his thought.

Finally, a plant's developed form possesses an underlying coherence and forms 'an organic unity'. Seeing phenomena as wholes rather than parts is essential to organic, or holistic, thinking, and Coleridge famously expressed this by contrasting mechanic and organic ways of understanding form:

> The form is mechanic when on any given material we impress a pre-determined form, not necessarily arising out of the properties of the material [...] The organic form, on the other hand, is innate; it shapes as it develops itself from within, and the fullness of its development is one and the same with the perfection of its outward form.[35]

Murry's 'organic whole', which is organized according to the secret principle of its inner life, derives from Romantic thinkers like Coleridge, and Sangharakshita makes sense of Buddhism in the *Survey* in a similar way:

> I increasingly found that the more I related Buddhism to the spiritual life of the individual Buddhist the more I saw it in its deeper interconnections within itself, and the more I saw it in its deeper interconnections within itself the more

I saw it not as a collection of miscellaneous parts but as an organic whole.³⁶

The plant in Sangharakshita's parable displays all the features of organic thinking. The seed has the potential to become a lotus, but without the sun's kindling influence it would continue to sleep in darkness. That potential meant a great deal to Sangharakshita, but potential alone is not sufficient. Sunlight strikes the seed, as the inspiration of Perfect Vision stimulates individual growth, and the plant responds to the sun with reverence and gratitude. As it swells into maturity under the sun's sustaining influence, the developing plant offers an image for spiritual growth. Looking ahead to the terminology Sangharakshita favoured in later years, we could say the plant goes for refuge to the sun as human beings go for refuge to buddhahood, or that it follows the path of the Higher Evolution. Finally, the plant is all of these things combined into a living, organic whole.

Buddhist Romanticism

In his book *Buddhist Romanticism* Ṭhanissāro Bhikkhu – a prolific scholar and translator of Pāli texts – argues that westerners often misunderstand Buddhism because they view it through a Romantic prism. Westerners who think Buddhism teaches intrinsic human goodness, for example, have, in his view, learned their faith from humanistic psychology, which derived it, in turn, from Romanticism. That makes them Romantics at two removes, and their unconscious worldview shapes their understanding of Buddhist teachings, even when those teachings flatly contradict it.

While Sangharakshita felt close to Romantics, he was far from the sort of unwitting Romantic Ṭhanissāro criticizes. He also stressed the importance of critically examining received views, and shared many of Ṭhanissāro's criticisms of the filters through which westerners perceive Buddhism. He agreed, for example, that believing in intrinsic human goodness can obscure the Buddhist teaching that we can act either skilfully or unskilfully, and he thought seeing spiritual life in terms of 'experience' could produce 'neurotic craving for higher spiritual experience'.³⁷

But this is not the whole of the Romantic legacy. The movement was diverse and famously impossible to define, and, rather than the single Romantic religion Ṭhanissāro envisages, we find an array of differing Romantic philosophies. The opposition to reductive rationalism that unites them is, above all, a matter of feeling, and Sangharakshita entitled the first full collection of his poems *The Enchanted Heart* (a phrase from Shelley's 'Lines Written in the Bay of Lerici') because he valued the enchantment the Romantics associated with nature, love, beauty, and symbols. While Ṭhanissāro considers the teachings of the Pāli Canon timeless and beyond culture, Sangharakshita didn't think its timeless truth could be defined so narrowly. In his view, the spirit of the Dharma needed to be re-expressed, and through the Romantics and others he found inspiration in his own culture.

The thousand-petalled rose

In the absence of a reliable spiritual guide in the early part of his Buddhist career, Sangharakshita explored these issues for himself. But he wasn't entirely alone. Born Ernst Lothar Hoffmann in Germany in 1898, Lama Govinda was twenty-seven years Sangharakshita's senior. Reading Schopenhauer on the cusp of the First World War convinced him of the truth of Buddhism. He enjoyed a bohemian post-war artistic life, but in 1928 he travelled to Ceylon, became an *anagārika*, took the name Govinda, and established a hermitage near Kandy. In 1931 he accepted an invitation to a conference in Darjeeling, intending to uphold the Theravāda against Vajrayāna 'demon worship and weird beliefs'.[38] But tantric art stirred him mysteriously and the Tibetan monks impressed him deeply.

Govinda shared Sangharakshita's low opinion of modern western culture, and saw Tibet's conflict with the Chinese as a spiritual battle in which 'the organic connection with a fruitful past is destroyed for the chimera of a machine-made prosperity.'[39] Sangharakshita didn't share Govinda's idealized view of Tibet, but he recognized him as just the kind of contributor he wanted for *Stepping Stones*. Govinda, for his part, saw his own approach to Buddhism mirrored in Sangharakshita's journal and responded with encouragement, advice, and a stream of articles – the start of a lengthy correspondence. When Govinda visited Sangharakshita in Kalimpong (along with his partner Li Gotami), Sangharakshita felt he had more in common with the German than with any Buddhist he had met.

Govinda had resolved issues with which Sangharakshita was still wrestling, particularly the relationship of Buddhism and art and the relations between differing approaches to Dharma practice. Sangharakshita listened enthralled as Govinda explained that it was possible to take up practices of different sorts according to one's spiritual needs, adding new practices to the old ones until they formed a complex matrix or mandala. This offered a way to reconcile the view of the Buddhist path as a 'progression from stage to stage, or level to level', which Sangharakshita had principally favoured, with the philosophy of 'interpenetration'. As Govinda spoke, Sangharakshita realized spiritual practice could be 'an unfolding from an ever more truly central point into an ever increasing number of different aspects and dimensions', and had a vision of 'petal being added to petal, or facet to facet, until one had a thousand-petalled rose or a thousand-faceted crystal ball complete in all its glory'.[40]

* * *

Sangharakshita's mature formulations of the Buddhist path developed from the balanced perspectives of 'Above Me Broods...', the radiant vision of Amitābha, the image of the growing lotus, and the thousand-petalled rose that combined the elements of Dharma practice within an enchanted whole. But another element was important in his makeup: his passionate love of beauty.

Chapter Six

Love and Beauty

The Veil of Stars

If the central intellectual challenges of Sangharakshita's Indian writing were seeing Buddhism as a unified tradition and working out a coherent understanding of the Buddhist path, the emotional challenge was aligning his spiritual goals with his emotions. He wrote in 1951:

> The central problem of the spiritual life is [...] not so much a matter of the intellectual understanding of this or that doctrine as of the concentration of the total psychic energy of the individual – now dissipated in so many directions – along the line of its eventual realization. Since this energy is nothing but the energy of desire in the widest possible sense of the term, and since emotion is only the 'long-circuiting' of desire, it is with the concentration and sublimation of desire and the reorientation of emotion that the spiritual life is above all else concerned.[1]

Beauty was tremendously important to him, and he thought artistic beauty shared something essential with Buddhism. He wrote, also in 1951:

> It has been recognized even in the West (by Schopenhauer) that all great art contains an element of self-transcendence akin to that which constitutes the quintessence of religion. When this element of self-transcendence is consciously cultivated in poetry, in music, or in painting and sculpture,

instead of the element of mere sensuous appeal, art ceases
to be a form of sensuous indulgence and becomes a kind
of spiritual discipline, and the highest stages of aesthetic
contemplation become spiritual experiences.[2]

The Religion of Art (1953) describes what it means to follow this path, either as a creative artist or as an appreciator of art:

At first the mind shrinks from the artist's touch; but it
soon discovers that to be stretched is, after all, not such an
unpleasant experience as it had supposed. Eventually, the
experience becomes a positive delight, dearer, perhaps, and
more rewarding, than any hitherto known. The spiritual life
claims another devotee.[3]

Since Goethe and Schlegel, people had argued that art could fill the gap created by the decline of established religion:

In these days when, all over the world, conventional religion
so often fails to move the hearts of men, the Religion of Art
may enable some people at least to experience, through the
instrumentality of Beauty, those supreme values of life which
in former centuries were generally mediated by Religion.[4]

What Sangharakshita valued in art excluded most modern art and, especially in his twenties, he could be disdainful of the 'emotional muck-heaps'[5] of popular culture and people who 'are content to be human beings, just as a pig is content to be a pig'.[6] His tone changed in later life, but not his underlying view of art:

[A]ny art which is worthy of the name finds itself in a
sort of hierarchy. At the lowest level there is art that
simply organizes sensuous impressions into pleasurable
formal relations. Above this level you can then find art
that expresses, through those formal relations, the artist's
sensibility. A still higher form of art communicates, through
that sensibility, the artist's sense of values. And in the very
highest form of art, that sense of values, communicated in

that way, is capable of transforming the lives of the observer, listener, or reader.⁷

• • •

The Veil of Stars, which Sangharakshita wrote between 1951 and 1954, is his major poetic achievement.⁸ It comprises 119 epigrammatic stanzas each of which, as Lama Govinda says in his 'Introduction', 'forms a complete unit in itself'.⁹ The verses sometimes echo the aphorisms of *Thus Spake Zarathustra*, but the poem takes its form from Rabindranath Tagore's serene 1916 work *Stray Birds*. Sangharakshita's subject is the turbulent emotions of the Lover – the poem's protagonist who is perhaps close to Sangharakshita, if not identical with him – as he experiences the pleasures and pains of unreciprocated erotic love and finds a way beyond them.

It begins with the declaration that love has arrived unexpectedly, 'mysterious as the flight of a bird from unknown lands' (i), awakening a passion within the Lover 'that had slept for a thousand years' (vii). The Beloved's beauty entrances him, and his love has an inexpressible fineness, like 'the music of the stars [...] and the melody o' the moon' (xviii). He feels a connection with something precious that is woven into nature, 'like the thread of gold that runs through the texture of all my dreams' (xi).

But the Lover's happiness depends entirely on the Beloved, who is unresponsive:

I sit in a breathless agony of suspense in your presence,
As though upon a single flicker of your eyelid hung the
    destiny of a world. (xxxii)

The Lover realizes bitterly that the Beloved is unresponsive because he is indifferent, and 'All the joy of love now turns into pain.'¹⁰ His anguish is profound, but it eventually stirs deeper reflections, and he recognizes the limitations of his attachment:

> Love is like ice and trickles away in tiny streamlets between
>   the fingers
> of the hands that seek to grasp it too tightly. (lxi)

'Tired out with continual weeping' (xxviii) he reaches a turning point. Echoing Keats and Baudelaire, he realizes his suffering holds an important lesson:

> He must pass beneath the arch of Pain who desires to enter
>   into the shrine of Love.
> He must enter into the shrine of Love who seeks to gaze upon
>   the face of the image of Wisdom. (lxv)

Sitting in the 'silence and peace of the old hills' (lxxiv), he feels nature's healing power and understands that his desire for the Beloved had masked a deeper yearning – 'a hunger unappeasable for the stars' (xci). Going beyond erotic love, he has found something greater:

> When Love has conducted you into the golden presence of his
>   master Compassion he bows to the ground before him and
>   departs. (xciii)

This is the bodhisattva's compassion for the world, and by the poem's conclusion the Lover has entered an entirely new form of existence.

The poem's true subject is not so much love as its transcendence. By its conclusion the Lover has achieved the goals of Buddhism, making it a poem about the relation of mundane experiences like romantic love to transcendental states such as the bodhisattva's compassion:

> It is the smile of the Bodhisattva that flashes upon me from
>   the heart of the golden sunset,
> And the flood of his Compassion that inundates my soul with
>   streams of love. (cx)

Platonism, compassion, and the path of beauty

A Neoplatonic temperament

The Veil of Stars' message that erotic emotion is a means to transcendence echoes the tormented professions and idealizations of Romantic poetry and the older tradition of courtly love. Behind both is the much older tradition of Platonism. Sangharakshita defined a Platonist as one for whom 'it was self-evident that there existed a higher, spiritual world',[11] and reflected in 2009 that, 'leaving aside any sort of doctrinal or metaphysical issues', he was 'a Neoplatonist by temperament as Shelley was [...] in the sense of a sort of idealism, and a sort of upward movement'.[12] He discovered Plato and Neoplatonism (the tradition that developed Platonism's mystical aspects in art and religion) as a teenager when he read Plotinus's *Enneads*, Dean Inge's *Philosophy of Plotinus*, and, above all, Plato's *Symposium*. The Platonic influence is palpable in his Indian writings, even though he had little access to Platonic works, but following his return to the West he read all the relevant texts he could find and came to consider Neoplatonism (rather than Christianity) 'the major spiritual tradition of the West'.[13]

For all its appeal, Sangharakshita recognized the fundamental differences between Buddhism and Neoplatonism. The central Platonic tenet is that, beyond the individual good or beautiful things we perceive through our senses, is a realm of pure forms where we encounter the good and beautiful themselves. While most people cannot see beyond particulars, says Plato, the true philosopher is one who 'believes in the beautiful itself [and] can see both it and the things that participate in it'.[14]

However, the basic Buddhist metaphysical understanding, as Sangharakshita himself describes it in *The Three Jewels*, is fundamentally different. The teaching of *anatta/anātman*, or 'not self', denies the existence of an unchanging substance behind phenomena:

> Abstracted from its green and red colour a leaf is not an independent entity but only a name. When it changes its colour what really happens is that, as the traditional formula would have it, in dependence upon a green leaf a red leaf arises.

In this way, he recognizes, 'Buddhist thought as a whole adhered faithfully throughout the long course of its development to the strict nominalism inherent in its doctrine of insubstantiality.'[15] Things can't be both dynamic and eternally unchanging – these are different ways of understanding the world – and, according to the classical Buddhist analysis, the Platonic outlook is a form of 'eternalism'. The Buddhist position, as Sangharakshita expressed it, is that 'it is the absence of any permanent, unchanging self-nature that makes religious progress possible.'[16]

However, Buddhism combines its denial of absolutes with a belief that a mind entirely freed of craving is so radically different from ordinary consciousness that it represents an entirely different order of reality. Between the two are levels of reality through which we can ascend. For Sangharakshita, this mirrored the Neoplatonic belief that love and beauty offered ways to approach the ideal. Consequently:

> [S]uch affinities as exist between Buddhism and the religious traditions of the West are to be found in Neoplatonism rather than in Christianity, notwithstanding the fact that Christian theology and mysticism are both deeply indebted to Neoplatonism.[17]

The path of beauty
Sangharakshita reflects in his memoirs that he was, by nature, 'a lover of beauty',[18] and the Platonic tradition in art and poetry as well as in philosophy was important for him because it accommodated both his idealism and his response to beauty. Again, the relationship with Buddhism is not straightforward. Buddhist sources sometimes say that, as well as being unsatisfactory (*dukkha*), impermanent (*anicca*), and insubstantial (*anatta*), conditioned existence is *asubha* – 'not beautiful' or 'ugly'. For the Theravādins Sangharakshita encountered, this meant that all sense pleasures should be spurned, and nirvāṇa was conceived negatively. Against this, *The Three Jewels* cites a passage from the Discourses in which the Buddha speaks of 'the Release called the Beautiful' and proposes a different understanding of *subha*:

Subha, literally 'purity', really means beauty, though beauty of the spiritual rather than of the sensuous order. It is pure beauty in the Platonic and Neoplatonic sense of something shining in a world of its own above and beyond concrete things, which are termed beautiful only in so far as they participate in its perfection. When Buddhism insists that all things are *asubha*, it does not mean that we have to regard a flower, for instance, as essentially ugly, but only that in comparison with the beauties of a higher plane of reality, those of a lower plane are insignificant.[19]

Guided by scholars like Caroline Rhys Davids, Sangharakshita found a seam of imagery, stories, and poetry in the unwieldy Pāli Text Society translations of the Discourses that Theravādin Buddhists had largely overlooked. In excluding beauty, he thought they had misunderstood their own tradition and cut themselves off from a source of emotional sustenance. The Buddha, he reflected, wasn't moved to go forth from worldly life by seeing its defects:

The first three sights turned him away from conditioned existence, but it was the beauty of that fourth sight, the sadhu in his yellow robes, the wanderer, that moved him to go forth in the direction of Nirvāṇa.[20]

He thought failure to allow space for beauty, and therefore for emotional engagement, had contributed to the 'spiritually moribund' condition of much of the Theravādin world.[21]

Against the Theravādins he often cited the story from the *Udāna* of Nanda, the Buddha's nephew, who has become a bhikkhu but is distracted from Dharma practice by thoughts of a young woman. The Buddha transports Nanda to the Tāvatiṃsa heaven and shows him 500 dove-footed nymphs, and Nanda declares that, by comparison, the woman resembled a mutilated monkey. He re-engages with meditation so that after death he can 'attain the nymphs', but outgrows this dubious motivation and eventually becomes an *arahant*. The Pāli commentaries interpret Nanda's story as an example of the Buddha's 'skilful means', but Sangharakshita thought it described Nanda's ascent 'through a series of worlds, each representing a successively higher, more refined sublimation of feeling', and even suggested 'the soul's ascent from a lower to a higher beauty'.[22]

Tuning to Mahāyāna Buddhism, Sangharakshita found a surfeit of beauty, particularly in the sutras' eloquent devotion and visionary poetry. He writes in *A Survey of Buddhism*:

> The Mahāyāna emancipates Buddhism from its comparatively drab terrestrial and historical context and transfers it to a celestial context of dazzling beauty and irresistible emotional appeal; it mounts the priceless jewel of the Dharma in a ring of gold.[23]

The 1996 paper *Extending the Hand of Fellowship* says of the Pure Land sutras:

> [W]hat we are presented with, in these three *Sutras*, is the vision of an ideally beautiful Buddha in ideally beautiful surroundings. The contemplation of beauty gives rise to love, and when the beauty contemplated is the sublime beauty of Buddhahood, as manifested in the radiant figure of Amitābha, that love takes the form of faith and devotion, through which the devotee is assimilated to the object of his devotion and achieves, in the symbolic language of the *Sutras*, rebirth in Sukhāvatī.[24]

This is a more straightforward way to become joined to beauty than the tortuous path of *The Veil of Stars*, but the destination is the same.

In the period that followed the publication of *The Veil of Stars*, tantric initiation gave Sangharakshita a way to engage with visual beauty in meditation. A late reflection entitled *Green Tārā and the Fourth Lakṣaṇa* describes the effect of the practice. Contrasting Tārā's beauty with the ugliness of ordinary existence, he says, leads to 'the *samādhi* of pure beauty', which opens a 'door of liberation', or *vimokṣamukha*. He concludes:

Historically speaking, Buddhism has not developed a spiritual path in which the goal is envisaged in terms of ideal beauty and the path in terms of increasing love for that beauty. There is no reason, however, why such a path should not be developed within the general framework of Buddhist practice, especially as we have models for such an approach within the Western spiritual tradition.[25]

Love and compassion

Of all Platonic and Neoplatonic texts, *The Symposium* was particularly important to Sangharakshita, especially Diotima's description of the soul's ascent to heaven, which he summarizes in a 1993 essay:

> Beauty is the object of love, for as Diotima tells Socrates in Plato's *Symposium*, Love is a lover of Wisdom because Wisdom is beautiful and 'Love is love of beauty'. [...] Earthly love is the love of earthly things, while heavenly love is the love of the things of heaven. The soul ascends from earth to heaven as it learns to love the things of heaven more than the things of earth, and it loves the things of heaven more than the things of earth as it perceives the greater beauty of the things of heaven, earthly beauty being but the faint, distorted reflection of heavenly beauty in the mirror of sense.[26]

In this account of Diotima's speech, earthly love has seemingly little value except as a step on the ladder to heavenly love, but *The Veil of Stars* is closer to what Diotima actually says:

> When a man, starting from this sensible world and making his way upward by a right use of his feeling of love for boys, begins to catch sight of that beauty, he is very near his goal.[27]

In 1949 the combination of physical and spiritual beauty for Sangharakshita coalesced in a figure glimpsed through the door of a hut in Ramana Maharshi's ashram:

> Inside was a single small room, completely bare, and inside the room, almost directly facing us, there sat, meditating, the most beautiful young man I had ever seen. Slim and fair-complexioned he sat there, with closed eyes, beautiful not only on account of his perfectly proportioned body, naked save for a small cloth but, even more so, on account of the beatific smile that irradiated his face. He was quite oblivious to our presence. Unable to take our eyes off him, we stood there for several minutes. Then, having closed the door behind us even more gently than we had opened it, we slowly made our way back to the ashram.[28]

To the end of his life, Sangharakshita cherished the image of the youth, who was 'not only physically beautiful but spiritually beautiful'.[29]

Physical beauty was important because it engaged the emotions. Edgar Wind explains in his classic study *Pagan Mysteries in the Renaissance* (1958) that for Neoplatonists

> Desire alone, without Beauty as its source, would not be Love but animal passion, while Beauty alone, unrelated to passion, would be an abstract entity which does not arouse Love.[30]

This is the key to *The Veil of Stars*, where the Lover embraces the emotion that comes to him like 'a bud at midnight' (ii). His anguish is equally intense, but it is a necessary step towards transcendence: 'pain that bore to me in careful hands the bottomless cup of joy' (lxx).

Here, as elsewhere, Sangharakshita believes, '[a]n ounce of practice and experience is worth a ton of theory and conceptualization',[31] and we must be true to what we honestly feel, he believes, rather than indulging in spiritual fantasies. Loving kindness, or *mettā*, he says in the *Survey*,

> consists not in thinking of oneself as expanding the feeling of love until it becomes all-embracing but in expanding the actual feeling of love itself – a subtle but supremely important distinction.[32]

Of course, *The Veil of Stars* is a poem, not autobiography, but the intensity of the emotions it describes surely tells us something about the feelings of the earnest and scholarly Bhikkhu Sangharakshita as he taught the members of the Kalimpong Young Men's Buddhist Association. There is no reason to doubt that Sangharakshita maintained his vows of celibacy, but the Lover declares feelings that are far from monastic detachment:

> Round and round in the ever-recurring starless night of
>   frustration
> The black flame of my love pursues your golden youth. (xliv)

The Symposium and Neoplatonic philosophy offered a place for such unruly emotions within a spiritual path leading to selfless compassion. Sangharakshita writes in the 1953 essay *Advice to a Young Poet*:

> The poet is compelled to give vent to his emotions in verse because they cannot be realized through any human relation: they refuse to terminate, in the noble words of Plato, on finite and particular objects, but protract themselves into the infinite and universal realm of poetry and Truth. It is in this capacity of protraction or penetration into Reality that the strength of an emotion truly consists.[33]

By the conclusion of *The Veil of Stars*, the lover's experience retains the affective intensity of earthly love, but it is more disinterested and universal than any mere emotion, and opens to wider forces: 'Sitting for hours and hours among the calm, quiet, kind old hills, I feel that somewhere behind the veil of things there is a Friend' (lxxv). This Wordsworthian thought makes compassion a mysterious power that echoes the life force Sangharakshita sometimes sensed in nature. It emerges, unforced, when the conditions are right: in one poem he calls it the unseen flower 'that springs up in the emptiness which is when you yourself are not there'.[34] If the mystery is *anatta* ('not self') or *śūnyatā* ('emptiness'), what emerges is the bodhicitta. He wrote in 1947:

The flower does not consider or take thought before it sends forth its perfume on the breeze, but does so naturally and unconsciously. Similarly, the bodhisattva, engaged in the plenary realization of *bodhi*, does not consider or take thought to be compassionate; but his compassion radiates naturally and superconsciously from his realization of non-duality. *Karuṇā* is the world's name for its dualistic understanding of the bodhisattva's realization of unity.[35]

The force that drives the Lover by the poem's end is much greater than romantic longing or any other form of desire:

> It is this great rhythm of joy that, having given birth to
>   millions of stars in the sky,
> Now pours down into my heart and ecstatically begets there
>   the unending mystery of my love. (cxiii)

This is the cosmic love that Neoplatonism describes, which 'makes the planets join hands together in their dance of joy about the sun' (cxii). It is also the bodhicitta of Mahāyāna Buddhism – the selfless motivation that defines a bodhisattva:

> It is the smile of the Bodhisattva that flashes upon me from
>   the heart of the golden sunset,
> And the flood of his Compassion that inundates my soul with
>   streams of love. (cx)

But, even when he has transcended egocentricity, the Lover recognizes that the lower, erotic love was indispensable to his journey, and the truth can only be found through the error:

> What I thought was my love for you is, now I find, in reality
>   compassion for all sentient beings.
> Thinking to pick up a glow-worm from the grass, lo! I plucked
>   down a galaxy of stars from the sky. (xcvi)

• • •

These are rarefied reflections, but compassion also had a practical meaning for the young Sangharakshita. Shortly after Bhikkhu Kashyap left him in Kalimpong to 'work for the good of Buddhism', Sangharakshita scribbled a haiku in his notebook:

> Behind me the old
> Gate shuts. Before me opens
> A new gate of gold.[36]

For the previous three years, he explains, he had been concerned with the needs of his own spiritual life; now it was time to start paying attention to others, and passing through the golden gate meant expressing outwardly the compassion that had accompanied his vision of Amitābha.

It manifested in small moments of connection. One day in 1949, while Sangharakshita was living as a wanderer, he sheltered overnight in a cowshed and woke to find a white calf asleep beside him:

> To me that small life did impart
> A kind of aching tenderness,
> Such as may fill a mother's heart
> To see her infant's helplessness.
>
> And in the deepest depths of me
> I felt that I had understood
> In one clear flash the mystery
> Of universal brotherhood.[37]

For Sangharakshita, compassionate action particularly meant teaching Buddhism, and he taught from the start of his time in Kalimpong. Many of his strongest experiences as a Dharma teacher came through working with the followers of Dr Ambedkar, whose poverty was beyond anything he had known. The prejudice he witnessed sometimes haunted him for months, but he felt at home among them, made friends, and experienced a connection with his listeners that was more important than the differences in their situations. Years later, he told an Ambedkarite audience:

> Deep down, we are all the same: we are all just human beings.
> That is why we can understand one another, and why we
> can be friends. [...] I believe that it is possible for any human
> being to communicate with any other human being, to feel for
> any other human being, to be friends with any other human
> being.[38]

Notwithstanding his tendency to introversion, Sangharakshita's responsiveness to friendship, communication, and connection added another dimension to his sense of a rounded spiritual life. He sometimes experienced moments of profound awareness when he was most active, and learned that

> external activity and inner spiritual experience were
> not necessarily incompatible, and [...] however valid the
> distinction between 'introvert' and 'extravert' might be on
> the psychological level it was one that was transcended by
> the bodhisattva's non-dual experience of the Wisdom that is
> Compassion and the Compassion that is Wisdom.[39]

● ● ●

Lama Govinda writes in his 'Introduction' to *The Veil of Stars*:

> It rests on the inner parallelism between the most fundamental
> human emotions and the highest experiences on the path of
> liberation and enlightenment, the relationship between love
> and wisdom, the individual and the universal, the moods of
> Nature and the moods of the human heart.[40]

This means that a lower love points the way to transcendence, but it also means that compassion is immanent within earthly love. Sangharakshita writes in *The Awakening of the Heart*:

> For since everything in the universe reflects, and is in turn
> reflected by, every other thing, the Buddha-nature is mirrored
> in the depths not only of every human heart but in every
> grain of dust and blade of grass that is. As Aśvaghoṣa says,

everything is perfumed with the fragrance of True Suchness. Even the meanest and vilest of things enshrines immaculately within itself the Jewel of Enlightenment, of Buddhahood.[41]

We might say that transcendence and immanence coexist, but this is too abstract, and the poem says it better:

> Reality is reflected in my heart as love, and this love of mine is
> in turn mirrored in the all-embracing bosom of Reality,
> As though the moon lay reflected in the depths of the ocean,
> and the ocean in the calm clear heart of the moon. (cxvi)

The Beloved and the poet's love are images that disclose a greater reality and, in contemplating them, we come closer to Sangharakshita's imagination. To go further, we must explore his understanding of images themselves.

Chapter Seven
Imagination and the Path

The image

Many traditions associate physical objects, visual images, and sounds with an invisible, or abstract, higher meaning that can be intuited by dwelling on the object. Platonism developed a distinctive understanding of symbols, which Neoplatonism and hermeticism developed into elaborate esoteric philosophies. Renaissance thinkers drew on these sources, and the High Romantics followed them as they sought alternatives to both mainstream Christianity and rationalism. As Frank Kermode says in his book *Romantic Image*, the role of the Romantic artist is 'dwelling upon the image' and thereby acquiring 'symbol-making power'.[1]

Sangharakshita's response to images stemmed, in the first instance, from his response to nature, art, and poetry, his visions and dream life, and even the images stored away in his 'strong visual memory'.[2] He read widely in all these sources, and his interests also encompassed the nineteenth- and early-twentieth-century figures who continued the Romantic project into movements like Symbolism. As a young man he also read popularizers of esotericism like Mme Blavatsky, who claimed to have deciphered 'the "Mystery language" of the prehistoric ages, the language now called symbolism'.[3]

Sangharakshita didn't share the esotericist's desire to be privy to a mystical key that eludes the rationalist mainstream. He was closer to the poetic tradition in which images evoke an elusive reality, and says of an image in one Buddhist sutra: 'Like all true symbols, it has many meanings, and at the same time it is more than all its meanings.'[4] But he was acutely aware, like Romantics and esotericists, of the modern culture's inability to accommodate the dimension to which symbols had traditionally pointed. In 1952, as Sangharakshita was writing his Romantically tinged polemics about the saving role of art, Eric Heller wrote in *The Disinherited Mind*:

> The predicament of the symbol in our age is caused by a split between 'reality' and what it signifies. There is no more any commonly accepted symbolic or transcendent order behind them.[5]

This change preoccupied the modernists of the generation that preceded Sangharakshita, but he had little interest in their answers.

In Kalimpong Sangharakshita mixed with other Europeans seeking alternatives to modern culture. Lama Govinda started adult life as a painter in the tradition of German Romanticism, and his Buddhist thought combined Romantic and Tibetan views of the symbol. Meditation was a meeting ground:

> [W]hile using the forms of the external world, [art] never tries to imitate nature but to reveal a higher reality by omitting all accidentals, thus raising the visible form to the value of a symbol, expressing a direct experience of life. The same experience may be gained by a process of meditation. But instead of creating a formal (objectively existing) expression, it leaves a subjective impression, thus acting as a forming agent on the character or the consciousness of the meditator.[6]

Another Kalimpong friend, Marco Pallis, believed the modern world was disconnected from 'the whole body of thoughts, practices, and institutions coming down from antiquity insofar as these are informed by principles belonging, ultimately, to the metaphysical order'.[7] That chimed with Sangharakshita's intuition, and *A Survey of Buddhism* (1957) laments 'the progressive dissociation of more and more activities of life from the unifying and integrating dominance of Tradition'.[8] Within a traditional civilization, Sangharakshita declares, every branch of knowledge, and every kind of activity, is integrated with conceptions of a metaphysical order. Every aspect of life, even the lowest and most mundane, is given a transcendental orientation that enables it to function, in a general way, as a support, if not for the actual living of the spiritual life, then at least for a more or less constant awareness of the existence of spiritual values. [...] Nurtured in such an environment, in which the whole of existence appears to be a great Smaragdine Tablet, constantly reminding us that 'the things below are copies' and that the originals are above, sensitive hearts and minds become more subtle and sensitive still. To them 'rocks, and stones, and trees', and other natural objects, are not simply lumps of matter of various shapes and sizes, but 'huge cloudy symbols of a high romance' traced, not by the 'magic hand of chance', but by the irresistible finger of omnipresent spiritual law. Nature is not dead, but alive with many voices, and to an eye accustomed to see and to hear things that point beyond themselves even

An old pine tree is preaching wisdom,
And a wild bird crying out truth.[9]

The notion of the Smaragdine Tablet is found in the *hermetica* – a body of texts ascribed to Hermes Trismegistus, the legendary founder of the main branches of western esotericism and incorporated into Renaissance and Romantic Platonism. Its message is expressed in the formula 'As above, so below', which encapsulates the Platonic idea of correspondence between sense objects and a higher reality. Sangharakshita was less inclined to idealize traditional cultures in later years, perhaps influenced by his engagement with victims of the 'traditional' Hindu caste system. But his belief that a healthy culture supported a connection with a higher dimension of experience never changed, and he saw the FWBO as the basis of a 'New Society' that did the same.

Sangharakshita had a natural affinity with the symbol-laden traditions of Mahāyāna and Vajrayāna Buddhism. He says in a lecture in the 1972 series published as *Creative Symbols of Tantric Buddhism*:

> [A] symbol is not a sign. It does not stand for something that could be known in some other way. The whole point is that you can only get any sense of what the symbol represents, or get any feeling for it, through the symbol itself. [...] They are like dreams, which leave a vivid impression, a strong feeling, but cannot be expressed in words.[10]

Sangharakshita took care over how he used words such as 'symbol', 'image', 'myth', and 'archetype' and sometimes drew distinctions between them, but it was more important that they all expressed what he called the 'realm of undefined meanings'[11] and addressed 'our hidden, even secret, depths'.[12] He observes in *A Survey of Buddhism* that the Mahāyāna was 'much more keenly aware of the purely relative value and symbolical significance of words and concepts in relation to the Absolute',[13] and this was one reason he thought it was more attuned to the spirit of Buddhism than its 'Hīnayāna' precursors.

Sangharakshita recognized the affinity between Vajrayāna and Neoplatonic ways of understanding symbols, which he explored in some of the lectures he gave in the years after he returned to the West. He says in *Symbols of Tibetan Buddhist Art* (1966):

> A true symbol can be defined as an object or a phenomenon on a lower order of existence which stands for, represents, or takes the place of, a corresponding object on a higher order of existence. This definition of a symbol is based on the conception of a hierarchically ordered system of reality. [...] Though they themselves are material or mundane, they remind us of the existence of a higher order of being, and in a sense they even put us in touch with that higher order and enable us to communicate with and experience it.[14]

The Vajrayāna draws symbols into elaborate systems in which a pattern on one plane corresponds to a pattern on another. The major example is the mandala of five buddhas, each with their own iconography and associations, who together form a pattern, or mandala. Tantric practice depends on the correspondence between these archetypal forms and our immediate experience, especially the experience of the body:

> By repeating the mantra and assuming the mudra of any Buddha or bodhisattva, as well as by the manipulation of the various phenomena in which he is reflected, one can not only place oneself in correspondence or alignment with the particular order of reality which he personifies but also be infused with its transcendental power.[15]

The general principle of correspondence was more important to Sangharakshita than the details of tantric ritual, which require many years of training, and it suggested the affinity with buddhahood that made Enlightenment possible. He says in *The Three Jewels*:

> Thus there is not only a general correspondence, in the Hermetic sense, between the realm of conditioned and the realm of unconditioned existence, but also a particular, indeed a special, correspondence between the human condition and Buddhahood. This correspondence is the foundation of all such affirmations as 'I am the Buddha' and 'I am Vajrasattva' – or whatever other Buddha-form it is occupies the centre of the mandala.[16]

The relation between earthly love and transcendent compassion in *The Veil of Stars* is a correspondence of this sort. Understood platonically, a higher meaning is immanent in a symbol, and the work of art uses the symbolic form to make that meaning available to others. Sangharakshita remarks in his 1958 essay *Paradox and Poetry in 'The Voice of the Silence'*:

> just as the efficacy of the sacramental action of the tantras is ultimately due to the essential truth of the *sutra*'s teaching, so does the power of the image to induce poetic experience ultimately derive from the fact that its comparisons are not merely fanciful but strike a deep root into the very nature of things.[17]

The true poet, he says, understands that 'Images are perceptions of real correspondences',[18] and reveal a higher truth. Myths, symbols, and archetypes do the same and, as Sangharakshita writes in *A Survey of Buddhism*:

> Knowledge stops short at conceptual symbols; wisdom passes beyond them to apprehension of the realities indicated by the symbols. But if the nature of that realization is to be communicated, recourse to those same symbols must again be had.[19]

In the absence of a traditional Buddhist term for the faculty that perceives the higher meaning of an image or experience, Sangharakshita followed platonically minded Romantics in naming it 'the Imagination'.

Blake and the Imagination

Sangharakshita derived his use of the term 'Imagination' from Samuel Coleridge (1772–1834) and especially William Blake (1757–1827). He loved Coleridge's *daemonic* poems, and Coleridge's organic thinking paralleled his own, but what he principally drew from Coleridge was his account in the *Biographia Literaria* of the imagination as a power within human consciousness that reflects a primal force in the universe. Coleridge distinguishes between the 'Primary Imagination' – a transcendent, Platonic absolute – and the 'Secondary Imagination', which is 'an echo of the former [...] and differing only in degree and in the mode of its operation'.[20] Coleridge's account of the relation between the two is famously convoluted – as Byron wrote, 'Explaining metaphysics to the nation / I wish he would explain his explanation.'[21] Sangharakshita commented:

> Coleridge, as a thinker, was a sublime abortion. He had greater mental endowment than any Englishman perhaps ever had, and he would have been one of the greatest religious thinkers of all time. But he was severely hampered, crippled even, by his attachment to orthodox Christianity. His inability

to reconcile the Trinitarian Christian in him with his own true, original genius was the cause, not the effect, of his famous indolence.[22]

Sangharakshita's engagement with William Blake went much deeper. He first encountered Blake as a teenager when he saw the mythic figures depicted in Blake's engravings and read the prophetic wisdom of *The Marriage of Heaven and Hell*. Sangharakshita's sense of spiritual affinity with Blake grew after his return to England, and in 1977 he wrote an essay entitled *Buddhism and William Blake*. Sangharakshita's abiding concern was that 'Buddhism will not really spread in the West until it speaks the language of Western culture.' Blake's work offered a unique western example of 'a non-theistic imaginative vision of rare intensity and integrity'. Blake himself was a 'combative and fiery genius'[23] who fought against both conventional Christianity and the mechanistic science and psychology of the Enlightenment. Aligning Buddhism and Blake therefore meant engaging with western culture as a field of contesting values, and taking sides.

Like Sangharakshita, Blake was a Londoner of humble origins, largely self-educated and set apart by his spiritual vision. Blake offered a model of what it meant to be a true individual who 'thought and felt and spoke for himself, without fear and without favour'. His fundamental insight, as Sangharakshita expresses it, was that 'Man is in reality not a natural but a spiritual being, and his essence is eternal.'[24] The faculty that recognizes this is the imagination:

> It is not just a human faculty but the man himself, in the deepest and truest sense, and without it there can be no true art and no true religion. It is the Divine Vision or Divine Humanity, in which all things have their existence.[25]

For Blake, as for Buddhism, the reality we inhabit depends on our minds because the mind actively colours its perceptions: 'Every eye sees differently. As the Eye, such the object.'[26] We do this according to our capacity, as Blake's interpreter Northrop Frye explains:

> The 'visionary' is the man who has passed through sight into vision [...] If there is a reality beyond our perception we must increase the power and coherence of our perception, for we shall never reach reality in any other way. If the reality turns out to be infinite, perception must be infinite. To visualize, therefore, is to realize.[27]

Blake's elaborate myth, with its symbolic patternings, offered an archetypal account of humanity's fall from a state of divine vision and how we can restore it. *The Four Zoas* dramatizes the fall as a conflict between various faculties that are represented through mythic personae. Imagination separates from Sense, Reason, and Emotion, leaving humanity in a fallen state in which the faculties are at war. Individual and collective redemption is possible if the faculties are reunified or, as Sangharakshita would say, 'integrated'; but this is a profound and difficult process that must occur on psychological, archetypal, and political levels.

Blakean integration means rising from lower to higher levels of consciousness and being. The lowest level is that of the body and its instincts, and 'single vision' is the limited, 'corporeal' perspective Blake called 'Newtons sleep'.[28] Twofold vision adds reason; threefold vision adds the emotions; and fourfold vision – 'the supreme delight' – includes the liberating faculty of imagination. Sangharakshita's 1975 poem 'Homage to William Blake' expresses his own yearning for Blakean wholeness:

> Therefore will I, all I can,
> Build up complete the Fourfold Man,
> Head and heart, and loins fine,
> And hands and feet, all made divine.[29]

In comparing Blake's system with Buddhism, Sangharakshita sets it beside the symbolic patterns of Tantra:

> Both Blake and Vajrayāna Buddhism see the whole of
> existence as one vast and complex system of correspondences.
> Both use the hermetic principle, as it may be termed, as
> a principle of order, as a means of organizing the more

prominent features of our experience into a beautiful and meaningful pattern, i.e. into a mandala, and in this way achieve integration.'³⁰

For Sangharakshita, the mandala is primarily an image of the 'horizontal integration' that comes from resolving psychological tensions and balancing the five spiritual faculties – faith with wisdom, and energy with meditation. 'Vertical integration' means aligning the lower mandala with a higher one. Spiritual wholeness, for both Blake and Sangharakshita, therefore requires integration along both axes, but Blake's particular importance for Sangharakshita was what he had to say about vertical integration.

Critics debate whether Blake learned his thinking from Neoplatonism, whether it is a version of Christian prophecy or a more individual genius, but Plotinus's description of a hierarchy of vision certainly parallels Blake's. Plotinus writes in his *Essay on the Beautiful* that the 'corporeal eye' gives way to the 'intellectual eye', closing which 'we must stir up and assume a purer eye within, which all men possess, but which is alone used by a few.' We can perceive the absolute in this way because something in us corresponds to it: 'The sensitive eye can never be able to survey the orb of the sun unless strongly endued with solar fire.'³¹

Sangharakshita's understanding includes the same model of ascending levels depending on a hierarchy of perception, and he found a Buddhist hierarchy of vision in the teaching of the Five Eyes (which appears in slightly different versions used in the Pāli commentaries and Mahāyāna sources). Echoing Blake and Plotinus, it envisages a 'fleshly' eye at the base; then the 'divine' eye of clairvoyance; the 'Dharma' eye – the 'inner spiritual vision, with which you "see" the truth of things'; the *arahant*'s Eye of Wisdom; and the Universal Eye of the Buddha.³² Vision and imagination are closely related in Sangharakshita's thought. In his account of the eightfold path, Perfect Vision arises when the Dharma Eye opens, even briefly, offering 'a vision of the nature of existence' that is 'direct and immediate, and more of the nature of a spiritual experience than an intellectual understanding'.³³

Vision and Imagination overturn conventional ways of seeing the world, including religious ones. Blake thought organized religion developed when 'men forgot that all deities reside in the human breast',[34] and his version of Christianity rejects everything that is normally associated with it. His belief that religious teachings should be understood poetically anticipates Sangharakshita's critique of established Buddhism, and Sangharakshita writes:

> Even when [Blake] does use the language of belief he uses it in his own way, i.e. not literally and dogmatically but metaphorically and symbolically. According to him this is in fact the right way to use it, for all religion is 'decayed poetry' and to understand it poetically is to understand it as it was originally meant to be understood. Then as now, it is the poetic genius, the man of imagination, who is the truly religious man.

Blake's message that 'man should develop his own imagination, his own divine humanity, and become what, in the depths of his being, he truly is'[35] echoes Sangharakshita's determination to understand Buddhism through the medium of the spiritual imagination. He wanted to channel Blake's genius as he distinguished Buddhism's spirit from the shell of literalistic understanding and expressed it in fresh ways that were true to its imaginative core.

Nature and transcendence

Blake says, 'Where man is not nature is barren',[36] and Sangharakshita explains:

> Nature has, indeed, no existence apart from man, and like man is fundamentally spiritual, being simply 'a portion of soul [i.e. the emotions] discerned by the five senses, the chief inlets of soul in this age'.[37]

To regard nature as a portion of the soul is close to repudiating merely physical or biological existence, but, like Sangharakshita, Blake valued concrete knowledge over concepts on the principle expressed in *The Book of Thel*:

Does the Eagle know what is in the pit?
Or wilt thou go ask the Mole:
Can Wisdom be put in a silver rod?
Or Love in a golden bowl?

Blake meant that neither love nor wisdom is an abstraction, and the mole's tactile knowledge is as valuable as the eagle's lofty vantage point. At the same time, Blake believed the body must be elevated into the Human Form Divine through the power of imagination, or else, as Harold Bloom says, a person 'merely has his body and is finally possessed and imprisoned by it'.[38]

Sangharakshita placed more faith than Blake in sensory appreciation. He says in *The Religion of Art* (1953):

> The poet [...] is rooted in the objective world as a plant is rooted in the soil. The nutriment that he derives therefrom is transformed into the invisible sap of aesthetic experience and creative potency, re-emerging thence into visibility not as earth and water but as the marvel of a leaf or the miracle of a flower. For the true poet seeks not only to enrich his experience through observation of, and sympathy with, life in all its multitudinous forms, but also to refine it, to raise it to the highest possible pitch of intensity, by solitary reflection on its meaning.[39]

But, like Blake, he valued nature as the imagination transfigured it. He says in his lectures on the *Sutra of Golden Light*:

> Those human energies which are part of nature can be placed at the service of the golden light – they can be transformed. But nature herself cannot be placed at the service of the golden light. Nature herself cannot be transformed. All that we can transform is our attitude to nature, and that is sufficient.[40]

The 1995 poem 'The Call of the Forest' reflects Sangharakshita's belief that transcendence means a different experience of nature and the body. It starts with a response to the literal forest:

> What does the forest whisper
> With every wind-stirred leaf,
> From many-centuried oak tree
> To hour-old blossom-sheaf?
> What does the forest whisper
> When nightingales are dumb
> And cicadas fall silent?
> The forest whispers, 'Come'.

This mingles the Buddhist myth of renouncing the world with a Romantic feeling for nature, and the following stanzas lament the usurpation of the ancient forests by urban life. But the forest whispers its deeper meaning with the voice of the imagination:

> The whisper's a dream-whisper,
> But dreams are of the Soul
> And Soul itself a forest
> Beyond the mind's control.
> The whisper's a Soul-whisper,
> That like a muffled drum
> Calls, 'From your mind-built Cities,
> O Man, to Freedom come!'[41]

Engaging the imagination in this way depends on the individual who has developed an imaginative faculty and learned to apply it. We must therefore trace what the imagination meant for Sangharakshita.

Chapter Eight

Sangharakshita's Imagination

The world of the image

In the summer of 1966 Sangharakshita and his friend Terry Delamere stepped into the Basilica of St Apollinare in Classe, outside Ravenna, on the northeastern coast of the Adriatic, and walked along the nave. They had driven across France and northern Italy, stopping at Milan, Bergamo, Verona, Vicenza, Venice, and Padua, visiting as many churches and museums as their schedule permitted and soaking themselves in the art they contained. Renaissance art had been important to Sangharakshita since he read the seven volumes of John Addington Symonds's *Renaissance in Italy* aged eleven or twelve, but they had come to Ravenna for its Byzantine churches, especially the mosaics that survived from its late-classical heyday, and the Basilica of St Apollinare was acknowledged to be the finest of them all.

Flanking the nave were columns of cipolin marble, and at the end the visitors looked up to the shimmering tesserae of a mosaic depicting St Apollinare, the first bishop of Ravenna, in a green valley filled with trees amid a row of sheep. Above the saint was a jewelled golden cross and, hovering over it, in a sky streaked with gold, were two winged figures. When the American novelist Henry James stepped into the church a century earlier, during his own artistic pilgrimage, its distinctive atmosphere and lonely setting filled him with 'melancholy stillness'.[1] As Sangharakshita gazed at the mosaic, taking in its vibrant colours, the light saturating the church, and the power of its symbolism, he felt deep peace spreading through him.[2]

Sangharakshita and Terry continued through Italy, crossed from

Brindisi to Greece, and travelled on to Delphi, the ancient shrine of Apollo that was the journey's true destination. Stepping into the precincts, Sangharakshita felt

> the very earth was holy, and [...] this holiness penetrated the rocks and trees and permeated the air, so that one felt it in the warmth of the sun and drew it in with every breath.[3]

Sitting in the famous theatre, he read Euripides's *Ion*, which is set there, and engaged with the story so intensely that he recalled: 'I could see the drama unfolding before me [...] not buskined actors but living human beings moving and speaking there.'[4]

The art Sangharakshita saw in Italy and the sites he visited in Greece touched him on many levels. The journey was a way to reconnect, after two decades in Asia, with his deep love of European art and literature and to experience himself as a 'Western Buddhist' for whom these sources of inspiration were important both psychologically and spiritually.

Sangharakshita recalled the 1966 journey to Italy and Greece in the 1984 essay *The Journey to Il Convento*, which he wrote when he was in Italy again for a three-month ordination retreat in a former monastery in Tuscany. He knew that crossing the Alps from northern Europe into Italy had come to mean 'exchanging the Gothic for the classical, Christianity for paganism, religion for art, melancholy for joy'.[5] He adds that for him it meant a transit

> from the surface of things to the depths, from the conscious to the unconscious mind, from brain cells to bloodstream [...] from the modern to the archaic, from the present to the past, from the rational to the irrational.[6]

That made Italy a mythic realm, at least in its artworks, and, in responding to what he saw, Sangharakshita entered what he later called 'the world of the image' – a mode of experience that was at the heart of his character. This was an intuitive process. As he wandered through the churches, an 'irrational wisdom' guided him towards images that represented, in archetypal form, the fundamental concerns of his life. Images of St Jerome (the translator of the Bible into Latin) and images of angels had an especially strong resonance. Both were emblems of the vertical dimension of experience, one representing the depths and one the heights.

St Jerome

The image of St Jerome in the wilderness and outside mainstream society resonated for Sangharakshita at the time of his Italian journey when he felt he was leaving 'the "Rome" of collective, official, even establishment, Buddhism' and inhabiting the metaphorical wilderness beyond it.[7] In other depictions, Jerome is in a cave or a study, and the essay *St Jerome Revisited*, also written at Il Convento in 1984, explores the cave as an image of inner life. 'In order to see himself as a spiritual being,' says Sangharakshita, 'man has to stop viewing himself only as a physical body, as nature does, and *enter into the cave of the heart*.' The translator resembles the alchemist who renders old meanings afresh. As there are degrees, or levels, of knowledge, to be a translator in the fullest sense is to become 'an interpreter of one degree of knowledge, or one level of reality, to another [...] even, a mediator between different planes of existence or different worlds'.[8] St Jerome, the archetypal translator, symbolized for Sangharakshita what it meant to 'fathom the uttermost depths of what one is trying to translate so that one may translate it faithfully, i.e. bring its meaning to the surface, or from darkness into light'.[9]

This mirrored the change in Sangharakshita's life in the mid-1960s as he absorbed the implications of his return to the West. It affected how he lived, how he expressed Buddhist ideas in his lectures at the Hampstead Buddhist Vihara and elsewhere, and his increasing disregard for what others expected of him as a bhikkhu. He says in *The Journey to Il Convento*: 'In order to travel towards the region of light and life, we have to travel towards – and through – the region of darkness and death.'[10] This period of Sangharakshita's life was a kind of 'spiritual death' – a process of letting go that meant touching the depths of his experience. Padmasambhava, the demon-tamer, offered a Buddhist image of contacting the depths. A second Buddhist parallel was

Nāgārjuna, the great Mahāyāna Buddhist philosopher, who receives the Perfection of Wisdom texts from *nāga* princesses who have preserved them in the depths of the ocean. All these figures, hovering between the transcendental and the mundane, were images of Sangharakshita's task as a Dharma teacher in the West.

Representations of Jerome sitting at a desk in a cell in the desert, 'gigantically crouched in little room', as he writes in a 1967 sonnet, represented his profound solitude and the inwardness of the search for truth:

> In a world of sin
> The Empire changes hands, the Churches fight
> Factious as dogs. By day the old man, stung,
> Magnificently answers Augustine,
> Then, dredging from the deep, night after night
> Translates THE WORD into the vulgar tongue.[11]

The conclusion of *St Jerome Revisited* echoes Walter Pater's famous description of the *Mona Lisa* as an image of an ancient mode of being: 'older than the rocks among which she sits [...] a diver in deep seas'.[12] For Sangharakshita, Jerome represented a universal human process, occurring far below conscious awareness, which mirrored what Sangharakshita was himself attempting:

> What the artists of the Italian Renaissance depict is not so much St Jerome in his study, translating the Bible, as man in the cave of his own heart where, having subdued his lower nature and separated himself from the social order, he devotes himself to the pursuit of his distinctively human activities. What they depict is man as interpreter and creator, bringing up into consciousness what he has experienced in the depths of his own being and giving it appropriate expression for the benefit of all. What they depict [...] is man as a spiritual being who, in the shadow of time and death, strives to fathom the mystery of existence.[13]

Angels

If St Jerome, like Padmasambhava, symbolized engagement with the depths of experience, angels, like bodhisattvas, represented the heights. Sangharakshita's response to images of angels in Italian churches was part of a lifelong attraction. The archangel Michael captured his attention when he read *Paradise Lost* as a young teenager. He drew angelic figures, began his own epic poem, and poured over reproductions of Fra Angelico's angels. Gazing at their gold aureoles and multicoloured wings, he sensed their correspondence with something within him that was 'as yet hidden and undeveloped'.[14]

In India, Sangharakshita absorbed Indian mythology, including canonical Buddhist accounts of the angelic *devaloka*s ('god realms'), and angelic imagery, akin to that of Shelley and Rilke, appeared in his poems:

> We cry that we are weak although
> We will not stir our secret wings;
> The world is dark – because we are
> Blind to the starriness of things.[15]

On his return to England, Sangharakshita visited the medieval and Renaissance sections of the London art galleries, and in Italy he gave the exploration his full attention. Representations of the annunciation (the episode from Luke's Gospel in which the archangel Gabriel tells Mary that she will conceive a child through the Holy Spirit) offered 'an archetypal image of receptivity on the part of the human soul to some higher influence, a messenger from some other realm'.[16] Images of the youth Tobias and the angel who leads him by the hand expressed spiritual friendship, and perhaps angelic guidance.

Sangharakshita's engagement with Christian imagery coexisted with his rejection of Christianity. Aged eighteen, he wrote in *The Middle Way*:

> I believe that Christianity is dead, that its life is only a
> movement as it were of worms in a dead body. [...] But I
> mourn it, for I owe much to it.[17]

In a poem written two years later, his ancestors demand: 'Why does he go after strange gods?' He replies: 'I go not after strange gods / But after mine own heart.'[18] But the spiritual needs that drove him East had not finished with Christianity, and Christianity had not finished with him. *The Journey to Il Convento* suggests that, behind the Christian images that drew him, lies a truth deeper than any culture or religion:

> [T]hey are Christian only in the sense that in them an archetype which is of universal significance and value has been clothed in a Christian, Italian, Renaissance form – even in a form peculiar to a particular artist. [...] What the Buddhist is drawn to is not so much the Christian form of the image as the archetype of which that image is an embodiment, and it is therefore really the archetype that is of significance to him.[19]

The form is, nonetheless, important. Sangharakshita recoiled from depictions of the crucified Christ, and eventually traced his mixed responses to Christianity in the book-length study *From Genesis to the Diamond Sutra*.[20] What drew him in Christian art was 'not so much the Christian form of the image as the archetype of which that image is an embodiment'. But, though we may sense a correspondence between a Christian image and a Buddhist 'counterpart' – Jerome and Nāgārjuna, the Virgin Mary and Guanyin, angels and bodhisattvas – the Christian form, being western, possessed an additional emotional power for a western Buddhist like himself. And yet, he reflects in *The Journey to Il Convento*, we live 'in the midst of the ruins of Christian civilization and culture'.[21] The images he contemplated were broken because the culture and worldview that gave them meaning had lost its power. He longed for a time before the images were broken, and a culture that still recognized its connection to a transcendent dimension. Sangharakshita's spiritual life put him in contact with that dimension, but Christian imagery had a distinctive resonance that Buddhist images sometimes lacked.

Sangharakshita remarks that the retreatants to whom he addressed *The Journey to Il Convento* and *St Jerome Revisited* had made a literal journey to Italy, perhaps pausing along the way to see some art. But this was a metaphor for another, ascending journey from one level of being to another. He distinguishes a hierarchy of images 'in accordance with the degree to which they are the embodiments of a particular archetype' and, in contemplating angels and bodhisattvas, Sangharakshita felt himself ascending a stratified spiritual reality towards the archetype of Enlightenment, activating and deepening the faculty that enabled him to access it. That faculty was 'the imagination', and refining it offered a way to perceive reality more truly. He concludes that 'one arrives at the conception of a hierarchy of levels of the imagination, or imaginal *faculty*, corresponding to a hierarchy of levels of images and archetypes, or imaginal *world*.'[22]

* * *

Aged ninety-two and a few months away from death, Sangharakshita wrote a short story in which a beautiful young angel with golden hair and iridescent wings appears beside his armchair. Sangharakshita tells the angel that he is surprised to see him. If he had expected any such visitor, he thought it would have been a bodhisattva. The angel asks if it has ever occurred to him that bodhisattvas might be angels in disguise. The blurring continues when the Virgin Mary and Guanyin appear beside the angel (along with Māra), and the two female figures disagree politely about which of them is a form of the other. As for who is correct, the angel comments, only a senior cherub or seraph could say. The first angel then tells Sangharakshita that, throughout his life, he has been under angelic protection:

> Your guardian angel takes on many forms, even Buddhist ones, and in the course of your life he has helped and protected you more often than you knew. You have been in quite a few tight corners, and you have always thought that it was your good luck or your good karma that extricated you from them. In fact, it was your guardian angel, working behind the scenes, who did so every time.[23]

The story suggests that, even as Sangharakshita's strength declined, the angelic presence remained in his life. He sometimes suggested that his students think of the bodhisattva figure they visualize as a guardian angel – the Buddhist term is *puṇya-devatā* – in the sense of a 'slightly higher self'.[24] Perhaps the guardian angel in Sangharakshita's story represents his own angelic faculty; perhaps it represents a dimension of experience that is usually invisible but somehow protects us as we navigate the world; or perhaps it really is an angel. In any case, the story expresses Sangharakshita's sense that the outward events of his life occurred within a wider space than either the senses or concepts could encompass.

The world of the sutras
Sangharakshita describes many other ways in which he accessed the imagination, including meditation, art, and contact with nature. Buddhist scriptures were particularly important because they clarified and elevated his experience. He remarks in his commentary on the *Songs of Milarepa*:

> [A]fter reading the classics of Western literature or listening to the Western musical repertoire, if I then immerse myself in a Mahāyāna *sutra*, the atmosphere is totally different and goes completely beyond even the best of Western culture. [...] It leaves it completely behind. My real inspiration definitely comes from such sources.[25]

The memoirs describe an especially intensive period of engagement with Buddhist canonical literature as Sangharakshita wrote *The Eternal Legacy* in the early 1960s. Reading the Discourses, he says, he found himself in the world of ancient India where the Buddha taught 'now in a village moot hall, now beneath the spreading branches of a banyan tree, now to invisible presences in the silence of the night'.[26] The Discourses could be dry, but he detected a buried emotionality:

> certain pages of the Pāli canon thrill with a quiet enthusiasm, or glow with a serene happiness, or flash out in dazzling ecstasy. [...] Like a vibration of a pitch too high to be

perceived as sound by human ears, the very delicacy and refinement of the emotional element in the Pāli scriptures, wholly free as it is from the turbidity and violence of ordinary human passion, has perhaps caused it to escape attention.[27]

Reading the Mahāyāna sutras, he was 'transported to another world', perhaps 'an archetypal world inhabited by innumerable Buddhas and bodhisattvas and resounding with the sublime tones of the Dharma'.[28] In this realm, he wrote elsewhere, 'Deep seems to be answering deep from abysses of realization unfathomable by thought.'[29] Unsurprisingly, he sometimes found it hard to return to 'a world in which one had to keep accounts and pay bills'.[30]

For several months, aged eighty-nine, he and his companion Paramartha spent their evenings reading and reflecting on the *Śūraṅgamasamādhi Sūtra*:

> [I]t was only after we had spent two or three evenings on it that I began to feel at all at home in its radiant world. It was a world inhabited by Buddhas and bodhisattvas, by gods and goddesses of various kinds, and towards the end of the *sutra* there appears the cunning and malignant figure of Māra, the Evil One. As the weeks and months of study and discussion went by I felt that I was not merely a spectator of this world but living in it and breathing its unique atmosphere.[31]

At the sutra's centre is the bodhisattva Mañjuśrī, and though Sangharakshita had practised the *sādhana* on the figure he had received from Jamyang Khyentse Rimpoche, these evenings of study brought 'a much more vivid awareness of his presence and of his true nature', and Sangharakshita reported that he felt a consciousness behind it'.[32] 'The world of the *sutra*', he says, 'is as much beyond time as it is beyond space, and while I was in it I too was beyond time.'[33]

In a series of lectures on the Mahāyāna text known as the *Vimalakīrti Nirdeśa*, later published as *The Inconceivable Emancipation*, Sangharakshita reflected on what it meant to engage in this realm. Mahāyāna sutras, he explains, are concerned with 'the Dharma as a living spiritual reality' and, while the Discourses portray the Buddha in a recognizably historical setting, they universalize the Dharma by setting it in

> an ideal, archetypal realm, flashing with light and glowing with all the colours of the rainbow, a realm where everything was made of jewels, and the air was filled with music and perfume.[34]

Often in his lectures, and even more in his poems, Sangharakshita expresses a yearning to dwell in such an elevated, mythic realm. The *Vimalakīrti Nirdeśa* lectures reflect on its meaning:

> Reading the Mahāyāna scriptures, we are emancipated from the contingent and the determinate, from time, space, and causality, from historical reality. We experience archetypal reality, myth, the realm of undefined meanings. In technical terms, we encounter the *sambhogakāya*. That is, we encounter the Buddhas and bodhisattvas of the Mahāyāna in their archetypal forms. Through this experience we contact something within us of which we were not previously aware. Something is sparked off that even the Pāli scriptures were unable to spark off. And this happens because the realm of archetypal reality, of myth, of undefined meanings, corresponds to something within us.[35]

Notwithstanding Sangharakshita's confidence, many readers are likely to be baffled by the sutras' paradoxes and 'phantasmagoria'. Sangharakshita's meaning becomes more apparent if we recognize that he is speaking from his own experience and encouraging others to participate in it.

At the same time, Sangharakshita recognized the difference between his situation and that of his audience. The lectures came at the end of the long London Buddhist Centre building project, and his listeners had been working hard to finish the building and set up new businesses. His role was to remind them of the inspiration that made it all meaningful:

> The movement in London [...] needed, I felt, to be lifted, at least for a few hours, to a totally different plane, a plane on which transcendental truth was conveyed by means of marvellous phantasmagoria.[36]

That required him to remain on this level for the full two months in which he was working on the lectures and delivering them, and make it available to his listeners. He connected the sutra with the urgent and personal desire 'to contact the realm of the archetypal':

> Meaning must be meaning *for you*, something that you personally experience. Our quest for meaning is therefore our quest for ourselves, our quest for the totality, the wholeness, of our own being. On one level we belong to the realm of historical reality; but on another, we belong to the realm of spiritual reality. The Mahāyāna scriptures reveal this world to us. So does myth; so does poetry. And they reveal it to us not as something external to ourselves, but as our own world, as a world in which we ourselves actually live, usually without knowing it.[37]

Sangharakshita's message was that, with a receptive mind and a little effort, through reading the sutras his listeners could enter this archetypal world. Doing so, they would find themselves, in their wholeness and totality, as participants in the realm of spiritual reality.

Il Convento revisited

At the end of *The Journey to Il Convento* Sangharakshita observes that he could engage with images because he possessed 'at least the rudiments of what has been termed the imaginal faculty'.[38] He took the term 'imaginal' from Henry Corbin, the writer on Islamic mysticism who used it to describe the supra-sensory realm evoked in medieval Iranian Sufism that comprised 'an intermediate world' between the world we perceive through the senses and the ultimate, imageless truth. This is 'the world of Idea-Images, of archetypal figures, of subtile substances, of immaterial matter' in which, as Ibn Arabi says, 'the spiritual takes body and the body becomes spiritual.'[39] Sangharakshita echoes Corbin when he speaks of St Jerome as 'an image that had its existence in a world of images or in an imaginal world – a world to which one has access by virtue of the imaginal faculty'.[40]

With this reflection Sangharakshita arrives at a central expression of his understanding of spiritual life:

> The imaginal faculty is, in reality, the man himself, because when one truly perceives an image one perceives it with the whole of oneself, or with one's whole being. When one truly perceives an image, therefore, one is transported to the world to which that image belongs and becomes, if only for the time being, an inhabitant of that world. In other words, truly to perceive an image means to become an image, so that when one speaks of the imagination, or the imaginal faculty, what one is really speaking of is *image perceiving image*. That is to say, in perceiving an image what one really perceives is, in a sense, oneself.[41]

This account of imaginal experience, burnished here into a luminous quintessence, takes us to the core of Sangharakshita's spiritual understanding: his desire to abandon the bounds of selfhood and be reborn as an image in an archetypal or imaginal world. This is the true significance of Sangharakshita's experiences of dwelling in the world of a Mahāyāna sutra, joining with a buddha figure in meditation or recognizing himself and the unspoken depths of his life in the figures of St Jerome and angelic messengers. In tracing that experience, we are also tracing Sangharakshita's 'secret biography'. The world of image is also 'the world of dreams, recollections of which sometimes mingle with the stream of waking consciousness only, more often than not, to be quickly forgotten'.[42]

The imagination was also central to Sangharakshita's presentation of the Dharma. It was central to the writings and teachings through which, over seven decades, he offered a distinctive account of Buddhism. We must turn, therefore, to those teachings, approaching Sangharakshita's work as a thorough presentation of the path to buddhahood, its nature, and what it means to practise it.

Part Three
Tracing the Path

To create a little flower is the labour of ages.

William Blake, *The Marriage of Heaven and Hell*,
'Proverbs of Hell'

Chapter Nine

The Unity of Buddhism

Simply a Buddhist

Sangharakshita comments in *Facing Mount Kanchenjunga* that, from the outset of his Buddhist life, 'I had always regarded myself not as a follower of this or that school of Buddhism but simply as a Buddhist.'[1] Like other westerners drawn to Buddhism, he mainly encountered it through English-language translations of Mahāyāna sutras and Pāli suttas, which he read with avid interest, finding an essential unity beneath the outward differences:

> [T]he scenes depicted by the *Larger* and *Smaller Sukhāvatī-vyūha Sūtras*, with their rivers fifty miles wide and twelve miles deep, their jewel lotuses ten miles in circumference, and their myriads of golden-bodied Buddhas and bodhisattvas, are very different from the sober pictures drawn by the Pāli texts; but the waves of the great rivers murmur, and the birds in the jewel trees sing, the same refrain as the Hīnayāna scriptures: *dukkha, anicca, anatta*.[2]

As well as reading Buddhist scriptures with an attitude of faith, Sangharakshita also read the modern scholarship that fundamentally challenged traditional understandings of them. Theravādins held that everything ascribed to the Buddha in the Pāli literature was literally spoken by him, but scholars had long concluded that the Discourses had changed in the centuries before they were committed to writing. They thought the Vinaya, or 'monastic code', had developed over many centuries, and they relegated analytical Abhidhamma texts and Pāli commentaries to later periods entirely. This meant the Buddha's original teaching had to be reconstructed, but there was no agreement about what it had contained.

Similarly, Mahāyāna Buddhists held that the sutras they followed literally contained teachings of the historical Buddha that he had reserved for more advanced students. Scholars, however, believed the Mahāyāna movement and its texts had emerged some centuries after the Buddha – in many cases, all that can be said is that their origins are mysterious and unknowable. Sangharakshita thought it was possible that a germ of the sutras might date back to the Buddha, but he broadly accepted the scholarly interpretation, even though it meant rejecting the Mahāyāna account of the sutras' origins. At the same time, he never doubted their spiritual value and continued to ask why the Mahāyāna had developed, how its account of the Buddhist path related to that of the Discourses, and how the Mahāyāna schools related to one another. In time, he applied the same critical perspective to the Vajrayāna, the third tradition, which claimed its own esoteric texts and practices represented higher teachings still.

These were grounds for doubting the claims of the various schools to present the exclusive or highest version of Buddhism, and setting these claims aside made it plausible to regard Buddhism as a unity. But no amount of scholarship could define Buddhism's true meaning. As Sangharakshita asserts in *A Survey of Buddhism*:

> The scientific study of Buddhism will, therefore, be *a priori* limited to those aspects of the Dharma which are susceptible of an intellectual understanding, while the Dharma as a whole, being concerned exclusively with the Path of Emancipation, and more particularly with those actualities which, we are expressly told, exist 'beyond the reach of reasoning' [...] will transcend the sphere of its investigations.[3]

The *Diamond Sutra* experience gave Sangharakshita a perspective from which he could investigate Buddhism, and he quickly developed a view of the tradition that accorded with his initial insight. His very first published article, entitled 'The Unity of

Buddhism', appeared in *The Middle Way* (the Buddhist Society magazine) in 1944, when he was just eighteen. It argued that Buddhist ethics couldn't be separated from Buddhist 'metaphysics', as some of its critics wanted, and Buddhism needed to be taken as a whole:

> Buddhism is not only (I will not say 'merely') a system of ethics, it is also a philosophy, a religion, a science, and much more besides. It is not one road to Enlightenment, but many – although in a deeper and more hidden sense all ways (*dharmas*) are one.

This hidden sense in which all *dharmas* are one was the theme of Sangharakshita's doctrinal writing in the following years, but 'The Unity of Buddhism' expressed the principle that guided him:

> Buddhism is not sectarian, since it recognizes that the whole of its own teaching, like that of all other religions, is only a finger pointing to the moon – a means, not the end.

Sectarianism was, in fact, an expression of the very craving Buddhism sought to overcome in endeavouring to 'release men from bigoted belief in *any* of its many insidious forms by pointing out the opposite of everything to which they cling'.[4] By 1945 Sangharakshita was already describing Buddhism in terms that would become central to his later thought:

> To take refuge in the Buddha, the Dharma, and the Sangha means that we become first of all convinced of the supersensuous existence of an eternal spiritual reality – either by association with some living holy person, or by reading of such a life in some book or scripture; that we endeavour to realize that reality which he has realized before us by practising certain of the disciplines which he suggests to us, and that we finally, by means of such continued practice, become firmly established if not in that transcendental state, at least in the road which ultimately leads to it.[5]

Sangharakshita maintained this outlook when the British Army dispatched the eighteen-year-old Private Lingwood to Ceylon, and he encountered the reality of a Buddhist country that failed to live up to the ideal. He thought Buddhism in the country was 'dead or at least asleep',[6] and wrote privately: 'If Ceylon is Buddhist, cannibals are Christian.'[7] His faith was equally unswayed by his admiration for some of the Hindu monks and teachers he encountered in his wandering period. Monastic ordination was a way to affirm this commitment to Buddhism *per se*, not to join the Theravāda school, and once he was established in Kalimpong – as a bhikkhu but without a monastic community around him – he practised in his own way, inhabiting the space *between* traditions. He quickly established the magazine *Stepping Stones* to share his own writing and present Buddhism as a united tradition, drawing inspiration from many sources.

Sangharakshita had to maintain his stance in the face of the alternatives. To the Tibetans in Kalimpong, he was a double oddity: an *inji gelong* ('English monk') with both white skin and yellow (rather than red) monastic robes, who begged for alms food in the Kalimpong bazaar like the bhikkhus of old:

> I was in their eyes an antiquated figure out of the remote, legendary Indian past of Buddhism – a figure such as they had seen, if at all, only in paintings of episodes from the life of the Buddha.[8]

They were relieved to learn he wasn't a Hīnayānist, pursuing merely personal salvation, and that, like them, he followed the compassionate bodhisattva path. But, if that made Sangharakshita acceptable to Tibetans, it didn't make him an exclusive follower of their traditions.

Sangharakshita was keenly aware that, arguably for the first time in Buddhist history, the different strands of Buddhism had been thrown together and their scriptures were available to any interested reader. His response was to ask what united the traditions; others responded by asserting the primacy of their own. The fortnightly Ceylonese newspaper *Buddhist World* declared the Theravāda represented 'the pure Dhamma' while other traditions were 'so many corruptions and degenerations of the one pure faith'.⁹ Sangharakshita's editorial in the July 1951 issue of *Stepping Stones* was a tirade against the *Buddhist World*'s attitude. The sole purpose of Buddhist teachings, he declared, was helping people cross the ocean of *saṃsāra*, like the raft in the Buddha's well-known analogy, whose function is taking travellers across a stream. Praising the Theravāda on the grounds of its antiquity was like clinging to the raft and thereby betraying the Buddhist teachings. Worse still, he added, the 'shrunken and aberrant form of Buddhism' to which these writers adhered 'had been for centuries unable to produce even a single *arahant*'.¹⁰

But knowing he opposed Theravādin sectarianism didn't mean Sangharakshita had resolved his own position. He wanted to translate his intuitive sense of Buddhism's unity into a coherent understanding. He took seriously the goal presented in the Discourses of becoming a stream entrant and then an awakened *arahant*, but also responded to the Mahāyāna ideal of the bodhisattva who defers their own Enlightenment to help other beings attain it for themselves. He said some years later:

> We may not be able to correlate the teachings of Stream Entry and the arising of the *bodhicitta* point by point, but we need to be able to correlate them to some extent in the interests of our own spiritual life and development. Otherwise we find ourselves in the impossible situation of having to choose between the 'Mahāyāna' and the 'Hīnayāna', the bodhisattva ideal and the *arhant* ideal, as though they represented distinct paths.¹¹

In his developed understanding, the tension between the two is unnecessary. He said in 1981:

> You cannot really gain Enlightenment for the benefit of others unless you are a person of considerable spiritual development yourself, and you cannot develop spiritually yourself unless you are at the same time mindful of the needs of other people. In the long run spiritual individualism and spiritual altruism coincide.¹²

The same understanding appears in his early work, at least as an intuition. Seeing what this meant as an understanding of the Buddhist tradition was much harder, but it was important to Sangharakshita. He wanted to marry a sense of Buddhism's indefinable essence with a clear understanding of its many teachings, and to practise accordingly. Once again, Lama Govinda was able to help.

'Buddhism as Living Experience'
Along with Sangharakshita's editorial, the July 1951 issue of *Stepping Stones* included an article by Govinda entitled 'Buddhism as Living Experience', which expressed his own response to Theravādin sectarianism. 'Spiritual things can be "fixed" as little as living things', he wrote. 'Where growth ceases, there nothing but the dead form remains.'[13] In his view, Buddhism depended on this aliveness, not the antiquity of its traditions or the proximity of its scriptures to the Buddha's words, and it came alive when it was practised: 'Truths have to be continually rediscovered, they have ever to be re-formed and transformed, if they are to preserve their meaning, their living value or their spiritual nutritiousness.' The individual who practised Buddhism in this way was therefore 'the link between the past and the present', and, through them,

> history is again reshaped into present life, becomes part of our own being and not merely an object of learning or veneration which, separated from its origins, and the organic conditions of its growth, would lose its essential value.

Buddhism is, in fact, akin to a living organism, and the different phases of Buddhist history represent aspects of its growth:

> The essential nature of the tree, however, is neither confined to its roots, nor to its trunk, its branches, twigs or leaves, nor to its blossoms or its fruits. The real nature of the tree lies in the organic development of all these parts, i.e., in the totality of its spatial and temporal unfoldment.[14]

Govinda's radical redefinition of 'tradition' expressed something Sangharakshita intuited but had not fully articulated. He writes in his memoirs that the German's words

> sounded, as though on some mighty organ, notes that struck a responsive chord in my own heart and set up there reverberations that were to grow rather than diminish in volume as the years went by.[15]

A book with a mission

Sangharakshita's twenties, when he was a wanderer and then a newly ordained bhikkhu, were a time of 'strenuous study and prolonged and intense contemplation'.[16] He reflected on conditionality, the four noble truths, and the three characteristics of conditioned existence, reporting that, 'as I meditated, flashes of insight into the transcendental truths of which [the Buddha's teachings] were the expression in conceptual terms would sometimes spontaneously arise.'[17] He wanted both a direct apprehension of the truth towards which the teachings pointed and a theoretical understanding of the path and its relation to nirvāṇa. He sought the unity beneath the outward divisions of the traditions that inspired him. As he wrote in 1956: 'Only a united Buddhism will be able to contribute to the building of a united world.'[18]

Sangharakshita completed the process, at least for the time being and to his own satisfaction, in *A Survey of Buddhism*. In 1954, when he was twenty-nine, the theosophically based Indian Institute of Culture in Bangalore invited him to give an overview of Buddhism in a series of lectures. Preparing the lectures, he recalled, demanded a 'tremendous intellectual and spiritual effort', and so powerful was his engagement when he came to deliver them that it seemed 'time almost stood still.'[19] Turning the lectures into a book required three further years of painstaking effort, but the finished work, published in 1957 when Sangharakshita was thirty-one or thirty-two, retains the intensity of the lectures. Over 500 pages in length, the *Survey* approaches the Buddhist tradition as a living entity whose purpose is offering a path to nirvāṇa. It is a wide-ranging and closely argued profession of his faith. 'Everywhere', Lama Govinda wrote to him on reading it, 'one feels a profound conviction stands behind your words.'[20]

The *Survey* is the centre of Sangharakshita's thought about Buddhist teachings and expresses the core of his understanding of Buddhism. In subsequent years he worked out the implications of the *Survey*'s approach, and this sometimes led to fresh conclusions, but, looking back in 1980, he wrote: 'I find no reason to change my approach to Buddhism or my method of treatment, even in matters of detail.'[21] His later teachings, he says, 'were not only based on, or grew naturally out of, the fundamental principles adumbrated in the *Survey*, but also served to confirm the validity of the approach to Buddhism' it contained.[22] The late papers outlining his developed doctrinal position, composed in collaboration with Subhuti, were recognizably an extension of the ideas Sangharakshita had outlined six decades earlier.

Perceiving Buddhism's unity

A Survey of Buddhism is a book with a mission. Expressed abstractly, the mission is to present Buddhism as a unity by identifying the core that organizes its various expressions. As Sangharakshita says in the 1980 preface:

> I was concerned to see Buddhism in its full *breadth* and in its ultimate *depth*, that is to say, I was concerned (1) to see Buddhism as a whole and (2) to see it in its deeper interconnections both within itself and in relation to the spiritual life of the individual Buddhist.[23]

He calls this core 'basic Buddhism', or, in its more developed form, 'Integral Buddhism'.[24] It also marks an important stage in the process Sangharakshita describes in *The History of My Going for Refuge* of distinguishing the spirit of Buddhism from the elements of the Buddhist tradition that complicated or obscured it. As Stephen Batchelor comments, the *Survey* testifies to Sangharakshita's 'capacity for synthesis and his innate grasp of essentials',[25] but it wasn't simply an intellectual exercise. Even when Sangharakshita addresses matters requiring complex philosophical thought, he continually reverts to his conviction that Buddhism's essence cannot be captured in words or concepts, and suggests we come closest to seeing its character and purpose when we recognize its living spirit. It is written for those who 'wish to transcend the intellectual barriers which seemingly separate school from school and *yāna* from *yāna* and know the heart, the essence, of Buddhism as an integrated whole'.[26]

Sangharakshita knew this wasn't the only way to understand Buddhism, and the *Survey* names the basic difficulty:

> Divergences in both institutional religion and personal religion being so numerous, and in many cases so radical, are we justified in speaking of Buddhism at all? Or are we not rather concerned with a number of practically independent religious movements, all more or less nominally Buddhist? Is Buddhism one or many? Obviously, there is no external uniformity. There is not always even unity of doctrine. What, then, constitutes the fundamental ground of unity in Buddhism?[27]

In the next generation, the English academic Paul Williams, recognizing the questions Sangharakshita poses but approaching them with scholarly disinterestedness, warns in his book *Mahāyāna Buddhism* against 'the essentialist fallacy' that, he believes, 'occurs when we take a single name or naming expression and assume that it must refer to one unified phenomenon'.[28] For Williams, there is no such thing as 'Mahāyāna Buddhism', and we could extend the same principle to 'Buddhism' as a whole. Sangharakshita recognized the logic behind Williams's position, and the *Survey* itself asks if 'Mahāyāna' is 'just a convenient collective designation for a jumble of contradictory teachings having no clearly defined relations with one another'.[29] It even outlines the Buddhist critique of essentialism, which regards each seemingly solid 'thing' as merely 'a transitory assemblage of evanescent parts'.[30] Sangharakshita didn't apply this critique to Buddhism, but didn't explain why. His starting point, it seems, was an intuitive sense of something behind Buddhism's outward diversity.

Buddhism as an organic whole

In the preface to the 1980 edition of the *Survey* Sangharakshita comments that he hadn't wanted to offer a superficial overview that simply described Buddhism's major historical forms one by one:

> If I wanted really to do justice to them I had to show that they were all interconnected, which meant exploring their common basic principles, and show what bearing they had on the spiritual life of the individual, for the sake of which, after all, Buddhism had originally been promulgated. I was therefore concerned to see Buddhism not only in its full breadth but also in its depth. Indeed, I discovered that I could not see it in its breadth without seeing it in its depth.[31]

He adds in *The History of My Going for Refuge* that this meant seeing Buddhism 'not as a collection of miscellaneous parts but as an organic whole'.[32] As the discussion of organic thinking in Chapter Five suggests, this was a congenial mode of understanding for Sangharakshita, and in the *Survey* it enabled him to grasp a meaning behind Buddhism's outward forms. In general terms, organic thinking means perceiving phenomena as wholes and as processes, and organic analogies represent this in images. Sangharakshita understands that Buddhism is neither a plant nor a person, but describing it in these terms, as the *Survey* frequently does, makes its character concrete. As a plant is more than an assemblage of roots, branches, and leaves, it suggests, Buddhism is more than its individual schools, doctrines, and methods. They are parts of a larger organic form, like the branches of a tree, all growing from the same trunk. Describing the various early Buddhist meditation practices, Sangharakshita outlines a method for understanding their connections that he used in the book as a whole:

> [T]he bare branches of the tree of Buddhist meditation enable us to see the structure, to grasp the underlying principle, of the whole system of practice, all the more clearly for

their being naked of that luxuriant crop of special methods
and elaborate techniques which later on sprang up, like
an exuberant growth of leaves, on the basis of the broad
principles indicated by the prescriptions of the Original
Teaching.[33]

The trunk, we may say, unifies the tree. Similarly, the phases of Buddhist history are stages in the growth, decay, and fresh growth of a living organism. That whole is dynamic and alive, and its aliveness derives from the common purpose towards which all authentic expressions of Buddhism are directed:

The unity of Buddhism consists in the fact that, through
differences and divergences of doctrine innumerable, all
schools of Buddhism aim at Enlightenment, at reproducing the
spiritual experience of the Buddha. The Dharma is therefore
to be defined, not so much in terms of this or that particular
teaching, but rather as the sum total of the means whereby
that experience may be attained.[34]

The *Survey* systematically describes Buddhism according to this principle. The first chapter mainly examines the teachings of the Buddha himself, as we encounter them in the Discourses. It emphasizes that the Buddha regarded those teachings as 'symbolical merely, reflecting, as though through darkness well-nigh impenetrable, only a faint glimmer of the infinite light of his realization'.[35] The teachings point us towards Buddhism's transcendental core, approaching which, Sangharakshita writes, 'We have begun to hear, as though from a great distance, the muffled heartbeat of Buddhism.'[36]

The Discourses sometimes evoke this core, and the figure of the Buddha embodies it. They also render it in concepts, but these are aids to following the path: 'relative truth' but not 'absolute truth'; 'method' rather than 'doctrine'; and a raft, not a destination. Sangharakshita later said the Buddha simply pointed in the direction of nirvāṇa, saying, 'If you go in that direction you will see what I saw.'[37] But if conceptual expressions of Buddhism are secondary, that doesn't make them unimportant:

The answer to the question 'What is the use of retaining doctrines such as conditioned co-production and the four truths if they are only relatively true?' is therefore the same as the answer to 'What is the use of a raft if we cannot take it with us after reaching the further shore?'[38]

As we shall see in the next chapter, the *Survey* presents the teachings as essential, provided they are understood to be provisional and metaphorical.

Hīnayāna and Mahāyāna

'Hīnayāna' means 'Lesser Vehicle' while Mahāyāna means 'Great Vehicle', and Mahāyāna sources use the terms to contrast a lesser understanding of the Buddhist path that leads to becoming an *arahant* (one said to seek Enlightenment for their own sake) with the greater path of the bodhisattva, who seeks the Enlightenment of all sentient beings.[39] More broadly, the Mahāyāna argument, which Sangharakshita largely accepts, is that 'Hīnayāna' followers had forgotten the true meaning of the Buddha's teaching. He identifies five characteristics that distinguish the two *yāna*s. The Mahāyāna, he says, is '[p]rogressive and liberal-minded, caring more for the spirit than for the letter of the scriptures'; it is '[m]ore highly emotional and devotional in attitude'; '[m]ore positive in its conception of Nirvāṇa and the Way'; it gives 'increased importance to a dedicated household life'; and it 'developed the altruistic aspect of Buddhism and preached the bodhisattva ideal'.[40]

Although Sangharakshita never thought of himself as a follower of the Mahāyāna alone, these characteristics express some of the central themes of his approach to Buddhism. We will consider each in the following chapters, but the first – valuing the spirit of the teachings rather than the letter – is fundamental, especially in the context of Buddhist unity.

In Sangharakshita's account, the Mahāyāna concern for 'the spirit [rather] than for the letter of the scriptures'[41] explains the outward differences between Mahāyāna teaching and that of the Discourses. 'Spirit' here means everything that is involved in reproducing the Buddha's experience, and, in principle, this characterization isn't contentious:

> All Buddhist schools, whether of the Mahāyāna or of the Hīnayāna, were concerned not with the theoretical determination of truth as an end in itself, but with its practical realization in life. What divided them, therefore, was not differences of opinion over what was true and what untrue in the scientific, descriptive sense of that term – for all agreed that truth, being indescribable, was a matter for personal experience – but differences regarding which doctrines, as well as which ethical observances and which meditational techniques, could in practice function as the means for the attainment of Enlightenment.[42]

This may sound like an ecumenical position that uncritically accepts all Buddhist schools on their own terms, but it implies a distinction between an authentic Buddhism, which understands that its teachings are rafts, and an inauthentic Buddhism that literalizes those teachings and makes them ends in themselves.[43] Sangharakshita thought the 'Hīnayāna' followers' preoccupation with analysis meant they 'started treating intellectual formulations of the Doctrine as possessing ultimate validity',[44] leading to 'spiritual individualism' and all the other faults to which the Mahāyāna responded. The Mahāyāna was 'an attempt to recapture the spirit of the Original Teaching',[45] and Sangharakshita largely endorses its criticisms of the 'Hīnayāna'. In fact, he thought it was possible to go further than the Mahāyāna with the help of a modern historical perspective that revealed elements in the Discourses that expressed a Mahāyāna-style outlook. The thrust of his closely argued analysis in the first chapter is that teachings originally intended as aids to practice have been turned into points of intellectual analysis, but their meaning can be reclaimed if we recognize their purpose.

Three of the *Survey*'s four chapters concern the Mahāyāna, but Sangharakshita's central point is that it inherited the Buddha's founding inspiration:

> The least that can be said for the Mahāyānists is that they are undoubtedly right in claiming to be in the direct line of spiritual descent from the Buddha, though they must be understood as having transmitted, not this or that doctrine, in the sense of a more or less elaborate conceptual formulation of transcendental verities, but rather that to which all such formulations pertain and point, namely, the Buddha's own experience of Enlightenment.[46]

Sangharakshita calls the Buddha's inspiration a stream or current of energy (the same image we have seen at work in his own life), making the Mahāyāna 'the main channel for the transmission of [the] mighty waters' that flowed from the Buddha, while the Theravāda 'may be regarded as a quiet but stagnant backwater'.[47]

Organic unity
To speak of the 'broad principles' connecting the meditation practices is to speak in abstract terms; to say that they are connected as the trunk and branches of a tree connect the leaves is to make the same point through a concrete image. To perceive Buddhism in terms of this metaphor is to imagine it, and throughout the *Survey* Sangharakshita imagines Buddhism's meaning by envisaging it as a living organism that develops like a tree growing from a seed into a mature adult. Its guiding principle is the distinction between what is essential to the Buddhist tradition as a living, changing spiritual force and the deadening elements that too often surround it.

A starting point is Buddhism's relation to the conditions from which it emerged:

> The relation between Buddhism, on the one hand, and the various philosophical speculations and religious practices flourishing in north-eastern India in the sixth century BCE, on the other, may be compared to that existing between a seed and the soil of the pot in which it is planted. The seed is not *produced* by the soil, but it could not germinate, or put forth roots and shoots, or go through all the remaining stages of a

plant's unfoldment, unless the soil was there to supply it with nutriment.⁴⁸

Moving on in Buddhist history, Sangharakshita describes the relation of the different Buddhist schools to the Buddha's teachings through the metaphor of organic growth:

> Even after their emergence as separate branches, all the various schools continued to preserve, not merely their own distinctive teachings, but also their own versions of the common stock of primitive traditions; each, while putting forth its own leaves and flowers, continued to clasp firmly the parent trunk.⁴⁹

Later in the book Sangharakshita refines the analogy:

> The Buddha's transcendental realization is the root, his Original Doctrine – the 'Basic Buddhism' of Chapter 2 – the trunk, the distinctive Mahāyāna doctrines the branches, and the schools and sub-schools of the Mahāyāna the flowers.⁵⁰

When Sangharakshita considers the teachings in more detail, he continues to look for signs of spiritual aliveness. He sees the Mahāyāna's disorganized variety as a sign of its authenticity, while the Theravāda, which had always resisted change, is 'a cosmos frozen by the magic wand of scholasticism practically into immobility'.⁵¹ In organic terms:

> [T]he spiritual individualism of the Hīnayāna, having become complete, powerfully reinforced that individualism and, like a rotten fruit that, falling from the bough, nourishes with its decay the tree that bore it, contributed to the further development of that one-sided conception of the *arhant*.⁵²

These images culminate in a passage that presents the Mahāyāna as the living re-expression of the original teaching:

> The Mahāyāna is related to the Original Teaching as a flower
> to its parent germ. And as the flower produces fresh seed
> so does the Mahāyāna contain within itself the possibility of
> perpetually renascent spiritual life. The Hīnayāna literalism
> against which the Mahāyānists inveighed may be compared to
> the husk which, while it protects the seed in the early stages
> of its growth, must be burst asunder and cast aside if the
> germinating life within is to find room for development.[53]

This account of the Mahāyāna is also a manifesto for the work Sangharakshita saw himself doing as a writer and teacher during his time in India as he laboured to revive Buddhism as a living force. When he returned to West, he often used the language of nurturing the living plant of Buddhist life – discarding the lifeless husk of unhelpful teachings, setting forth fresh seeds, and helping them grow – and described the FWBO as a plant growing from the seeds.

The growth of a plant suggests it is a unity in the sense of a single, developing phenomenon; its symmetry presents that unity as a harmonious form. When Sangharakshita comes, in the third chapter, to the Mahāyāna schools' relation to one another, he understands their interconnections as 'the mutually divergent manifestations of a single principle, of one supreme law, which despite or even because of their differences binds them together into unity'.[54] He links the schools by connecting them with the pattern of Buddhism's five spiritual faculties, which relate to one another like the petals of a flower:

> The Madhyamaka, the Yogācāra, Devotional Buddhism, and
> the Tantra, are the fully unfolded and perfectly developed
> forms of germinal elements contained in the Original
> Teaching. If the Mahāyāna is the fully-open flower of
> Buddhism its four main schools represent the four petals of
> the flower and the faculty of mindfulness its calyx. Just as one
> who gazes at a single petal will never be able to appreciate the
> beauty of the rose, so he who studies the doctrines and follows
> the practices of one school only, ignoring the rest, will be
> unable to understand the Mahāyāna.[55]

The image of a person who appreciates the whole rose evokes Sangharakshita himself as he surveys Buddhism with the faith that things of value coexist as elements of an interconnected whole. His capacity to appreciate the Mahāyāna in this way derives from his sense of the coherence of his spiritual life, as Buddhist practice has shaped it. 'Madhyamaka and the Buddhism of Faith and Devotion, the Yogācāra and the Tantra, are historically interdependent', he says, 'because the corresponding spiritual faculties are psychologically interdependent.'[56] These aren't historical arguments of the sort that would satisfy a scholar like Paul Williams, and, in later years, Sangharakshita recommended Williams's book in preference to the third and fourth chapters of the *Survey* as a source of information about the Mahāyāna, if not its interpretation. Instead, these arguments are a sincere attempt to connect the various elements of the Mahāyāna tradition from the perspective of a practitioner who wishes to learn from them all.

* * *

Others have created maps of the Buddhist tradition that note the shared foundations of the different schools,[57] but Sangharakshita did something distinctive in approaching it through the prism of spiritual practice. In his foreword to the *Complete Works* edition, Subhuti comments that *A Survey of Buddhism*

> locates Buddhist practitioners today in their true context, enabling them to see their relationship to the whole tradition, going back to the Buddha himself, rather than merely in relation to one modern version of any particular school.[58]

At the time of the *Survey*, Sangharakshita's approach had more in common with the Mahāyāna than any other tradition, and he argues that the 'Hīnayāna' and the modern Theravāda, which displayed the same tendencies, misrepresented Buddhism. For him, the Mahāyāna showed the Theravāda what it ought to be and could still become: 'Just as the development of the flower cannot be understood without reference to the seed, so the significance of the seed cannot be understood apart from the flower.'[59] His editorials in the *Maha Bodhi* journal sometimes call for a reformed Theravāda, but the *Survey* suggests that such a revival would first require a radical reappraisal:

> Only an influx of Mahāyāna Buddhism as a living spiritual force will save the Theravādin countries from the stereotyped scholasticism that now passes for doctrine and the rigid formalism that has taken the place of method, and enable them fully to appreciate the real significance and true value even of their own tradition.[60]

In the years after the book's publication, Sangharakshita developed a more critical approach to the Mahāyāna, but he never changed his view that the Mahāyāna had continued Buddhism's living spirit or that any authentic re-expression of that spirit would descend from or recapitulate the Mahāyāna spirit in a fresh historical situation. He envisaged the FWBO/Triratna as

> a branch of the mighty tree of Buddhism which, for more than 2,500 years, has sheltered a considerable portion of humanity [...] the same vital juice that circulates in the older, bigger branches of that tree circulates in our younger, smaller branch too, even if it circulates in it a little more vigorously than it does in some of them.[61]

The authority to judge

Sangharakshita's work as a whole and the *Survey* in particular raise a fundamental question: on what basis does he make his judgements about Buddhism, particularly such indeterminable questions as Buddhism's essence? How can we know which Buddhist teachings, in the whole, vast tradition, are spiritually alive and therefore capable of leading people to Enlightenment? One answer is to refer to the Buddhist scriptures, as Sangharakshita evidently did, but we must still decide which scriptures to emphasize and how to interpret them. We may also look to tradition, especially as it is articulated by a realized teacher, but, again, we face the challenge of knowing which traditions truly express the Dharma and which teachers are realized.

For Sangharakshita, the Buddha was the ultimate arbiter of 'right view', meaning that we should sift the scriptures to discover what was most likely to reflect his teaching. At the same time, he says, '[t]he criterion of what is or what is not Buddhism is ultimately pragmatic',[62] and scripture must be tested in the light of 'the spiritual life of the individual'.[63] What he calls 'the fundamental ground of unity in Buddhism' is therefore recognized 'not by an appeal to logic but by an appeal to spiritual life'.[64]

At least in the first instance, the individual in question can only be Sangharakshita himself, and in practice his approach involves alternating between textual authority and personal experience, and then aligning them with the help of the faculty the *Survey* calls 'intuition awakened by spiritual practice'.[65] This suggests something less than fully enlightened wisdom but greater than 'mere subjective feeling'. It can also be tested against the realization of the great teachers:

> Personal experience, or the realization of the individual Buddhist, will, if genuine, be in line with tradition, not, indeed, with – or not necessarily with – tradition in the merely bookish sense of the term, the authority of which the Buddha in fact repudiated, but rather with tradition in the sense of that unbroken succession of Enlightened beings upon whose existence the very life of the Dharma depends, and who, like torches that are lit from torches in a midnight marathon, alone illumine the darkness of the ages.[66]

Those sympathetic to Sangharakshita will regard this as a realistic, incremental approach. They will also note that he didn't claim an authority based on blinding revelation, merely that he was able to discern what the tradition was saying when it was true to its own principles. This is the approach of any reformer who is inspired by a tradition's founding values but thinks its present expressions fail to live up to those values or that it must adapt to changed circumstances.

The sociologist Philip Mellor expressed a more critical perspective when he argued that Sangharakshita followed a 'Protestant' model, according to which authority resides in the individual rather than time-honoured institutional forms, and that his innovations depended on his personal 'charismatic' authority.[67] Sangharakshita's book-length response, *The FWBO and 'Protestant Buddhism'*, sets out how he views his own 'authority':

> First one becomes able, by virtue of study and meditation, to distinguish between what is essential Buddhism, and what is not, and then one is understood as having personal authority because, appealing to their reason and experience, one enables people to see the difference for themselves.[68]

He thought this sort of judgement was intrinsic to any effort to follow the Buddhist path that went beyond simply adhering to its customs or perpetuating one of its schools. 'All the great spiritual masters who were founders of schools', starting with the Buddha himself, had done something similar:

> There is no question of their authority having its source in ecclesiastical position or political power, or in the supernatural in the Judaeo-Christian sense. There is not even any question of its having its source in tradition, in that tradition does not exist in the abstract, as it were, but only as embodied in individuals, so that even 'traditional' authority is *spiritually* efficacious only to the extent that it is mediated by 'charismatic' individuals.[69]

He explained elsewhere that this was the authority he claimed as a Buddhist teacher:

> I have studied the Buddhist scriptures to some extent; I have tried to put their teachings into practice; I have some experience of spiritual life and some experience of dealing with people. To that extent I have some 'authority' to make judgements about right and wrong views. I can't enforce my conclusions (nor would I wish to do so), but those people who have confidence in me, especially those who say they are my disciples, will at least give careful consideration to the conclusions at which I have arrived.[70]

At the same time, Sangharakshita repeatedly asserted that Buddhism's essence wasn't accessible through reasoned judgement, helpful though that could be. It was everything that was embodied in the Three Jewels and the individual's response to them; it was the current of spiritual energy that flowed from the Buddha into the Mahāyāna. His own task was discriminating between 'what is essential and what is not essential – what is living and what is dead'[71] in the tradition he inherited.

Triyāna and going for refuge

The Triyāna view

Throughout the 1950s and early 1960s Sangharakshita maintained his position as an independent, non-sectarian Buddhist and was accepted as such by the Buddhists of many traditions with whom he mixed. His writing and teaching drew inspiration from early Buddhism, the Mahāyāna schools, Tibetan Vajrayāna, and modern figures like Anagārika Dharmapāla and Dr Ambedkar. By his own testimony, he was able to encompass these disparate influences, and, through works like the *Survey*, he clarified how they related. He was developing a new way to approach Buddhism that responded to the modern encounter of its different forms, but these were complex matters, and his understanding of Buddhist unity was still developing.

In March 1957, a few days after giving Sangharakshita the Tārā initiation, Chattrul Rimpoche appeared unexpectedly at Everton Villas, where Sangharakshita was living. Sangharakshita told the Rimpoche he wanted to establish a permanent monastic centre dedicated to 'the study, practice, and dissemination of the total Buddhist tradition',[72] and the Rimpoche declared his confidence that this would soon happen. He added that it should be called the Triyana Vardhana Vihara – 'The Vihara Where the Three Yānas Flourish (or Blossom)' – and pronounced a blessing:

> In the sky devoid of limits, the teaching of the Muni is
> The sun, spreading the thousand rays of the three śikṣās [i.e. morality, meditation, and wisdom];
> Continually shining in the radiance of the impartial disciples,
> May this Jambudvīpa region of the Triyāna be fair!

The verses suggest that the Buddha's teaching is expressed in various ways but is universal, like the sun. However, the Rimpoche may not have appreciated the difference between Sangharakshita's understanding of 'Triyāna' and that of his own Vajrayāna tradition. The Tibetan understanding of Triyāna was that the Buddha had taught all three vehicles, addressing them to disciples of differing capacities. It accepted the 'Hīnayāna' path but considered it inferior to the Mahāyāna bodhisattva path, while the Vajrayāna path encompassed and superseded both.

For a while, Sangharakshita was happy to be called a Triyāna Buddhist, but his understanding of the Buddhist tradition differed from that of the Vajrayāna. He believed the most basic Buddhist teachings, as recorded in the Discourses, expressed its essential meaning. These were the teachings of the historical Buddha, and the *Survey* calls them the 'unshakeable foundation' of the later tradition.[73] He couldn't think them inferior to anything that followed. The Mahāyāna was a return to the essential spirit of the Buddha's teaching, and the Vajrayāna had done the same in its own time. But it was clear to Sangharakshita that both Mahāyāna and Vajrayāna were later developments, and their scriptures hadn't literally been spoken by the Buddha.

It took some time for Sangharakshita to understand the difference between his view of the *yāna*s and that of Tibetan Buddhism. He read *The Jewel Ornament of Liberation*, the manual by the twelfth-century Tibetan teacher Gampopa, when it was published in English in 1959. It presents the *yāna*s as successive stages of a 'gradual path', and, seeing them laid out in this way, Sangharakshita concluded that Gampopa had misunderstood the relations between them:

> For him both the Hīnayāna and the Mahāyāna had been taught by the Buddha. He was therefore unable to see them as representing successive developments from the Buddha's original teaching, and because he was unable to see them in this way he was unable to appreciate (1) that historically speaking the Mahāyāna was to a great extent a restatement of the original teaching in terms more in accordance with the spirit, as distinct from the letter, of that teaching than

were those of the Hīnayāna, and (2) that in the Mahāyāna restatement of the original teaching the place of Going for Refuge was occupied by the arising of the *bodhicitta*.[74]

This was more than a historical observation. The Mahāyāna and Vajrayāna claims that they offered higher – and still higher – teachings suggested that the highest *yāna*s were the most important. Stacking the *yāna*s in this way complicated and divided the tradition and distracted from the most basic teachings, which contained Buddhism's essential meaning. Sangharakshita observed in 1972:

> The stack has got so high by now that it would really make sense to drop all the later developments and go back to the original teaching of the historical Buddha himself (as far as we can tell what it was) – hence my own concern to stress the importance of Going for Refuge.[75]

If the basic teachings contain the whole path, we must simply devote ourselves to realizing them in our experience more and more deeply. Doing so also makes sense of the variety of Buddhism, as the trunk of a tree makes sense of the branches. Rather than defining Buddhism through its concepts, this makes it a matter of experience and commitment.

The refuge tree
On 22 October 1962, the day following the Padmasambhava *abhiṣeka*, Sangharakshita set out from the Vihara at the western end of Kalimpong along the ridge-top road to the bazaar in the centre of the town. Following the rains, he wrote, the countryside burst into life with 'the warm golden sunlight glistening on the grass', and zinnias, marigolds, and dahlias growing wild in the hedges. 'The sky', he wrote, 'spreads like a canopy of blue silk above the earth'.[76] Brightly dressed Gurkhas, Tamangs, Lepchas, Newars, Sherpas, and Bhutanese, who had come to Kalimpong to buy or sell their produce, typically thronged the market amid stalls piled high with fruit and vegetables.

Sangharakshita ventured behind the vegetable stalls to the small Tibetan street-market where refugees sold whatever possessions they owned to fend off destitution. He saw a Tibetan monk squatting at the roadside, probably a refugee himself, selling a small bundle of xylographs – sheets printed from embossed wood blocks – and on an impulse he bought them, even though he couldn't understand the writing. Back at the Vihara, Kachu Rimpoche told him the text was the *Tharpe Delam*, or *The Smooth Road to Emancipation,* which gave detailed instructions for performing the Nyingma *mūla-yoga* practices, mostly focused on Padmasambhava.

The *mūla-yoga*s are 'root practices' performed as preliminaries to tantric initiation, and the most significant of them for Sangharakshita was the going for refuge and prostration practice. Each of the four major Tibetan Buddhist schools has its own refuge tree – an icon centring on the founder of the school. In the case of the Nyingma refuge tree, the guru is Padmasambhava who sits on a central lotus with four other lotuses arranged around it, all springing from the same stem. On each of these lotuses we see an array of figures representing the Three Jewels or Refuges as well as a lineage of human teachers through whom the school's teachings have been transmitted. The practitioner visualizes the tree and prostrates before it while reciting a refuge prayer:

> *Oṃ āḥ hūṃ,* to the best of all refuges I go. To the lama the Buddha, the lama the Dharma, the lama the Sangha; to the lama the Śrī Mahā Heruka; to the lama the All-Performing King; to the Three Jewels and the three roots in one, Guru Rimpoche, for refuge I go.

Then they stand, prostrate again and repeat the process as many times as possible.

The prostration practice expressed Sangharakshita's growing belief in the centrality of going for refuge, and he practised it daily for two years. The tree signified to him 'the whole conception of refuge, in its historical background, its universal perspective, and its immediate practical application'.[77] He said more about its universality in the 1972 talk 'The Cosmic Refuge Tree and the Archetypal Guru':

[I]t is formed by the intersection of the horizontal and vertical dimensions – or, one might say, the exoteric and esoteric dimensions, the horizontal, exoteric dimension comprising the Buddha, the Dharma, and the Sangha, while the vertical, esoteric dimension comes in the form of the gurus, the *yidams*, and the *ḍākas*, *ḍākinīs*, and guardians.[78]

The vertical dimension – here associated with esoteric meanings – includes a transcendent awareness that is both beyond and within the practitioner. In this sense, the practice is an imaginative enactment of going for refuge, using symbolic language in 'the rich and colourful mode of the Indo-Tibetan Tantric tradition'.[79]

Because the refuge tree has a range of meanings, it affects the practitioner on every level. Stretching one's body before a physical image of the Buddha and a visualized image of Padmasambhava while reciting verses, Sangharakshita notes in *The History*, engages body, speech, and mind, signifying that 'one goes for Refuge [...] with the whole of one's being'. The practice is transformative, 'even to the extent of bringing about a radical change in one's mental and spiritual outlook', because it expresses commitment to the Three Jewels completely. For that reason, 'it also represented a restoration of Going for Refuge to something like its original place in Buddhism and in the Buddhist life'.[80]

Going for refuge
All Buddhist traditions recognize going for refuge as the act that makes one a Buddhist, but most regard it as a preliminary matter. *The History of My Going for Refuge* describes Sangharakshita's first experience of taking *pañca-sīla* (the five lay precepts), his *śrāmaṇera* ordination, and his bhikkhu ordination in November 1950. In each case going for refuge was treated as a formality, and *The History* describes how Sangharakshita gradually recognized this neglected observance as the central act of the Buddhist life and 'the unifying principle, therefore, of Buddhism itself'.[81] As we have seen, Sangharakshita's exploration of the Buddhist path turns on the relationship between the individual and buddhahood, and going for refuge entails the individual's commitment to realizing it. He writes in the *Survey* that going for refuge depends on the conviction that

the Buddha has attained the Transcendental, that the Dharma is the means to the Transcendental, and that the members of the Sangha, by which is meant in this context the Āryasaṅgha, have gained the transcendental path.[82]

The History calls it 'the response of one's total being to the Truth'.[83] Above all, going for refuge is an *act*, just as the Dharma is a path we must actively follow. The prostration practice embodied that, as Sangharakshita said 1965:

> You don't just *accept* the Three Refuges; you *go* for Refuge. This action is a total, unqualified reorientation of your life, your existence, your striving, in the direction of the Three Jewels or Refuges. When you say 'I go for Refuge' you are not only acknowledging that the Three Jewels are the most supremely valuable things in existence; you are also acting upon that acknowledgement. You see that the Three Jewels provide a possibility of escape into a higher spiritual dimension, and so you *go* – you completely redirect and reorganize your life in the light of that realization.[84]

What's more, Sangharakshita repeatedly said, the act isn't performed just once: 'it's an act the significance of which continually deepens',[85] meaning that it can be undertaken at ascending levels and therefore includes the whole path. In this way, it is 'essentially a profound inner experience, a spiritual rebirth or "conversion", as a result of which one's whole life is transformed and reoriented'.[86]

Because going for refuge is common to all the Buddhist schools, it unites the tradition and does so not through elaborate doctrinal synthesis but by focusing on commitment to the path to buddhahood. And, as all members of the Buddhist community go for refuge to varying degrees, it cuts across the division between monastic and lay followers. If the various schools failed to recognize its significance, Sangharakshita thought, that was because they had overemphasized secondary matters such as the monastic lifestyle, particular meditation practices, or tantric initiation.

For Sangharakshita, going for refuge expressed the fundamental reorientation that was implicit in other formulations of the path. A

1981 talk entitled 'Going for Refuge' places it alongside the arising of the bodhicitta, the opening of the Dharma eye, stream entry, and going forth – 'five different aspects of a single basic, crucial, and unique spiritual experience'.[87] None of them fully expressed that experience, but in Sangharakshita's view going for refuge was its most basic expression. Other expressions of the path could be understood as aspects of the same process.

The altruistic dimension and the bodhisattva ideal

The bodhisattva ideal of 'dedicating oneself, for innumerable lifetimes, to the attainment of Supreme Enlightenment for the benefit of all living beings'[88] sustained Sangharakshita through the practical difficulties he faced in his early years in Kalimpong. Later, he responded to the bodhisattva spirit he saw in Dhardo Rimpoche and others, and wove the figure of the bodhisattva into all aspects of his thought. The *Survey* presents the bodhisattva ideal as the unifying factor of the whole Buddhist tradition. Sangharakshita calls it 'the perfectly ripened fruit of the whole vast tree of Buddhism'[89] because the tree's growth has culminated in it. Its significance lay, as much as anything else, in its emotive power:

> Doctrines and ideals can, of course, both function as unifying factors; but inasmuch as the heart of man is more profoundly moved and his conduct more powerfully influenced by the latter than by the former, it is the bodhisattva ideal which, for practical purposes at least, must be recognized as the unifying factor *par excellence*.[90]

At the same time, the bodhisattva ideal was ill-suited to uniting the tradition when the Mahāyāna held it up against the 'Hīnayāna' ideal of becoming an *arahant*. This was the same dichotomy that Sangharakshita confronted in the distinction between the three *yānas*, and, in valuing the bodhisattva ideal, he didn't want to become a Mahāyāna Buddhist as opposed to a follower of the historical Buddha. Recognizing the centrality of going for refuge enabled Sangharakshita to see the bodhisattva ideal as the altruistic dimension of the same basic process it expressed. This in no way diminished its significance. On one level, the bodhisattva path was a guide to daily living; on the other, the bodhicitta, as Sangharakshita later wrote, was 'something vast, cosmic, sublime, which descends into and penetrates and possesses those who are receptive to it'.[91]

This was a unified understanding but not a diminished one, and in Dhardo Rimpoche Sangharakshita had found someone who 'manifested in his life to a high degree the "perfections", [...] the practice of which for the benefit of all beings made one a bodhisattva'.[92] He felt ready to 'give formal expression to my acceptance of the bodhisattva ideal',[93] and on 12 October 1962, ten days before the Padmasambhava *abhiṣeka*, he received the bodhisattva *saṃvara*, or 'ordination', from Dhardo Rimpoche.

Going for refuge and lifestyle
Sangharakshita's growing recognition of the centrality of going for refuge affected his view of the Buddhist community. In India he was committed to being a monk, but his writing testifies to his profound disillusionment with the Theravādin monastic sangha. The *Survey* calls Theravādin monastic life 'little more than a convenient means of livelihood for idle people', and says the Vinaya (the monastic code) had been reduced to a single obligation – 'the obligation of not being found out'.[94] He added in 1980: 'I do not retract a word of what I wrote', only adding that 'the canker of formalism' was present in other forms of Buddhism as well.[95]

In Kalimpong, Sangharakshita broadly aligned himself with Mahāyāna attitudes to monasticism that focused less on its formal aspects and recognized the value of a dedicated household life. But he increasingly felt the division of the Buddhist community between monastic and lay members was a secondary matter and often an obstruction. Much more important was the division between people who were nominally followers of Buddhism and those who were actually practising it, and his Nyingma teachers Dudjom Rimpoche and Dilgo Khyentse Rimpoche were both married lamas and 'towering spiritual personalities'.[96]

In this way, Sangharakshita writes in *The History*,

> I came closer to seeing that monasticism and the spiritual life were not identical and closer, therefore, to realizing that what really mattered was not whether one was a monk or a layman but the depth and intensity of one's Going for Refuge.[97]

He could also understand his own Buddhist identity in these terms:

> Since the arising of the *bodhicitta* – and becoming a bodhisattva – was in fact the altruistic dimension of Going for Refuge, this in turn had the effect of making me think of myself simply as a monk who went for Refuge, or even as a human being who went for Refuge and who happened to live in monastic or semi-monastic fashion. Commitment was primary, lifestyle secondary.[98]

It was a relatively short step to the view that he was 'neither a monk nor a layman', and a new kind of ordination focused on going for refuge and on the principle 'commitment is primary and lifestyle secondary'.

Sangharakshita's understanding of commitment was largely (though not fully) worked out by the time he conducted the first ordinations into the Western Buddhist Order on 7 April 1968. It was important to him that others were going for refuge in the way he had come to understand it, with him as their witness, and the Order represented a new phase in his life. Later chapters will consider this in more depth. Before that, we must return to the understanding of the path he set out in his Indian writings, and particularly *A Survey of Buddhism*.

Chapter Ten

Conditionality and the Path

Nirvāṇa and conditionality

Buddhist unity doesn't depend just on a shared intention to go for refuge and follow the path. It also requires a shared understanding of reality. Sangharakshita worked out his understanding in the philosophical and doctrinal essays he wrote between 1947 and 1954, and the *Survey* draws his thoughts together. The material is complex because he both presents his understanding and argues against alternatives, negotiating a range of philosophical issues along the way. Nonetheless, behind the complexity is the same understanding of the Dharma as a principle of spiritual aliveness, creativity, and growth that we have already encountered. The two central elements of his discussion are nirvāṇa and conditionality.

Conceiving nirvāṇa

Nirvāṇa – the state attained at Enlightenment – is an inherently elusive subject, and Sangharakshita's discussion in the *Survey* proceeds with great care. His starting point is that, as all Buddhist schools agree, the nature of nirvāṇa cannot be adequately expressed through words or concepts. For this reason, he says, the Buddha preferred to remain silent rather than pronouncing on such matters as what happens to an enlightened person when they die. If he had declared that, as a buddha, he would live on after death, he would have implied the existence of a God-like Absolute; if he said his death meant annihilation, he would have implied that the material substance that made up his body was its ultimate reality. Silence represents the Buddha's middle way between 'eternalism' and 'nihilism'.

However, Sangharakshita says, 'Even silence, literally interpreted, might be misunderstood.'[1]

The Discourses cannot avoid speaking about nirvāṇa, but they usually refer to it in negative terms as the 'unborn', 'uncompounded', 'unbecome', and so on. Sangharakshita thought this a reasonable linguistic strategy, but he thought negative descriptions had themselves come to be seen as definitions that possessed 'an absolute validity'.[2] Defined in these terms, all we can say about nirvāṇa is that it is the absence of everything we know: 'the cessation of the saṃsāric process [...] the extinction of the phenomenal'.[3] That simply didn't express the spiritual ideal that inspired Sangharakshita or the qualities the Buddha displayed. In his view, '[A]fter all negations (including the negation of negation itself), there remains a spiritually positive residue.'[4]

The issue, for Sangharakshita, isn't whether nirvāṇa really 'exists': '[F]rom the standpoint of doctrine, all conceptual formulations of reality, whether positive or negative, were equally invalid.'[5] The issue is which way of thinking about nirvāṇa is more helpful. He points out that the Discourses contain many positive epithets for nirvāṇa, whose purpose is 'to awaken the dormant spiritual energies of the disciple not by addressing his intellect but by making an appeal to his imagination'.[6] To reconcile the two approaches, Sangharakshita introduces the distinction between absolute and relative truth that is found in the Discourses and became a central tenet of the Mahāyāna. The Buddha recognized both the absolute truth that nothing can be said about nirvāṇa and the relative truth that something must be said if the path is to be followed. In the same spirit, the Mahāyāna said that all conceptions are empty, but maintained that, 'from the standpoint of method, positive formulations, being more easily understood and more attractive than negative ones, were generally of greater practical help to the average Buddhist.'[7] Consequently, the Mahāyāna account of buddhahood includes an array of transcendent qualities and enlightened figures:

> These positive conceptions stand out against the omnipresent background of Voidness not as actors against the drop curtain of a stage, but rather as panes of glass of gradually increasing

degrees of opaqueness might stand out against the sunlit blue of the sky. The Light of the Void shines, in varying degrees of intensity, through them all.[8]

Sangharakshita's term for the rigid belief that a concept is absolutely true is 'literalism', and throughout his work he pointed out the tendency to literalize understanding. The *Survey* suggests that Buddhist teachings ask us to see that something can be relatively but not absolutely true. It opposes the tendency to literalize the Buddha's teaching, celebrates the alternatives, and views Buddhist history as a contention between literalism and the imagination:

> From one point of view the history of Buddhist thought, and of the various schools which contributed to its development, is the history of the setting up for practical purposes of one indication of reality after another, each to be ruthlessly discarded the minute it came to be regarded as true in the absolute sense.[9]

Conditionality and the path

If nirvāṇa can be conceived positively, what about the path leading to it? As the path involves developing consciousness, this means asking how consciousness works, and particularly how it changes. Sangharakshita again proceeded with care because, as he writes in the *Survey*, the Buddha's 'conception of, or rather insight into, the nature of phenomenal existence, is not readily comprehensible to the mundane intelligence'.[10] However, the Buddha did conceptualize his understanding in the teaching of *paṭicca-samuppāda / pratītya-samutpāda*, which, following Edward Conze, Sangharakshita translated in the *Survey* as 'conditioned co-production'. We can render it more simply (though less precisely) as 'conditionality'. This is the centre of the Buddhist account of how experience comes into being, how it brings suffering, and how that can change – in fact, the whole Buddhist path. Sangharakshita calls it 'the conceptualized formulation of the content of the Buddha's experience of *sambodhi*'[11] and 'the primary formulation of the Buddha's Enlightenment on the intellectual plane',[12] from which all later Buddhist thought developed and to which it may be reduced.

As a general principle, conditionality is expressed in the formula 'This being, that becomes; from the arising of this, that arises; this not being, that does not become; from the ceasing of this, that ceases.' This principle applies to all phenomena, including consciousness, and to understand it fully is to understand life itself. Speaking less formally in later years, Sangharakshita said that thinking in terms of conditionality means:

> You see that when things happen, they happen because of certain definite causes and conditions – and that this holds good not only of the external world, but also of your own mind. The realization that we are not fixed beings, but can change if we make the effort, and that if we set up appropriate conditions, desirable consequences will follow, is the key to spiritual development.[13]

At the same time, it is the core insight of the Buddha's Enlightenment:

> The scriptures tell us that when the Buddha surveyed the universe in the light of his supreme spiritual experience, he saw one prevailing principle or truth at work. He saw that the whole vast range and sweep of existence, from the lowest to the highest, in all its depth and breadth, was subject to what he subsequently called the law of conditionality.[14]

It is possible, at least up to a point, to align conditionality with scientific descriptions of the physical universe, but its importance within Buddhism is what it means for consciousness.

If conditionality is a general principle, the Discourses also apply that principle in particular contexts, and the *Survey* presents various formulations of the Buddha's teaching, including the four noble truths, as applications of conditionality. The most prominent formulation in the Discourses is the sequence of twelve *nidānas* ('causal links') that produce typical human experience, which is characterized by *dukkha*, or 'suffering'. Simplifying somewhat, the common list of *nidānas* begins with ignorance and presents a cascade of reactions that produce the experience of suffering. Suffering creates more suffering, and for this reason we can call the process 'cyclic conditionality'. The 'Hīnayāna' account of conditionality (which the Theravāda school inherits) often identifies conditionality exclusively with this formulation of the *nidāna*s, and Sangharakshita argues that it loses sight of the principle it expresses:

> [T]he flesh is more than raiment and an understanding of the principle of universal conditionality of far greater moment to the spiritual life than an understanding of any of its specific applications, however important or interesting these might be, in the form of one or another of the doctrines of Buddhism. But this truth the Hīnayānists speedily forgot.[15]

The result, he thinks, was a view of the path as a purely negative process of abandoning craving, aversion, and ignorance, and that distorted its meaning.

But if, as a general principle, conditionality is simply a description of how things happen, there is no reason why it should apply only to the cycle of suffering:

> [A]t each causal stage it should be possible to speak, not only of a cessation of this or that condition making for rebirth, and hence for suffering, but also of the production of positive factors which progressively augment one another until with the realization of *sambodhi* the whole process reaches its climax.[16]

Sangharakshita found support for a progressive form of conditionality in an essay by the Indian Buddhist scholar B.M. Barua entitled 'Buddhism as Personal Religion'. Barua argued that the Discourses presented conditionality in two modes. Cyclic conditionality produces suffering, but in another mode:

> the reaction takes place in a progressive order between two counterparts or complements or between two things of the same genus, the succeeding factor augmenting the effect of the preceding one.[17]

Conditionality and the Path

He later commented:

> Apart from the scriptures themselves, this short work has had a profounder and more lasting effect on my thinking about Buddhism than anything I have ever read on the subject, besides strongly influencing my philosophical and religious outlook in general. [...] At one stroke Buddhism was shown to be a positive rather than a negative teaching and the spiritual path shown to be firmly based on a philosophical principle.[18]

The English translator of Pāli texts Caroline Rhys Davids found further justification in a text called the *Upanisa Sutta*, which lists twelve positive or progressive *nidāna*s that emerge from the cyclic *nidāna*s. These start with suffering and proceed in 'a causal sequence of joy and happiness' to rapture, serenity, and nirvāṇa itself.[19] She admits that this *sutta* differs from many others on the same theme in the Pāli Canon but says that, for this reason, it stands out like an oasis in the parched landscape.

If cyclic conditionality accounts for most of our ordinary experience, progressive conditionality explains the path. The *Survey* cites other 'positive' formulations of the path in the Discourses, but the positive *nidāna* sequence explains the principle of progressive conditionality on which they depend. This is central to Sangharakshita's understanding of the Dharma:

> The second [progressive] trend is not merely the negative counterpart of the first, but possesses a positive character of its own. Upon this second trend the spiritual life is based.[20]

Sangharakshita pithily concludes: 'Instead of being a mere defecation of things evil the spiritual life becomes an enriching assimilation of ever greater and greater goods.'[21]

The 1949 essay *Philosophy and Religion in Original and Developed Buddhism* already identifies conditionality, understood as a broad principle, as the shared basis of the various Buddhist schools:

> The differences between them are to a large extent differences of method and approach rather than differences of belief.

Only in the light of this conviction is it possible to regard the
development of Buddhist philosophy as an intelligible process
of organic growth instead of as a bewildering succession of
conflicting doctrines and mutually exclusive creeds.[22]

The distinction between cyclic and progressive conditionality
also enabled Sangharakshita to conceive the path, in all its
manifestations, as a movement away from one and towards the
other. His early philosophical papers had argued that the teaching
of *anatta*, or the absence of inherent selfhood, meant existence
was a dynamic process, and that following the path meant living
according to 'the nibbānic trend of becoming'.[23] Conditionality
explained how this occurred.

Saṃsāra and nirvāṇa

Barua had observed that the relation between conditionality and
nirvāṇa was a perennial problem within Buddhist thought, which
had created antagonistic schools and 'baffled even the intelligence
of Buddhaghosa'.[24] Sangharakshita's answer (following Barua) is
that conditionality encompasses nirvāṇa:

> This doctrine is an all-inclusive reality, or formulation of
> reality, within which are included two trends or orders of
> things, one cyclic between opposites, the other progressive
> between factors which mutually complement and augment
> each other.[25]

Conditionality, in its different modes, doesn't just operate within
reality – it is reality, or at least a way of formulating it. The cyclic
trend encompasses *saṃsāra*; the progressive trend describes the
conditions that lead from *saṃsāra* to *nirvāṇa*; and at their higher
stages the progressive *nidāna*s describe the process of liberation.
Our view of nirvāṇa will depend on which of these trends we
consider:

> In relation to the first trend Nirvāṇa may be described only
> negatively, in terms of cessation; from the viewpoint of the
> world it will inevitably appear as a purely transcendental and,

as it were, 'static' state. In relation to the second trend Nirvāṇa may be described as the farthest discernible point of the increasingly positive and progressive series of reactions away from the *saṃsāra*; here it appears as 'dynamic' rather than static, the archetype of time rather than of space.[26]

This suggests that buddhahood shares the character of the dynamic and creative path that leads to it. The 1953 essay *The Religion of Art* describes the unlimited experience for the true artist, who imagines 'beauty rising and shining beyond beauty as the mountaineer sees range upon range of hills rising up one behind another, each one loftier and grander than that beneath it'.[27] This is not quite a description of nirvāṇa, but it is a description of a creative mind, which is, in principle, unlimited.

Understanding conditionality as an all-inclusive formulation of reality also suggests that following the path means engaging with an aspect of existence that has an affinity with buddhahood. The *Survey* quotes Lama Govinda's expression of this idea:

> the quality of enlightenment is inherent in the universe, or more correctly, latent in every form of consciousness, and therefore must come to maturity, according to universal law, whenever the conditions are favourable. That this law does not work with the mechanical regularity of clockwork, proves it to be a living force.[28]

The context is a discussion of the appearance, according to Buddhist cosmology, of a sequence of buddhas throughout the history of the universe, each of whom rediscovers the Dharma in their own experience, but the implications extend much further and colour the whole of Sangharakshita's teaching. This means that nirvāṇa, or a prefiguration of it, is immanent in the path.

Conditionality expanded

Making conditionality accessible

Sangharakshita reflects in *The Three Jewels*, 'To the extent that it keeps in touch with living experience Buddhist thought is always in the making.'[29] The *Survey* set out his basic understanding of conditionality, in its cyclic and progressive modes, but he returned to the subject throughout his work. After 1964, he usually expressed that understanding more simply, without discussing alternative views. A series of talks, given at the Hampstead Buddhist Vihara in 1965 and published as *The Meaning of Conversion in Buddhism*, introduced the principal terms he used in subsequent years:

> [C]onditionality is of two kinds: the 'cyclical' and the 'progressive' or 'spiral'. [...] The cyclical mode of conditionality, in which you go round and round, governs the *saṃsāra*, the round of conditioned existence, but the spiral mode, in which you go up and up, governs the spiritual life, especially as embodied in the path or way laid down by the Buddha, and the goal of that path, Enlightenment.[30]

This is still abstract, but Sangharakshita also explained what it meant in the immediate experience of his listeners:

> [W]hen sensations and experiences impinge upon us we do not have to react with craving and thus perpetuate the cyclical movement of existence. We can react instead in a positive way.[31]

In 1971 Sangharakshita found a succinct way to express this understanding in the lecture 'Mind Reactive and Creative', which became a staple of teaching in the FWBO/Triratna. The reactive mind, he says, reacts automatically to stimuli, without choice or awareness, and in that sense is mechanically conditioned. Our ideas come from other people and, driven by habits, we stumble through our lives like somnambulists. The alternative is the creative mind, and spiritual life begins with the transition from reactive to creative modes that happens when we become aware and can start to guide our mental states. This simple act of mindfulness and choice, which we can make in any moment, is a key to the whole path:

> Awareness puts, as it were, a brake on the wheel. For this reason the cultivation of awareness occupies a central place

in the Buddhist scheme of spiritual self-discipline. It is the principal means of transition from the reactive mind to the creative mind, from the wheel to the path, from the circle to the spiral – ultimately, from *saṃsāra* to *nirvāṇa*.[32]

This connects conditionality with the language of imagination and growth, and Sangharakshita says the creative mind is aware, alive, and spontaneous. It is 'the Spirit of Life itself rising like a fountain from the infinite depth of existence'.[33]

In his central period (1964–87) Sangharakshita presented the path in many ways and associated it with numerous practices, but all these formulations expressed the underlying model of cyclic and progressive conditionality. He spoke extensively about the practice of ethics, meditation, friendship, sangha, devotion, work, the arts, and other methods, each of which offered a way to move from the wheel to the spiral and from reactivity to creativity. In a sense, each was both a path in its own right and an aspect of a single path that balanced various faculties: effort with meditation, and faith with wisdom, masculine qualities with feminine ones. As we shall see in detail in Chapter Twelve, he described following the path as an organic process of growth and development, and suggested that every aspect of the path could be practised on ascending levels, as ways of traversing the vertical dimension of being.

The terms 'reactivity' and 'creativity' echo the stimulus-and-response psychology of the period, and in recent years many teachers of Buddhism and mindfulness have developed these parallels. However, several aspects of Sangharakshita's account distinguish it. The philosophical underpinning of conditionality shows the universal principle behind mindfulness practice without which most psychological accounts of Buddhist practices move rapidly away from Buddhist terminology towards secular and scientific language. He also used symbolism to evoke the meaning of the path, often drawing on traditional Buddhist sources. The basic structure of his presentation is the wheel, representing cyclic conditionality and ordinary existence, and a path leading away from it and eventually reaching nirvāṇa. He often describes the wheel by using the composite symbol known as the wheel of life, at the centre of which we see a cock, a snake, and a pig, representing craving, aversion, and ignorance. As early as 1948 Sangharakshita had used the 'spiral' as a figure of speech to describe the path,[34] but *The Meaning of Conversion in Buddhism* makes it a constituent part of his thought. Sometimes his language took flight:

> The path seems to straighten out, to stand up; it becomes a great ladder stretching from heaven to earth and from earth to heaven. It's a ladder of gold, a ladder of silver, a ladder of crystal. But again the symbol changes. The ladder becomes slender and solid and turns green; it becomes the stem of a gigantic tree with enormous blossoms, blossoms that are bigger the higher up they are. At the very top of the tree, shining like a sun, is the biggest blossom of all. In the centre of each of these blossoms sit all kinds of beautiful and radiant figures: Buddhas and bodhisattvas, *arhants*, *ḍākas*, and *ḍākinīs*.[35]

Sangharakshita sometimes reminded his listeners that formulations of the Buddhist path, many of which come in the form of lists, were ways to access a spirit or an experience, and, discussing a Pāli source, he said:

> It might be better to imagine a day of unfettered inspiration and free-flowing energy, a day in which you were able to be completely true and clear in your communication, a day in which you felt so real a connection with others.[36]

Even 'the path' was a metaphor, albeit a useful one, for a process that finally eludes any expression:

> Language is only language. Even when one speaks of the Buddhist path it is only a figure of speech, but it is a very useful figure of speech and one that lies at the heart of Buddhism. If you take the figure of the path too literally you will think that when you move on to the succeeding stage you leave behind the preceding stage. But that would be transferring what is true of the path in the literal sense

to the path in the metaphorical sense. We cannot but speak metaphorically, but we have to remain aware that we are speaking metaphorically.[37]

Levels of conditionality

The spiral path and the golden ladder both describe an ascent through a vertical dimension of being and consciousness. But, if the path ascends, does progressive conditionality operate in a single way at every level, or can we distinguish ascending levels?

The 'Aspects of the Bodhisattva Ideal' lectures (1969) engage with the paradoxical character of the bodhisattva path that the Mahāyāna teaches. In its early stages, Sangharakshita presents the path as a steady 'spiral' progress, but it also requires 'the patient acceptance that *dharmas* do not in reality arise or pass away'.[38] In other words, within Mahāyāna thought, causality is only provisionally true. It is another model, or metaphor, or finger pointing at the moon. How does that fit with an understanding of conditionality as an all-embracing formulation of reality that encompasses both *saṃsāra* and *nirvāṇa*?

Early Buddhism identifies a transition in an individual's fundamental mode of being at stream entry, and the Mahāyāna identifies a comparable change with the arising of the bodhicitta. Sangharakshita concluded that both terms describe a roughly equivalent shift in orientation:

> At this point one's personal centre of gravity has permanently shifted from the conditioned to the Unconditioned, so that from now onwards one is not just oriented in the direction of Nirvāṇa, but actually moving irrevocably towards it. From this point on progress is assured, because one has reached that part of the spiral which is not subject to any gravitational pull from the mundane, from the wheel of life.[39]

But what happens as one moves towards nirvāṇa in this way, and what kind of conditionality is at work? In *The Bodhisattva Principle* (1983) Sangharakshita says that, at lower stages of the path, when it is still possible to fall back, conditionality is both progressive and regressive (i.e. spiral and cyclic). But, past a certain point, it becomes 'irreversibly progressive',[40] and reaching this point is the real object of the spiritual life. His language kept evolving: in the 1986 lecture 'Discerning the Buddha' he said Enlightenment meant 'becoming involved in an irreversible and unmeasured transcendental process',[41] and in 1990 he spoke of a transition from 'the saṃsāric to the nirvāṇic mode'.[42] But what is this mode or process, and what form of conditionality does it express?

The five *niyama*s
Caroline Rhys Davids had asked similar questions a generation before Sangharakshita. She argues in *Buddhism: A Study of the Buddhist Norm* that the early Buddhist understanding of conditionality aligned it with modern science, with the difference that science is concerned with the physical and organic world while Buddhism addresses a moral and spiritual level of experience. Both extrapolate general laws from particular observations, and the Dharma expresses 'a vision of universal natural law [...] applying to existence as a whole' that is 'as natural, as necessary, as *inexorably*, inevitably sure, as the way of sun and moon, the dying of all that is born, the reaction of sentience to stimulus'.[43] She says of the 'law' of karma:

> Now the sutras do not assert, but they leave it clear enough, that rights and wrongs and those consequences of actions which we call justice, retribution, compensation, are as truly a part of the eternal natural or cosmic order as the flow of a river, the process of the seasons, the plant from the natural seed.[44]

To explain how physical and organic laws relate to spiritual ones, she turned to a formula in Buddhaghosa's commentaries on the Pāli discourses. The five *niyama*s identify the different aspects of 'the order the Buddha saw in the universe':

> Five branches, strands, phases were discerned: *kamma-niyama*, order of act-and-result; *utu-niyama*, physical (inorganic) order; *bīja-niyama*, order of germs, or seeds (physical organic order);

citta-niyama, order of mind, or conscious life; *dhamma-niyama*, order of the norm, or the effort of nature to produce a perfect type.[45]

Sangharakshita learned of the *niyama*s from Rhys Davids and found them helpful for the same reasons.[46] *The Three Jewels* calls them five distinct 'orders of conditionality' or categories describing different ways in which conditionality works. His main point, following Rhys Davids, is that karma doesn't explain everything that happens to us: 'though [the Buddha] teaches that every willed action produces an experienced effect he does not teach that all experienced effects are products of willed action or karma.'[47]

The 1970 lecture 'Karma and Rebirth' again presents conditionality as a naturally occurring law, and karma as a middle way between the fatalistic belief that everything we experience is the result of past actions and the nihilistic belief that our ethical actions have no future effects. Sangharakshita calls it 'the principle of conditionality operative on the moral plane'. However, when he comes to the *dharma-niyama* – the 'spiritual or transcendental' level of conditionality – he simply says, 'Exactly how it works, however, has not always been made very clear.'[48] Sangharakshita appreciated the Buddha's 'metaphysical reticence'[49] – his reluctance to speculate about the nature of reality beyond what could be observed – and it is telling that his most eloquent expression of the relation between progressive conditionality and nirvāṇa in the 1970s is an extended organic metaphor describing a bodhisattva's mode of existence in *Wisdom beyond Words*:

> Just as the sap flows up through the tree quite spontaneously and naturally, so the power needed for the practice of wisdom flows spontaneously from the bodhisattva's being, rooted as it is in ultimate reality. By sending roots ever deeper into the Dharma the bodhisattva enables the energy to flow ever more freely and abundantly. But just as the tree is only artificially separate from the sap that flows through it, so there is no distinguishing between the bodhisattva and the energy that springs from the source of ultimate reality. When you are

totally absorbed in something creative, you and the energy are one.[50]

The *dharma-niyama*

The History of My Going for Refuge (1987) began a retrospective phase in which Sangharakshita's main literary project was his memoirs, along with short works and papers spelling out the significance of going for refuge. He supervised the editing of many earlier works, compiled his *Complete Poems*, and gradually handed on his responsibilities within the FWBO and the Order. But he continued to reflect on the nature of conditionality and its relation to nirvāṇa and to the higher stages of the path. In the late papers Subhuti sets out the last phase of Sangharakshita's thoughts about conditionality, and we will consider them here, even though this takes us beyond the accounts of the path in his central period that are described in the following chapters.

The first of the late papers is *Revering and Relying upon the Dharma*. It begins with a question: 'What are we to make of [Sangharakshita's] various ways of speaking about Right View, whether those derived from tradition or of his own coinage?'[51] His various expressions of the path are bound up with his understanding of conditionality and particularly its progressive trend. But now he introduces a fresh distinction between two ways things happen *within* that progressive trend. The first is *karma-niyama*, which operates when we act 'skilfully' – making a conscious effort to develop, for example through practising ethics or meditation. That much is familiar from Sangharakshita's previous expositions, but *Revering and Relying upon the Dharma* identifies a second kind of conditionality and equates it with the *dharma-niyama*.

The formulation emerged, in part, from Sangharakshita's reflections on bodhicitta – the indefinable motivation that makes one a bodhisattva. He wrote of the *Diamond Sutra* in 1948, just six years after the shattering experience of first reading it:

> In the ultimate sense there exists no separate personality or individuality which may emancipate or be emancipated. Since the illusion of 'thou' and 'I' is not present in that moment

of supravolution which we personalize as a bodhisattva
we conclude that he is incapable of self-referring or other-
referring activities. He is a supra-personal cosmic force
making toward Enlightenment.[52]

Sangharakshita means that, because a bodhisattva experiences no sense of being a subject in relation to objects, 'he' should be viewed as a force or current of spiritual energy – 'a suprasensuous continuum of pure becoming'. One strand of Sangharakshita's thought addresses this state from the perspective of the individual who aspires to it, and the same 1948 essay urges spiritual practitioners to 'Remove the thorn of self-reference with the thorn of service and then pluck out the thorn of other-reference with the thorn of contemplation'.[53] A decade later, *The Meaning of Buddhism and the Value of Art* identified an 'expansive movement in consciousness' that comes when we progress 'from egoism to selflessness'.[54]

Another strand of Sangharakshita's thought presents it as a force or stream beyond the individual. We have already discussed his experience in Nagpur in 1956 of being 'not a person but an impersonal force' and his sense, as he developed the FWBO/Triratna, that 'a supra-personal energy or force was working through me'.[55] The 1969 lectures on the bodhisattva ideal call the bodhicitta – the indefinable motivation that makes one a bodhisattva – 'supra-individual but not collective' and 'a disembodied impersonal spiritual energy'.[56] And in a seminar on *The Bodhicaryāvatāra*, a classic guide to the bodhisattva path, he says it is

> supra-individual, supra-personal, in the sense that it is
> not just the ordinary empirical 'you'. It's something much
> greater, much wider and more powerful, that as it were takes
> possession of you.[57]

Finally, we have seen that Sangharakshita aligned the bodhicitta with the stream that carries the practitioner forward from the point of stream entry. *Revering and Relying upon the Dharma* understands this force or stream as the form of conditionality that predominates when we let go of ego-clinging:

As consciousness emerges in more and more sensitive and pure forms, it becomes less and less self-referenced and it is increasingly attuned to the way things truly are. Gradually the tendency to egoistic clinging weakens enough for a new process to come into play: progress in accordance with the *dhamma-niyama*.[58]

This means more than acting with a compassionate motivation or a selfless attitude. The *dharma-niyama* is what happens as one lives according to the truth that one is not a fixed subject separate from others and the world:

> The sequence of conditioned arisings, categorized under the *dhamma-niyama*, transcends self-consciousness, just as self-consciousness transcends instinctual consciousness, and develops within the individual independent of egoistic volition, spontaneously unfolding in more and more rich and satisfying forms. It is now the chief motive force of the one in whom it flowers, increasingly replacing the old self-referent willing, however refined.[59]

This also offers a way to understand nirvāṇa as a process of dynamic unfoldment. Sangharakshita described it in these terms in his 1976 commentary on Nāgārjuna's *Precious Garland*, for example:

> Nirvāṇa is a term used to indicate the unlimited nature of the process of growth and development, a final term to designate the fact that there can be no end to that positive process, no final turn of the spiral. Enlightenment is [...] a living process that continues beyond time, indeed, beyond the very distinction between time and timelessness.[60]

The *dharma-niyama* is, in one sense, simply a term for that process, and the late papers present nirvāṇa mainly through its embodiment in the Buddha, describing him as 'the fulfilment of the progressive trend in conditionality'.[61] However, their principal concern is not to define nirvāṇa but to suggest how we can approach it. The transition from *karma-niyama* to *dharma-niyama* is gradual, suggesting that selfless and even 'transcendent' forces can operate within our experience long before we make a decisive spiritual breakthrough. In more metaphysical language, this offers a fresh way to explain how transcendental qualities can be present within conditioned experience and available to unenlightened beings. This is a characteristic feature of Sangharakshita's account of the path, and with this in mind we can return to his central period – the time when he returned to England and founded the FWBO.

Chapter Eleven

The Path in Practice

The central period

During his time in India Sangharakshita gave thousands of talks but they were unrecorded, and we only know of his thought up to that point through his written work. *A Survey of Buddhism* is particularly important because it establishes his underlying approach, but it does so largely in abstract, doctrinal terms. His lectures and seminars in the two decades following his return to the UK are very different and, in many ways, this spoken material is the heart of his teaching. At the Hampstead Buddhist Vihara he often gave three talks a week, sometimes more, usually covering fresh material in each one, and with the establishment of the FWBO he had an audience of eager listeners. Many of the talks and some of the seminars have been edited into books that are included in his *Complete Works* and contain some of his most characteristic and persuasive prose. He delivered extended lecture series, including several commentaries on Buddhist texts and traditions, and many individual talks. He sought fresh expressions of ancient Buddhist teachings that integrated divergent teachings with his own distinctive understanding of the path, and formulated a message that matched the intensity of his inspiration. As he spoke, he sometimes felt himself taken over by a force that inspired him to extended passages of image thinking.

Sangharakshita's teaching changed in some respects in the mid-1970s as he entered his fifties. The FWBO was becoming a 'movement', so some lectures formulated his approach in terms Order members could use in their own teaching, and he saw new needs as his disciples grew in experience. He wrote in 1984 that his later teaching was 'based on, or grew naturally out of, the fundamental principles adumbrated in the *Survey*',[1] and it continued to develop as he pursued the implications of those principles.

Versions of the path

Throughout his career, Sangharakshita's view of the Buddhist path turned on the relationship between ordinary experience and buddhahood. He set out his basic understanding in the 1969 lecture series on the bodhisattva ideal:

> As human beings we are related to ultimate reality both directly and indirectly. We are related to reality directly in the sense that in the very depths of our being is something which all the time connects us with reality, a kind of golden thread which, though it may be gossamer thin, is always there. In some people that thread has become a little thicker, a little stronger, in others it has strengthened almost into a rope, while in those who are Enlightened there is no need for a connecting thread at all, because there is no difference between the depth of their being and the depth of reality itself.[2]

This suggests that reality is always immanently present within our experience, even if we must still work to realize its presence. The indirect relation is through our place in 'the hierarchy of being': we must feel ourselves to be in contact with the bodhisattva figures who embody enlightened qualities and friends who are 'spiritually more advanced than we are ourselves'.[3] They represent, or direct us towards, a transcendent reality.

Sangharakshita presented the path in many ways, and he most often described it as a journey towards a transcendent destination. But his presentations always include a sense that the qualities of buddhahood, or perhaps their reflection, are available to us as we practise. Conditionality explains this because – as he remarked in a seminar on the *Satipaṭṭhāna Sutta* – '[t]he transcendental is implicit in the very nature of the spiral path.'[4] Sangharakshita's accounts of the path in the central period of his teaching included both.

Vision and transformation

Sangharakshita's 1968 lecture series 'The Buddha's Noble Eightfold Path' is structured around two stages of practice. The first is the path of vision, which comprises only the first stage, *sammā-diṭṭhi* (Pāli), or *samyag-dṛṣṭi* (Sanskrit). Standard Theravādin accounts of the eightfold path translate the term as 'right view', but, as Lama Govinda wrote to Sangharakshita in 1956, *sammā/samyak* really means 'perfect or complete' while *diṭṭhi/dṛṣṭi* refers to 'a perfectly open, unprejudiced attitude of mind, which enables us to see things as they really are'.[5] Sangharakshita settles on 'perfect'. Right view, he says, denotes an intellectual grasp of Buddhist teachings, but Perfect Vision suggests something 'direct and immediate, and more of the nature of a spiritual experience'.[6] If we regard the path in this way, 'it is as though a whole new world has opened up'.[7]

The remaining seven stages comprise the path of transformation. If vision represents 'the realization of truth by the conscious mind',[8] transformation means its descent 'into the depths of our being', affecting 'every aspect and department of our lives'.[9] Eventually, one reaches the last stage, Perfect Samādhi, at which point Perfect Vision 'reigns supreme at every level of one's being and consciousness'.[10] Sangharakshita likens its role to the spread of sap through a tree:

> First you have a sapling rooted in the earth, and then one day the rain falls, perhaps quite heavily. The rain is absorbed through the roots of the sapling, the sap rises and spreads into the branches and twigs – and the tree grows. [...] The following of the Eightfold Path is like that. First there is a spiritual experience, a glimpse of reality, or in other words a moment of Perfect Vision. This is like the falling of the rain. And just as the sap rises and spreads into the branches and twigs, so Perfect Vision gradually transforms the different aspects of our being.[11]

Like a tree absorbing sap, following the path involves a deepening engagement with transcendental qualities that affect us from the start.

According to the traditional explanation, Perfect Vision arises only after the unshakeable insight of stream entry. This is how Sangharakshita explains it in a 'Prefatory Note' to the 2000 edition of the published talks,[12] but his explanation doesn't do justice to the method of the talks themselves. He says Perfect Vision can easily pass from our minds, and 'after a short time [...] [i]t is as though it had never been.'[13] It is an inspiration that prefigures a lasting insight rather than Insight itself, but one that can affect us profoundly if we cherish it as a source of inspiration, like keeping a mountain peak in sight as we travel towards it.

In fact, the talks work on multiple levels, addressing the people in Sangharakshita's audience who were entirely new to Buddhism along with those who were more experienced; addressing the struggles of daily life and relating them to Buddhist ideals. More precisely, they address different levels of experience that may be at work at the same time within an individual. As Sangharakshita wrote in 1957:

> Just as an object may be lit up now by a beam of white light, now by a beam of red, so the doctrinal formulas of the four noble truths, the five *khandhas* etc., can be the objects of both the mundane and the transcendental kinds of *sammā-diṭṭhi*.[14]

The bodhisattva ideal

In 1969, a year after the eightfold-path lecture series, Sangharakshita presented another traditional version of the path. The bodhisattva-ideal lecture series (later published as a book of the same name) describes the bodhisattva as 'a living contradiction [...] a synthesis of *nirvāṇa* and *saṃsāra*',[15] standing between the two and representing two fundamentally different ways of comprehending reality. The bodhisattva path has the flavour of both dimensions, and the series is Sangharakshita's fullest exploration in this period of the issues that most fundamentally concerned him.

One becomes a bodhisattva through the arising of the bodhicitta, which Sangharakshita usually translated as 'the will to Enlightenment'. It is 'the manifestation, even the irruption, within us of something transcendental: the emergence within our ordinary experience of something of a totally different nature'.[16] The bodhicitta represents the meeting of the individual and buddhahood, and for that reason it has two aspects. The 'absolute *bodhicitta*' is an aspect or dimension of nirvāṇa, and 'in its ultimate essence it is beyond thought and beyond speech'. The 'relative *bodhicitta*' is the individual's experience of nirvāṇa as a compassionate desire for the Enlightenment of all beings. More precisely, it is 'the reflection of the absolute *bodhicitta* in the web of conditioned existence, the stream of time, the cosmic process'.[17] It represents the presence of nirvāṇa deep in our minds – like a jewel lost in a rubbish heap or concealed in our clothing. These two aspects of *bodhicitta* coexist, but it is impossible to say how, and Sangharakshita's explanation is that they employ different categories of thought and language:

> Absolute *bodhicitta* is [...] conceived of in terms of space – that is, as fixed, permanent, unchanging. Relative *bodhicitta* is *bodhicitta* thought of in terms of time, which implies change. [...] But they are really the same – or rather, they are 'not two', as the traditional phrase has it, just as *saṃsāra* and *nirvāṇa* are said to be 'not two'. In one sense Enlightenment is eternally attained, in another sense it is eternally in the process of attainment, and these senses ultimately coincide.[18]

The absolute bodhicitta is transcendent and, in a sense, unknowable; the relative bodhicitta is immanent, and suggests that 'the reality towards which we are progressing is not, in the ultimate sense, foreign to us; nor are we, in the ultimate sense, foreign to it.'[19] To explain how the relative bodhicitta connects us to the absolute bodhicitta, Sangharakshita cites the Neoplatonic idea of correspondence: 'the eye could not behold the sun if there was not something sun-like in the eye.'[20]

The final lecture of the series, 'The Buddha and Bodhisattva: Eternity and Time', develops the theme. Those who follow the bodhisattva path, Sangharakshita says, do so in time and may think they will arrive at 'the wonderful gateway of Nirvāṇa, all glistening and golden'. But the buddhahood towards which they travel is entirely different from the path they follow. At its end, he says, is a precipice or empty space. The path, represented by the bodhisattva, and the goal, represented by the Buddha, are fundamentally different:

> We thus have two principles: a principle of Buddhahood in the dimension of eternity, and a principle of bodhisattvahood in the dimension of time. One is transcendent, the other is immanent. One represents perfection eternally complete, eternally achieved; the other represents perfection eternally in the process of achievement. And the one does not lead into the other; the two are discontinuous.[21]

In the *Survey*, the category of 'time' stands for conditionality, which Sangharakshita presents as the principle underlying both the path and buddhahood,[22] while space implies a purely transcendental understanding of nirvāṇa. In other words, for one who has attained nirvāṇa, it is unconditioned, but from the perspective of someone on the path it arises at the end of a path one must follow step by step.

The Bodhisattva Ideal expresses the connection paradoxically by saying 'Enlightenment is not reached by following a path. But this doesn't mean that the path should not be followed.' Both perspectives are important, and holding them together implies a fluid approach to Buddhist practice:

> It can be seen in terms of advancing from stage to stage, but it can also be seen in terms of deepening one's experience of what is already there. We need both. If one thinks one-sidedly of the spiritual life as a progression from stage to stage, one is liable to become too goal-oriented. But if one thinks only in terms of deepening one's present experience, unfolding from a deep centre within oneself, one may become rather inert. It is perhaps best to think of operating in both modes at the same time, or alternating between them at different periods of one's life. [...] Sometimes you may feel as though you are unfolding like a flower; at other times spiritual life may feel more like

climbing a mountain. [...] Thus in our spiritual life we are trying all the time to achieve that which we already have. We have to do both: realize that we already have it, but at the same time go all out to achieve it.[23]

A critical assessment

This account of the pragmatic and transcendent elements of Sangharakshita's teaching is relevant to the recent study *The Thought of Sangharakshita: A Critical Assessment* by Robert Ellis. He appreciates Sangharakshita's capacity to make 'the process of practice' accessible in many ways, but criticizes the idealistic framing of his teachings. For example, he says, using 'perfect', rather than 'right' in presenting the eightfold path has meant

> generations of Triratna Buddhists may have thought of themselves in unnecessarily idealistic terms [...] rather than practising the level of ethical speech or mindfulness that is practically sustainable for them.[24]

The result, Ellis concludes, is that Sangharakshita's work is an inconsistent mixture of differing modes of thought – sometimes acknowledging the limits of our knowledge and sometimes speaking from the 'absolute' perspective of Enlightenment. Ellis argues – here and throughout his Middle Way philosophy – that only the first of these is legitimate:

> If one claims to know about 'Reality' in the way [Sangharakshita] evidently claims in his writing, one is taking insufficient account of the limitation of one's own standpoint as a human being [...] and assuming the ontological standpoint of God. [...] Whatever the aspect of Buddhist teaching, his followers have found much of practical value in his interpretation of it, but at the same time they are asked to hold in mind traditional absolutist views that contradict and undermine that practical value.[25]

Ellis's fundamental disagreement isn't with Sangharakshita but with Buddhism – in fact, with any system or philosophy that bases its teachings on 'metaphysical claims'. Buddhism, at least, has a response, which Sangharakshita follows. It depends at every stage on two sources of knowledge. The first is awareness of suffering and the patterning of our mental lives, and this develops pragmatically and incrementally. The second is the understanding that comes through the experience of Enlightenment. The basis of Buddhism is that, having attained this knowledge, the Buddha, and later other realized teachers, knew something unenlightened people can't know, and he shared it with them through the formulations and practices of the Dharma. The Buddha's enlightened understanding is therefore embedded in the Dharma, and, though the form of the teachings is contingent, the insight they express is not. In that sense, any authentic expression of the Buddhist path is illumined by something beyond what one currently knows, which is to say, something transcendent.

Ellis believes this transcendental knowledge is unrealistic, alienating and ultimately oppressive. Sangharakshita's view is that, while this aspect of the Dharma can be misunderstood, it contains something that cannot be accessed through pragmatic experience alone. As he wrote in a 1997 review of Stephen Batchelor's *Buddhism without Beliefs*:

> *Logically* speaking [Dharma practice] begins with the 'existence' of what may be described as a transcendent Absolute, for as the Buddha declares in the *Udāna*, 'There is, monks, an unborn, unbecome, unmade, uncompounded; if there were not, there would be known no escape here from the born, become, made, compounded' (i.e. there would be no ending of anguish).[26]

Buddha nature and the path of regular steps

As the FWBO developed, Sangharakshita was able to observe what his students made of his teachings and particularly his advice that they regard buddhahood as both transcendent and immanent. The immanence of Enlightenment is central to the 1965 lectures later published as *The Essence of Zen*, the 1966 lectures on Tibetan

Buddhism, and the 1969 series on 'Creative Symbols of the Tantric Path to Enlightenment'. He says of the Vajrasattva *sādhana*:

> [I]f you go deep enough into your own mind, beyond all thoughts, words, and deeds, even beyond all the other Buddhas and bodhisattvas, you encounter the fundamental intrinsic purity of Vajrasattva. He symbolizes the primeval, original purity of one's own mind, its transcendental purity beyond space and beyond time.[27]

Chanting Vajrasattva's mantra, he says:

> you feel cleansed, pure, bright, resplendent, crystalline. You begin to recover what is called your original purity, your original nature. [...] And as you realize that, you become gradually suffused with the sense of reality, and even with the power of reality. You become Vajrasattva.[28]

The vividness of these teachings no doubt reflects the continuing inspiration he drew from practices he had only learned in his later years in India.

This aspect of Sangharakshita's teaching powerfully affected people encountering the FWBO, as Subhuti attests in an essay entitled 'Three Myths of the Spiritual Life'. Like that of many of his peers, Subhuti's interest in Buddhism began with drug-induced glimpses of non-duality. Buddhist teachings articulated his sense that the highest truth was immanent in every moment of experience, and he responded positively when Sangharakshita expressed this outlook in his teaching. The connection deepened when Subhuti took up a *sādhana* practice on Mañjughoṣa (the bodhisattva of wisdom), in which the bodhisattva is both a transcendent object of reverence and the epitome of the practitioner's inner purity. Subhuti says he regularly experienced 'a sense of reality unfolding naturally, without any conscious effort on my part'. When he heard Sangharakshita reading a Dzogchen text, he realized Sangharakshita understood its message: 'And as I listened to him, I felt that I too was at one with it. Every word seemed to come from that experience of reality-as-immediately-present.'[29]

The dangers of Buddha nature

The 'primeval, original purity' that Sangharakshita recognized in the depths of his mind wasn't a conceptual understanding, but the Buddhist schools offered ways to conceive it, most notably the teachings of buddha nature or *tathāgatagarbha*. Sangharakshita sometimes used this language in his early writing, but he warned in *The Three Jewels*:

> Used indiscriminately, [these teachings] are extremely dangerous. A purely theoretical concept of Buddhahood may, in effect, be superimposed upon the ego, with disastrous results. For this reason Buddhism generally prefers to speak the language not of identity but of analysis and change.[30]

When Sangharakshita spoke of intrinsic Enlightenment and the like in the early years of the FWBO, he drew attention to the metaphorical character of these ideas, and he later sometimes called them 'poetic philosophy'.[31] He says in *The Bodhisattva Ideal*:

> Buddhahood may perhaps be said to be immanent within us in potential, but to realize that potential, we will need to do more than become aware of it: for most of us, it will be a process requiring a great deal of time and effort.[32]

This way of expressing the path is an important theme in his 1971 lectures on the *White Lotus Sutra* with their inspirational revelation of the eternal buddha, but thereafter Sangharakshita largely stopped speaking in these terms. The 1975 lecture 'The Path of Regular and Irregular Steps' explains that the sudden publication of thousands of texts deriving from the whole Buddhist tradition had changed the profile of Buddhism in western countries. These texts were often consumed uncritically and without guidance, leaving some people confused while others concluded they had mastered the teachings simply by reading about them. In truth, Sangharakshita sometimes told his listeners, we do not understand Buddhism at all. He made a similar point in a seminar on the *Udāna*:

[T]hese teachings were communicated by teachers to their disciples when they thought the disciples were ready to hear them. Nowadays anybody can pick up a book that says, 'You don't have to do anything. Just realize that you are Buddha.' Perhaps thinking that 'realizing' means understanding intellectually, people think, 'Well yes, I *am* Buddha. There's no need for me to do any religious practice.'[33]

In 1973 the Tibetan lama Chögyam Trungpa Rimpoche (whom Sangharakshita had known both in India and in Britain) published *Cutting through Spiritual Materialism*, which also recognizes the tendency for western Buddhists to 'deceive ourselves we are developing spiritually when instead we are strengthening our egos through spiritual techniques'.[34] Trungpa Rimpoche also recognized the need for commitment, but his message was that effort was necessary only as a preliminary to entering a state of relaxed, open awareness:

> We begin to realize that there is a sane, awake quality within us. In fact, this quality manifests only in the absence of struggle [...] we need only drop the effort to secure and solidify ourselves and the awakened state is present.[35]

Trungpa Rimpoche inherited the immanence-based Mahāmudrā teachings of his Kagyu school and responded to the cultural issues on their terms. Sangharakshita's principal reference point was the message of the Buddha that he found in the Discourses, which emphasized a developmental path. This was the yardstick against which he considered whether later doctrines 'represent a departure from the Buddha's original teaching'.[36]

The distinction between the paths of regular and irregular steps in fact originates in the Chinese text *Dhyāna for Beginners*, which Sangharakshita's lecture broadly follows. He acknowledges that exposure to the highest levels of wisdom may be powerful, but doubts the effects will last:

> [W]e find, sooner or later, that we are slowing down. We seem to be up against an invisible obstacle. Apparently

in a sort of spiritual doldrums, we are going through the motions, but nothing is happening: we don't seem to be getting anywhere.[37]

Following the path of regular steps means recognizing the stage of spiritual progress we have reached and practising in a way that's appropriate to it. Rather than thinking we have moved beyond basic teachings, we should first establish our practice of ethics, as the foundation of meditation practice. Wisdom is a culmination of the path, not the place to start.

The problem with the popularization of buddha nature is that it strips away the context of spiritual commitment and experience. Reviewing a volume on Zen in 1975, Sangharakshita comments:

> [T]he Zen stories and sayings are essentially *precepts*, that is to say, they are personal teachings directly relating to the individual spiritual needs of the disciple concerned, and should not be read out of context, or taken as applying to people whose spiritual needs may, indeed, be the exact opposite of those of the disciples for whom the teachings were originally meant. Unless this is borne in mind, armchair followers of 'Zen' in the West will continue to regard themselves as having transcended the traditional Buddhist virtues when they have, in fact, yet to develop them.[38]

Sangharakshita returned to the *White Lotus Sutra* in the 1987 lecture 'The Priceless Jewel', which discusses the sutra's 'Parable of the Return Journey'. A man gets drunk and falls asleep in the house of a friend who sews a priceless jewel into the drunk man's clothing, and then travels to a foreign country where he falls destitute. He doesn't know that the answer to his problems has been with him all the time. The Buddha explains that the jewel represents the bodhicitta, which hides within human consciousness. The image reminds Sangharakshita of his sense that the *Diamond Sutra* merely reminded him of something he already knew, but he also warns that the image can be misunderstood:

> The fact that the priceless jewel is tied within the man's garment does not mean that the truth, or reality, or ideal, which is potentially existent within us lies just below the surface of consciousness and is immediately accessible. [...] We also have to follow the spiritual path which, leading from ethics to concentration and meditation and from concentration and meditation to clear vision or wisdom, will enable us eventually to achieve a state of pure awareness or knowledge.[39]

The danger is thinking we can possess nirvāṇa or the bodhicitta without changing. The alternative is more challenging:

> In order to overcome internal and external factors alike, we shall have to be prepared to encounter a truth, or a reality, that far transcends anything we had previously thought or imagined. We shall have to regain the higher spiritual ideals which we perhaps have, individually and collectively, forgotten.[40]

The heroic ideal
The problems Sangharakshita found in buddha-nature teachings were partly inherent in the very concept, and partly related to the needs he saw in the people he was teaching in the early 1970s. He commented in 1980:

> Had I spoken of relaxing in the early days, this would have been the very thing that people wanted to hear, and they would have relaxed in the sense of subsiding into sloth and torpor and laziness. I can remember the days when I walked into the Pundarika centre in Balmore Street and I had to step over the bodies of people lying around on the floor. Many of our friends were hippies and thought that taking drugs was the quick and easy way, and that you didn't have to bother to meditate.[41]

By 1975 a highly committed group of young disciples had emerged as leaders of the FWBO and, with Sangharakshita's encouragement, they threw themselves into establishing single-sex residential communities and starting FWBO centres. The huge, derelict Victorian fire station that was to become the London Buddhist Centre was bought in this year, and converting it required an immense effort. Sangharakshita's talk of 'the heroic ideal' entered FWBO discourse, and Nagabodhi wrote in the *FWBO Newsletter*:

> If the spiritual life is about the transformation of our whole being, it follows that it is not enough for us to be 'Buddhists' with our peaceful, passive sides only. We have to learn to incorporate all our energies and drives into the process.[42]

In 1977 Sangharakshita noted with satisfaction that

> the Movement has expanded to an extent that hardly anyone could have foreseen, and changes have taken place at virtually all levels. People are less problem-oriented, and more ideal-oriented, than they were previously. There has been a shift of emphasis from the 'psychological' to the 'spiritual' end of the spectrum of personal development – from the red of mental health to the violet of transcendental awareness. More energy is in circulation, and there is a higher degree of emotional positivity.[43]

Sangharakshita's predominant model of the path in these years was taking regular steps towards a distant goal. This required disciplined practice, and meant renouncing some things and cultivating others. Outsiders sometimes criticized the FWBO as overly masculine, emphasizing effort (*vīrya*) rather than receptivity (*kṣānti*), and in Chapter Seventeen we shall come to some of the problems in the movement's ethos and collective character in this period. But the heroic ideal was only one aspect of the path Sangharakshita presented, and we must turn to an overview of that path that draws out its basic character. To do this, the following chapter picks up a thread that has run through this book: Sangharakshita's organic thinking and his framing of the path as a process of growth and development.

Chapter Twelve

Growth and Development

Growth and the path

The fifth lecture in Sangharakshita's 1971 series on the *White Lotus Sutra*[1] begins by evoking the efflorescence that occurs when the monsoon breaks at the end of the Indian hot season:

> Just like magic, the yellow, parched land suddenly becomes entirely green and vegetation of every kind springs up. The rice fields are filled with emerald shoots, and even the most stunted bushes and shrubs burst into leaf. The bamboo and the plantain shoot up inches in a single night. Every shrub, every tree, every bush, every plant, starts to grow.[2]

This seemingly miraculous change is the inspiration for the 'Parable of the Raincloud', which likens rain pouring from the sky to the Buddha's teaching, and the 'Parable of the Sun', which represents the Buddha as the sun and the plants that spring up as the beings who respond to the teaching. The meaning of the parables, says Sangharakshita, is that Dharma practice means growth.

These images inspire a cascade of associations: the Buddha's vision of humanity as lotuses in various stages of unfoldment, which lies behind the imagery, and even the title of the *White Lotus Sutra*; the lotuses representing the chakras in Tibetan tantra; and the three lotuses held by the bodhisattva White Tārā, which 'represent the process of growth and unfoldment which is the spiritual life'.[3] All of them present the Dharma as a natural source of nourishment, fostering individuals in distinctive ways. This is the spirit of the path, and it is more fundamental than the divisions between Buddhist schools, between reason and emotion, or between religion and secularism:

> What really matters is to feel, through the concepts, through the images and symbolism, that which informs and gives life to them all – the experience of emancipation from all conditions whatsoever. In other words, we are trying to feel at least to some degree the absolute consciousness of the Buddha, the Enlightened consciousness from which all the teachings originally came.[4]

* * *

As we saw in Chapter Five, from early in his Buddhist career Sangharakshita connected the Buddhist path with the image of a growing plant, and in Chapter Nine we saw that *A Survey of Buddhism* uses the analogy with a living organism to describe the pattern of Buddhist history. The *Survey*'s account of conditionality is more abstract and principial, but, by the time Sangharakshita wrote *The Three Jewels* five years later, the analogy between progressive conditionality and organic growth was explicit:

> Human life represents a transformation of energy in dependence on which any other transformation of energy, mundane or transcendental, can arise. [...] As when a seed produces a flower, or when rough ore is smelted into gold and the refined metal wrought into an ornament, a number of intermediate steps connect the beginning with the end of the process. In the case of conditioned sentient existence the transformation takes place through the operation of the laws in accordance with which individualized consciousness determines being [...] the intermediate steps being set forth in the negative and positive counterparts of the twelve *nidānas*.[5]

The comparison of the 'spiral' *nidāna*s with a living process depends on the nature of the causality they describe. It isn't mechanistic causation in which 'a' causes 'b', like one billiard ball hitting another; instead, 'b' arises in dependence upon 'a': it emerges naturally when the conditions are right, just as a plant grows from a seed that is fed and watered. In 1969 Sangharakshita defined 'spiritual development' (a synonym for 'spiritual growth') as 'a type of dependent origination or conditionality',[6] and in the 1970s he would often speak of the path as a process of organic growth, without explaining the conceptual underpinning. He comments on the *Udāna* passage comparing the Dharma to the ocean:

> You could say that the concept of becoming liberated is contained in the concept of growth and development [...] the Dharma has one flavour, the flavour of growth and development.[7]

In the 1966 lecture 'The Stages of the Spiritual Path' (later incorporated into *What Is the Dharma?*), Sangharakshita says spiritual life 'unfolds' in accordance with conditionality:

> Just as out of the bud grows the flower, and out of the flower the fruit, so out of one spiritual experience there grows another, out of that yet another, and out of that another still, each one higher, more refined, more beautiful, a little nearer to Nirvāṇa. Each stage is a spiritual experience in the process of transition to another, more advanced experience. The stages aren't fixed or static; you don't proceed up the spiral path like going up the steps of a staircase, even a spiral staircase. [...] The path itself grows, just as a plant grows, one stage passing over into the next so that there's a constant upward movement.[8]

Sangharakshita's suggestion is that we come close to understanding the path if we envisage it in these terms. It isn't something to be grasped conceptually: the image of a growing plant can help us imagine it.

* * *

The language of growth was everywhere in Sangharakshita's teaching after his return to the UK. He said in a 1979 talk introducing the FWBO:

Buddhism is simply whatever helps that individual to grow, whatever helps him or her to develop from lower to higher levels of being and consciousness. At the same time, the Dharma does not represent just a vague general principle of growth; it is embodied in specific spiritual practices.[9]

The 1975 poem 'Four Gifts' encapsulates the FWBO's message in four images. The first is the lotus, which, Sangharakshita comments, represents 'the whole process of human development', including the experience of growth and the conditions that support it:

The plant needs soil, air, water, and space in which to grow. In the same way, human beings need to be rooted. They need to have the light of friendliness or compassion shining on them and giving them support.[10]

The 1975 lecture 'The Path of Regular and Irregular Steps' contrasts the model of growth with that of buddha nature, concluding that, if we do use this language, we should recall buddha nature is described as a seed: '[F]rom the seed comes forth a little shoot, which grows into a stem, from which leaves and finally buds and flowers are produced.'[11] Regular practice, Sangharakshita says, is like the steady growth of a plant, and ethics, meditation, and wisdom are 'natural stages in the spiritual and transcendental development of the individual'. Believing we are already enlightened is like trying to make a plant grow by forcibly opening the tiny buds with one's fingers, or building a house without foundations:

Instead of pulling open the buds one has to water the roots. One doesn't start building anything until one has dug the foundations. As Buddhists, the flower that we want to see blooming is the thousand-petalled lotus itself, so plenty of water is needed. The tower we want to build is the tower that reaches up into the very heavens, so a very firm foundation is required.[12]

The following year, 1976, Sangharakshita gave a lecture entitled 'Enlightenment as Experience and Non-Experience', which situates these ideas within a cultural context. The modern condition, he says, is one in which

> we gradually lose contact with our feelings; when we lose contact with our feelings we lose contact with ourselves; and when we lose contact with ourselves we lose contact with life.[13]

The mechanical repetitions of modern society produce a compulsive desire for consumption and diversion, and the same tendencies shape our view of Enlightenment. We value exoticism, project inflated qualities onto guru figures, and fixate upon techniques, making Enlightenment an experience to be possessed. But that's like tying a flower to a dying plant that has been stolen from somebody else's garden.

Sangharakshita suggests three alternatives. We can approach Enlightenment as 'work', as 'duty', and as a process of growth:

> The process is absolutely continuous. Growth doesn't lie only at the end of the process; if we are working our way up we are growing. All such effort is growth. We may say that the spiritual life, the Path, is like the plant, and Enlightenment, the goal, is like the flower. In one sense, of course, the flower is separate from the plant. However, in another sense the flower is part of the plant, the natural product of the plant, the culmination of its growth.[14]

Like a plant, a spiritual life requires conditions that support development, and through these years Sangharakshita said a great deal about what these conditions entail. Some were internal, concerning mental states and attitudes; others more external, including friendship, communication, and a conducive lifestyle. The FWBO was attempting to create supportive conditions, including communal living and working situations, and Sangharakshita envisaged these developments as the basis of a western Buddhist culture that would support the whole breadth of Buddhist practice:

> Buddhism is not just ethics, not just meditation. It is a lot more than these two things, great and important as they are. Buddhism is a doctrine, a teaching, even a philosophy. It is a whole series of great myths. It is a body of legends. It is a complex of social institutions. It is a regular pattern of festivals and celebrations. It is a treasure-house of the arts. It is ritual. It is work.[15]

What Sangharakshita meant by 'growth' differed from what it meant within humanistic psychology and the looser Human Potential Movement. In the 1970 talk 'Buddhism versus Psychotherapy', Sangharakshita acknowledges the commonalities but emphasizes the differences:

> So far as Buddhism is concerned, meditation forms part of a complete and coherent system of spiritual self-development. It is one stage on a path leading from a state of ignorance to Enlightenment, from simple consciousness to absolute consciousness. Moreover this system, or this path, represents the direct practical application to human existence of a whole philosophy of existence, a total view of reality.[16]

This aligned spiritual development with the underlying nature of existence and especially the principle of conditionality. It followed that the process of development was patterned.

The system of practice

Unlike most Buddhist teachers of his generation, after the FWBO's early years Sangharakshita didn't focus on leading meditation retreats. The path he presented included many elements – of which meditation was just one (albeit an important one) – that aligned his approach with the texts he explored in his lectures and seminars. Formal meditation was part of his own practice, but so was reading sutras, writing, friendship, and much else. In later life, visitors would find him sitting quietly, perhaps gazing out of his window, not reading and, seemingly, not even thinking – at the centre of a strong and distinctive atmosphere.

Despite not leading meditation retreats, Sangharakshita guided Order members personally and spoke extensively about meditation, often embedding what he had to say in his presentation of the path as a whole.[17] If the path was a process of organic development, meditation was 'a means of personal development':

> We want to grow [...] simply because we are living beings. Every living being wants to fulfil the law of its own nature, which is to develop. We want to actualize our own deepest potential, to become what we really are, to achieve in time what we are in eternity.[18]

In 1978, a decade after the Order's establishment, Sangharakshita clarified the connections between the practices he had taught in a talk to Order members entitled 'A System of Meditation'. He used the word 'system' advisedly, alert to its mechanistic connotations, insisting he meant 'an organic, living system', not something 'dead, mechanical, artificially created'.[19] The four main elements are integration, positive emotion, spiritual death, and spiritual rebirth, while a fifth element, the just-sitting practice, accompanies and balances each stage. The stages are both progressive and themes to which the practitioner must keep returning, and Sangharakshita returned to the 'system' at the end of his life when he presented it as the pattern of spiritual life. With Sangharakshita's blessing, Subhuti renamed it a 'system of Dharma life'.

Integration
As a meditation instructor, Sangharakshita shared practices that had been important for him, and as a Dharma teacher he generalized their significance. Stationed in Singapore in 1945, he learned a form of the *ānāpāna-sati*, or mindfulness of breathing, from the Theravādin monk Soma Thera. Returning to his barracks, he sat beneath a mosquito net and practised what he had learned:

> My mind became at first buoyant, then filled with peace and purity, and finally penetrated by a 'quintessential, keen, ethereal bliss' that was so intense I had to break off the practice.[20]

For a decade, the mindfulness of breathing was the 'sheet anchor' of his spiritual life, and, in the 'System of Meditation' talk, he spoke of it as the meditation practice that exemplified the larger process of integration.

Sangharakshita's accounts of integration often began by describing ordinary consciousness as an array of often conflicting selves that must be brought together. He said the conflict between Sangharakshita I and Sangharakshita II had prompted him to think in these terms, and resolving it meant integrating two competing aspects of his character.[21] Failing to become integrated, he thought, left important aspects of experience untouched by the Dharma, and liable to exert a 'gravitational pull' away from the path.[22] Resolving inner conflicts aligned psychic and emotional energies so they could be directed to the path. To be integrated in this way was to become an individual. Such a person, he said, is self-aware and emotionally positive, takes responsibility for their actions, and is sensitive, intelligent, creative, spontaneous, independent, receptive, imaginative, and faithful.[23]

Concentrating the mind in meditation is a 'direct method' because it works directly on the mind and, practised effectively, integrates 'our total being, conscious and unconscious, intellectual and emotional'.[24] In almost all cases Sangharakshita thought it needed the support of 'indirect methods of development', including a conducive lifestyle, devotional ritual, and Dharma study. Physical practices like yoga and T'ai Chi guarded against the 'alienated awareness' he had observed at the Hampstead Vihara. They supported an 'integrated awareness' that meant

> learning to experience yourself more fully, to be more aware of what you experience in your physical body, and in your feelings and emotions, particularly those feelings that you like to think you don't experience.[25]

Becoming whole and reclaiming disowned aspects of experience countered the alienating influence of a culture that, he said, lacked 'stable, universally accepted values' and encouraged people to repress emotions and bodily sensations.[26] For most people, integrated awareness therefore required a community, especially a sangha, in which individual experience could be acknowledged with emotional positivity. Sangharakshita called this 'horizontal integration', but becoming whole, individual, and truly human also involved 'vertical integration'.

Sangharakshita discussed these ideas many times, with variations and some inconsistencies in his terminology. Horizontal integration in meditation often referred to the act of focusing the mind, though it could also mean the harmonious unfoldment represented by a thousand-petalled lotus:

> [T]he Enlightenment factors can be thought of as emerging like the petals of a flower from the bud. With the unfolding of each petal a state of greater refinement and beauty arises, until eventually all the petals of the flower of Enlightenment stand complete around the centre.[27]

Vertical integration principally meant ascending spiritual heights, particularly through meditative absorption, or *dhyāna*, but doing so required the practitioner to integrate unconscious energies more often associated with the psychic depths. Part One of this book suggested the importance, in this period of Sangharakshita's life, of contacting his own psychic depths, and he repeatedly discussed these themes in the 1969 lecture series 'Aspects of Buddhist Psychology'. 'Repression is no solution', he said in one lecture. 'The shadow must be saturated with awareness and resolved.' We must look at the shadow, 'recognize it, accept it, and transmute it into what the Tantric tradition calls a guardian'.[28]

The main reason for integrating the depths, in Sangharakshita's understanding, is that doing so makes the heights accessible. He said in another talk from 1969:

> Buddhists are more concerned with the heights than with the depths of the mind. Buddhism envisages heights of mind beyond mind with a view to climbing those heights – that is, with the expansion of awareness beyond its present upper limits to ever higher spheres of consciousness. And the way this is achieved – according to all schools of Buddhism – is

through the practice of meditation. In fact, meditation may be defined, for general purposes, as the systematic expansion of awareness or consciousness.[29]

He later suggested that the depths could be seen as the buried counterpart of the heights:

When experienced as rising from the depths, the forces of inspiration seem to bring us up with them; when experienced as descending from the heights, they seem to bend down and catch us up to their exalted level. In either case, the experience is the same – we are lifted to a higher level.[30]

A talk on 'The Mandala: Tantric Symbol of Integration' suggests the need for 'some third, reconciling factor, something that will combine the clarity, sharpness, and crystalline purity of the conscious mind with the richness and colour of the unconscious'. This is the function of mandalas and buddha figures:

They represent a resolution, or at least the beginnings of a resolution, of the conflict between the conscious and the unconscious, a reintegration of the psyche on higher and higher levels in which nothing is left out, no element is excluded or repressed, everything finds its place in a complete, harmonious, organized, and unified pattern.[31]

Integrating the different aspects of experience makes it possible to access 'higher states of awareness, new levels of consciousness'.[32] Traditional accounts of mindfulness, for example, usually speak of developing the four *satipaṭṭhānas*, meaning four different areas of experience (body, feeling, mind states, and *dhamma*s), but Sangharakshita integrates this into a developmental scheme that presents awareness of things, oneself, others, and reality as four ascending 'levels of awareness'.[33] Similarly, he identifies levels of meditative consciousness in various ways, especially through his presentation of the *dhyānas*.

Levels of experience

The combination of horizontal and vertical elements in Sangharakshita's teaching reflects his underlying model of experience. To be wholly integrated means engaging the various aspects of life at all levels. What we experience at a lower level corresponds with a higher level, as a seed corresponds to a plant, and its meaning is only fulfilled through the plant's development:

> just as the lotus consists of many layers of petals, some without, some within, so both the universe and the individual consist of many different layers, many different levels, some lower and others higher. So in this way the lotus comes to represent the whole process of development, of unfoldment stage by stage, level by level, degree by degree, from the bottom to the top – development both cosmic and human.[34]

Sangharakshita thought Buddhists too often observed the outer form of Buddhist teachings while ignoring their inner meaning, and, conversely, that by looking into basic teachings more fully we could recognize ascending levels of their meaning and significance. He presents friendship, meditation, sangha, engagement with the arts and imagination, and other practices as paths that can be undertaken at different levels. The most prominent example, in relation to which he works out the basic pattern, is his exploration of the levels of going for refuge. The *Survey* already recognized that the external observance that made one nominally a Buddhist in fact contained much more:

> effective refuge, of which the formal refuge is at once the expression and the symbol, can be taken only by one who has an understanding of the true nature of the Triple Gem. [...] Taking refuge in the Triple Gem is not, therefore, an act to be done once and for all time, but something which grows with one's understanding of Buddhism. The refuge is complete when one's understanding of Buddhism is complete, that is to say, when one attains Enlightenment.[35]

The 1978 talk 'Levels of Going for Refuge' calls nominal going for refuge the 'cultural' level, after which come 'provisional, effective, real, ultimate, and cosmic' levels. Effective going for refuge means 'actually committing oneself to the Three Jewels';[36] real going for refuge occurs with stream entry or the arising of the bodhicitta; and ultimate or absolute going for refuge is equivalent to full Awakening. In this way, going for refuge is 'not simply a devotional practice. It's not even just a threefold act of individual spiritual commitment. The Going for Refuge is the key to the mystery of existence itself.'[37]

Positive emotion

The second stage of the system is positive emotion, a quality that was present in Sangharakshita's love for nature, his affection for people, and the heartfelt devotion to Buddhist ideals of his youthful poetry. The *mettābhāvanā*, or 'development of loving kindness' practice, which he had learned in the 1950s, epitomized positive emotion. The *mettābhāvanā* and similar compassion-based practices are common within Buddhism, but Sangharakshita emphasized it far more than most other teachers of Theravādin meditation practices. Returning to England in 1964, he was shocked to find how 'negative', 'alienated', and 'neurotic' many British Buddhists were, and he was determined to make the FWBO different. He introduced puja (devotional practice) as a means to developing positive emotion, and encouraged friendship and altruistic activity. '[T]he more we progress in our individual growth and development', he says in one commentary, 'the more positive and creative will be our effect on everyone with whom we come into contact'.[38]

Positive emotion is the affective counterpart of positive, or progressive, conditionality. Sangharakshita says in his commentary on the *Udāna*:

> Without a basis of emotional positivity, very little spiritual
> development is possible, so it is very important indeed
> to stress those aspects of the teaching that encourage the
> development of positive states of consciousness, especially the
> series of positive *nidānas*: faith, joy, rapture, bliss, and so on.

> We must have a strong emphasis on the emotionally positive
> – not just a theoretical emphasis, but the actual generation
> of positive emotional states – otherwise we will not get very
> far.[39]

Positive emotion, we might say, is what it feels like to follow the spiral path:

> Positive emotion, whether it is devotion or *mettā* or anything
> else, is expansive by its very nature. If one's sense of devotion
> is not broadening its scope, it is thus not really a positive
> emotion at all. Like *mettā*, its tendency is to become universal.
> *Mettā* should go on expanding, renewing itself, growing
> brighter and stronger as it does so. If it really is *mettā* you are
> feeling, you will never feel you have had enough.[40]

Sangharakshita wanted the FWBO to be a practical expression of positive emotion. He considered friendship the proper basis of sangha – 'the soil from which you grow and develop' – while the kindness of others is 'like the sunshine that stimulates your growth'.[41] 'Positive emotion', he told Order members in the 1978 'System of Meditation' talk, 'is the lifeblood of the Order. If there's no positive emotion in the Order, there's no life in it at all.'[42]

Sangharakshita believed that, like integration, *mettā* could be experienced at different levels. Along with ethics, mindfulness and *mettā* are the basis of the path Sangharakshita taught, and he asked people to become established in them before taking on other practices:

> If we are dissatisfied with the *mettā bhāvanā*, to ask for higher
> and more advanced practices is self-defeating. Naturally we
> would like something different for the sheer novelty of it, and
> we may even persuade ourselves that we are ready for more
> advanced training. [...] It probably means that we have not
> prepared for the practice adequately, or that we need to be
> more imaginative, perhaps more intuitive or devotional in our
> practice.[43]

But he believed *mettā* could lead to insight, and what he said about it mirrors his account of the bodhicitta and looks ahead to his account of *dharma-niyama* as a mode of existence that becomes available when ego-clinging is abandoned:

> The Stream Entrant *lives* his or her knowledge, experiencing it in the form of a fully developed positivity. [...] As our capacity for positive emotion grows stronger, self-reference becomes ever more difficult to detect, because it becomes harder for us to tell just where the boundaries of the self lie.[44]

Spiritual death and spiritual rebirth
With the third and fourth stages, spiritual death and spiritual rebirth, the system of meditation overtly reflects the cycles of nature. Sangharakshita learned insight, or vipassanā, practices from Yogi Chen in the early 1960s and passed them on to Order members who already had a grounding in the mindfulness of breathing and the *mettābhāvanā*. It is not enough to think solely in terms of steady growth:

> If one thinks in terms of growth and development, then one has to think in terms of a growth and development from which one does not fall back. You don't want to have this week a spiritual development which you lose next week. But so long as your experience is confined to *dhyāna* or *samādhi* this is in fact what happens. The only thing that can fix the development, the only thing that can make it permanent, is insight.[45]

In the natural world, growth depends on death, and this is how Sangharakshita speaks of the process of spiritual death and rebirth in 'Transformation of Life and World in the *Sutra of Golden Light*', his lecture series given in 1976 on this Mahāyāna text:

> [I]f we allow ourselves to think and feel deeply, this is surely what we are looking for: to die and be reborn – but not necessarily in the flesh. What we seek is a withering of the roots of our being and a truly radical rebirth [...] to emerge

like a butterfly from the chrysalis of all our old conditions
into an entirely new life of greater freedom and joy, greater
awareness and spontaneity.[46]

This primal human wish is at the heart of Buddhism:

[E]very Buddhist scripture is a Book of the Dead, because
the whole purpose of any Buddhist scripture is to act as the
agent of transformation. That's what it's there for. If we're not
prepared to die, we cannot become a bodhisattva.[47]

The most important insight practice in Sangharakshita's teaching is the contemplation of the six elements, which he learned from Yogi Chen in Kalimpong. It involves seeing the aliveness of the elements within our experience, and then recognizing their impermanence and ungraspability. That shows the place of spiritual death within an experience of life:

[T]he touch of reality on the conditioned self [...] feels like
death. In fact, for the conditioned self it *is* death. [...] When
you see the truth you die, as it were; or perhaps one could say
that when you die, you see the truth.[48]

Theravādin formulations of the path conclude at this point, using the language of cessation as an equivalent term to 'spiritual death'. But the thrust of Sangharakshita's work is that this is inadequate. In the realm of spiritual experience, something follows spiritual death, as spring follows winter in the natural world. This is the glorious existence celebrated in the Mahāyāna as the bodhisattva path and the enlightened qualities embodied in buddha and bodhisattva figures. For this reason, the 1978 'System of Meditation' talk relates spiritual rebirth to *sādhana* practice, meaning meditation on a buddha or bodhisattva. Within *sādhana*, Sangharakshita said:

out of the experience of the death of the mundane self the
transcendental self arises [...] in the midst of the sky – in the
midst of the Void – where we see a lotus flower. On the lotus

flower there is a seed in the form of a letter. This letter is what we call a *bīja* mantra. This *bīja* mantra is transformed into a particular Buddha or Bodhisattva figure.[49]

Because it depends on the progressive trend in conditionality, the whole path is, from one perspective, a process of spiritual rebirth. When obstacles have been removed, illusions shattered, and unskilfulness abandoned or purified, progressive conditionality can express itself freely in the operation of the creative mind.

The 'System of Meditation' talk also mentions the just-sitting practice as a balance to more active practices. Within a buddha-nature approach, 'formless' practices such as Mahāmudrā, Dzogchen, and zazen are important, but Sangharakshita didn't want to formulate or conceptualize receptive awareness as if it were an activity in its own right. He saw it as the completion, or absorption, of the prior stages. He would simply say: 'Don't try to make an effort and don't try not to make an effort.'[50]

The late papers

The late papers bring together Sangharakshita's formulations of the path into a comprehensive 'system of Dharma life' that integrates his understanding of *karma-niyama* and *dharma-niyama* with the system of meditation. The stages of integration and positive emotion both engage the *karma-niyama* processes in the sense that they describe what happens when we act as 'responsible ethical agents' and foster skilful states. This is especially clear in the stage of positive emotion:

> One will experience deeper and richer states of consciousness emerging – not merely at the time of meditation. One will have a more abiding sense of satisfaction and self-confidence, one will feel a deeper harmony with others and a stronger sympathy, one will have a more subtle aesthetic sensibility, one will dwell more frequently in dhyana.[51]

Positive emotion allows the sense of self to become more fluid, lessening the sense of separation from others. This goes much further when we renounce 'the illusion of an independent self' in the stage of spiritual death, which allows space for 'a new order of conditionality' – the *dharma-niyama* – that functions beyond our willing. Spiritual rebirth follows:

> The Stage of Spiritual Rebirth trains us to 'revere and rely upon' the *dharma-niyama* completely, resting in it as what unfolds within us when we give up our self-attachment. It means allowing a new supra-personal motive force to operate through us, now that we have relinquished self-referent willing.[52]

The final stage, here called 'The Stage of No Practice', means 'allowing the evolutionary trend to unfold naturally within one, without any effort to bring anything into being'.[53] This completes Sangharakshita's sense of the path as a balance of complementary practices that can be experienced at ascending levels:

> Sangharakshita sees the elements of the system not only arranged hierarchically and sequentially as *stages* of the spiritual path, but also as *aspects* of Dharma practice, all of which must be engaged with at each and every such stage and thereby brought to perfection at the highest stages.[54]

Chapter Thirteen
Wider Contexts

The Higher Evolution

If Sangharakshita taught a path of spiritual development that could be divided into distinct stages, he also viewed it in relation to its 'wider contexts'. *The History of My Going for Refuge* lists three – 'the social or communal, the higher-evolutionary, and the cosmic':[1]

> Between the act of Going for Refuge and the context within which it takes place there is an organic connection – a connection which I tried to express [...] by speaking of the individual who goes for Refuge as being himself a part of the common framework within which he and others go for Refuge.[2]

The 'social' context is sangha, in the sense of a 'spiritual community' to which we will return in a later chapter. As we have seen, Sangharakshita thought the spiritual vitality of an effective sangha could only come from '(true) individuals, or those who are self-conscious, independent, sensitive, emotionally positive, responsible, and creative'.[3] These individuals act together not as a 'group' but guided by something else, perhaps 'a third order of consciousness' – for which there is no adequate expression, at least in English – that surpasses the consciousness of both the group and the individual. In this way, a sangha exists on several levels, the highest of which can only be expressed symbolically, perhaps as the Thousand-Armed Avalokiteśvara.

The second context is the Higher Evolution, which had been one of the central themes of Sangharakshita's teaching in the early years of the FWBO and located personal growth within the development of life as a whole. Thinkers like Kant and Goethe, and then the German and English Romantics, had prepared the way for evolution to be seen as an overarching theory of life that combined spiritual life with biology. Following the publication of Darwin's *Origin of Species* in 1859, many religious and spiritual thinkers connected his theory of evolution with their own messages. Mme Blavatsky declared in *Isis Unveiled* (1877) that the evolution of monkeys into men was merely a precursor to the evolution of men into higher beings, and she enlisted ancient 'wisdom traditions', including Buddhism, into a theory that embraced evolution in 'both the physical and spiritual aspects'.[4]

Blavatsky's book affected Sangharakshita in various ways, but the idea of higher evolution remained below the surface of his thoughts.[5] One early essay suggests that the teaching of *anatta* 'implies the possibility of endless spiritual evolution',[6] and *The Three Jewels* speaks of 'the Higher Evolution from a mundane to a transcendental consciousness'.[7] On returning to England and finding himself in a predominantly secular culture, Sangharakshita wondered if traditional, 'religious' terms would constrain the Dharma's message, and whether sticking to them was 'unimaginative and unrealistic'.[8] He was wearily familiar with rationalized, western accounts of Buddhism that stripped away ritual and the transcendent dimension of experience. He wanted something else, and, writing in 1971 to R.C. Zaehner, the author of *Evolution in Religion*,[9] he described the development of his thoughts. The starting point for his thoughts was the teaching of conditionality, which, he said, he had come to understand as including the progressive *nidāna*s and a path of development. Next, he recognized that the path 'consisted of a sequence of psychological and spiritual experiences', which 'constituted a process of continuous growth and development by which the individual advanced from lower to higher states of being and consciousness'. This process, he thought, could be termed 'an evolution'. Thirdly, having returned to the West, he sought a new way to express Buddhist teachings:

> In 1964, however, having spent twenty years in the East, I returned to England, and soon felt the need, purely as a 'skilful means' (*upāya-kauśalya*), of a principle sufficiently familiar to the modern mind not to require much explanation and capable, at the same time, of being generalized in such a way as to provide a medium for the exposition of Buddhism. One day, while preparing a lecture, it flashed on me that the concept of evolution was such a principle. At once everything fell into place. Science revealed how far man had come. This was the lower evolution. Buddhism, as the Path, showed how far he still had to go. This was the higher evolution. Though not strictly continuous the two phases between them constituted the two halves of a single process. Science and religion, the lower and the higher evolution, were comprehended in one gigantic sweep.[10]

In 1969 and 1970 Sangharakshita gave two series of lectures on the Higher Evolution[11] with the intention of

> laying out the Buddhist system of thought as a whole in terms that should be sufficiently familiar to all of us as a way of looking at the world as not to require much explanation.[12]

He explored the topic in many other lectures in this period, relating it to meditation, culture, and the bodhisattva ideal, and returned to it in the 1983 paper 'The Bodhisattva Principle'.

The Lower Evolution includes biological development on the phylogenic scale, which goes 'from amoeba up to man-like animal', while the Higher Evolution takes the individual 'from animal-like man up to Buddha or Enlightened man'.[13] Human beings governed by the dictates of the Lower Evolution remain in the realm of the group, he says, and are not truly conscious of their motivations and choices. Awareness, and particularly *reflexive awareness*, changes this by introducing the possibility of acting as an individual who takes responsibility for both their actions and their mental states:

in the mind there lies the possibility of a continued development. [...] In a sense, we are mind rather than body, and if our future lies anywhere, it lies in the mind.[14]

Beyond reflexive awareness lie 'transcendental consciousness' and 'the higher spiritual reality that embraces both oneself and all conditioned existence'.[15]

Some more conservative Buddhist teachers criticized Sangharakshita for seemingly abandoning traditional terminology, and scientifically informed students in the FWBO/Triratna have sometimes objected to the use he makes of biology. But this misunderstands his intention:

> The purpose of bringing evolution into a discussion of Buddhism is not so much to explain evolution in spiritual terms as to use the idea of evolution to throw light on the spiritual development of the individual. It is not meant to suggest anything merely scientific, historical, or even religious. It is a way of describing a process within ourselves as individuals. It concerns ourselves as continually growing – *evolving* – beings, as beings who are capable, indeed, of infinite development.[16]

This was a new way to continue what Sangharakshita had been doing throughout his career: expressing the essential message of Buddhism and its meaning for the individual in fresh and effective ways:

> What I have come to call the Higher Evolution represents a complete restatement in contemporary terms of the essentials of the Buddha's teachings. Indeed, we may even claim that in principle it represents a restatement of all that is essential, all that is truly significant, in human culture and religion.[17]

Sangharakshita says in *Living with Awareness*: 'For all human beings, not only saints and sages, the implicit purpose of human existence is to evolve and develop.'[18] In doing so, we participate in a vast process that includes the epochs of biological evolution, and engage the potential for growth that is built into the structure of life. This, he says in *A History of My Going for Refuge*, is Buddhism's true meaning:

> In Buddhism there were many doctrines and disciplines, many moral rules and devotional observances, but they were all secondary. Even meditation was secondary. What was important, for Buddhism, was that man should grow and develop – that he should evolve. Buddhism was not a matter of thinking and knowing, or even of doing, but of being and becoming. In other words, Buddhism was a matter of following the path of the Higher Evolution.[19]

Nietzsche and breaking through
If Romanticism foreshadowed Sangharakshita's ideas about the Higher Evolution, Romanticism itself was a diverse movement, notoriously hard to define with an even more diverse legacy.[20] Sangharakshita's 'favourite modern philosopher',[21] Friedrich Nietzsche, lived two generations after the High Romantics but drew on them in his own, distinctive philosophy, and such was Sangharakshita's inspiration when he first read *Thus Spake Zarathustra* aged eighteen that its words seemed to be 'written across the blue sky in scarlet letters'.[22] Zarathustra famously declares that God is dead, and Nietzsche's subject is finding meaning in a world without God. For Sangharakshita, Nietzsche captured modern man's existential predicament:

> We are on our own, and therefore have to try to understand ourselves afresh. We can't accept ready-made answers any more. We find ourselves here and now, in the midst of the starry universe, standing on the earth, surrounded by other living beings like ourselves, with a history behind us, and perhaps a future before us, and we each have to ask ourselves – not anybody else because there's nobody else to tell us – the crucial question, 'Who am I? What am I?'[23]

Zarathustra descends the mountain to proclaim a new conception of humanity, declaring: 'I teach you the overman ["the *Übermensch*"]. Man is something that shall be overcome.'[24] Stripped of the racial connotations, which Nietzsche didn't intend, the 'overman' or 'superman' represents a stage of evolution beyond ordinary human existence. Sangharakshita equated this with the Buddhist path. That parallels the true individual who has abandoned emotional reactivity, stands apart from the group, and follows the path of the Higher Evolution. The individual represents a new kind of existence: 'As the ape in a sense created human beings, so we ourselves must now create a new kind of being.'[25]

The heroic superhumanity Nietzsche celebrated opposed the Christian embrace of human frailty, rationalized Enlightenment accounts of human meaning, and the Romantic belief in intrinsic human goodness. He rejected all these cultural influences as 'illusions', and his writing attempts to shatter them. Nietzsche's desire for a more primal, pre-Christian mode of experience resonated with Sangharakshita's identification with the timeless spirit that remained once cultural expressions and literalized doctrines were stripped from historical Buddhism. This engaged his prophetic, and even apocalyptic, strain, and the overtly Nietzschean 1969 poem 'New' declares a yearning to start anew:

> New words
> Come to me from the stars
> From your eyes from
> Space
> New words vibrant, radiant, able to utter
> The new me, able
> To build for new
> Men a new world.[26]

Sangharakshita commented that the newness the poem proclaims is 'that which has no connection with time but which irrupts into, or manifests within, the temporal process, from another dimension'. It is the '"Behold, I make all things new" of the Apocalypse'.[27]

A 1969 lecture entitled 'Breaking Through to Buddhahood' proposes an alternative to understanding the path as a process of steady, organic growth. Sometimes, Sangharakshita says, the path is blocked, and we require 'an abrupt transition from one level or dimension of experience, or one mode of being, to another'.²⁸ At such junctures we must break through barriers with forcible effort. One barrier is *negative emotion*, which limits us within 'a cold, hard, tight knot of separate selfhood'; then come psychological conditionings, which make us 'machines rather than human beings'; and a third is the rational mind, at least if it excludes whatever is 'unharnessable, unmanageable, the untamable'. Finally, we must break through the time sense, in the sense of 'clock time', which divides time into seconds, minutes, and hours:

> [I]n this way the natural self-regulating rhythm of the organism is disrupted, and one's experience of organic time, of pure duration, lost. Our life's experiences don't emerge and flower from the depths of the eternal now. We see them strung out, like washing on a line [...] We draw up programmes and diaries and so on because, basically, we don't trust ourselves [...] we feel insecure.²⁹

Breaking through to the newness of 'the eternal now' restores our alignment with life's natural pattern. This matched the countercultural desire for revolutionary alternatives to the *status quo* in the years after 1969 and added a radical edge to Sangharakshita's message:

> Buddhism, properly and deeply understood, and thoroughly and extensively applied, is *revolutionary*. It is revolutionary, that is to say, within the context of the established order. It is in this realization that our breakthrough consists: in the realization of the fact that Buddhism has to transform every aspect of our lives and be not just something that we theoretically understand, not just a little hobby with which we occupy ourselves once or twice a week.³⁰

In an era of student protests and political radicalization, Sangharakshita declared in aphorisms that followed those of Blake and Nietzsche: 'Awareness is revolutionary', and 'The true revolutionary does not play other people's games – including the game of violence.'³¹

Cosmic perspectives

Let me summarize Sangharakshita's understanding as these chapters have traced it. All phenomena exist according to the principle of conditionality, which has two modes – one cyclic and one progressive. Therefore, the progressive trend of conditionality inheres in existence, and it can be expressed in the language of evolution. Buddhist practice means engaging with conditionality in a creative way, and its traditional formulations can be re-expressed as the path of the Higher Evolution. This means the individual's engagement with the path engages them in a universal process. That brings us to the third, 'cosmic' context that Sangharakshita mentions in *The History of My Going for Refuge*. He told Zaehner:

> The Buddhist scriptures, especially those of the Mahāyāna, quite clearly envisage a universe (in the fullest sense of the term) in which, under the guidance of Buddhas and bodhisattvas innumerable, all sentient beings are ultimately destined to Enlightenment. [...] In this sense one may therefore speak of Buddhism as the religion of evolution, of spiritual evolution, on a cosmic scale.[32]

This includes the entire evolutionary process because 'each form of life aspires to develop into the next higher form' and, in that sense, 'all living beings go for Refuge.'[33] One manifestation is the 'law' of karma, or the moral patterning that preserves the universe's ethical equilibrium as an organ preserves the body:

> Perhaps there is something in the world, or in the universe, that is analogous to that subconscious intelligence – a sort of intelligence which is capable of intervening to protect the safety and well-being of the organism (in this case the world or even the cosmos) as a whole.[34]

The processes Sangharakshita later termed the *karma-niyama* were part of his thinking in this sense long before he formulated his full account of the five *niyamas*, and his explorations of the bodhisattva and the bodhicitta included another element before he identified that with the *dharma-niyama*. In the *White Lotus Sutra* series of lectures, Sangharakshita calls the bodhisattva 'one in whom the urge to grow which is present in every living being has become self-conscious'.[35] The bodhicitta represents the full expression of this urge, and, when it arises in an individual, they experience something more than their individual selfhood. The act of going for refuge can therefore be seen as engagement in a much larger process, meaning that 'the individual's act of Going for Refuge takes place within the cosmic *bodhicitta* and, therefore, within the wider context of the bodhisattva ideal in the broadest sense.'[36] Sangharakshita therefore comes to speak of 'cosmic going for refuge'.

The 1983 paper *The Bodhisattva Principle: Key to the Evolution of Consciousness, Individual and Collective* begins with a call, in the spirit of the Romantics, to restore a perspective on life that supports a sense of meaning and purpose:

> If we are not to become the hapless victims of destructiveness
> without limit, power without restraint, and chaos without
> end, we shall need a richer and more abundant creativity,
> a purer and more ardent love, and a more harmonious and
> stable order, than the world has ever known before.[37]

While Sangharakshita doesn't suggest that Buddhism alone can supply these needs, he says it recognizes the principle on which a solution depends. This is 'the principle of perpetual self-transcendence', or 'the Bodhisattva Principle' that is woven into the texture of reality:

> Buddhism sees in the figure of the bodhisattva the highest
> embodiment of that urge to Enlightenment which is
> immanent in all forms and spheres of life. That urge becomes
> conscious, so to speak, in the process of the Higher Evolution,
> which in turn finds its fullest and clearest expression in
> the path, particularly in that part of it which consists of the
> development or evolution of consciousness. [...] In terms of
> Western thought, the bodhisattva principle is the principle
> of perpetual self-transcendence. Self-transcendence is the

ultimate nature of Higher Evolution and Lower Evolution alike. Self-transcendence is the ultimate nature of existence.[38]

This resounding declaration of faith expands Sangharakshita's understanding of organic growth to cosmic proportions. He said relatively little about these topics in the following decades, but the late papers return to them.

Evolution and the *niyamas*

The scope of Sangharakshita's ideas about evolution and spiritual life reflects the universal scope of conditionality, and the *niyamas* identify ascending levels at which conditionality operates. The lower *niyamas* describe the physical and biological processes of the Lower Evolution, while the Higher Evolution depends initially on *karmic* effort and later upon *dharma-niyama*. As Subhuti says, Sangharakshita sees this progression as 'a continuous sweep' of conditionality in different modes and phases, the common element being 'an upward momentum, lifting on to the next level'.[39] This 'always possible upward momentum' in the whole of existence is cosmic going for refuge.

Subhuti acknowledges that these are unwieldy ideas that raise the questions that accompany any universal, metaphysical point. Sangharakshita combined their sweep with respect for the Buddha's metaphysical reticence and an acute awareness of the indefinability of reality. *Revering and Relying upon the Dharma* comments that there is no need to speculate about why things function according to conditionality or why conditionality works in particular ways:

> All we are required to say is that we can observe, directly and by reliable report, regularities in the world around us and within us that do enable a progression from simpler to more complex and sensitive organisms and onward to higher human states, if not further.[40]

The *niyamas* express an impulse to growth that we can observe in the organic realm and experience personally:

> What one feels as an urge within oneself is not merely accidental. It is a trend, even a momentum, within things that now emerges in one's own consciousness. The universe cooperates with you in your efforts to follow the Path – or, rather, your own conscious efforts cooperate with the evolutionary trend in the universe.[41]

The teaching of the *niyama*s, organic thinking, and even the principle of conditionality are all ways of approaching a mystery, not literal expressions of the truth. Sangharakshita said as much in *The Bodhisattva Ideal*:

> one sees that in reality there is no conditionality, no causality, and one is able to face up to this fact even though it goes against all one's suppositions. One sees the whole of existence as being like a mirage, not really coming into existence and therefore not really going out of existence either. And what seals the genuine mystery of this realization is that one is all the more compassionate for it.[42]

Nonetheless, to approach the mystery we must envisage it in some way. For Sangharakshita, one way to do this is to approach the Dharma as a living force pulsing through the universe and echoing in our spiritual lives. Another way is to reflect on its embodiment, especially in the figure of the Buddha.

Chapter Fourteen

Imagining the Buddha

Meeting the Buddha

Among the many books that Sangharakshita planned but never wrote was a life of the Buddha based on Pāli sources. His approach would have been 'both philosophical and devotional', and brought together

> the historical Buddha and the legendary or archetypal Buddha in such a way that the reader would see and feel them as the mundane and transcendental aspects of a single undivided personality.[1]

Even without the book, we have many lectures and seminars and a great deal of writing about the Buddha that present the same 'doubleness of aspect'.

The Discourses, which Sangharakshita read from his teenage years in the often-ponderous Pāli Text Society translations, are our source for understanding the historical Buddha. The texts range from simple accounts in collections like the *Udāna* and the *Sutta Nipāta* to the lengthy suttas of the *Dīgha Nikāya*. In the latter, teachings are more abstract and conceptualized, and the mythology is more elaborate. Influenced by historical scholarship, Sangharakshita identified the simpler teachings as an earlier stratum and therefore closer to the Buddha himself. The interpretative principle he eventually formulated was: 'the more abstract the mode of expression the less authentic it is in expressing the Buddha's teaching, and the more concrete the more authentic.'[2]

As he reread the Discourses to write *The Eternal Legacy* in the early 1960s, Sangharakshita found a very different figure from the saint or bhikkhu conventionally depicted in Buddhist art as 'well-groomed, clad in brand-new yellow robes, and carrying an embroidered shoulder bag'. Sangharakshita envisaged a figure closer to the Hindu sadhus he had met on his travels: 'unshaven, clad in ragged, dust-stained garments'.³ A poem from 1961 evokes this version:

> Lean, strenuous, resolute, He passed His days
> Trudging in dust-stained clouts the forest paths;
> Stood as a beggar at the beggar's door
> For alms, and more than kingly, spoke with kings.

But this figure had been buried beneath layers of conventional religiosity:

> They carved Him out of sandal, chipped from stone
> The Ever-moving, cast in rigid bronze
> Him Who was Life itself, and made Him sit,
> Hands idly folded, for a thousand years
> Immobile in the incensed image-house;
> They gilded Him till He was sick with gold.⁴

Sangharakshita also rejected the romanticized images of the Buddha as 'a ghostly figure in a yellow sheet gliding around India and gently rebuking people for not being kind to animals'.⁵ The 1969 lecture 'The Heroic Ideal in Buddhism' praises Mathura depictions of the Buddha as 'a powerfully-built man in the prime of life, firmly erect, like a great tower or a massive tree'.⁶ This embodied the determination he thought was 'intrinsic to the quest for Enlightenment' and 'at the very core of the essential nature of the Buddha'.⁷

Sangharakshita understood that the way we envisage the Buddha shapes our understanding of the path. He was particularly drawn to the start of the Buddha's career, as depicted in the *Udāna*, which presents the Buddha as the meditating holy man who has burned up all his impurities and is glowing with spiritual heat and no doubt giving off spiritual light as well, who is absorbed in the *dhyānas*, who is seeing things as they really are, and whose doubts, therefore, have vanished.[8]

This is 'pre-Buddhistic Buddhism', a time when '[t]he Buddha, out of the depths of his own experience, is just represented as using ordinary language to explain to himself, as it were, what is happening.'[9] These early expressions describe the basic elements of the Buddha's experience. These include the process of conditionality, but even the simplest formulations, as Sangharakshita remarks in the *Survey*, are 'symbolical merely, reflecting, as though through darkness well-nigh impenetrable, only a faint glimmer of the infinite light of his realization'.[10]

Sangharakshita commented in 1966:

> Buddhism is essentially trying to communicate a mystery, the mystery of the Buddha's Enlightenment, to unenlightened human beings, in such a way we can participate in it to the measure of our capacity.[11]

On the other side is the individual Buddhist who looks up to the Buddha, aspires to reach buddhahood and senses that, in their depths, they are already connected to it. To approach that realization, or to feel its echo in ourselves, Sangharakshita suggests, we need myths and symbols as well as concepts. In the decade after 1964 his accounts of the Buddha presented him as a figure with human, symbolic, and archetypal dimensions. The 1967 lecture 'Archetypal Symbolism in the Biography of the Buddha', for example, retells the story of Māra, his daughters, and the demon army that assails the Buddha on the eve of his Enlightenment. Sangharakshita interprets these figures as 'the unregenerate forces of the unconscious mind, the passions and cravings that swirl about in the pit of the unconscious'.[12] The Buddha's triumph over Māra, he says, represents the integration of these forces, and the serpent-king Mucalinda, who winds his coils around the Buddha in the weeks after his Awakening, embodies its effect. The legends express a 'poetic, imaginative, even spiritual truth':

> We have to take in these archetypal symbols, open ourselves to them, listen to them, and allow them to speak to us in their own way, especially to our unconscious depths. We have not just to think about them, but to experience them, assimilate them if we can, and eventually allow them to transform our whole lives.[13]

The three bodies

The account of the Buddha in *A Survey of Buddhism* stresses that, even in the Discourses, the Buddha has a timeless aspect. A lineage of previous buddhas stands behind him, and his appearance in recorded history is the fruit of innumerable previous lives. He embodies the eternal Dharma, which 'is new only in the sense that it is never out of date', and his human biography is 'the story of the mystic marriage of the human and the divine, the individual and the universal, the terrestrial and the cosmic, the immanent urge and the transcendental ideal'.[14] Unless we see this, we will not see the Buddha:

> we may have faith in Gautama the Rationalist, or in Gautama the Reformer, and so on, but faith in Gautama the *Buddha* we shall not have, though it is faith in this sense alone that conduces to Enlightenment.[15]

The Mahāyāna *trikāya* doctrine offered a framework for perceiving the Buddha, in all his dimensions. Without understanding this teaching, Sangharakshita remarks in *The Three Jewels*, 'the *raison d'être* of much that is most precious in the tradition is likely to remain obscure.'[16] The teaching distinguishes three aspects, or 'bodies', of the Buddha. The first is the *nirmāṇakāya*, and at this level the Buddha appears as a being in the world, but this is merely the outward expression of a spiritual reality that is more fully expressed in a visionary level called the *sambhogakāya*. The highest truth, the *dharmakāya*, is beyond representation altogether.

In one sense, this teaching is metaphysical, but Sangharakshita was most concerned with what it offered the person wanting to perceive the Buddha more deeply. *The Three Jewels* calls it 'an attempt to explain systematically the deepening spiritual experience of the devotee of the Buddha in his quest for absolute reality'.[17] The three bodies represent ascending truths that become accessible as our perception expands:

> the ordinary man, the yogi, and one possessing *prajñā* all see the same Buddha. All see the *dharmakāya*. But so gross is the ordinary man's perception, so darkened his mind by unwholesome emotions and erroneous views, that, like one almost totally blind who sees instead of the sun only a faint glimmer of light, he sees not the *dharmakāya* but the *nirmāṇakāya*.[18]

This mirrors Blake's fourfold vision, the ascending spheres of Neoplatonism, and the hierarchy of eyes mentioned in the Buddhist commentaries. By contemplating the lower levels, the practitioner can perceive the higher truth they intimate. As Sangharakshita writes in the *Survey*:

> [W]e stand face to face with the Buddha not only when we perceive his *nirmāṇakāya*, or physical body, but also when, through the exercise of imagination or by the practice of meditation, we are able to behold, not with a fleshly but with a spiritual eye, his body of glory or *sambhogakāya*.[19]

The Bodhisattva Ideal lectures ask what the ascending levels of perception tell us about the Buddha and buddhahood:

> Although the Buddha as a historical person may have existed within time, Buddhahood itself exists outside time, in the dimension of eternity. We can in fact think of the Buddha as existing simultaneously on two levels: on the level of time, as a human, historical figure, and on the level of eternity, as reality itself. Then in addition to these two we can think of him as existing in an intermediate, as it were archetypal realm.

This intermediate realm is especially important:

> The *sambhogakāya* represents an archetypal richness of endowment beyond the limitations of any actual historical situation. In that sense the archetypal Buddha is the Buddha beyond space and time, beyond history, but endowed with all the perfections of all the historical Buddhas and more.[20]

The three bodies express the 'correspondence, in the Hermetic sense',[21] that Sangharakshita discusses in *The Three Jewels* between the conditioned and the unconditioned. The Buddha we perceive with the physical senses points us towards the glorious body of the visionary Buddha, and that in turn discloses the imageless reality of buddhahood.

Reimagining the Buddha

Contemplating buddhas and bodhisattvas by meditating on them in a *sādhana* practice, or immersing oneself in the sutras that describe them, were central practices for Sangharakshita. In their turn, Order members took on a *sādhana* devoted to a particular buddha or bodhisattva figure (the *yidam*), and Sangharakshita encouraged them to make it the centre of their spiritual lives. Through the practice, one comes into relationship with buddhahood in the concretized form:

> Perhaps one could say that there is a sort of mutual tuning in. When you become aware of a bodhisattva not in an abstract conceptual sense but with your whole being, when you tune in to a bodhisattva, you are in contact with them, even if it is in a very subtle, attenuated, distant way. Something passes from them to you.[22]

The tradition describes what passes as transcendental knowledge (*jñāna*) and blessings, to receive which the practitioner must engage with an attitude of 'love, respect and faith', but the *yidam*'s form has its own power:

The *yidam* is thus that special aspect of the Dharma,
that special aspect of reality, through which the disciple
approaches the Enlightenment experience [...] the whole of the
Dharma is contained, embodied, in your *yidam*, and you direct
all your attention to that.[23]

Sangharakshita recognized that this engagement could come in other forms, but contemplating a buddha or a bodhisattva by visualizing them and chanting their mantra had a distinctive power. The practitioner could *evoke* the qualities of buddhahood, and *invoke* an energy that was beyond them:

The energy is the energy of the Void, if one can use that
expression, and the particular figure that you evoke and
invoke determines the particular form that that energy takes.
It may be an energy of love and compassion or an energy of
wisdom or an energy of purification.[24]

This isn't the divine gift a theistic tradition might seek – it goes along with insight into impermanence and insubstantiality:

In the course of the practice the image comes intensely and
vividly to life while at the same time one reflects that it has
arisen in dependence on causes and conditions, and is thus not
completely real. Reflecting in this way, one sees that neither
the concept 'real' nor the concept 'unreal' is sufficient to
exhaust the true 'reality' of the situation. 'Reality' transcends
real and unreal, existence and non-existence.[25]

Buddhophany, sādhana, and the refuge tree

Other teachers of Tibetan meditation practices might describe *sādhana* in these terms, but Sangharakshita added something that illustrates the distinctiveness of his general presentation of the Dharma. This is the imagination: the subject of *Reimagining the Buddha*, the second of the late papers that emerged from Sangharakshita's discussions with Subhuti. Sangharakshita produced his own summary in a short piece entitled *Buddhophany*.

It begins with the individual's relation to nirvāṇa:

> A successful Dharma life requires an imaginative connection with the Goal, some definite sense of reality beyond self-clinging. If there is no such connection and sense then spiritual life becomes no more than a refinement of self-identity, at best.[26]

Without the connection to buddhahood that we have traced throughout Sangharakshita's work, all we have is a 'refinement of self-identity'. The expression suggests the limitations, from his perspective, of secular and psychological ways of understanding Buddhist practice (however valuable they might be in their own terms). The 'imaginative connection with the Goal' has also threaded through this account, both explicitly and implicitly. Describing the path as a process of growth, for example, uses the image of a growing plant to suggest that Dharma practice touches something dynamic and alive that is both within and beyond ourselves. That aliveness (which can be expressed as progressive conditionality) inheres in the very way consciousness functions and prefigures the experience of unbounded creativity that is nirvāṇa.

To experience the path in this way is to engage the imagination – 'the essential vehicle of all genuine moral, aesthetic, and spiritual life', as Subhuti calls it.[27] The imagination unifies our experience, combining intellect, emotion, and will into 'a single harmonious act of awareness'.[28] It also allows us to contact levels of experience that are beyond the scope of our normal consciousness – the process Sangharakshita calls 'vertical integration'. As he remarks in a seminar:

> The quest for holiness, which the study of the Dharma subserves, is a quest for spiritual wholeness, for complete integration of the 'personality' not with any subjective principle merely, but with Reality.[29]

Symbols are the imagination's natural medium, which is why *sādhana* – contemplating the symbolic forms of buddhas and bodhisattvas – is central to Sangharakshita's system of Dharma life.

However, the relation between the imagination and traditional forms is not straightforward, and the complexity springs from Triratna's relation to other Buddhist schools and what it means to practise Buddhism in a new culture. Sangharakshita writes in *Buddhophany*:

> The Triratna Buddhist Order and Community is not a continuation of the Tibetan tradition, or of any other particular Buddhist tradition. The particular iconographic, theoretical, and ritual frameworks of Tibetan or other traditions are not our reference point.[30]

This states Triratna's position clearly and names an issue Sangharakshita had already addressed in relation to the refuge tree. For many years, Order members visualized and prostrated before the Nyingma refuge tree, which had been so important to Sangharakshita. But, in this form, the tree's specific meaning is devotion to Padmasambhava (as the embodiment of buddhahood) and the lineage of teachers who continued his teachings though the Nyingma school. For a time, it was possible to disregard the anomaly, but, in the early 1990s, the newly appointed public preceptors raised it with Sangharakshita, and he devised what came to be known as the refuge tree of the Triratna Buddhist Order.

The Triratna version of the refuge tree shares the structure of the Tibetan versions, but the figures it contains reflect Sangharakshita's understanding of the Buddhist tradition. Śākyamuni, the Buddha of history, is at the centre, rather than Padmasambhava, because, as Sangharakshita writes in *Buddhophany*: 'The Buddha Śākyamuni – his life, teaching, person, and image – is our central and key reference point. It is through him that we know of Enlightenment.'[31] The Triratna refuge tree includes many figures besides the Buddha. On a lotus to the Buddha's left are *arahant*s – the Buddha's enlightened followers; to his right are bodhisattvas; and behind him is a collection of Dharma books. Above the Buddha are several tiers of figures. Highest, because they are earliest in time, are the Indian Buddhist teachers, particularly Nāgārjuna and Asaṅga, who represent the major philosophical trends; then come the major Tibetan teachers; below them are Chinese Buddhist teachers; and, finally, the principal teachers of Japanese Buddhism.

The presence of these teachers doesn't imply that Triratna follows all their teachings – for one thing, they contradict one another. The figures on the tree constellate around the Buddha because, as Sangharakshita writes:

> All later developments in Buddhism emerge from his realization and teaching. Going for Refuge to the Buddha in the first place means Going for Refuge to the Buddha Śākyamuni as teacher and embodiment of the Ideal.[32]

The other figures are sources of inspiration, but their teachings should be understood in the light of the Buddha's teachings, and within Triratna 'whatever practices are done in the Order depend on principles derived from the Buddha himself.'[33] Sangharakshita's role in Triratna is clarifying what this means, so he appears along with his eight main teachers on the lotus in front of the Buddha.

Sangharakshita's understanding of buddha and bodhisattva figures follows this understanding of the Buddhist tradition:

> The Archetypal Buddhas and Bodhisattvas, that emerged later in Buddhist history, are all to be understood as 'hypostases' or imaginative embodiments of the Buddha's Enlightened experience and qualities. They cannot therefore be truly understood without there first being a deep understanding of, and feeling for, the Buddha of history.[34]

This means that the familiar buddha and bodhisattva forms are not what is fundamentally important about them. The insight had a long gestation. Sangharakshita recalls in his memoirs that his visionary connection with Amitābha, which had prompted his decision to take monastic ordination in 1949, resurfaced in 1956 but with an important difference:

> I also experienced feelings of intense love and devotion towards the Buddha (especially in the form of Amitābha) and Avalokiteśvara, which was not often the case with me. Sometimes these feelings were accompanied by the

corresponding visionary experiences, but more often there would be an awareness of the transcendental 'person' in question without my being conscious of any particular form.[35]

In a similar spirit, in the 1969 *Bodhisattva Ideal* lectures Sangharakshita suggests bodhisattvas will take on different forms in the West because people will perceive and experience them differently. At some point in a practice devoted to Mañjughoṣa, he says, one has to put aside the traditional iconography and ask oneself: 'What is Mañjughoṣa? What is the reality behind this term Mañjughoṣa? What do I experience?'[36] Finding a new form is not something to be done casually, but in a new culture it is inevitable:

> We will probably need to start off with the traditional Eastern iconography. [...] Such depictions may give some clue to what those bodhisattvas are – but not necessarily. Sooner or later we have to work our way from the traditional appearance of a bodhisattva to what that appearance is meant to represent.[37]

Buddhophany adds the historical reflection that 'The various images of Buddhas and Bodhisattvas emerged in a natural and unselfconscious process of historical unfolding as later Buddhists continued to imagine the "world" of Enlightenment.' What we should draw from that is the example of a 'process of imaginative unfolding [...] not primarily the forms it created'. In a modern setting, the imagination should be free to respond to buddha and bodhisattva figures:

> Our effort should especially be to allow imagination to unfold naturally, not to force it into any particular iconographic mould, especially one from a culture not our own. We should consciously allow images of the Buddha and his Enlightened experience to arise from our own cultural circumstances.[38]

To 'reimagine the Buddha' is not unprecedented, or unorthodox, so far as Sangharakshita is concerned. We cannot help imagining. As Subhuti writes:

> As imagination begins to flourish more and more freely, it becomes clear that it is not merely a power of the mind that we own, but the mind itself. It is not something we have, but something we are. It is not part of us, but the whole. We are imagination.[39]

If truth is beyond expression, everything from Buddhist teachings to the form of the Buddha is a metaphor or symbol. This means, as Lama Govinda had written in Sangharakshita's magazine six decades earlier: 'Truths have to be continually rediscovered, they have ever to be re-formed and transformed, if they are to preserve their meaning.'[40]

The buddha image is important because it has been charged with meaning by the devotion of generations of Buddhists: it is an 'illumined image'. But more important is the faculty that perceives it: 'the illumined imagination',[41] which perceives spiritual realities to the degree to which it has been liberated from ego-clinging.

Buddhophany asks what it means to reimagine the Buddha in these terms. Sangharakshita's presentation of the path is an exercise in reimagining the Dharma. We must now turn to his efforts to reimagine the sangha as he developed a Buddhist Order and movement.

Part Four

Creating a Movement

The fundamental principle of my philosophy
is that power and value do not coincide.

Sangharakshita, *A Stream of Stars*[1]

Chapter Fifteen

Sangharakshita's Roles

Sangharakshita was forty-one in 1967 when he started to teach under the auspices of the Friends of the Western Buddhist Sangha. He commented in 1990 that in the intervening years the Order and movement had 'occupied the very forefront of my consciousness, there being hardly a day when my thoughts were not concerned with it, either directly or indirectly'.[1] Through the FWBO/Triratna, he put his teachings into practice, and it is impossible to separate what he said from the people to whom he spoke: the community his teachings attracted and members of the Order he started in 1968. This is not to say that Sangharakshita had a plan that he enacted through the FWBO/Triratna. He says in *The History of My Going for Refuge* that he came to understand what he was doing in the act of developing it: 'the act becoming more adequate to the idea as the idea itself became clearer, and the idea becoming clearer as the act became more adequate'.[2]

The movement's successes, challenges, and history are too complex to treat briefly, in part because it was a joint creation that evolved through the lives of first dozens and then thousands of people. Its story has been told many times and, rather than offering another such account, here I will consider how the understanding of the Dharma this book has traced shaped the movement.[3] This chapter explores how Sangharakshita envisaged his role as founder and teacher; the next places his teaching in the context of other approaches to Buddhism in the West. Then come the myths that underpinned the movement, particularly in its early decades, and we must consider their role in both its successes and its difficulties. The concluding chapter draws the threads together.

• • •

Sangharakshita was sometimes modest about his role in creating the movement. His 1990 paper *My Relation to the Order*, his fullest reflection on the subject, concludes:

> One of the illusions about myself that I do *not* cherish is that I was the most suitable person to be the founder of a new Buddhist movement in Britain – in the world, as it turned out. I possessed so few of the necessary qualifications; I laboured under so many disadvantages. When I look back on those early days, and think of the difficulties I had to experience (not that I always thought of them as difficulties), I cannot but feel that the coming into existence of the Western Buddhist Order was little short of a miracle.[4]

At the same time, Sangharakshita thought carefully about what he was trying to create and the tensions that attend spiritual organizations. In the 1970 talk 'Is a Guru Necessary?' he notes that a true guru isn't the head of a religious group, a teacher who imparts knowledge and information, a father substitute or a problem-solver. He wanted to engage with the people who were learning from him, and recognized that this involved what he called the 'vertical communication' that occurs 'between people one of whom is on a consistently higher level than the other'.[5] He wanted his disciples to be *individuals* who thought for themselves, and the Order and movement to be free from authority and power. '[R]eal spiritual teachers', he said, 'do not make claims about themselves. [...] They are not after power.'[6] Instead, he found alternative ways to envisage his position.

Gardener and architect

Having left the Hampstead Buddhist Vihara in 1967, Sangharakshita started his own activities in a small basement room named the Triratna Meditation Centre and Shrine Room, located beneath Sakura, a shop owned by one of his supporters in London's West End. One day, he opened his eyes at the end of a period of meditation and saw what was happening in a kind of vision:

> As the last gong-stroke dies away,
> Shiver on shiver, into the deep silence,
> Opening my eyes, I find myself
> In a green-mossed underground cave
> Overarching still waters whereon
> White lotuses, half open, are peacefully smiling.[7]

This is another version of the Buddha's vision of humanity as a bed of lotuses and the Dharma as natural growth. The meditators were growing like lotuses in the environment he had created. He was creating a lotus pool, or a garden.

By 1973 Sangharakshita had led hundreds of classes and meetings. He decided to take a sabbatical from active engagement in the FWBO and spent a year with a friend in a chalet in Cornwall. In a 'Personal Message to All Friends' published in the *FWBO Newsletter*, he explained that he wasn't taking the sabbatical because he was tired or because he was disappointed at the movement's slow progress. He was more convinced than ever that the movement had a 'vast potential [...] which is only just now beginning to be realized'.[8] But he thought he was often regarded

> not as an individual but as a piece of well-oiled religious clockwork – as a machine, in fact, for giving lectures and taking classes, for answering people's questions about Buddhism and solving their personal problems.[9]

He felt powerful 'unprogrammed and unprogrammable' energy growing within him that needed space to emerge.

If Sangharakshita wasn't a machine, what was he? Perhaps he was a gardener. 'Like a tender growing plant', he wrote in the 'Personal Message', 'a movement as young as ours needed constant attention, and this, as the only full-time gardener then available, I felt perfectly happy to give'.[10] By then, several 'assistant gardeners' had emerged, and it would be their responsibility to ensure that the young plant gets both rain and sunshine in the right quantities, that the soil in which it grows is kept well aerated, that caterpillars are picked off the leaves, and that, periodically, its branches are sprayed with insecticide.[11]

He was confident that the living spirit of the Dharma was alive within the movement and would continue to develop without his constant involvement.

By 1990, assistant gardeners were fulfilling most of Sangharakshita's responsibilities, and *My Relation to the Order* concludes with an extended account of the movement that expresses his satisfaction, and even incredulity, at its growth:

> Now, hundreds of lotuses are blooming, some of the bigger and more resplendent flowers being surrounded by clusters of half-opened buds. During the last twenty-two years a whole lotus-lake has come into existence, or rather, a whole series of lotus-lakes. Alternatively, during the last twenty-two years the original lotus plant has grown into an enormous lotus-tree not unlike the great four-branched Refuge Tree – has in fact grown into a whole forest of lotus-trees. Contemplating the series of lotus-lakes, contemplating the forest of lotus-trees, and rejoicing in the strength and beauty of the lotus-flowers, I find it difficult to believe that they really did all originate from that small and inadequate pot, which some people wanted to smash to bits, or cast into the dustbin, or bury as deep as possible in the ground.[12]

* * *

Sangharakshita insisted he didn't plan the array of centres, residential communities, and team-based right-livelihood businesses that developed in the 1970s. They grew organically, and the FWBO offered itself 'not as an organization but as a spiritual community'.[13] But this didn't mean there was no organization:

> Everything that is alive is organized, and disorganization means death. If you look at a plant, so long as it has life, it has

structure, it has organization, and when it dies, it withers and disintegrates.¹⁴

Sangharakshita's role, along with that of leading Order members, was to structure the movement's growth. Letting go of the organic metaphor, he sometimes thought of the movement, with its centres, communities, and co-operative businesses, as a building and himself as the architect. What those involved in the movement were developing was the beginning of a much wider social change: they were designing 'A Blueprint for a New World'.

This was the title of the fourth lecture in a series Sangharakshita delivered in the ornate surroundings of the Royal Brighton Pavilion in 1976. He explains that this blueprint isn't an abstract plan to be enforced in the manner of a political programme – a spiritual community isn't a power structure. In any case:

> Buddhists distrust abstract theories, theories not directly related to the needs of the concrete human situation. Buddhism delineates general principles but leaves the specific application of those principles to the individual.¹⁵

This made Sangharakshita a very unusual kind of architect: he shaped things by speaking about values that he encouraged people to embody, and guided them in how to put these values into practice. He was an architect and a gardener combined. Perhaps, he says at the talk's conclusion:

> We already have a detailed blueprint for a new world, or something that is perhaps even better: the living, growing seed of a new world. The acorn is the real blueprint for the oak tree.¹⁶

Sangharakshita refined his account of the movement as a building in the 1991 talk 'The Five Pillars of the FWBO'. Twenty-three years after its foundation, he thought participants in the FWBO were often like people who couldn't recognize the shape of a building because they were standing inside it. Speaking personally, he said:

> I see it as a tree, or perhaps a sapling – a sapling that has
> sprung from a seed planted twenty-three years ago and
> is already bearing fruit, already providing shelter and
> nourishment for people in many parts of the world. I see the
> FWBO also as a bed of lotuses, a garden, a road, a raft. I see it as
> a magnificent temple, which began twenty-three years ago as
> a tiny improvised shrine.[17]

The talk pursued the architectural metaphor by saying the temple, which was still being constructed, was supported by five pillars: ideas, practices, institutions, experiment, and imagination. He didn't mean there were only five pillars or that they were fixed and rigid pillars of stone. They might equally be pillars of light, or perhaps the pillars of cloud or fire that are mentioned in the Bible. Nonetheless, these pillars created the temple's structure, and it was important that people in the FWBO recognized them. That meant recognizing the value of ideas, which we easily take for granted when they become familiar to us; practices, especially meditation, which could transform consciousness; and 'spiritual institutions' – specifically, 'centres, communities, and co-ops' – which made transformation a shared process. Without carefully conducted experiments, he said, 'the FWBO may not succeed in establishing itself in a new environment and may not even survive in the old environment'. Finally, people wishing to develop the temple should recognize that it also rested on imagination, hard as it may be to locate:

> Look for imagination in the realm of myth, especially in the
> myth of the Order, the myth of the Movement, in archetypes
> and ideals, in poetry in the broadest sense of the term. More
> concretely, look for it in ritual and ceremony, in meditation,
> and in the scriptures, especially some of the great Mahāyāna
> *sutras*. Look for it in the fine arts.[18]

This meant that, in addition to being a gardener and an architect Sangharakshita was also, at least by analogy, an artist.

Artist, translator, visionary

In 1972 Sangharakshita wrote a short story (one of six he published in his lifetime) entitled *The Artist's Dream*. A figure called 'the Artist' dreams that the sky opens, and before him, as though depicted on a great wall, he sees a visionary representation of 'a new heaven and a new earth'. The scene imprints itself on the Artist's mind in all its detail, and, when a monastery commissions him to paint a large fresco, he knows this is the scene it must depict. To start with, he works alone and progress is slow, so he trains a group of young men to be his assistants. The passion the Artist feels for 'the great work' seizes some of the helpers as well, and they, too, start to feel there is 'nothing better than painting one's dreams on empty walls'.[19]

The young men's wives and sweethearts believe they have lost them to the project and come to the monastery demanding they return home. The Artist assures the women he has no wish to keep the men any longer than is necessary, but this only angers them further. Uproar ensues, and the authorities take the women's side. Most of the men leave, progress slows, and the Artist's strength fails. But one morning, as he paints, he notices that the whole scene is miraculously complete and 'all at once in the midst of the intensity of his joy, he knew that he had died, and that the new heaven and the new earth were eternal, and himself for ever a part of them.'[20]

Sangharakshita acknowledged the story as a parable of his efforts to establish the FWBO.[21] We will come to the resemblance between the Artist's conflict with the women and tensions within the movement around gender and families, but the most important elements for understanding Sangharakshita's role are the figure of the Artist, his revelatory vision, and his struggle to realize it.

The Artist's intuitive sense that he must realize his vision echoes Sangharakshita's experience in the founding of the Order. He says in *The History of My Going for Refuge*:

> [F]or me, there could be no question of first clarifying an idea or concept and then acting upon it, i.e. acting upon it in its

clarified form. An idea or concept was clarified in the process of its being acted upon.[22]

This presumably meant he didn't have a fixed idea of how the Order should develop, and came to understand its nature only by engaging with it. It also echoed his description two decades earlier of the artist who begins with 'a vague sense of something that he or she clarifies and intensifies in the process of creating the work of art'.[23]

The implication is that Sangharakshita regarded his work in establishing the FWBO as a creative endeavour akin to an artist's creation of his work. Stephen Batchelor writes of Sangharakshita in his book *The Awakening of the West*:

> While confessing a romantic, intuitive impulse at the root of his actions, he was able to realize his vision because of his rational gifts as a synthesizer of ideas and an organizer of people.[24]

It would be more accurate to consider Sangharakshita a creator of ideas than a synthesizer, and a creative force rather than an organizer. He reflects in *The History* that the course of his life had been determined 'by impulse and intuition rather than by reason and logic',[25] and said much later: 'I'd like to describe myself as a creative person, someone whose life has been an expression of creativity, even if only in a small way.'[26]

• • •

The Artist in the story is also a visionary, and Sangharakshita's vision was a world transfigured. He described the movement in these expansive terms in the 1976 Brighton talks:

> [A] new world [...] exists only in the imagination, only as a dream, but it is no less worthy of our attention for that. The imagination, after all, has its uses. What we imagine today we may do tomorrow; the dream of the night may become the reality of the morning. Let us imagine, let us dream,

and we may find that we are closer to reality than we had thought.[27]

What he had in mind wasn't an improved version of the existing society, but something radically different:

> This new world will be a world in which we relate to one another as individuals, a world in which we are free to develop to the utmost of our potential, and in which the social, economic, and political structures will help us to do that. The new world will be, in short, a spiritual community – a spiritual community writ large. Our aim, therefore, must be to transform the present world into a spiritual community. This is the only new world that is worth having, the only new world worth working for.[28]

Sangharakshita's intuition as he created the FWBO/Triratna was itself guided by deep forces that could only be expressed in images and symbols. As we have seen, he saw himself as a translator like St Jerome who was re-expressing Buddhism by bringing the meaning of the Dharma from the depths of consciousness to the surface. Like an artist, he wanted to give an outward form to deep energies, and that form was principally the Buddhist movement he established.

Sangharakshita was never an ordinary member of an FWBO community, and he never worked in a right-livelihood business. He was involved in organizational matters and willing to help with practical ones, but he never donned overalls in the burned-out shell that slowly became the London Buddhist Centre. His role was to offer personal counsel and practical advice, to be a spiritual friend and to teach. More diffusely, he drew out the deep meaning he saw in the movement's activities and institutions, particularly through image and myth. He told people in the movement that they weren't just practising Buddhism in the West: they were creating western Buddhism; they weren't just making connections with western culture, they were establishing *a new Buddhist culture*; and they weren't just finding conducive conditions for Dharma practice, they were *building a New Society*. This made Sangharakshita a mythmaker as well as a translator and visionary, and the myths he developed weave through the account that follows.

Teacher and friend

We must add a more obvious role to this account of Sangharakshita as a gardener, architect, artist, and visionary. He was the FWBO/Triratna's founder and teacher, and he qualified the authority this implied by calling himself a spiritual friend. To start with, he taught Order members in person, and even those he never met usually learned about Buddhism by listening to recordings of his lectures. But, as the movement grew, he ceased to know all its members and was even further removed when he handed on responsibility for conducting ordinations (a process that started in the late 1980s and continued for several years). By the time of his death, those he had ordained personally were a small proportion of the total.

Sangharakshita discussed his role in these changed circumstances in the 1990 paper *My Relation to the Order*, which described his role as a preceptor and recalled the first ordinations in 1968. The people he had ordained

> all went for Refuge with a certain understanding of what was meant by Going for Refuge. That understanding coincided with my own understanding of what was meant by Going for Refuge, at least to some extent. It coincided with it because having studied and practised Buddhism under my guidance the men and women in question shared my views. In other words they were not just ordinands and I was not just their preceptor. They were also my pupils, my disciples, and I was their teacher.[29]

Although Sangharakshita's role as teacher later became controversial for some, the paper states it straightforwardly, as something that was generally understood and accepted. Nonetheless, he is emphatic:

> What I mean, when I say that I am the teacher of the Order, is that the Dharma studied, practised, and propagated by Order

members is the Dharma as elucidated by me. This is not to say that I have elucidated the Dharma at every single point, only that I have elucidated it in certain fundamental respects.[30]

As those he had ordained conducted ordinations in their turn, the Order was increasingly understood as a lineage of teaching, witnessing, and discipleship. This was an alternative to thinking in terms of transmission, empowerment, or appointing people to an ecclesiastical position. Calling himself a spiritual friend had a similar implication.

Friends were important to Sangharakshita throughout his life, and, once the movement was established, the great majority of his friendships were with people who were involved in it. He recognized that many of those friendships had what he called a 'vertical dimension' in the sense that he was the more experienced party. The lecture 'Is a Guru Necessary?' describes what happens between guru and disciple as 'existential communication',[31] but he usually preferred to avoid such elevated language. He said in *My Relation to the Order*:

> We have in Buddhism the wonderful term 'spiritual friend' and this I am more than content to apply to myself and to have applied to me by others. Indeed, there are times when I think that 'spiritual friend' is almost too much and that just 'friend' would be enough.[32]

Contact with a spiritual friend was a matter of personal connection and communication, and it wasn't necessary to inflate the spiritual friend's status.

Like many of Sangharakshita's descriptions of the community he founded, this is an idealized version of it. The notion of a community of individuals is inherently complex, and the larger it grows the greater the complexity becomes. The group dynamics that affect every community – however self-aware and ethical it may be – will inevitably be in operation, at least to some degree. But the roles Sangharakshita adopted were intended to alleviate these tensions, and they went along with a conception of sangha, or 'spiritual community', that was just as idealized, and just as subtle.

Chapter Sixteen
Spiritual Community

The Order

In developing the Order, Sangharakshita reimagined what it meant to be a committed Buddhist; and, in developing the movement, he reimagined what it meant to live a Buddhist life. The Order gave an outward form to his understanding of Buddhism, and he called it 'my *chef-d'œuvre*, the principal work of my life'.[1]

The Order began in modest circumstances. *The History of My Going for Refuge* starts with Sangharakshita's diary entry for 7 April 1968, the date of the first public ordinations into the Western Buddhist Order: 'Arrived at Centre House at 10.15. Found nothing ready. Cleared and arranged room, set up shrine etc.'[2] One of the ordinands, who received the name Vangisa, later described the equally mundane circumstances of his private ordination the previous night:

> There was no build up to the occasion, no retreat in progress, no quiet departure one by one from the silence of the meditation room, just Monmouth Street in the long dusk of a Spring evening, discarded newspapers blowing in the breeze and taxis honking outside the window as we waited our turn in the shop.

Nonetheless, Vangisa reflected: 'Looking back, I can only say that a seed was planted that began to flower.'[3]

The precepts and lifestyle
Sangharakshita used the same imagery of seeds and plants to describe the Order's development, sometimes varying the

metaphor to speak of a living spirit or a developing organism. That evokes his sense of the Order's meaning, but traditional Buddhist language expressed how he understood it with much greater precision. He says in *The Ten Pillars of Buddhism*, a 1984 paper on the ten precepts taken by Order members:

> One goes for Refuge to the Buddha, the Dharma, and the Sangha – or, in more contemporary idiom, commits oneself to them – when one decides that to attain Enlightenment is the most important thing in human life, and when one acts – or does one's best to act – in accordance with that decision. This means organizing one's entire life, in all its different aspects, in such a way as to subserve the attainment of Enlightenment.[4]

He calls the ethical precepts 'the prolongation of the act of Going for Refuge itself into every aspect of one's existence',[5] and combines the traditional formula with its organic significance:

> Going for Refuge, or commitment to the Three Jewels, is one's lifeblood as a Buddhist. Observance of the precepts represents the circulation of that blood through every fibre of one's being. By its very nature blood must circulate. If it does not circulate this means that the organism to which it belongs is dead, and that the blood itself, stagnating, will soon cease to be blood.[6]

Order members, he said, should follow the principle of 'more and more of less and less', which is to say, 'trying to go more and more deeply into the so-called basic teachings of Buddhism rather than trying to hurry on to teachings which are allegedly more advanced'.[7]

At the same time as addressing the ethical issues that arise in daily life, Sangharakshita elevates the precepts by tying them to underlying ideals. Using an architectural metaphor, he calls going for refuge the foundation of the great temple of the Dharma, while the precepts are 'pillars' supporting a dome of meditation and a spire of wisdom. Infused by transcendent qualities, the precepts are like pillars made of precious metals and stones.

The first precept – abstaining from taking life – expresses an attitude to life that is both basic and elevated:

> [O]bservance of the first precept means that, as a result of our imaginative identification with others, we not only abstain from actually killing living beings but operate more and more in accordance with the love mode and less and less in accordance with the power mode. In this way there takes place within us a change so great as to amount to a change in our centre of gravity, so to speak, and this change manifests both as observance of the first precept and, to the extent that their individual natures permit, as observance of all the other precepts as well.[8]

The precept of not killing implies an orientation in the whole of one's life that frames much of what Sangharakshita says about the Order. He comments in the *Vimalakīrti Nirdeśa* lectures, for example:

> Within a spiritual community, within a Buddhist order, there can be no question of law and punishment, because law and punishment are based at least to some extent on the power mode, and by its very nature a spiritual community is based on the love mode. One member of the Order cannot punish another, because that would mean invoking the power mode.[9]

The shift to the love mode ripples through the remaining precepts, which address various areas of life. The result is a temple that is also a growing plant:

> The ten precepts are not only ten pillars; they are ten petals, the ten petals of a magnificent flower, of which meditation is the stamen, and wisdom the seed or fruit. We ourselves are that flower, both individually and 'collectively', and we grow and we bloom not for our own sake only, but for the sake of all living beings.[10]

Connecting ethical observances with the principles they express also means that Order members can choose how to apply them. That doesn't make lifestyle unimportant, but means commitment to the three refuges and ten precepts is more fundamental:

> A member of the Western Buddhist Order is first and foremost simply a Buddhist, simply one who is committed to the Three Jewels. Whether he or she lives more or less as a monk or nun or more or less as a member of the laity depends on the nature of his or her spiritual needs, and those needs are not necessarily the same from one year to the next.[11]

Following the precepts in this way produced a different attitude to 'lifestyle' from that of the bhikkhu sangha and, in that sense, the Order expressed Sangharakshita's rethinking of the principles that guide a Buddhist life. It corrected the tendency, which he thought particularly characterized the Theravāda, to associate commitment to the Buddhist path with monasticism, and to divide Buddhists into monastic and lay followers:

> When one has refined the crude ore of popular Buddhist ethical and pseudo-ethical observance, whether 'monastic' or 'lay', when one has removed the accretions and excrescences, and picked out the foreign bodies [...] one has left those ten great ethical principles which, as prolongations of the act of Going for Refuge into every aspect of one's existence, govern and eventually transform one's life.[12]

The ten ethical precepts followed by Order members were a 'fundamental moral code' (*mūla-prātimokṣa*) that was equivalent in the ethical sphere to going for refuge in the Buddhist life as a whole, and unified the tradition by restoring its fundamental principles:

> Such a reduction represents a return to, and a renewed emphasis upon, the basics of Buddhism. It can be regarded as innovative only by adopting a standpoint from which

those basics are ignored or from which they cannot be seen for the accretions and excrescences by which they have been overlaid.[13]

The Order and the FWBO

Order members weren't obliged to be involved in the activities of the movement:

> It is a free association of committed individuals, of people who take Enlightenment as their ideal, who try to develop as individuals, who experience for themselves, in themselves, the successive stages of the spiritual path, who enjoy spiritual fellowship with one another, and who help, encourage, and inspire one another.[14]

Nonetheless, an altruistic dimension was intrinsic to Sangharakshita's understanding of going for refuge, and that included an ambition to help others and, thereby, to change society. The Order was the core of a spiritual community, which was itself the nucleus of a New Society. In its first two decades, the wider community around the Order was often called 'the Friends' and sometimes 'the movement', and Sangharakshita carefully crafted its guiding principles.

In both India and England, Sangharakshita had experienced Buddhist organizations that were controlled by non-Buddhists. So a basic principle was that Order members should control FWBO/Triratna bodies. Individual centres were autonomous, with 'no centralization, no headquarters, and no organizational pyramid to hold them together'.[15] The common commitment Order members had made united them, but it was a 'spiritual rather than organizational'[16] unity, and, while co-ordination was important, more fundamentally, it grew from friendship, communication, and commitment to a shared vision. Similarly, there was no single template for FWBO activities:

> Since the single purpose of all these activities is to help people in their personal development, they are variously designed to serve the spiritual needs of all who care to come along.[17]

The leading role of Order members also introduced a principle of 'spiritual hierarchy' that influenced the movement's culture as a whole, but the basis of that hierarchy (at least in principle) was the capacity to operate ethically, subordinating the 'power mode' to the 'love mode'.

The myth of the Order
Sangharakshita reflected in his 1969 lectures on the bodhisattva ideal, when the Order was still very small, that the bodhicitta might arise out of 'the intensive interaction of true individuals'.[18] As the Order and movement developed, he began to speak of a distinctive kind of consciousness that was 'not the sum total of the individual consciousnesses concerned, nor even a kind of collective consciousness, but a consciousness of an entirely different order'.[19] As Sangharakshita wrote in his 1973 letter to the movement, this way of seeing the FWBO crystallized as an image:

> [A] vision rises before me [...] of a figure multiple-faced and multitudinously-armed. It is Avalokiteśvara, 'the Lord who Looks Down', the embodiment of compassion [...] the manifestation in which eleven radiant countenances look with smiles of compassion in the eleven directions of space, and a thousand arms, radiating like so many light rays from their single sun-like source, extend their benign operations into the remotest corners of the universe. Much as the full moon in all its glory may be reflected in a puddle, it is a tiny reflection of this figure that the FWBO aspires to be.[20]

This matched Sangharakshita's sense that existence comprised numerous levels, and that a phenomenon on one level could correspond with a more elusive equivalent on a higher level. In that sense, a platonic correspondence could be said to exist between the Order and the higher truth Avalokiteśvara embodied, and the true meaning of being an Order member was enacting this mythic truth in one's life. Sangharakshita says in *The History of My Going for Refuge*:

With every day that passes we should have a more decisive realization of the fact that we are, each one of us, an arm, or a hand, of that Avalokiteśvara who is the embodiment of the cosmic will to Enlightenment and, therefore, the embodiment of the cosmic Going for Refuge.[21]

As Avalokiteśvara embodies the bodhicitta, the Order could be said to manifest, or at least reflect, it. Sangharakshita returned to the theme in 1999 as he prepared to hand on the last of his responsibilities:

Now I want to focus on what happens when a number of people achieve this non-egoistic Going for Refuge, this non-egoistic arising of the *bodhicitta*, when this stream of non-egoistic spiritual energy starts manifesting through a number of people simultaneously. Those people will be literally hands or arms, or even faces, of Avalokiteśvara. There will be no question of any conflict between them. [...] Our Order has a future only to the extent that it is such a sangha, or contains such a sangha as its nucleus.

This anticipates Sangharakshita's later presentation of the five *niyama*s. The Order was a conditioned phenomenon that existed physically in the form of Order members, karmically as the sum of their behaviours and mental states, and supra-personally, in a form that could be envisaged as Avalokiteśvara. Sangharakshita was saying what he thought the Order needed if it was to have a future, not that it had already achieved it, adding: 'The future of the Order, of the Movement, is in your hands.'[22] But his comments also suggest that he thought the Order already expressed his vision, at least to a limited degree.

Creating sangha

Guiding principles
In a talk on the day of the first ordinations in 1968, Sangharakshita told the new Order members that the Order's purpose was

to enable people to commit themselves more fully to the
Buddhist way of life, to provide opportunities for spiritual
fellowship, and to provide an 'organizational' base for the
propagation of Buddhism in the United Kingdom.[23]

The context changed as the movement developed, but more or less everything else followed from these simple principles.

But what *were* the conditions for spiritual fellowship? Reviewing a book about D.H. Lawrence's abortive attempts to create a community of like-minded friends, Sangharakshita reflected on why Lawrence had been unsuccessful. He drew out four principles of spiritual community, which 'as a result of our own efforts to put the Buddhist ideal of spiritual community into practice in the West, we have found to be true'.[24]

Firstly, the spiritual community 'consists of individuals', meaning, as Sangharakshita said elsewhere, that it comprises people who have 'accepted responsibility for their own lives, and have decided that they want to develop as human beings'.[25] In Sangharakshita's view, individuality was a diminishing quality when set against the reach of the state and mass culture, and he pithily defined the FWBO as 'a spiritual movement of Buddhist origin which is concerned with the protection of the individual from the group'.[26] Lawrence hadn't recognized the need for a community to be made up of individuals or the principles that followed.

Secondly, and controversially, Sangharakshita declared, 'The couple is [...] the enemy of the spiritual community.'[27] He thought one reason Lawrence's experiment had failed was that his own role within it was inseparable from that of his wife, and the people he invited to join them were also married couples. We shall return to questions of sex, relationships, and families in the next chapter because they are so difficult to navigate and Sangharakshita's ways of resolving them came at a cost.

Thirdly, he said, 'the spiritual community is not a group.'[28] This set it against the normal character of collective enterprises, including power dynamics, factionalism, and much else. He thought Lawrence's attempts to create a community were undermined by his feeling that 'he had to be their leader; he had to ask them to follow him.'[29] Sangharakshita had thought carefully about his own leadership role, and set out to foster a community of individuals in a manner more akin to that of a gardener or an artist than the director of an organization. He told one person:

> I do not want disciples who are meek and obedient and afraid to speak their mind. I want disciples who are bold, self-confident, and independent and who are capable of standing against the whole world if necessary.[30]

We should add that the FWBO was nonetheless subject to group dynamics, and many people did regard Sangharakshita as a leader.

Finally, and crucially, the spiritual community must have 'a common ideal and a common method of practice'.[31] Such a community, Sangharakshita said,

> comes into existence only when a number of people work on themselves – and on one another – in such a way that they actually become individuals and are able to relate to one another as individuals.[32]

He had in mind a community of practitioners, all developing themselves according to shared principles. Community living was itself part of the practice.

This is a subtly balanced set of principles. Shared ideals imply a spiritual hierarchy because individuals will embody the ideals to varying degrees, but the hierarchy is checked by the emphasis on individuality and alertness to group traits. Forty years later, when the Order has nearly 3,000 members and has developed elaborate systems for internal communication and for managing issues such as ordinations, it still recognizably adheres to these principles, and faces the same challenges.

Friendship: horizontal and vertical
A final element in Sangharakshita's conception of spiritual community was arguably even more important than the four he mentioned in the book review: the network of friendships that bound the community together. On one level, 'friendship' simply meant that its members

> help one another, support one another, encourage one another, inspire one another [...] bearing one another up when they get into a difficult and disturbed condition, or when they get depressed.[33]

This was an essential basis of psychological wellbeing and an effective Dharma practice:

> As we spend time with spiritual friends in this way, we will get to know each other much better and learn to be more open, more honest. We will also be brought up against our own weaknesses, especially against our natural inborn tendency to operate in accordance with the power mode. But if we have spiritual friends, they will help us to learn to operate in accordance with the *mettā* mode and become less selfish, more egoless.[34]

This sustaining connection with peers, or *horizontal* spiritual friendship, was perhaps the most important way to foster positive emotion:

> Your spiritual life has to be warm, and that warmth comes from your own emotional positivity, generated to some extent through meditation experience, to some extent through your experience of the fine arts, but perhaps above all for most people from your experience of horizontal spiritual friendship.[35]

Vertical spiritual friendship meant 'the friendship you have with those who are spiritually more developed than yourself, particularly with your spiritual teacher'.[36] In a lecture in the bodhisattva ideal series Sangharakshita says:

> It is of the utmost importance for us to be in contact with people who are at least a little more spiritually advanced than we are ourselves, through whom the light of reality shines a little more clearly than it shines through us. Such people are known traditionally in Buddhism as our spiritual friends, our

kalyāṇa-mitras, and they are more important to us than even a Buddha would be.[37]

In the FWBO's early years only Sangharakshita could offer vertical *kalyāṇa-mitratā* (spiritual friendship), but, within a decade, experienced Order members were also fulfilling this role, at least on their own level, and living and working with other Buddhists were seen as ways for friendships to develop. Sangharakshita recognized that westerners often saw Buddhism as a path of 'personal development', while Indian Buddhists inspired by Dr Ambedkar usually saw it in social terms, but friendship and sangha were relevant to both: 'If you want to evolve spiritually, you have to evolve in free association with others.'[38]

The network of horizontal friendships gave the Order its warmth and openness, while vertical friendships maintained the focus on shared ideals and aspirations. A crucial hierarchical distinction existed between Order members and those outside the Order, and a hierarchy also developed within the Order itself, especially with the emergence of private and public preceptors. But this was largely informal, and the movement generally avoided stratified ecclesiastical roles, grand titles, and ceremonial attire.

New Society, new culture

The movement had a mission. Subhuti declared in *Buddhism for Today: A Portrait of a New Buddhist Movement* (1983): 'The creation of the New Society is the purpose of the FWBO.'[39] Many who became involved with the FWBO had already rejected conventional values and lifestyles under the influence of the 1960s counterculture, and Sangharakshita offered a way to relate their social idealism to spiritual ideals. He had reflected on the social implications of Dharma practice from the start of his career, and his work with the followers of Dr Ambedkar, many of them very poor, showed their importance:

> I saw as a result of my connection with them the need to transform the whole of one's social life. It was not enough just to transform one's individual life. In fact, it was hardly

possible, certainly for the majority of people, to transform
their individual life without a corresponding transformation
of the collective life of society itself.[40]

Back in the UK, Sangharakshita spoke of the need for supportive conditions and did his best to create them through Dharma activities and retreats. On retreat, participants felt immersed in the Dharma and, with his encouragement, some explored how they could extend this to the whole of their lives. Residential communities and right-livelihood businesses developed naturally – *organically* – and matched the path Sangharakshita was teaching. A Buddhist lifestyle made spiritual practice a shared activity, put Buddhist ideals such as altruism and renunciation into practice, and gave an outward form to the wholehearted commitment implied in going for refuge.

By the mid-1970s Sangharakshita was calling these new FWBO institutions 'The Nucleus of a New Society' and declaring they could prompt a wider social change.[41] Characteristically, he expressed this both as a practical way to influence wider society and as a mythic endeavour. In 1976 he gave a series of lectures on the Mahāyāna *Sutra of Golden Light*, which were later published along with seminar material as *Transforming Self and World*. The talks evoke the sutra's visionary world, combining it with a sustained reflection on the social and cultural application of the teachings Sangharakshita distilled from it. The sutra centres on a dream in which its protagonist, Ruciraketu, sees an array of buddha figures gathered around a magical drum. For Sangharakshita, this was an image of transfigured perception:

> The world in Ruciraketu's dream has been so completely transformed that it is no longer 'world' out there at all. [...]
> The transformed self interpenetrates the transformed world so that there is no self, no world, no subject, no object. The two have become interfused.[42]

This is the perspective of the bodhisattva who 'transcends individual personality altogether to become what we might call a "suprapersonal" stream of spiritual energy'.[43] The implication is that, if individuals commit themselves to something greater, the boundaries of selfhood will dissolve, and they will perceive the world as a bodhisattva perceives it.

This could also happen collectively, and Sangharakshita thought the FWBO could embody the living bodhisattva spirit at the heart of the Buddhist tradition that had repeatedly been lost amid rigid outer forms and overliteral understanding. As the movement gained in confidence and grew in dynamism, he increasingly described it in these terms. It was the Windhorse, 'a current of positive, emotional and spiritual energy'[44] or a manifestation of Avalokiteśvara: the reflection of a transcendent force at work in the world.

This is a visionary or prophetic view of the movement, and Sangharakshita's descriptions of the FWBO in the 1970s sometimes had a Blakean strain of revolutionary, even apocalyptic, idealism. Harold Bloom calls Blake a 'heroic vitalist' who casts out dualism to make the world afresh,[45] and Sangharakshita sometimes associated the FWBO with the same heroic idealism. In his poem *Milton*, Blake urges: 'Rouse up O young men of the new age! Set your foreheads against the ignorant hirelings!' Sangharakshita's 1979 poem 'Blake Walked among the Stones of Fire...' demands the same:

> Rouse up, young men of Albion,
> Blake calls you from the fire,
> Gives you his fiery chariot
> And arrows of desire.
>
> Go forth, young men of Albion,
> To harrow, forge, and plough,
> And build more than Jerusalem
> In Albion – now.[46]

* * *

If the FWBO was a kind of bodhisattva, it must find practical ways to manifest bodhisattva qualities, and the *Sutra of Golden Light* lectures suggest various ways in which ideals can be translated into practices. Discussing a passage in which a goddess helps a monk, Sangharakshita says: 'Here we have Buddhist economics in its purest form, the economics of giving.'[47] Within FWBO right-livelihood settings this produced the principle 'Give what you can; take what you need.' Another lecture describes the four great kings of Buddhist cosmology who uphold the ethical order. Sangharakshita uses Erich Fromm's language of the 'love mode' and the 'power mode' to translate this into the terms of the FWBO, insisting that, within the spiritual community, power should always be subordinated to love. It is hard to act according to such principles, but the Dharma makes it possible, in part because the Dharma brings a transcendent illumination into our lives: '[T]here is only one way of transforming one's own self and the world, and that is by making them receptive to the golden light, the light of the transcendental.'[48] This is another version of the illumined path that Sangharakshita taught in every aspect of his work.

Perhaps the most striking feature of the lectures is Sangharakshita's confidence that transformation is possible. The world, he says,

> can be transformed through teams of spiritually committed individuals taking up different human activities and orienting them in the direction of the golden light in such a way that they conduce to the spiritual development both of those who carry out the activities and those who come into contact with them.[49]

This is the mythic meaning of the FWBO's activities.

* * *

Buddhist lifestyles and institutions were just the outer form of a new Buddhist culture that would be the true transforming agent. Sangharakshita meant something quite distinct when he spoke in these terms. He didn't mean adopting the art and culture of Japan or Tibet that appealed to many Buddhists in the West. Much as he appreciated Asian Buddhist culture, his approach had always involved distinguishing it from the more essential values and teachings that were Buddhism's essence. At the same time, 'western Buddhism' didn't mean integrating Buddhism with mainstream western life in the manner of the vipassanā movement or secular Buddhism:

> Western culture, as it stands as a whole, is quite incompatible with Buddhism and there can be no question of our seeking to express Buddhism in terms of that culture. It is a question, rather, of Western Buddhism finding expression in a *new* Western culture, a culture which would in its own way, on its own level, help people to develop, if not spiritually then at least psychologically. In creating that culture we would of course keep the best elements of the traditional Western culture, but a lot would have to go.[50]

Sangharakshita explained in the *Sutra of Golden Light* lectures that a western Buddhist culture needed to grow organically from the experience of people 'deeply imbued with the spirit of Buddhism'[51] who would replicate, in a new form, the traditional society he had described in *A Survey of Buddhism*, where every aspect of life is given a 'transcendental orientation' and becomes a support for 'a more or less constant awareness of the existence of spiritual values'.[52]

Sangharakshita thought this culture could develop through the shared experience of the Order, provided its collective life was sufficiently intensive. He told an interviewer in 1977:

> Our main objective should be to make the whole Movement a world within a world, a culture within a culture, a community within a community, where everything is as it should be, or at any rate as near as we can get. And this community should grow and extend until it is virtually conterminous with society.[53]

Sangharakshita never ceased to believe that something of epochal significance could emerge from the movement he had founded. He sometimes evoked Schopenhauer's prediction that a 'Second Renaissance' would be born of western contact with the 'treasures of oriental literature'.[54] The catalyzing element was the great literature, art, and classical music that inspired Sangharakshita and that he shared with others. Waves of engagement with Plato, Goethe, Blake, Shelley, Nietzsche, D.H. Lawrence, and others rippled through the movement in the 1970s, along with Botticelli, Mozart, and J.S. Bach. The key, Subhuti wrote in his 1983 book *Buddhism for Today*, was that people approach their works 'with genuine sensitivity and receptivity to the message of transformation'.[55]

It is one thing to enjoy music and literature, another to find in them a way to enter an archetypal world. Many years later, in a lecture on 'Eros and Beauty', Subhuti called Sangharakshita's teachings on art and imagination 'the real western Tantra'.[56] Both Tantra and great art engage unconscious psychic forces through the medium of images in which they find a language for experiences that are elusive, and in that sense esoteric. This is overtly true of Tantra, which is intended for advanced disciples rather than general audiences and kept secret from the uninitiated, but the same might be said of art, as Sangharakshita understood it. This sort of engagement has always been an elite activity, and Sangharakshita's Romantic and Platonic sensibility accentuated this. He preferred high art to popular culture, sublimity to naturalism, and poetry to novels. In the twenty-first century these tastes have become esoteric, and yet they are a large part of what Sangharakshita meant when he spoke of expressing Buddhism in the language of western culture.

Sangharakshita's aesthetic sensibility was diffused through the movement in the myths he developed and the approach to Dharma practice that inspired it. In the 1990s he described his stance as a Dharma teacher as a marriage between the aesthetic absolute, according to which imaginative artists may do and say whatever they like, and the religious absolute, which holds sway in absolutist religion. The conflict between Sangharakshita I and Sangharakshita II reflected the same opposition, and his own approach reflected his recognition that, in the modern world, the two must coexist:

[N]owadays you cannot really have the religious teacher in the old sense, as representing the religious absolute. Some people in the Buddhist world are not very happy with the way in which I'm doing things, but they have to recognize that the FWBO is successful – which surely has something to do with this 'conflict' of mine.[57]

Politics and social change

Sangharakshita's social message can't easily be identified with a particular political position. In his terms, political parties of both left and right operate within the realm of the group. He mistrusted leftwing collectivist solutions that spoke of class conflict and envisaged an increasing role for the state, and he reserved a particular distaste for 'modern, egalitarian, "politically correct"' views that implied 'no one is more spiritually developed than anyone else'.[58] At the same time, he instinctively opposed such rightwing values as nationalism, snobbishness, consumerism, and the power of money. He read the conservative British newspaper *The Daily Telegraph* but he didn't share its enthusiasm for the British establishment. He sometimes pondered engaging directly with societal and political issues, and did so to a limited extent by speaking out on subjects like the blasphemy laws and the threat of nuclear war. But he thought both leftwing and rightwing approaches contributed to 'the brute mass of corporate existence'[59] that dominated modern societies, and he recognized the gulf between his way of thinking and almost all conventional political discourse. His views could possibly be called a form of anarchism or libertarianism, but only if those terms are fundamentally redefined in terms of a spiritual outlook and a hierarchy of being.

Sangharakshita in fact put his energy into developing the FWBO as an alternative social model that expressed his ideas. Perhaps that simply meant, as Sangharakshita said in the 1978 *Vimalakīrti Nirdeśa* lectures, that,

> to the extent that our spiritual aspirations have a common object, they will be united; and to the extent that they are united, they will be a force for good in the world.[60]

That is a more achievable ambition than transforming the world into a pure land bathed in golden light, but mythic thinking doesn't set out to be pragmatic. When the aspiring bodhisattva vows to lead all beings to Enlightenment, even though beings are numberless and filled with faults, they commit themselves to a mythic endeavour, not a social-change agenda. The mythic vehicle is the creation of a pure land or buddha field, which Sangharakshita presented as a version of the ideal society to which the FWBO aspired. In such a society, Sangharakshita said,

> when all the different activities that make up the world have placed themselves at the service of the spiritual development of the individual, the world will be transformed by the golden light.[61]

Although the buddha land is the sphere of a buddha's influence, it must be purified through a joint effort:

> It has to be built by a number of people – bodhisattvas and would-be bodhisattvas – working together. One of them may be more advanced than the others, may have more vision, may even be the first to attain Enlightenment and then help the others to take that final step. But all must be inspired by the same ideal, the ideal of supreme perfect Enlightenment for the benefit of all beings.[62]

Sangharakshita was steeped in Blake's vision of a new Jerusalem that could be built in England's green and pleasant land and Shelley's belief in *A Defence of Poetry* that poets were 'the mirrors of the gigantic shadows which futurity casts upon the present'. Functioning as an artist and mythmaker, he intended the collective myths with which he described the movement to connect its activities with mysterious and powerful forces that couldn't be expressed in any other way. If Sangharakshita considered the Order his *chef-d'oeuvre*, the movement was his great poem: a space free from both capitalism and 'pseudo-egalitarianism' where Buddhist values could flourish, echoing the mythic splendour of another realm.

The challenges of community

Alongside the myths, we must set the unavoidably messier, more complex, and less ideal reality of the FWBO/Triratna. Few human beings are entirely free of conformity to group norms or individualistic reactions against them, and, however well-designed organizational structures may be, tensions and power dynamics are inevitable. Most accounts of the FWBO in the 1970s and 1980s recognize at least some problematic aspects, but there are many interpretations. Some describe a group of relatively young people committed to a grand project who could be excessively zealous but created something extraordinary. The most critical accounts evoke a self-enclosed culture deluded by a sense of its own importance, which magnified the flaws of its founder, including his aversion to women and family life, and encouraged a culture in which coercive and predatory behaviour could flourish.

My own view, based on my experience over many years (and therefore of course partial), is that, while the movement has had difficulties, the most critical accounts bear little relation to reality. Nonetheless, it is important to consider the difficulties and the extent to which they grew from Sangharakshita's teaching. A full study would also take account of the changes in the movement that make it, in many respects, a different entity in the 2020s from what it was in the 1970s. Here, it is only possible to identify a few areas of tension. A starting point is how individuals related to the ideals Sangharakshita propounded.

Idealism and its discontents

An interview with a leading Order member called Lokamitra, published in the *FWBONewsletter* in 1976, suggests how members of the early FWBO communities tried to apply their ideals skilfully and with awareness:

> Whatever happens you always come back to that ideal if you are sincerely trying to follow it, trying to live according to what the ideal requires. That doesn't mean that the other sides can be denied. When one is trying to develop, one inevitably comes up against one's worst sides and one is always

confronted by these, face to face. [...] Living in a community, you cannot just cut half of yourself off. You have to be there completely, so all your sides have to come up.[63]

Dhammadinna wrote in a 1981 issue of the *Newsletter* that such settings were 'hopefully' free from 'group values of competition, power games, desire for status etc.' However, she also warned:

If the spirit of friendship is lacking or diminishing, if willpower begins to take the place of *mettā*, if coercion, even of the subtlest kind begins to supercede inspiration and encouragement, then we shall cease to live in a Spiritual Community.[64]

In practice, motivations are always mixed, and coercion can be hard to recognize, especially when one is working hard for a cause. In the same issue of the *Newsletter*, an Order member called Padmaraja described his understanding of what it meant to be a *kalyāṇa-mitra* (spiritual friend): 'The *kalyāṇa-mitra* is Ideal-oriented, his emotions flow in the direction of the Ideal, are completely caught up in the Ideal.' For the junior partner (the mitra), he says, the *kalyāṇa-mitra* embodies the ideal and the mitra may even fall in love with them. As he describes it, the relationship is intense and may include sex, but he is confident it will be free from unhealthy emotional entanglement: 'If one has very intense ideals to which one is committed in a very intense way, one has fewer emotional problems.'[65]

The *kalyāṇa-mitra* is likely to be less ideal, and the mitra more vulnerable, than this account allows. The writer was the chair of the centre I was attending as a teenager, drawn by the excitement and confidence such idealism generated. But, by 1988, protests against its unhealthy internal culture and accusations of bullying had engulfed the centre. When Sangharakshita threatened to close it, Padmaraja stepped down as chair and then resigned from the Order. In 1998 I reflected on what had happened:

Idealism [...] can bring pride and narrowness and leads people to reject ideas, emotions, and even relationships that do not fit in. In part, the pressure to succeed came from the FWBO's imperative to show that its ideas of alternative lifestyles and new economic forms could be translated from theory into practice. [...] The outside world, including other FWBO centres, was looked down on, and this made people blind to internal failings.[66]

Psychologists who consider the problems of spiritual practitioners and communities sometimes speak of spiritual bypassing: 'the tendency to use spiritual ideas and practices to sidestep or avoid facing unresolved emotional issues, psychological wounds, and unfinished developmental tasks'.[67] I think that's what happened at this centre, and the ethical failings at this centre were particularly pronounced, but they were echoed, to varying degrees, elsewhere in the movement. Teachers in the vipassanā community mainly look to psychotherapeutic insights to counteract this tendency, but Sangharakshita's antidote was the path of regular steps and a practice that remained grounded in ethical awareness, communication, and friendship. Integration and spiritual maturity grow from such sources. As I wrote in 1998:

> I stayed involved in the FWBO because I could see it becoming steadily more mature, individually and collectively. I saw a growing awareness of the sometimes painful gulf between our aspirations of what the FWBO might be and the reality – as well as a growing ability to work with these issues with patience, humanity and humility.[68]

In subsequent years, I think this maturation has continued. The movement's increased size has brought increased complexity, but – unlike the movement's early decades – there are now many people with several decades' experience of Dharma practice who are equipped to address the tensions of community.

Sex, relationships, and families
Sangharakshita often insisted on the importance of recognizing the views we hold on all sorts of matters from the nature of existence

to relations between the sexes. Within Buddhist thought, even 'right views', which conduce to the path, are not held to be true in an ultimate sense, and Sangharakshita often insisted on their provisional and figurative character. Nonetheless, he said: 'Only a Tathāgata has no views; while this should certainly be one's aim, one can realize it only by taking one's stand upon right views.'[69] Right views are important because they define the nature of the path.

To some, Sangharakshita's more controversial views about gender, lifestyle, and sex were radical and outspoken; to others they were dangerous, dogmatic, and belligerent. Either way, to understand them we must recognize their origin in his distinction between the Lower and Higher Evolution. In his thought, the Lower Evolution is the domain of biological drives such as the need for sex and the desire to reproduce. Family life, child rearing, and 'the group' fall within it. The Higher Evolution, which is the province of the individual, means transcending the dictates of biology.

This had important practical implications. Ordination was neither monastic nor lay and didn't require Order members to follow a particular lifestyle. The principle was 'Commitment is primary, lifestyle secondary',[70] with the caveat that lifestyle should be 'an expression of one's observance of the ten precepts'.[71] But associating family life with the Lower Evolution (or, in more traditional terms, with craving and attachment) suggested that anyone serious about Dharma practice should avoid having a family, especially an 'emotionally overloaded' nuclear family.[72] Ideally, they would find a living situation, such as a residential community, that was more conducive to Dharma practice. Even outside a family, Sangharakshita considered emotional dependence on a sexual partner a particular barrier:

> If we're not careful, they have to be everything for us, sexual partner, friend, companion, mother – at least in the case of men – father, advisor, counsellor, and much else. We expect love from them, security, happiness, fulfilment and, in a word, we expect the sexual-romantic relationship to give meaning to our lives.[73]

Sangharakshita wrote in his review of the Lawrence biography:

> By the couple, in this context, one means two people, usually of the opposite sex, who are neurotically dependent on each other and whose relationship, therefore, is one of mutual exploitation and mutual addiction. A couple consists, in fact, of two half-people, each of whom unconsciously invests part of his or her total being in the other: each is dependent on the other for the kind of psychological security that can be found, ultimately, only within oneself.[74]

This didn't mean there was no place for sexual relationships or people with families, but it did mean that, in Sangharakshita's view, a spiritual community couldn't be built around them. The members of one of the Archway communities happened to all be young men, and a new and exceptional kind of friendship developed between them. With Sangharakshita's encouragement, single-sex communities became a model for FWBO living for both men and women, and the practice extended to right-livelihood working situations. Being free from 'inter-sex tensions',[75] he thought they could be places where 'men and women tend to develop, and integrate into their own spiritual life and practice, the "feminine" and "masculine" qualities which are normally projected on to the opposite sex'.[76]

The result was an intensive social experiment including dozens of people – and in time many more. It isn't hard to imagine some of the problems that arose: people with families felt they had been pushed to the periphery; men left their families and moved into a community, causing difficulties for the partners and children they left behind; women felt excluded when men's communities formed; and men whose determination to keep women at arm's length tipped into outright sexism.

The most controversial area in the long term was sex. It is hardly novel to suggest that getting married and having children bring responsibilities that might deflect from an intensive focus on spiritual life. But the alternative Sangharakshita proposed wasn't celibacy, and there was no bar against sex *between* community members. He thought psychological projection was, on the whole, less pronounced between people of the same sex, and in some quarters that made homosexuality seem less 'neurotic'. Although what followed was sometimes unproblematic, sex is usually emotionally loaded, and problems certainly did arise. It was also inevitable that these ideas would be criticized in later years on the grounds that they served those, including Sangharakshita himself, whose sexual interests were directed towards their own sex.

That isn't to say that single-sex FWBO residential communities were a pretext for abusive behaviour. Sex between community members was a small part of what happened in communities; in some cases, it was more common though not necessarily problematic. But this wasn't what community life was about, and communities in the FWBO/Triratna created an environment that supported both friendship and more intensive Dharma practice – and they still do. Their influence has been central to the deep sense of sangha that, in more recent years, has often been seen as the movement's most striking virtue.

Women and gender

Sangharakshita's association of family life with the Lower Evolution was also a comment on gender, because he thought women were drawn more strongly than men to everything family life involved. This didn't make him 'anti-women' as has sometimes been suggested. In India he actively advocated women's rights.[77] In the West he emphasized individuality and established an ordination that was equal for both men and women. He said he had no quarrel with 'feminism with a small "f"', meaning 'the attitude that a woman, no less than a man, should be free to develop whatever capacities and interests she has'. But he did criticize 'Feminism with a capital F', which presents women as victims and, he thought, 'tends to result in the development of hatred towards men'.[78]

Nonetheless, Sangharakshita placed greater value on the concerns and activities traditionally associated with men than those associated with women. As a teenager he imbibed Schopenhauer's account of women as 'childish, foolish, and short-sighted'[79] and driven by a wish to propagate. We hear its echo in the women of

The Artist's Dream who want their menfolk to return to domestic life. That view of women sometimes appears in the seminars, but Sangharakshita also offered a more nuanced account of spiritual psychology. 'Feminine' qualities such as receptivity, patience, and kindness were important within his presentation of Dharma practice, but he gave a leading role to traditionally masculine ones such as 'initiative, boldness, daring, courage, adventurousness'[80] because he thought they created the momentum that produced change. This isn't quite the same as valuing men more highly than women, and he reserved his highest praise for an androgynous state, beyond male and female identities and open to both men and women, in which 'one ceases to think of oneself as being a man or a woman in any absolute and exclusive sense'.[81] But before androgyny was possible, he thought, we must escape the gravitational pull of the Lower Evolution, and that required qualities usually associated with men.

Sangharakshita expressed a version of these thoughts in a somewhat opaque aphorism included in the 1979 collection *Peace Is a Fire*: 'Angels are to men as men are to women – because they are more human and, therefore, more divine.'[82] Ratnaprabha's introductory essay in the *Complete Works* calls this a 'weird little saying',[83] but it stems from Sangharakshita's understanding of the Higher Evolution as a journey through an ascending hierarchy of states, from the human to the transcendental. As this was a quintessentially human activity, a person with a greater affinity with the path could be said to be 'more human' than one with less affinity; and if, as Sangharakshita thought, men had a greater spiritual aptitude than women (because they had a greater affinity with masculine qualities), it followed that men could be said to be more human (and therefore more divine) than women.

A single aphorism could be regarded as a provocation akin to Nietzsche's more outrageous sayings, but Sangharakshita didn't want his views to be brushed aside. Subhuti discussed the aphorism in *Sangharakshita: A New Voice* (1994) in the course of surveying Sangharakshita's thought as a whole, and, when this discussion was criticized, he expanded it into a short book, published in 1995, entitled *Women, Men and Angels: An Inquiry into the Relative Spiritual Aptitudes of Men and Women*.

A fierce controversy ensued. Some women Order members embraced Sangharakshita's views as a challenge to move away from domesticity and free themselves from emotional dependence on men. They placed the aphorism beside his encouragement to women to become more self-reliant:

> Women should stop looking over their shoulders at men and trying to prove themselves equal to men. This does not mean that the sexes are unequal. It means that the concepts of equality and inequality are inappropriate. Women should simply do what is best for their own development as individuals without bothering about whether or not men are doing the same things or about where it leaves them in relation to men.[84]

Women's communities, and an array of women's activities, developed – slowly at first and then with growing confidence, and with Sangharakshita's strong encouragement. By the 2000s women held positions of responsibility at every level of the movement, and more women than men were being ordained (at least outside India, where the culture created extra barriers). But, to many, Sangharakshita's view that women's very biological makeup disadvantaged them was discouraging if not demeaning. It sounded like a new version of age-old sexist tropes that failed to take account of women's strengths and their changing place in society. Subhuti expressed his regret for *Women, Men and Angels* in 2004; it was withdrawn from publication, and in 2017 he issued a still more extensive apology:

> Unfortunately, the book drew attention to a relatively peripheral aspect of Sangharakshita's thinking, giving it a status it did not warrant and having effects that I did not anticipate. I especially regret that some people have been caused pain by it, and some have been put off involving themselves with Triratna.[85]

Sangharakshita never retracted his views, but in 2009 he commented that they expressed 'my observation, which I cannot prove and which has little bearing on the actual practice of the Dharma'. He didn't apologize as Subhuti had, but he acknowledged that the 'whole weight of current popular opinion' was against his view, and 'it would be wise not to insist on it, since it is not critical to someone's practice of the Dharma, and one doesn't want to discourage anybody without good reason.'[86]

Disagreement and discipleship

The controversy over *Women, Men and Angels* raised more fundamental questions. Did an Order member's relationship with Sangharakshita mean they must agree with his views? Clearly there must be a basic accord on fundamental matters, but at what point did disagreement mean an Order member ceased to be a disciple? And if an Order member who disagreed with Sangharakshita's views on gender was teaching in a Triratna centre, should they pass on their own views, or only his? Questions like these are intrinsic to any religious community, but they are especially pointed in one based in the principle of individuality. Sangharakshita told Order members they weren't obliged to agree with him on all points, but he wanted them to take what he said seriously and recognize that it was based on careful thought.

By the 2000s the majority of Order members no longer lived in residential communities or worked in right-livelihood businesses. Many of the founding generation lived alone or with their partners, and newer Order members often had families. Many right-livelihood ventures, as with many small businesses, were overtaken by changing economic conditions and the difficulty of retaining experienced staff. One, Windhorse:Evolution, prospered and set up local businesses around the movement, mainly in the UK, but it eventually faced the same challenges on a larger scale and closed in 2015.

The Order was also ageing. The average age of members of all western Buddhist movements, including Triratna, increased as the 1960s generation aged. For a variety of reasons, the movement cannot rely for its future on the children of Order members, and its growth – even its survival – means attracting new people and especially younger generations. Across western societies, lifestyles have become more individualistic, religious affiliation has declined, and many social-change movements, from trade unions to religious movements, have lost their appeal. Buddhism lost some of the cultural cachet it had enjoyed. Rather than asking whether the FWBO's New Society could change the world, it seemed more realistic to ask whether its institutions could survive at all.

Attitudes to Sangharakshita were also changing. The media coverage of his sexual behaviour discussed in Chapter Three affected his standing in the movement. The larger Order was far from the small band of disciples it had included in the 1970s. Some experienced Order members had developed their own approaches to Dharma practice or received teachings and initiations from other Buddhist schools. Were they still Sangharakshita's disciples? If they passed on what they had learned, did their teaching express the movement's approach? And, if so, what was that approach?

During his period of insomnia and anxiety in 2003, Sangharakshita withdrew from all involvement in FWBO matters and later described what happened in the reflective piece, *A Season in Hell*. It begins with a short parable. The good ship FWBO has been sailing along untroubled until the captain disappears from the bridge. Without his hand at the wheel, the ship veers to left and right, and the crew, who should have been steering, are nowhere to be seen. Some passengers, tired of always travelling in the same direction, criticize the captain and some of them jump ship. Then order returns:

> [T]he captain did not die, and eventually appeared on the bridge again, though less frequently than before, and looking paler and thinner. The liner was set on its old direct course, the crew was reorganized, the passengers reassured.[87]

An alternative view was that the issues facing the movement were more than a temporary disruption.[88] In 2000 Sangharakshita handed on the headship of the Order to the College of Public Preceptors – a small group of senior Order members with final responsibility for ordinations. But in 2004 Subhuti, the first chair of the College, declared they did not consider 'headship' an accurate description of their role. He wrote to Order members that a new consensus was needed:

> Revelations about Bhante's behaviour underline that questions must be asked about spiritual authority, including about who confers ordination and on what basis. I believe we need to debate this very widely so that we can try to reach a new common understanding on the subject.[89]

• • •

Although Sangharakshita handed on responsibility for ordinations and even the headship of the Order, some things were bound up with his role as the Order's founder and its definitive teacher, particularly the shared understanding of the Buddhist path that defined ordination. That could only mean the version he formulated.

In 2009, aged eighty-four, Sangharakshita thought it time to restate principles that had become unclear. His declining strength and virtual blindness made it impossible for him to write a substantial paper, but he could still share his views and have them published. He gathered three senior Order members at Madhyamaloka, and the ensuing discussion was published as *What Is the Western Buddhist Order?*

The first, and most basic, question Sangharakshita addressed was: 'What defines the Order?' The question arose because of the changing nature of the Order. As Order members discovered their own ways to practise, some gravitated towards traditions, and teachers representing them, from beyond the FWBO. Taken to its logical conclusion, this produced the view that 'the Order is what Order members collectively think it is', with no reference to Sangharakshita's place in the shared commitment made at ordination. He vigorously disagreed:

> My version is that, directly or indirectly, I decide. The Order cannot be redefined democratically. The Order was founded by me as the community of my disciples who are practising the Dharma in accordance with my teaching. [...] The duty of

my disciples is to adhere faithfully to the teaching they have received from me, to practice [sic] faithfully in accordance with that, and to do their best to hand it faithfully on to others.[90]

The reason for his insistence, he said, was the nature of the spiritual life: 'For commitment to be strong it has, in a sense, to be narrow.' He considered this a traditional attitude that most teachers would share: 'You need to follow a particular set of teachings and practices within a particular framework under a particular teacher in order to experience any real progress.'[91] He had offered a fresh presentation of the Dharma and founded an Order based upon it:

Every Sangha presupposes a Dharma: a particular Sangha presupposes a particular presentation of the Dharma. The Order and the FWBO presuppose the particular presentation of the Dharma which I have given over the years.[92]

This implied a clear answer to the question *What Is the Western Buddhist Order?*: 'The Order can be defined as the community of my disciples and the disciples of my disciples, and the disciples of my disciples' disciples and so on.'[93] In a short message prefacing the published version of the interview, Sangharakshita asked Order members to treat it as 'my Last Will and Testament', and, along with the papers that followed it, *What Is the Western Buddhist Order?* became required reading for people training for ordination.

The tenor of Sangharakshita's comments in the interview differs from the 1970 talk 'Is a Guru Necessary?' and the 1990 paper *My Relation to the Order*, but the role it outlines is the one that had been assumed throughout the Order's history. He didn't want it to be a melting pot of approaches, and thought coherence could only come from his teachings: 'Choosing this Order', he said, 'means choosing me as your teacher.' He knew many Order members were less concerned with principles than with the pragmatic question of what they found helpful to their Dharma lives, but he thought the Order was weakened by 'people who are in fact no longer members of the Order in this effective sense, who are no longer my disciples following my teaching'.[94]

This didn't mean Sangharakshita expected complete agreement. He didn't think an Order member was obliged to find his teachings on the Higher Evolution 'an acceptable presentation of the Dharma',[95] and he said of his views on the spiritual aptitude of men and women:

> I regard that as a difference of opinion that does not affect their discipleship. Although my view of the matter does come from my personal experience and relates to the Buddhist tradition through the ages.[96]

A few years later he added, in a postscript to the interview, that it wasn't even essential that Order members accept the term 'disciple'. But it was important that they 'share my understanding of the Dharma and follow practices that flow from that understanding'.[97]

Chapter Seventeen
Alternative Traditions

Theravādin contrasts

Sangharakshita wasn't alone in developing a Buddhist movement in the West after the late 1960s. In fact, a Buddhist world quickly developed in Europe and North America that included many movements comparable to, or larger than, the FWBO, along with smaller groupings gathered around individual teachers. This Buddhist world reflected the complexity of the Buddhist tradition in Asia and added fresh variants. Most Buddhist organizations were connected to the tradition in which the founders had trained – usually Zen, Theravāda, or Tibetan Buddhism. Some stuck closely to received forms, at least initially, while others adapted them to varying degrees. There were also temples catering to Asian Buddhist communities in western countries, and movements like Soka Gakkai that adapted to modern conditions in Asia before arriving in the West.

Sangharakshita's approach was always distinctive. In the 1979 talk 'Western Buddhists and Eastern Buddhism', he said:

> [T]he first thing that the Western Buddhist has to do is learn to distinguish what is really Buddhism from what is actually South-east Asian, or Chinese, or Japanese, or Tibetan, or even Indian culture.[1]

This had been his project in India. In England, as an independent teacher, he felt free to draw from Buddhist tradition as he saw fit and find fresh ways to express its essential meaning. He sometimes called his approach 'critical ecumenicalism' – an alternative to adhering exclusively to a single school, mixing them eclectically, or boiling the tradition down to a single practice such as meditation. His focus was the fundamentals of the Buddhist tradition. He sometimes said the FWBO was 'just Buddhist', meaning that he adhered to the basic principles he traced back to the Buddha and drew from the various traditions 'whatever [they] can find that contributes to the spiritual development of the individual in the West'.[2] The FWBO's task was to find ways to practise Buddhism in the modern world while staying true to Buddhism's essential meaning.

Monasticism

Two years before Sangharakshita was born in a nursing home in Stockwell, South London, a fifty-year-old Englishman died a couple of miles away in Eccles Road, Clapham Junction.[3] Born Allan Bennett, in the course of an eventful life he had been a scientist, a leading figure in the esoteric Order of the Golden Dawn, a teacher to the notorious magician Aleister Crowley, and only the second Briton to become a Theravādin bhikkhu. His Buddhist name was Ananda Metteya, and Crowley called him 'the noblest and gentlest soul I have ever known'.[4] Both Metteya and Sangharakshita disliked theosophy-style gossip about previous lives, and the younger man made little of his connection with his precursor. But the physical resemblance between them was so strong that, when visitors to the Hampstead Vihara saw a photograph of Metteya above the abbot's desk, some people thought it was a photo of Sangharakshita. The resemblance extended to aspects of their lives and their approach to Buddhism, though the differences were just as striking. Both combined intelligence with faith, and teenage 'mystical' experiences shaped both their lives. Like Sangharakshita, Metteya saw Buddhism as a universal teaching with a 'living, breathing Truth' at its heart,[5] and thought of the path as a matter of 'spiritual progress'.[6]

However, it seems unlikely that Metteya would have seen the movement Sangharakshita founded as the fulfilment of his hopes for Buddhism in the West. While both men received Theravādin ordination, Metteya considered the Theravāda 'the Traditional, Original, or Orthodox School',[7] and disrobed only reluctantly when ill-health made it impossible to continue. A generation later, Sangharakshita rejected the Theravāda in its modern manifestations (though not the scriptures it preserved), and refused any understanding of Buddhist orthodoxy that identified it with established forms.

Metteya's own writings often dispense with traditional Buddhist terminology, as Sangharakshita's do, but he never gave up his belief in the bhikkhu life.[8] More fundamentally, what Sangharakshita rejected wasn't monasticism but 'the identification of the spiritual life with the monastic life and the monastic life itself with pseudo-monastic formalism'.[9] He called this 'Vinaya-style monasticism', and contrasted it with a more flexible 'Sutra-style monasticism' based on chastity and renunciation but without the many Vinaya rules.[10] What *really* mattered, he concluded,

> was that one went for Refuge to the Three Jewels, after which, as an expression of that continuing act, one could live either as a 'monk' or as a 'layman'.[11]

Sangharakshita's solution was team-based right-livelihood businesses and a culture of supporting Order members to be full-time practitioners who 'may not be wearing yellow robes, but in certain important respects [...] live like monks'.[12] By the mid-1990s, when Sangharakshita had returned to celibacy, he described himself as 'a Sutra-style monk rather than as a Vinaya-style *bhikkhu*'.[13] A community of *anagārika*s developed within the Order, who undertook to be chaste and careerless and to have few possessions, and by the mid-2020s around seventy Order members practised in this way. This was a small proportion of the Order as a whole but a significant number by comparison with other Buddhist monastic communities.

* * *

Sangharakshita remarked in 1976: '[I]t is not possible to be a bhikkhu in most Western countries. [...] In fact, if you tried to beg for food from door to door, you might even be arrested.'[14] On one level that proved not to be correct. In 1978 American bhikkhu Ajahn

Sumedho (b. 1934) arrived in England with two other western monks. Sumedho had trained in Thailand with Ajahn Chah, a Thai bhikkhu renowned for his devotion to meditation and strict adherence to the Vinaya. Sumedho spent ten years in Thailand as a Thai Forest monk, and he was determined to maintain the bhikkhu lifestyle in the West. His early attempts to beg his food were as unsuccessful as Sangharakshita had predicted, but donors soon appeared and Sumedho and colleagues founded monasteries at Chithurst and Amaravati. These communities, which include mostly western monks and latterly some nuns, have maintained Vinaya monasticism, with some adaptations, and spawned a modest international network.

All the same, monks and nuns make up a tiny minority of Buddhists in the West, and many of those who ordain disrobe after a few years. Their commendable achievements are far from the influence on western culture Sangharakshita believed Buddhism needed to exert if it was to help alleviate the world's problems:

> The Buddhism that could do this is not the traditional Buddhism of south-east Asia and the Far East. It would have to be a Buddhism that was not identified with monasticism, and that had shed all unnecessary oriental cultural baggage. It would have to be a Buddhism in which commitment to the Buddha, the Dharma, and the Sangha was primary, and lifestyle secondary.[15]

Theravādin monastics are a small proportion even of westerners who follow Theravādin practices, and a much more widespread development is the broad movement that we can refer to as the vipassanā community.[16]

Joseph Goldstein and the vipassanā sangha

Joseph Goldstein, a leading figure in the global vipassanā movement, was born in 1944, nineteen years after Sangharakshita, and as a young man he learned vipassanā meditation in India from Anagārika Munindra. Munindra was himself a student of Mahasi Sayadaw (1904–82), who taught what was initially called the 'new Burmese *satipaṭṭhāna* method' and inspired a modernizing movement that systematized Theravādin meditation practices, separated them from the devotional, doctrinal, and cosmological aspects of the Theravāda, and made them accessible to lay people and non-Buddhists.

As fellow monks in the small world of Indian Buddhism, Sangharakshita and Munindra met and discussed Sayadaw's meditation method.[17] Sangharakshita declared in *A Survey of Buddhism* that, under its influence, 'the dry and dusty pitchers of modern Theravāda may well present once again to the parched lips of humanity a brim overflowing with the waters of spiritual life.'[18] However, at the Hampstead Buddhist Vihara he met people who were experiencing 'extreme nervous tension and a schizoid state' as a result of the practice. He coined the term 'alienated awareness'[19] to describe what had happened to them and banned the practice from the Vihara.

Goldstein returned to the West in 1974, disrobed, and two years later he and other former Theravādin monastics founded a retreat centre called Insight Meditation Society (IMS) in rural Massachusetts. In time, a network of independent insight meditation centres spread across North America and around the world, while many other vipassanā teachers and movements developed in parallel. Later still, a much wider 'mindfulness movement' developed, first in healthcare settings and then across western societies, that further popularized vipassanā-style approaches.

Goldstein's relationship with the Buddhist tradition resembled Sangharakshita's in some respects but differed fundamentally in others. Goldstein also wanted to distil the essence of Buddhism, and was willing to set aside its established forms. He said in 1989:

> I'm not so concerned with any labels or the cultural forms of the tradition, although I do appreciate the many ways they have evolved in Asian culture. Instead, what inspires me is the connection with the original teachings of the Buddha, with what, as far as we know, he actually taught during his lifetime. [...] What I would like to be doing, and what I hope I am doing, is teaching what the Buddha taught based on my own experience of it.[20]

For many years, Goldstein practised and taught Theravādin practices within the vipassanā network. But a wider American Buddhist world was developing that also included many Zen and Tibetan Buddhist teachers. In the 1990s Goldstein learned Dzogchen practices from a Tibetan master. It affected him deeply and became central to his practice. Seeing Zen-trained peers who were taking up vipassanā and Tibetan Buddhist practitioners who were learning Zen, he concluded that the categories of Asian Buddhism were breaking down. In 2002 he published a book entitled *One Dharma: The Emerging Western Buddhism*, which declared that a new kind of Buddhism was emerging that offered 'a skillful form for our times'.[21] That form was expressed in many ways as it was filtered through different practice traditions, but its essence remained the essential message of the Buddha, as Goldstein understood it.

This parallels Sangharakshita's approach, if only because he and Goldstein were asking similar questions. Andrew Rawlinson comments:

> The effect of these questions, which cut across traditional boundaries, is simple yet radical: it forces each Eastern tradition to be very clear about what is essential, and what is optional, in its own teaching.[22]

However, the method Goldstein proposes in *One Dharma* to ascertain Buddhism's true meaning differs from Sangharakshita's. Goldstein speaks of a fruitful meeting between 'the diversity and depth of the ancient Buddhist culture [...] [and] the openness and pragmatism of our contemporary western culture'. The key to navigating the tradition, he thought, was asking: what works to free the mind from suffering? What works to engender a heart of compassion? What works to awaken? For Sangharakshita, 'what works' in the experience of a Buddhist practitioner was only one side of a relationship with the transcendent values represented in the Three Jewels. He thought an authentic western Buddhism would only develop through commitment, or going for refuge, to these values.

The difference in outlook produced very different movements. It is hard to generalize about the Insight Meditation movement because it is a loose and diverse network, but its core has always been vipassanā meditation in the tradition of Mahasi Sayadaw, and a significant difference with the FWBO/Triratna concerns the conception of 'practice'. For most vipassanā teachers, practice predominantly means meditation and mindfulness, and the dialogue Goldstein had in mind in *One Dharma* largely meant sharing meditation practices. For Sangharakshita, these practices went along with other aspects of the Buddhist path, including ethics, faith, study, and much else. He didn't think this was just a matter of different styles. In *Extending the Hand of Fellowship* (a 1996 paper discussing the FWBO's relation to other Buddhists) he said of the vipassanā movement:

> Some of the movement's leading personalities not only emphasize meditation, in the sense of 'insight meditation', at the expense of Going for Refuge; they also ignore Going for Refuge completely. In extreme cases, having reduced meditation to '*vipassanā*', and *vipassanā* itself to a matter of mere technique, they take it out of its Buddhist context and seek to combine it with elements derived from other sources, so that it is no longer *vipassanā* in the traditional sense but something quite different.[23]

While ordination within Triratna meant dedicating oneself to Buddhism, centres in the vipassanā network often didn't call themselves Buddhist, and many teachers maintained an involvement in Christianity or Judaism. The central activity was offering retreats rather than developing a community, and retreats were led by a network of teachers rather than members of an order.

Theravādin monasticism, the vipassanā community, and Triratna offer three differing understandings of what it means to practise Buddhism in the modern world. Andrew Rawlinson wrote in 1997:

> The *bhikkhu sangha* regards the *vipassanā sangha* as grandiosely concerned with the higher stages of the path without having fulfilled the elementary steps; the vipassanā *sangha* sees the *bhikkhu sangha* as stuck in formalities.[24]

Sangharakshita agreed with vipassanā teachers that a lifestyle based on Vinaya rules was limiting and impractical. He agreed with the bhikkhus that an early emphasis on insight was an unhelpful 'path of irregular steps'. He thought both approaches focused on secondary matters, rather than the commitment to the fundamental values expressed in going for refuge from which a balanced approach to both lifestyle and 'practice' followed.

In some ways, the vipassanā movement's approach to reformulating Buddhism was much narrower than Sangharakshita's. Whatever Goldstein's personal interests may have been, the overwhelming subject of his teaching is how consciousness can transform through meditation, mainly meaning samatha practices that concentrate the mind and vipassanā practices aimed at gaining insight. But this narrowness has also given the vipassanā movement a tremendous reach. A fruitful dialogue developed between vipassanā teachers and psychological researchers, and many vipassanā and mindfulness teachers have also been trained psychotherapists. The focus on meditation and mindfulness also relegated beliefs and views, and the scholar Gil Fronsdal (a vipassanā teacher himself) commented that vipassanā teachers typically adhere to 'Western values, worldviews, and institutional preferences', including 'democracy, equality, feminism, and individualism'.[25] This meant that mindfulness meditation could be taken up with a western lifestyle and a liberal worldview, and in time within healthcare, education, and many other settings. These eventually reached millions of people across western societies.

Sangharakshita was cautiously open to popularizing Buddhist methods and to presenting them in non-Buddhist terms, provided these remained true to Buddhist values, but his conception of *western* Buddhism was very different from what Fronsdal describes in the vipassanā community. Goldstein and others spoke positively of the need to 'integrate' Dharma practice, which usually meant taking up meditation within a lay lifestyle. Sangharakshita called that Buddhism without withdrawing from worldly life, and added:

> What is really wanted is a Buddhism that is neither lay nor monastic in the traditional sense but which is firmly based on the centrality for the Buddhist life of the act of Going for

Refuge supported by the observance of the fundamental ethical precepts. The integration that is needed is not the integration of Buddhism into the world, but of the world into Buddhism.[26]

This was a fundamentally different conception of what it meant to be 'western'. *One Dharma* was written in the tradition of American pragmatism that aligned with a secularized outlook. Vipassanā teachers are much more likely to cite scientific papers than the predominantly European western philosophical and artistic tradition that was an important context for Sangharakshita's thought. He viewed western culture hierarchically, and his conception of 'western Buddhism' included the aspects he considered 'higher' while rejecting much else.

Chögyam Trungpa and crazy wisdom

Sangharakshita met Chögyam Trungpa Rimpoche (1939–87) in India and in Britain, where the Rimpoche began teaching in the 1960s before moving to North America. Both Chögyam Trungpa and Sangharakshita thought Buddhism's arrival in western societies marked a decisive historical juncture. As Chögyam Trungpa wrote:

> My journey to the overseas continent needs no copyright.
> For it has never been conducted in the same manner.
> It is the fresh meeting of man,
> The true meeting of living man.[27]

But Chögyam Trungpa's re-expression remained distinctly Tibetan. He founded a movement devoted to 'creating Enlightened Society', and eventually named it 'Shambhala' after the ideal city of Indian and Tibetan mythology. That paralleled Sangharakshita's talk of creating a New Society and building a buddha land (or 'Sukhavati'), but Chögyam Trungpa's approach included, among other things, presenting himself as a quasi-monarch at the centre of the Kalapa Court. Stephen Batchelor comments that this arrangement evokes Tibet's 'devotional Buddhism with feudal overtones'.[28]

In Tantric Buddhism the student surrenders his or her will to the guru, and Chögyam Trungpa embraced the role. He was thought to manifest 'the crazy wisdom of complete directness',[29] and continually challenged his students in the belief that 'The student of tantra should be constantly in a state of panic.'[30] He also smoked, drank heavily, often taught while drunk, and had sex with many of his female disciples. The justification was that his behaviour displayed the freedom the student could experience directly by opening to the natural state of awareness:

> Beyond that process of thinking and non-thinking there is some basis of nonthought, nonconceptualization. No matter how confused we might be, there is a dancing ground of experience that is common to everyone. [...] a basic state of mind that is clear and pure and natural.[31]

This message matched the countercultural spirit, and Chögyam Trungpa's followers included many creative artists in the Beat Generation. Perhaps the most prominent was Allen Ginsberg, who thought Sangharakshita was radical, but his poetry, with its rhyme, metre, and literary echoes, was 'square'.[32] He might well have said the same about Sangharakshita's presentation of a path of regular steps beginning with ethics and depending on an honest estimate of one's strengths and weaknesses.

Sangharakshita remarked in 1996 of the tantric understanding of the teacher's role:

> Though such an approach may have a certain validity, when correctly understood, in practice it results, only too often, in the lama being regarded as infallible (and his behaviour therefore as beyond criticism), as well as in a surrendering, on the part of the disciple, of his (or her) intellectual independence and moral and spiritual autonomy.[33]

Such a role suited neither his personality nor his emphasis on individuality. He was certainly a friend and *kalyāṇa-mitra*, but he warned in 1970: 'It is a great mistake to expect from a guru what we can only get, ultimately, from ourselves.'[34] We have seen that, throughout his life, Sangharakshita experienced powerful energies that seemed to be both an external force and the expression of his unconscious psychic depths. These were connected to his sexual activity, sometimes cut across 'conventional morality', and were arguably the source of the ethical questions he prompted, but he never justified his behaviour as 'crazy wisdom' or any other spiritual quality.

Chögyam Trungpa was a brilliant and complex figure who resists a simple assessment. He valued consistency and progression along with crazy wisdom, and his movement was dynamic and creative even after his death in 1987. But it also encountered successive ethical challenges arising from his behaviour and that of his Dharma heirs, and these were surely related to his teaching of crazy wisdom. Sangharakshita, for one, was not inclined to judge him. He remarks in one seminar:

> They might ask about a certain gifted but wayward Buddhist teacher, 'Is so-and-so a bodhisattva or is he a total fake?' Of course, the fact is that such a person is a complex human being and worthy of more than a snap judgement either way.[35]

Thich Nhat Hanh and interbeing

Thich Nhat Hanh (1926–2018) was born a year after Sangharakshita and received full monastic ordination a year before him in 1949. The Vietnamese teacher's early career was bound up with Buddhist efforts to oppose the Vietnam War, at the end of which the victorious Communist regime exiled him and he settled in the West. Like Chögyam Trungpa and Sangharakshita, Thich Nhat Hanh founded a sangha that grew within his lifetime into a worldwide movement and, like them, he was a prolific Dharma teacher who reformulated Buddhist teachings for the modern world. He was charismatic in a very different way from Chögyam Trungpa, often beginning his talks by standing silently until he had the audience's attention, ringing a meditation bell, and then speaking quietly on themes like awareness, peace, and innate goodness.

The main subject of his teaching was how we can live peacefully amid suffering by learning to see it correctly and remaining connected to a profound source of meaning. This was the inspiration of the Order of Interbeing, which he founded in 1966 at the height of the Vietnam War in the belief that Buddhist monks and nuns must step outside their monasteries and temples and engage with the world's difficulties alongside committed lay followers. He later shared this 'engaged Buddhism' with the wider world in both Asia and the West, where it proved popular.

Thich Nhat Hanh's principal lineage descended from Ch'an (the Chinese school from which Japanese Zen also developed),[36] and his philosophy derives ultimately from the *Avataṃsaka Sūtra*, *The Awakening of Faith*, and Yogācāra teachings, which also influenced Sangharakshita as a young man. Thich Nhat Hanh's modernized version of these teachings centred on the idea of *interbeing*:

> If we look into this sheet of paper even more deeply, we can see the sunshine in it. If the sunshine is not there, the forest cannot grow. In fact nothing can grow. Even we cannot grow without sunshine. And so, we know that the sunshine is also in this sheet of paper. The paper and the sunshine inter-are. [...] As thin as this paper is, it contains the entire universe.[37]

This implies an understanding of conditionality according to which phenomena, including pieces of paper, mental states, and human societies, arise together and – seen truly – are parts of an interdependent whole rather than separate entities. The illusion of separateness is the cause of suffering; recognizing interconnectedness and interbeing is the end of suffering. This interconnected reality is empty because the piece of paper is made up entirely of things that are not the piece of paper. Likewise with the individual: we don't exist independently; we 'inter-are' as parts of the interconnected web of existence. Thich Nhat Hanh equated this with the Emptiness taught by the Mahāyāna tradition, which, he said, is the shared ground of being: 'The ultimate is the ground that makes the historical dimension possible. It is the original, continuing source of being. It is nirvāṇa. It is the kingdom of God.'[38]

One way to compare this understanding of life with other Buddhist understandings is through the underlying conception of conditionality. The Discourses and early Buddhism – and Sangharakshita after them – understand causality as 'dependent arising': 'b' arises in dependence upon 'a'. The Discourses apply this not so much as a general metaphysical principle but as an account of individual experience: 'suffering arises in dependence upon craving.' It also implies individual ethical responsibility: consequences arise in dependence upon my actions, and therefore I am responsible for them. Thich Nhat Hanh speaks of 'the mutual co-arising of phenomena', which is to say: 'a' and 'b' arise together.

These differing ways of understanding conditionality produce different understandings of the spiritual life and the world. Thich Nhat Hanh's teachings imply that society's problems arise from a web of conditions of which we are part. As David McMahon comments in his book *Buddhist Modernism*, within Thich Nhat Hanh's thought 'moral responsibility is decentered from the solitary individual and spread throughout the entire social system.'[39] Thich Nhat Hanh himself describes Buddhist practice in his book *Being Peace* as 'a way of helping us stay in society'.[40] This aligns with the perspective of political liberalism, ecology, and humanistic psychology, and for many whose worldview is based on them, his teachings have added a spiritual dimension. By the end of his life, Thich Nhat Hanh was widely acclaimed as a prophet of the mindfulness movement, engaged Buddhism, interfaith dialogue, environmentalism, and peace activism.[41]

When the influence of the *Avataṃsaka Sūtra* and *The Awakening of Faith* was at its strongest, Sangharakshita sometimes echoed this perspective. As a teenager, he described the outlook of the bodhisattva who lives for the sake of all beings: 'He in them and they in him – a mutual interpenetration of being – this is his ideal.'[42] A few years later, he declared that 'the positive albeit symbolical complement of the doctrine of no-selfhood is that of the perfect mutual interpenetration of all the seemingly discrete "things".'[43] He retained a feeling for this approach throughout his life, but thought it was only meaningful if we recognize ourselves as individuals at different stages of realization, take responsibility for our actions and states of mind, and make an effort to develop.

If Thich Nhat Hanh taught original purity, interbeing, and equality, Sangharakshita taught the need to develop, individuality, and hierarchy. He remarked in a lecture on 'The Bodhisattva Hierarchy' that inequality was 'one of the most obvious things about life',[44] and he thought individuals should open themselves to the influence of the higher dimension and ascend the hierarchy of being. We are equal in the sense of having the same potential for Enlightenment, but Sangharakshita called the view that we are equal in a more pragmatic sense 'pseudo-egalitarianism'. In the 1992 book *The FWBO and 'Protestant Buddhism'* he used the term 'Rousseau-ism' to describe the belief within western culture that 'there exists a self which is pure [and] that this self is enslaved by socially imposed beliefs and customs.' He thought this view affected the whole of modern culture:

> It has encouraged the shifting of moral responsibility for one's actions from self to society. It has encouraged talk of rights rather than duties. Above all, perhaps, it has encouraged people to believe that they do not need to *work on themselves* but have only to change the social, economic, and political conditions under which they live. Such Rousseauism has nothing in common with Buddhism.[45]

The implication is that teachings like Thich Nhat Hanh's appealed to western people because they expressed their pre-existing Rousseauism and precluded an attitude of 'real devotion or reverence'.[46] Sangharakshita called his own worldview 'thoroughly medieval', because for him 'it was natural to think in terms of hierarchy and degree.'[47] If this made him unpopular, so be it. He observes in his memoirs that his character possessed

> a rock bottom of obstinacy that made it utterly impossible for me to retract or disown any opinion which I genuinely believed to be true even to save my life.[48]

In 1992 both Sangharakshita and Thich Nhat Hanh were speakers at the Congress of the European Buddhist Union held in Berlin. Western Buddhism had been growing for twenty-five years, largely in the form of independent Buddhist movements, and events like the Congress marked a new phase of dialogue. The subject of Thich Nhat Hanh's talk was living in the world with simple mindful presence, and he suggested this was all we really needed to change ourselves and the world. Engaged Buddhism, he said, meant embracing the world, with all its problems.

Sangharakshita had been asked to speak on the apparently similar theme of 'The Integration of Buddhism into Western Society', but he told his audience that the real meaning of being a Buddhist was going for refuge to the Three Jewels. This meant:

> [T]he whole-hearted recognition of the fact that permanence, identity, unalloyed bliss, and pure beauty are not to be found anywhere in mundane existence, but only in the transcendental nirvanic realm. [And secondly it consists in] the wholehearted resolve to make the great transition from the one to the other.

In conclusion, Sangharakshita declared that, although he had been asked to speak about the integration of Buddhism into western society, 'what we really have to do is to integrate Western society into Buddhism.'[49]

Sangharakshita and modern Buddhism

As a young monk Sangharakshita had no doubt that Buddhism could make a significant contribution to the world with all its problems. But in India, he saw, and wrote about, a tradition in decline, facing formidable foes, weighed down by its past, and – in the case of the Theravāda – bound up with what he thought were literalistic and unduly conservative understandings. He advocated reform and adaptation, and wanted to be part of a movement that unleashed Buddhism's transformative power, finding inspiration in figures like the Sri Lankan reformer Anagārika Dharmapāla and the great Indian Dalit leader Dr Ambedkar.

This mission stayed with Sangharakshita all his life. Buddhism is arguably more relevant than ever in an increasingly technology-filled, stressful, and unstable world, but he noted in 1996:

> In the course of my lifetime, at least, the portion of the earth's surface traditionally covered by Buddhism has shrunk dramatically [...] Buddhism is now the smallest and in certain respects the least influential of the three great world religions.[50]

Many Buddhist leaders in Asia recognize the challenge Buddhism faces in remaining relevant in a world that differs fundamentally from the traditional societies in which it developed. The same questions are accentuated in the West. Sangharakshita believed that Buddhism must adapt, and his principal contribution was proposing a basis for adaptation while maintaining the tradition's integrity. That meant going back to Buddhism's guiding purpose and stripping away the elements that didn't serve it, however revered they might have become.

This reaffirmed a view of Buddhism as a path to Enlightenment that Ajahn Sumedho, Chögyam Trungpa, and Thich Nhat Hanh would have shared, but Sangharakshita's teaching differed from theirs. Because it didn't stem from a single Buddhist school, he was free to ask fundamental questions, and he argued that Buddhist traditions too often lose sight of Buddhism's meaning by focusing too much on the tradition's outward forms. That willingness to strip away established forms resembled the approach of secular Buddhists, but he couldn't have been further removed from their willingness to dispense with ritual, devotion, and a sense of buddhahood as a transcendental state.

In Sangharakshita's lifetime, his influence on modern Buddhism never matched his ambition. His views were challenging, and some people found them abrasive. The falling out at the Hampstead Buddhist Vihara cast a long shadow, and coverage of his sexual behaviour and views on gender affected his public standing. Finally, the FWBO/Triratna's project of building a 'self-contained Buddhist world' inevitably brought a degree of insularity. For all these reasons, although Sangharakshita had supporters and opponents, by the time of his death there was relatively little awareness of the scope or depth of his contribution. It merits more attention than it has received, and its relevance to Buddhism's challenges has not been fully measured.

Chapter Eighteen
Seeds and Flowers

Sangharakshita and Triratna

The process that led me to write this book began seven years before I finally completed it. Sangharakshita was still alive when I started assembling my thoughts, and by the time I was done he had been dead for several years. I set out to write this book because I wanted to clarify the issues his life and teachings had raised for me. That meant distilling his essential approach and understanding his character, and, even though I had been familiar with his work for many years, what I found surprised me. The extent of his work was obvious, but I hadn't fully appreciated its scope, and in each area I considered I found levels upon levels of meaning. In bringing together the elements of his thinking, I often found he had preceded me by explaining not only what he taught but why he taught it. His writings balance what must be expressed for the sake of clarity with what can only be felt or intuited, and lead back to a more elusive spirit. He reflects at the end of the conversations published as *What Is the Western Buddhist Order?*:

> There is something about the movement, the Order and even about me that is not easily definable. There is a touch of something that cannot be buttoned down, something that cannot in the end be defined. Even the desire to button it down or define it is a mistake.[1]

In the *Survey* he encapsulates his view of the Buddhist tradition as the transmission of this spirit: 'Flame is lit from flame, and ultimately life's inspiration springs not from theories about life but from life itself.'[2]

• • •

The German sociologist Max Weber long ago noted the distinctive place of the founder in any movement, organization, or religion. He said the founder possesses a 'charismatic authority', which is not to be confused with charisma in the sense of a person's attractiveness. Charisma in Weber's sense stems from the founder's capacity to speak authoritatively about fundamental matters from their personal experience, rather than depending on precedents. Sangharakshita insisted the true authority in Buddhism is the Buddha's awakened understanding, but he recognized that, as a Buddhist teacher, he possessed charismatic authority in the sense of 'the ability to distinguish between what is, and what is not, Buddhism'.[3] This included rational analysis, but it also meant 'discriminating between what is essential and what is not essential – what is living and what is dead'.[4] In other words, Buddhism's meaning is something to be grasped through 'spiritual intuition',[5] or imagined – in the expanded sense of imagination this book has explored.

Sangharakshita passed on his understanding in three main ways: through his writings, through personal interactions, and through the Order and movement. His writings can be read as sources of information about Buddhism, but his underlying intention was to communicate his understanding of its meaning. His writings therefore ask to be read as Murry read a poet – for their 'deeper rhythm' as well as their surface meaning.

Max Weber's ideas about founders and organizations also clarify the challenge facing Triratna after Sangharakshita. Weber noted the difference between the way a charismatic founder operates and what is required of the organization or movement they establish. It must pass on the founder's unique inspiration, in part through the example of people they have trained but also through institutional forms and procedures. Weber called this 'the routinization of charisma'.[6]

Triratna closely fits the model. Sangharakshita withdrew slowly, and the Order's structures developed gradually, in a process that lasted for many years. It was able to continue without significant disruption after his death in 2018. The intention throughout was that the new structures would operate according to Buddhism's animating spirit, but that posed a challenge that will also determine Triratna's future. How can the spirit of the Dharma be maintained? One danger is repeating the mistake of the schools Sangharakshita criticized, and smothering the spirit one wishes to preserve by holding too tightly to the forms in which it has been embedded. Another is that the forms are so loose there are no shared ways to understand and practise Buddhism. Then the Order will dissolve into a sea of contradictory approaches.

Triratna's structures and values were intended as so many middle ways between these dangers. In 2006 Sangharakshita said he had initiated several lineages that, taken together, combined the spirit of the Dharma with the form that sustains it. The first was a lineage of teachings, meaning that Order members should study and pass on what he had taught and evolve new teachings on that basis. Then came a lineage of practices, especially meditation. The third was the lineage of inspiration flowing 'from me to others, and from others to yet others', which could only be 'transmitted' through personal contact, particularly in the context of a private ordination. Supporting these three lineages, Sangharakshita said, was a fourth lineage of structures and responsibilities (he later spoke of 'institutions') that should be 'continued and, in some cases, modified if they no longer fulfil their original purpose'.[7] Like the Order itself, these lineages derive from Sangharakshita, and Triratna's future fortunes will always be bound up with responses to him. The legacy of his sexual activity has complicated this, but for me that is part of a much larger picture that includes his life, his teachings, and the Order.

Reflecting on the spirit of the Dharma and Sangharakshita's efforts to express it returns me to my experience as a fifteen-year-old when I heard him evoke the taste of freedom through intricate webs of image thinking. I remained a Buddhist because Buddhist practice enabled me to connect with that spirit. I joined the Order and continued to study Sangharakshita's work because I found that, for all the difficulties, Buddhism was alive in them in a remarkably vivid and eloquent form.

Coda: 'The Sunflower's Farewell'

At the end of Sangharakshita's life, he recognized the strengths and challenges of the movement he founded, but said he had let go of anxieties about its future. In fact he reached a stage he had imagined in poems written forty years earlier, in the autumn of 1978. He was fifty-three, the FWBO was growing rapidly, and a dedicated band of workers were putting the finishing touches to the London Buddhist Centre. But he was in a reflective mood and wrote three autumnal poems. The first describes a decaying sunflower beside the Norfolk fields around Padmaloka:

> Aloft on its tall stalk the sunflower hangs
> As though half weary. Harvest long since reaped,
> It sees beyond the ivied crumbling wall
> Blue-vaulted stubble in faint sunlight steeped.
>
> Aloft on its dry stalk the sunflower hangs
> In silence: in the West, the round red sun.
> The yellow petals, once its glory, wilt:
> Its seed is ready and its work is done.[8]

'The Sunflower's Farewell' offers an image of exhaustion and completion, but Sangharakshita never rested in pathos, and, in his system of practice, spiritual rebirth follows spiritual death. 'Padmaloka', the third poem in the sequence, is perhaps the strongest of all his later poems. It evokes the gardens and trees around the house, the drifts of golden leaves and the sluggish river close by:

> In this quiet spot, girt by the reeds and rushes,
> The soul roots deeper, and the spirit hushes.

But autumn presages winter, and winter is followed by spring. The lilies on the margined pond prefigure an archetypal realm that beckons after death:

Thinking and dreaming, in this quiet spot,
Summer and Winter, I shall end my days,
Till like the rose I am remembered not,
And life has vanished with the sunset-rays.
Then, among silver lakes and golden mountains,
The new-born lotus smiles beside the crystal fountains.[9]

Notes

Epigraph

1 *The Three Jewels*, in *The Complete Works of Sangharakshita* (hereafter SCW), vol. 2, p. 59.

Introduction

1 'Last Word', BBC Radio 4, 9 November 2018.
2 The group called itself 'the Adhiṣṭhāna Kula' and eventually produced a report entitled *Addressing Ethical Issues in Triratna*, available at https://thebuddhistcentre.com/stories/ethical-issues/, accessed on 22 January 2025.
3 Theravādin bhikkhus or monks are often referred to as 'Bhante', a term of respect. People addressed Sangharakshita in this way in his time as a monk, and the practice continued when he founded the FWBO.
4 *Uposatha Sutta*, *Udāna* 5.5.
5 *The Taste of Freedom*, SCW, vol. 11, p. 52.
6 *The Taste of Freedom*, SCW, vol. 11, p. 52.
7 *The Taste of Freedom*, SCW, vol. 11, pp. 42–3.
8 *The Rainbow Road*, SCW, vol. 20, p. 84.
9 *A Survey of Buddhism*, SCW, vol. 1, p. 24.
10 *Introducing Buddhism 3: The Approach to Buddhism* (1966), SCW, vol. 12, p. 59.
11 *Wisdom beyond Words*, SCW, vol. 14, p. 373.
12 *The Rainbow Road*, SCW, vol. 20, p. 85.
13 The path of the bodhisattva that is followed within Mahāyāna Buddhism, rather than the early Buddhist path of the *arahant*.
14 *What Is the Sangha?*, SCW, vol. 3, p. 389.
15 *Buddhism for Today – and Tomorrow*, SCW, vol. 11, p. 170.
16 *Wisdom beyond Words*, SCW, vol. 14, p. 472.
17 *Revering and Relying upon the Dharma*, in *Seven Papers*, Triratna InHouse Publications, 2018, p. 47.
18 *The Three Jewels*, SCW, vol. 2, p. 54.
19 *The History of My Going for Refuge*, SCW, vol. 2, p. 428.
20 *An Old Saw Resharpened*, SCW, vol. 7, p. 326.
21 *Milarepa and the Art of Discipleship II*, SCW, vol. 19, p. 372. He states this position as 'the fundamental voidness of all dharmas', but adds that the Madhyamaka's philosophical understanding must be supplemented by the meditative realization of the Yogācāra. Madhyamaka and Yogācāra are the two principal trends in Mahāyāna thought.
22 *The Three Jewels*, SCW, vol. 2, pp. 132–3.
23 See SCW, vol. 12, p. 179 ff; vol. 16, p. 1 ff, and vol. 13, p. 113 ff.
24 *The Bodhisattva Ideal*, SCW, vol. 4, p. 148.

25 Samuel Coleridge, *Collected Letters of Samuel Taylor Coleridge*, ed. Earl Leslie Griggs, 6 vols, Clarendon, Oxford, 1956, vol. 1, p. 281.
26 *The History of My Going for Refuge*, SCW, vol. 2, pp. 405–6.
27 John Middleton Murry, *God: An Introduction to the Science of Metabiology*, Jonathan Cape, London, 1929, p. 47.
28 *The History of My Going for Refuge*, SCW, vol. 2, p. 498.
29 *The History of My Going for Refuge*, SCW, vol. 2, p. 405.
30 *The Path of the Inner Life* (1950), SCW, vol. 7, p. 359.
31 *The Rainbow Road*, SCW, vol. 20, p. 451.
32 *The Religion of Art*, SCW, vol. 26, p. 148.
33 See Andrew Rawlinson, *The Book of Enlightened Masters*, Open Court, Chicago, IL, 1997, pp. 501–8 and references throughout the book.
34 *Know Your Mind*, SCW, vol. 17, p. 617.
35 *The Three Jewels*, SCW, vol. 2, p. 54.
36 Personal communication with Subhuti.
37 *My Relation to the Order*, SCW, vol. 2, p. 530.
38 *Criticism East and West*, SCW, vol. 26, p. 319.
39 John Middleton Murry, *Discoveries*, Collins, London, 1924, pp. 13–14.
40 Helen Vendler, *Poets Thinking*, Harvard University Press, Cambridge, MA, 2004, p. 119.
41 One source of Vendler's understanding is St Augustine's theology of images.
42 *Moving against the Stream*, SCW, vol. 23, p. 182.
43 W.B. Yeats, 'At Stratford-on-Avon: Ideas of Good and Evil', quoted in Ted Hughes, *Shakespeare and the Goddess of Complete Being*, Faber & Faber, London, 1993, p. xvi.
44 James Hillman, *Revisioning Psychology*, Harper & Row, New York, 1975, p. x.
45 *Living with Awareness*, SCW, vol. 15, pp. 93–4.
46 *Milarepa and the Art of Discipleship I*, SCW, vol. 19, p. 212.
47 *Milarepa and the Art of Discipleship I*, SCW, vol. 18, p. 282.
48 Vidyadevi, preface to *The Essential Sangharakshita*, SCW, vol. 6, p. xvii.
49 'Third Letter from London' (April 1980), SCW, vol. 24, p. 148.

Chapter One

1 *Autumn Thoughts* (October 1951), SCW, vol. 7, p. 336.
2 SCW, vol. 7, p. 336.
3 *Facing Mount Kanchenjunga*, SCW, vol. 21, p. 436.
4 *The Rainbow Road*, SCW, vol. 20, p. 469.
5 Dhardo Rimpoche, 'Report of the Indo-Tibetan Buddhist Cultural Institute' (1963), quoted in Suvajra, *The Wheel and the Diamond: The Life of Dhardo Rimpoche*, Windhorse Publications, Glasgow, 1991, p. 110.
6 In *Precious Teachers* Sangharakshita wrongly states that the invasion occurred on 23 October, perhaps because this was when he heard of it. SCW, vol. 22, p. 545.
7 Sangharakshita gives this date in *Precious Teachers*, SCW, vol. 22, p. 472. *The History of My Going for Refuge*, SCW, vol. 2, p. 442, says it occurred on 24 October.
8 Khantipalo, *Noble Friendship*, Windhorse Publications, Birmingham, 2002, pp. 87–8. At this time Khantipalo was called Śramaṇa Sujīva.
9 *Triyana Vardhana Vihara Report, 1957–1962*, Kalimpong, 1963, p. 5.
10 Khantipalo, *Noble Friendship*, p. 16.
11 *A Complex Personality: A Note*, SCW, vol. 26, p. 639.
12 *Buddhism for Today – and Tomorrow*, SCW, vol. 11, p. 171.
13 'What Might Have Been' (2018), SCW, vol. 26, p. 585.
14 Khantipalo, *Noble Friendship*, p. 84.
15 *Fields of Creativity*, SCW, vol. 12, p. 636.
16 'Letter 22' (4 March 1963), in *Dear Dinoo: Letters to a Friend*, Ibis Publications, Birmingham, 2011, p. 96.
17 Christmas Humphreys, *Both Sides of the Circle: The Autobiography*

of *Christmas Humphreys*, Allen & Unwin, London, 1978, p. 211.
18 Ken Winkler, *A Thousand Journeys: The Biography of Lama Anagārika Govinda*, Element Books, Longmead, 1990, p.115.
19 *With Allen Ginsberg in Kalimpong*, scw, vol. 22, p. 566. Sangharakshita introduced Ginsberg to his own teacher, Yogi Chen, who in turn advised him to consult Dudjom Rimpoche. In Barry Miles's biography of Ginsberg, Sangharakshita and Yogi Chen are conflated into 'an old English lama with blackened teeth'. Barry Miles, *Ginsberg: A Biography*, Simon & Schuster, New York, 1989, p. 309.
20 *Triyana Vardhana Vihara Report*, p. 3 ff.
21 *Triyana Vardhana Vihara Report*, p. 6.
22 *Wanted: A New Kind of Bhikkhu*, scw, vol. 8, p. 327, and *Wanted: A New Kind of Upāsaka*, scw, vol. 8, p. 331.
23 *The Language of Scents*, scw, vol. 26, p. 493.
24 *Buddhism in India Today* (1959), scw, vol. 7, p. 468.
25 *The History of My Going for Refuge*, scw, vol. 2, p. 438.
26 Khantipalo, *Noble Friendship*, pp. 42 and 44.
27 'Letter 17', in *Dear Dinoo*, pp. 96.
28 'Letter 22' from Lama Govinda to Sangharakshita (6 March 1961), Sangharakshita Study Centre archive.
29 *What Might Have Been*, scw, vol. 26, p. 591.
30 *The Rainbow Road*, scw, vol. 20, pp. 301–2.
31 *Moving against the Stream*, scw, vol. 23, p. 60.
32 Nagabodhi, *Jai Bhim*, Windhorse Publications, Birmingham, 1996, p. 86.
33 *In the Sign of the Golden Wheel*, scw, vol. 22, p. 30.
34 *The Rainbow Road*, scw, vol. 20, p. 452.
35 *In the Sign of the Golden Wheel*, scw, vol. 22, p. 186.
36 *In the Realm of the Lotus*, scw, vol. 26, p. 247.
37 *Padmasambhava, Tantric Guru of Tibet* (1972), scw, vol. 12, p. 293.
38 *The Rainbow Road*, scw, vol. 20, p. 134, and *A Visit to a Tibetan Monastery* (1945), scw, vol. 7, p. 76.
39 *Padmasambhava, Tantric Guru of Tibet*, scw, vol. 12, p. 575.
40 *Facing Mount Kanchenjunga*, scw, vol. 21, p. 93.
41 *Facing Mount Kanchenjunga*, scw, vol. 21, p. 258.
42 *Creative Symbols of Tibetan Buddhism*, scw, vol. 13, p. 171.
43 *The Life of Service or the Life of Contemplation* (1948), scw, vol. 7, pp. 154–5. The scw note that 'This article was published in *Vedanta Kesari* vol. xxxv, no. 4 (August 1948) under the name of Anagārika Dharmapriya' (vol. 7, p. 156). It may have been composed earlier than 1948.
44 'The Stream of Stars', scw, vol. 25, p. 264.
45 Shelley, *Prometheus Unbound*, act 2, scene 5, lines 72–4.
46 *Colin Wilson Revisited*, scw, vol. 26, p. 572 ff. *The Outsider* was published in 1956, and Sangharakshita says he read it a few years after it was published.
47 *Colin Wilson Revisited*, scw, vol. 26, p. 572.
48 *The Rainbow Road*, scw, vol. 20, p. 18.
49 *The Rainbow Road*, scw, vol. 20, pp. 18–19.
50 'The Awakening of the Heart' (1949), scw, vol. 25, pp. 463 and 468.
51 *Colin Wilson Revisited*, scw, vol. 26, p. 579.
52 Diary entry for 19 July 1953, in *Diary Leaves 1953–4*, Sangharakshita Study Centre archive.
53 *Colin Wilson Revisited*, scw, vol. 26, p. 577.
54 *From Genesis to the Diamond Sutra*, scw, vol. 13, p. 610.
55 *What Might Have Been*, scw, vol. 26, p. 584.
56 *Colin Wilson Revisited*, scw, vol. 26, p. 578.
57 Preface to *Complete Poems 1941–1994*, Windhorse Publications,

Birmingham, 1995. This preface does not appear in SCW, vol. 25.
58 'Goldfish' (1950), SCW, vol. 25, p. 225. The poem can be interpreted non-sexually, but Sangharakshita told his interlocutors in the 2009 *Conversations with Bhante* that 'One has to read between the lines a bit, but it is fairly obvious what I am writing about.' Available at https://www.sangharakshita.org/articles/conversations-with-bhante, accessed on 23 January 2025.
59 *Conversations with Bhante*.
60 'Love's Austerity' (1957), SCW, vol. 25, p. 223.
61 Khantipalo, *Noble Friendship*, p. 47.
62 'Sonnet' (1956), SCW, vol. 25, p. 278.
63 *Creative Symbols of Tantric Buddhism*, SCW, vol. 13, p. 117.
64 *Tibetan Buddhism*, SCW, vol. 13, p. 92.
65 Quoted in Geoffrey Samuel, *Civilized Shamans: Buddhism in Tibetan Societies*, Smithsonian Institute Press, Washington, DC, 1993, p. 11. See Sangharakshita's review: *A Survey of Tibetan Religious Development*, SCW, vol. 8, pp. 351–3.
66 Marco Pallis, *Peaks and Lamas* (1946), 3rd ed., Woburn Press, London, 1974, p. 358.
67 Lama Anagārika Govinda, *The Way of the White Clouds*, Hutchinson, London, 1966, p. xi.
68 *New Currents in Western Buddhism*, SCW, vol. 11, p. 373.
69 *A Survey of Buddhism*, SCW, vol. 1, p. 377.
70 *Getting beyond the Ego*, SCW, vol. 7, p. 406.
71 *In the Realm of the Lotus*, SCW, vol. 26, p. 224.
72 *In the Sign of the Golden Wheel*, SCW, vol. 22, p. 363.
73 *Facing Mount Kanchenjunga*, SCW, vol. 21, p. 323.
74 See *The Purpose and Practice of Buddhist Meditation*, SCW, vol. 5, p. 37–8.
75 Thomas Merton, *The Asian Journal of Thomas Merton*, New Directions, London, 1975, p. 144.
76 Merton, *The Asian Journal*, p. 143.
77 *Precious Teachers*, SCW, vol. 22, p. 392.
78 Subhuti, *Sangharakshita: A New Voice in the Buddhist Tradition*, Windhorse Publications, Birmingham, 1994, p. 193. Sangharakshita said this to Subhuti in an interview recorded in 1989.
79 *The Meaning of Conversion in Buddhism*, SCW, vol. 2, p. 248.
80 *Precious Teachers*, SCW, vol. 22, pp. 400–1.
81 *Precious Teachers*, SCW, vol. 22, p. 407.
82 *What Is the Sangha?*, SCW, vol. 3, p. 516.
83 *The Bodhisattva Ideal*, SCW, vol. 4, p. 554.
84 The four *mūla-yoga*s are usually considered preliminaries to undertaking *sādhana* practice. The going for refuge and prostration practice is the first. The others are the development of the *bodhicitta* practice, meditation and mantra recitation of Vajrasattva, and the mandala offering.
85 *The Cosmic Refuge Tree and the Archetypal Guru*, SCW, vol. 13, pp. 216–17, 219.
86 *Creative Symbols of Tibetan Buddhism*, SCW, vol. 13, p. 162 and p. 684, n. 65, and *Precious Teachers*, SCW, vol. 22, p. 503.
87 *Creative Symbols of Tibetan Buddhism*, SCW, vol. 13, pp. 215–16.
88 *Precious Teachers*, SCW, vol. 22, p. 474.
89 Vishvapani, 'Return Journey' (interview with Sangharakshita), in *Dharma Life* 20 (summer 2003), p. 48; and *Lecture Tour in India 1981–2*, SCW, vol. 9, p. 330.
90 'The Present Emergency' (November 1962), SCW, vol. 8, p. 308 and p. 310.
91 Sangharakshita wrote to a lawyer named Mr Chaterjee on 21 April 1959: 'since Cou-En-Lai's [sic] last statement reaffirming a centre of anti-Chinese activity in Kalimpong, the Indian Government has begun to take an undue interest in my affairs which, together with the newspaper reports read by the general public, will seriously damage my reputation for integrity with the general public.' The newspapers included *The Blitz* of Bombay, the *New Delhi Times*, and *The*

New Age. Letter in the Sangharakshita Study Centre archive.
92 Subhuti, *Bringing Buddhism to the West*, Windhorse Publications, Birmingham, 1995, p. 93.

Chapter Two

1 *Moving against the Stream*, SCW, vol. 23, p. 80.
2 *Moving against the Stream*, SCW, vol. 23, p. 421.
3 Stephen Batchelor, *The Awakening of the West*, Parallax Press, Berkeley, CA, 1994, p. 333.
4 *New Currents in Western Buddhism*, SCW, vol. 11, p. 378.
5 *The Path of Regular Steps and the Path of Irregular Steps*, SCW, vol. 11, p. 58.
6 *From Alienated Awareness to Integrated Awareness* (1970), SCW, vol. 5, p. 104; SCW, vol. 12, p. 258 ff.
7 *The Heights and Depths of the Spiritual Life*, SCW, vol. 12, p. 23.
8 *Buddhism and the Language of Myth*, SCW, vol. 12, p. 107.
9 Vishvapani, 'Return Journey', p. 48.
10 Nagabodhi, *Sangharakshita: The Boy, the Monk, the Man*, Windhorse Publications, Cambridge, 2023, p. 164.
11 *Conversations with Bhante*.
12 *Moving against the Stream*, SCW, vol. 23, p. 103.
13 *Moving against the Stream*, SCW, vol. 23, p. 110.
14 Nagabodhi, *Sangharakshita*, pp. 165–6.
15 Quoted in *Moving against the Stream*, SCW, vol. 23, pp. 182–3.
16 *Moving against the Stream*, SCW, vol. 23, p. 183.
17 See *The Journey to Il Convento*, SCW, vol. 26, p. 264 ff.
18 Vangisa, 'Ten Years in the Golden Light', in *FWBO Newsletter* 34 (spring 1977), p. 4.
19 *Moving against the Stream*, SCW, vol. 23, p. 376.
20 Maurice Walshe, 'Editorial: New Year's Revolution', in *The Buddhist Path: Journal of the London Buddhist Vihara* (January 1968), p. 2.
21 A statement by Maurice Walshe in the July 1967 issue of *The Buddhist Path* adds a further twist: 'It is much to be regretted that temporary credence was given to certain damaging allegations respecting the moral character of Ven. Sangharakshita which are now known to be totally false. The exact source of these allegations, which seem to have been deliberately "planted" in several quarters, is not yet known, but their falsity is evident and they should be denied if further repeated. signed: Maurice Walshe, Chairman English Sangha Trust.' *The Buddhist Path: Journal of the London Buddhist Vihara* (July 1967), p. 3.
22 *New Currents in Western Buddhism*, SCW, vol. 11, p. 379.
23 Letter from Christmas Humphreys to Sangharakshita, 10 December 1966, Sangharakshita Study Centre archive.
24 *Moving against the Stream*, SCW, vol. 23, p. 393.
25 Letter to John Hipkin, quoted in *Moving against the Stream*, SCW, vol. 23, p. 406.
26 *Moving against the Stream*, SCW, vol. 23, p. 438.
27 Maurice Walshe, 'Editorial: Milestones', in *The Buddhist Path: Journal of the Buddhist Vihara* (November 1967), p. 3.
28 Walshe, 'Editorial: New Year's Revolution', p. 2.
29 'The Ven. Sangharakshita Sthavira', in *Sangha: Monthly Buddhist Journal of the Sangha Association*, vol. 8, no. 7 (July 1964), p. 2.
30 A gathering of bhikkhus recognized Sangharakshita shortly after his arrival as the 'Head of the English Sangha'. 'Statement Issued by the Sangha of English Monks of Great Britain', in *Sangha: Monthly Buddhist Journal of the Sangha Association*, vol. 8, no. 10 (October 1964), p. 3.

93 *Buddhism for Today – and Tomorrow*, SCW, vol. 11, p. 173.
94 *Precious Teachers*, SCW, vol. 22, p. 561.

31 Vishvapani, 'Return Journey', p. 50.
32 Vishvapani, 'Return Journey', p. 50.
33 *Moving against the Stream*, scw, vol. 23, pp. 376–7.
34 An organization named Friends of the Western Sangha was established on 4 April 1967. A charity named the Friends of the Western Buddhist Order was established on 1 April 1968. Sangharakshita conducted the first ordinations into the Western Buddhist Order on 8 April 1968.
35 'The Scapegoat' (1970), scw, vol. 25, p. 328.
36 'Letter to a Friend' (1992), available at https://alaya.thebuddhistcentre.com/index.php/s/A4A3l68TgSqJzWe#pdfviewer, accessed on 24 January 2025.
37 'Fourth Metamorphosis' (1967), scw, vol. 25, p. 319.
38 'Sex and the Spiritual Life', in *Golden Drum* 6 (August 1987), scw, vol. 11, p. 584.
39 'I Want to Break Out' (1968), scw, vol. 25, p. 309.
40 *Living with Carter*, scw, vol. 26, p. 608.
41 Quoted in Fabrice Midal, *Chögyam Trungpa: His Life and Vision*, Shambhala Publications, Boston, MA, 2004, p. 493.
42 'Letter to a Friend'.
43 'The Great Reader', scw, vol. 25, p. 327.
44 *The Bodhisattva Ideal*, (1969), scw, vol. 4, p. 43.
45 James Hillman, *Insearch: Psychology and Religion*, Scribner, London, 1968, p. 79.
46 *The Heights and Depths of the Spiritual Life*, scw, vol. 12, p. 26.
47 *The Bodhisattva Principle*, scw, vol. 4, p. 643.
48 *The Journey to Il Convento*, scw, vol. 26, p. 268.
49 *St Jerome Revisited*, scw, vol. 26, p. 305.
50 Friedrich Nietzsche, *Thus Spake Zarathustra*, trans. R.J. Hollingdale, Penguin Books, Harmondsworth, 1961, p. 108.
51 'New' (1969), scw, vol. 25, p. 313.
52 *Forty-Three Years Ago*, scw, vol. 2, p. 611.
53 The first edition of *The Eternal Legacy*, published in 1985, designates Sangharakshita in this way. In subsequent years he published as 'Sangharakshita' or 'Urgyen Sangharakshita'.
54 Nagabodhi, *Sangharakshita*, p. 189.
55 Buddhadasa, *On the First Rung: Reminiscences of the Early Years of the Triratna Buddhist Order 1969–1974*, Ola Leaves, Ledbury, 2014, p. 42.
56 *What Is the Sangha?*, scw, vol. 3, pp. 511, 512.
57 *The Young Man in the Hut*, scw, vol. 26, p. 599.
58 *Moving against the Stream*, scw, vol. 23, p. 446.
59 *My Relation to the Order*, scw, vol. 2, p. 531.
60 Subhutip (Alex Kennedy), *Buddhism for Today: A Portrait of a New Buddhist Movement*, Element Books, Salisbury, 1983, p. 34.
61 Barry Pilcher, 'New Sakura, Archway', in *FWBO Newsletter* 16 (July 1972), p. 7.
62 Buddhadasa, *On the First Rung*, p. 34.
63 'A Personal Message to All Friends', in *FWBO Newsletter* 18 (spring 1973), scw, vol. 11, pp. 514–15.
64 Ananda, 'Looking Back (A Personal Impression)', in *FWBO Newsletter* 34 (spring 1977), p. 11.
65 Michael Kennedy, 'An Open Letter to the Friends', in *FWBO Newsletter* 10 (December 1970). Michael Kennedy was later ordained as Abhaya.
66 Nagabodhi, *Sangharakshita*, p. 198.
67 Padmasambhava, *Tantric Guru of Tibet*, scw, vol. 12, pp. 293–5.
68 'A Personal Message to All Friends', scw, vol. 11, p. 515.
69 *FWBO Newsletter* 43 (summer 1979), p. 37.
70 This figure is cited in Ian Oliver, *Buddhism in Britain*, Rider, London, 1979, p. 160.
71 'First Letter from New Zealand, May 1979', scw, vol. 24, p. 11.
72 Ole Mallender, 'Foreword', in scw, vol. 26, p. 215. Mallender is describing a visit in 1978.

73 'First Letter from New Zealand, May 1979', SCW, vol. 24, p. 11.
74 'Say Padmaloka', SCW, vol. 25, p. 457.
75 'Before Dawn', SCW, vol. 25, p. 348.
76 See *Travel Letters*, SCW, vol. 24, pp. 1–147.
77 'First Letter from New Zealand, May 1979', SCW, vol. 24, p. 19.
78 *New Currents in Western Buddhism*, SCW, vol. 11, p. 350.
79 *Milarepa and the Art of Discipleship II*, SCW, vol. 19, p. 438.
80 Oliver, *Buddhism in Britain*, p. 196.
81 'Second Letter from New Zealand', SCW, vol. 24, p. 129.
82 'Padmasambhava Comes to the West', in *FWBO Newsletter* 43 (summer 1979), pp. 16–19, SCW, vol. 8, pp. 524–5.
83 *The Manu, the Buddha, the Guru and the Tertön*, SCW, vol. 12, p. 322.
84 *The Manu, the Buddha, the Guru and the Tertön*, SCW, vol. 12, p. 334.
85 *The Manu, the Buddha, the Guru and the Tertön*, SCW, vol. 12, pp. 333, 335.
86 *The Manu, the Buddha, the Guru and the Tertön*, SCW, vol. 12, pp. 334, 336.

Chapter Three

1 'Second Letter from London, July 1989', SCW, vol. 24, p. 340.
2 From Andrew Marvell's 'To His Coy Mistress'; *St Jerome Revisited*, SCW, vol. 26, p. 293.
3 'Dharmadhara told me that my blood pressure was only slightly less than Dayasri's had been when she had her stroke and that, without medication, my life expectancy was not more than five years, possibly as little as one or two years.' 'Letter From Wales' (January 1989), SCW, vol. 24, p. 307.
4 'Letter From Wales' (July 1989), SCW, vol. 24, pp. 306–7.
5 *Extending the Hand of Fellowship*, SCW, vol. 2, pp. 546–7.
6 'Guhyaloka, July 1998', SCW, vol. 25, pp. 424–5.
7 'Looking Ahead a Little Way' (1999), SCW, vol. 12, p. 600. In this talk Sangharakshita announced his intention to hand on the headship or the Order. The following year, he announced how that was to happen.
8 'Guhyaloka, September 1999', SCW, vol. 25, p. 435.
9 Personal communication with Subhuti.
10 *A Season in Hell*, SCW, vol. 26, p. 458.
11 *The Poetry Interviews*, SCW, vol. 25, p. 67.
12 *A Season in Hell*, SCW, vol. 26, p. 459.
13 'A Memoir of Mark Dunlop' (2017), Sangharakshita Study Centre archive.
14 Madeleine Bunting, 'The Dark Side of Enlightenment', *The Guardian* (27 October 1997).
15 *Conversations with Bhante*. See note 54 to Chapter One.
16 'Sex and the Spiritual Life', *Golden Drum* 6 (August 1987), SCW, vol. 11, pp. 577, 578.
17 *Conversations with Bhante*.
18 *Conversations with Bhante*.
19 Jamie Doward, 'Fears Mount over Scale of Buddhist Sect Sexual Abuse', *The Observer* (19 February 2017).
20 Adhiṣṭhāna Kula, 'Sangharakshita's Sexual Activity', in *Addressing Ethical Issues in Triratna*.
21 *Conversations with Bhante*.
22 'The Wind', SCW, vol. 25, p. 450.
23 *The History of My Going for Refuge*, SCW, vol. 2, pp. 405–6.
24 Percy Shelley, 'Ode to the West Wind' (1819). Other echoes include D.H. Lawrence's 'Song of a Man Who Has Come Through' and John's Gospel, 3.8.
25 *In the Sign of the Golden Wheel*, SCW, vol. 22, p. 364.
26 Letter from Sangharakshita to Subhuti (14 October 2011), quoted in '*A Supra-Personal Force or Energy Working Through Me*': The Triratna Buddhist Community and the Stream of the Dharma, Seven Papers, p. 160.
27 *A Supra-Personal Force or Energy Working Through Me*, Seven Papers, p. 163.

28 *A Supra-Personal Force or Energy Working Through Me, Seven Papers*, p. 165.
29 *Conversations with Bhante*.
30 *A Word on Mantrayana*, SCW, vol. 26, p. 698.
31 Sangharakshita, *Statement of Apology and Regret* (December 2016), available at https://www.sangharakshita. org/articles/a-personal-statement, accessed on 27 January 2025.
32 *Blake and the Gates of Paradise* (2017), SCW, vol. 26, pp. 647–8.
33 *Dreams: Old and New II*, SCW, vol. 26, p. 682.
34 'Argosies' (1952), SCW, vol. 25, p. 249.
35 *Dreams: Old and New II*, SCW, vol. 26, p. 682.

Chapter Four

1 *The Priceless Jewel*, SCW, vol. 16, pp. 232, 218. In *The Drama of Cosmic Enlightenment* Sangharakshita pairs the *Hymn of the Pearl* with the *White Lotus Sutra*'s 'Parable of the Return Journey': SCW, vol. 16, pp. 85–99.
2 From Aśvaghoṣa, *The Awakening of Faith in the Mahāyāna*. This translation is taken from *A Buddhist Bible*, ed. Dwight Goddard, Beacon Press, Boston, MA, 1966, p. 363, quoted in *Wisdom beyond Words*, SCW, vol. 14, p. 325.
3 *In the Sign of the Golden Wheel*, SCW, vol. 22, p. 17.
4 *The Language of Scents*, SCW, vol. 26, p. 498.
5 *Progress and Religion* (1948), SCW, vol. 7, p. 166.
6 *A Survey of Buddhism*, SCW, vol. 1, p. 20.
7 *A Note on Anatta*, SCW, vol. 7, p. 208.
8 *The Meaning of Buddhism and the Value of Art*, SCW, vol. 26, p. 111. This paraphrases the Buddha's reply to Mahā-Pajāpatī Gotamī (*Aṅguttara Nikāya* 4.280–1), which Sangharakshita often quoted.
9 *The Drama of Cosmic Enlightenment*, SCW, vol. 16, pp. 94–5.
10 William Blake, *The Marriage of Heaven and Hell*, 'Proverbs of Hell'.
11 *The Meaning of Buddhism and the Value of Art*, SCW, vol. 26, p. 111.
12 *The FWBO and the Path of Spiritual Development*, SCW, vol. 11, pp. 730–1.
13 *The Three Jewels*, SCW, vol. 2, p. 79.
14 The three *loka*s appear frequently within Sangharakshita's writing; these definitions are taken from *The Journey to Il Convento*, SCW, vol. 26, pp. 271–2.
15 *The Three Jewels*, SCW, vol. 2, p. 65.
16 *The Rainbow Road*, SCW, vol. 20, p. 73.
17 Unpublished early autobiographical writing, Sangharakshita Study Centre archive.
18 *Facing Mount Kanchenjunga*, SCW, vol. 21, p. 299.
19 See *In the Realm of the Lotus*, SCW, vol. 26, p. 226, and the account of later 'occult' experiences in *On the Edge of the Etheric*, SCW, vol. 26, p. 621 ff.
20 *Living with Awareness*, SCW, vol. 15, p. 137.
21 *The Lamas of Tibet* (1965), SCW, vol. 12, p. 12.
22 *The Lamas of Tibet*, SCW, vol. 12, p. 14.
23 *The Bodhisattva Ideal*, SCW, vol. 4, p. 169.
24 *Buddhism without Beliefs*, SCW, vol. 8, p. 574.
25 *The Lamas of Tibet*, SCW, vol. 12, p. 14.
26 *The Launch of 'Wisdom beyond Words'* (1993), SCW, vol. 14, p. 312.
27 *A Complex Personality: A Note*, SCW, vol. 26, pp. 638, 630.
28 'Third Letter from England', SCW, vol. 24, p. 168.
29 'Third Letter from England', SCW, vol. 24, p. 168.
30 *The Religion of Art*, SCW, vol. 26, p. 174.
31 'Third Letter from England', SCW, vol. 24, p. 169.
32 'Verses', SCW, vol. 25, p. 351.
33 *What Is the Dharma?*, SCW, vol. 3, p. 75.
34 Unpublished autobiographical sketch in the Sangharakshita Study Centre archive, LE26 (date unknown).
35 *The Bodhisattva Ideal*, SCW, vol. 4, p. 159.
36 *The Three Jewels*, SCW, vol. 2, p. 121.

37 *Milarepa and the Art of Discipleship II*, scw, vol. 19, p. 143.
38 See lecture 113, 'The Word of the Buddha', and the edited version in *Who Is the Buddha?*, scw, vol. 3, pp. 78–9. The image of the ocean is used in the *Laṅkāvatāra Sūtra*.
39 See lecture 139, *The Taste of Freedom*, and the edited version in scw, vol. 11, p. 43.
40 *Who Is the Buddha?*, scw, vol. 3, p. 80.
41 *Wisdom before Words*, scw, vol. 10, p. 568.
42 *In the Sign of the Golden Wheel*, scw, vol. 22, p. 17.
43 *The Bodhisattva Ideal*, scw, vol. 4, p. 33.
44 'Study Group Leaders Questions and Answers' on the lecture series 'Aspects of Buddhist Psychology' (September 1986), available at https://www.freebuddhistaudio.com/texts/seminartexts/SEM133_Aspects_of_Buddhist_Psychology_-_Unchecked.pdf, accessed on 30 January 2025. The discussion relates to the lecture 'Depth Psychology of the Yogachara'.
45 *The Language of Scents*, scw, vol. 26, p. 497.
46 *The Awakening of the Heart*, scw, vol. 7, p. 317.
47 *The Inconceivable Emancipation*, scw, vol. 16, p. 560.
48 *The Inconceivable Emancipation*, scw, vol. 16, p. 561.
49 *The Inconceivable Emancipation*, scw, vol. 16, p. 561.
50 *What Is the Dharma?*, scw, vol. 3, p. 263.
51 *Wisdom beyond Words*, scw, vol. 14, p. 472.
52 *A Survey of Buddhism*, scw, vol. 1, pp. 283–4.

Chapter Five

1 'Above Me Broods...' (1947), scw, vol. 25, p. 175.
2 *The Rainbow Road*, scw, vol. 20, p. 226.
3 *The Rainbow Road* also includes material about Sangharakshita's childhood, which Heinemann had cut, and Windhorse had published as a separate volume with the title *Learning to Walk*.
4 *Rainbows in the Sky*, scw, vol. 26, p. 672.
5 'Aspiration' (1947), scw, vol. 25, p. 181.
6 'Second Letter from England, October 1979', scw, vol. 24, p. 146.
7 *The Drama of Cosmic Enlightenment*, scw, vol. 16, pp. 173, 174.
8 *The Rainbow Road*, scw, vol. 20, p. 342.
9 *The Rainbow Road*, scw, vol. 20, pp. 341, 345.
10 *Creative Symbols of Tantric Buddhism*, scw, vol. 13, p. 196.
11 *The Bodhisattva Ideal*, scw, vol. 4, p. 148.
12 *The Essence of Zen* (edited from lectures given in 1965), scw, vol. 13, p. 341.
13 'The Lotus of Compassion' (1949), scw, vol. 25, p. 208. The poem was probably written after Sangharakshita's bhikkhu ordination.
14 Sangharakshita's bhikkhu ordination was held at Sarnath on 24 November 1950, while he was living in Kalimpong.
15 *The Rainbow Road*, scw, vol. 20, p. 470.
16 *Facing Mount Kanchenjunga*, scw, vol. 21, p. 48.
17 *The Awakening of the Heart*, scw, vol. 7, p. 316.
18 *Ariyapariyesena Sutta*, *Majjhima Nikāya* 26.
19 Ian McGilchrist is a recent exponent of holistic or organic thinking. He identifies the right hemisphere of the brain with a non-mechanistic understanding that allows us to perceive phenomena as wholes and processes. See Ian McGilchrist, *The Master and His Emissary*, Yale University Press, New Haven, CT, 2012.
20 *My Five Literary Heroes*, scw, vol. 26, p. 481 ff.
21 M.H. Abrams, *The Mirror and the Lamp: Romantic Theory and the Critical Tradition*, Oxford University Press, Oxford, 1953, p. 170.

22 *The Bodhisattva Ideal*, SCW, vol. 4, pp. 14–15.
23 *The Life of Service or the Life of Contemplation*, SCW, vol. 7, p. 147.
24 *A Survey of Buddhism*, SCW, vol. 1, p. 28.
25 *A Survey of Buddhism*, SCW, vol. 1, p. 30.
26 *Who Is the Buddha?*, SCW, vol. 3, p. 11.
27 Samuel Coleridge, *Aids to Reflection*, quoted in Abrams, *The Mirror and the Lamp*, p. 171.
28 *The Awakening of the Heart*, SCW, vol. 7, pp. 316–17.
29 *The Awakening of the Heart*, SCW, vol. 7, p. 317.
30 Samuel Coleridge, 'Monologue on "Life"', in *Frasers Magazine for Town and Country* 12 (November 1835), p. 495.
31 *The Rain of the Dharma* (1994), SCW, vol. 12, pp. 512–13.
32 Samuel Coleridge, *The Statesman's Manual*, quoted in Abrams, *The Mirror and the Lamp*, p. 172.
33 *The Three Jewels*, SCW, vol. 2, p. 15.
34 *Who Is the Buddha?*, SCW, vol. 3, p. 16.
35 Samuel Coleridge, *Lectures on Shakespeare*, quoted in Abrams, *The Mirror and the Lamp*, pp. 172–3.
36 *A History of My Going for Refuge*, SCW, vol. 2, p. 428.
37 *Enlightenment as Experience and Non-Experience* (1975), SCW, vol. 11, p. 80.
38 Lama Govinda, *The Way of the White Clouds*, p. 13.
39 Lama Govinda, *The Way of the White Clouds*, 'Foreword', p. xi.
40 *Facing Mount Kanchenjunga*, SCW, vol. 21, p. 259.

Chapter Six

1 *The Good Friend*, SCW, vol. 7, pp. 292–3.
2 *The Diamond Path*, SCW, vol. 7, p. 403.
3 *The Religion of Art*, SCW, vol. 26, p. 189.
4 *The Religion of Art*, SCW, vol. 26, p. 195.
5 *The Meaning of Buddhism and the Value of Art*, SCW, vol. 26, p. 130.
6 *The Religion of Art*, SCW, vol. 26, p. 173.
7 *The Realm of the Lotus*, SCW, vol. 26, p. 245.
8 *Complete Poems and Short Stories*, SCW, vol. 25, pp. 483–98.
9 Lama Govinda, 'Introduction' to *The Veil of Stars*, SCW, vol. 25, p. 477. Quotes from this poem in the pages that follow are given in the text using stanza numbers.
10 'Argument' of *The Veil of Stars*, SCW, vol. 25, p. 481.
11 *A Note on 'The Burial of Count Orgaz'*, SCW, vol. 26, pp. 314–15.
12 *Conversations with Bhante*.
13 *My Relation to the Order*, SCW, vol. 2, p. 537.
14 Plato, *Republic*, trans. G.M.A. Grube, Pan, London, 1974, book V, 475e–476d.
15 *The Three Jewels*, SCW, vol. 2, pp. 87–8.
16 *A Note on Anatta*, SCW, vol. 7, p. 213.
17 *The FWBO and 'Protestant Buddhism'*, SCW, vol. 13, p. 374.
18 *Moving against the Stream*, SCW, vol. 23, p. 317.
19 *The Three Jewels*, SCW, vol. 2, p. 82.
20 *Reflections on Going Forth* (1997), SCW, vol. 12, p. 551.
21 *The Three Jewels*, SCW, vol. 2, p. 85.
22 *Wisdom before Words: An Exploration of the Udāna*, SCW, vol. 10, p. 507. *A Note on 'The Burial of Count Orgaz'*, SCW, vol. 26, p. 314.
23 *A Survey of Buddhism*, SCW, vol. 1, p. 183.
24 *Extending the Hand of Fellowship*, SCW, vol. 2, p. 554.
25 *Green Tārā and the Fourth Lakṣaṇa*, SCW, vol. 26, p. 665.
26 *A Note on 'The Burial of Count Orgaz'*, SCW, vol. 26, p. 312.
27 Plato, *The Symposium*, trans. W. Hamilton, Penguin Books, Harmondsworth, 1981, p. 91, quoted in *A Note on 'The Burial of Count Orgaz'*, SCW, vol. 26, pp. 313–14.
28 *The Rainbow Road*, SCW, vol. 20, p. 344.
29 *The Young Man in the Hut*, SCW, vol. 26, p. 596.
30 Edgar Wind, *Pagan Mysteries in the Renaissance*, Norton, New York, 1958, p. 46.

31 *The Drama of Cosmic Enlightenment*, SCW, vol. 16, p. 112.
32 *A Survey of Buddhism*, SCW, vol. 1, p. 398.
33 *Advice to a Young Poet*, SCW, vol. 26, pp. 136–7.
34 'The Unseen Flower', SCW, vol. 25, p. 215.
35 *Puṇya and Upāya*, SCW, vol. 7, p. 140.
36 *Facing Mount Kachenjunga*, SCW, vol. 21, p. 24. The poem is quoted here but has been omitted from the SCW edition of the *Complete Poems and Short Stories*.
37 'The White Calf' (1949), SCW, vol. 25, p. 207.
38 *Dr Ambedkar's True Greatness* (1983), SCW, vol. 10, pp. 341–2.
39 *In the Sign of the Golden Wheel*, SCW, vol. 22, pp. 247–8.
40 Lama Govinda, 'Introduction' to *The Veil of Stars*, SCW, vol. 25, p. 480.
41 SCW, vol. 7, p. 317.

Chapter Seven

1 Frank Kermode, *Romantic Image*, 2nd ed., Routledge, Abingdon, 2002, p. 57.
2 *Moving against the Stream*, SCW, vol. 23, p. 182.
3 H.P. Blavatsky, *The Secret Doctrine*, vol. 1, The Theosophical Society, London, 1888, p. 309.
4 *Transforming Self and World*, SCW, vol. 16, p. 264. He is discussing Ruchiraketu's drum in the *Sutra of Golden Light*.
5 Eric Heller, *The Disinherited Mind*, Bowes & Bowes, Cambridge, 1952, p. 118.
6 *Art and Meditation*, Allahabad Block Works, Allahabad, 1936, quoted in *Facing Mount Kanchenjunga*, SCW, vol. 21, p. 251 and n. 55.
7 *Facing Mount Kanchenjunga*, SCW, vol. 21, p. 161.
8 *A Survey of Buddhism*, SCW, vol. 1, pp. 27–8. The mention of 'dissociation' echoes T.S. Eliot's idea of 'dissociation of sensibility', which he dated from the late seventeenth century.
9 *A Survey of Buddhism*, SCW, vol. 1, pp. 27–8.
10 *Creative Symbols of Tantric Buddhism*, SCW, vol. 13, p. 118.
11 *The Inconceivable Emancipation*, SCW, vol. 16, p. 532.
12 *The Drama of Cosmic Enlightenment*, SCW, vol. 16, p. 189.
13 *A Survey of Buddhism*, SCW, vol. 1, p. 246.
14 *Symbols of Tibetan Buddhist Art*, SCW, vol. 13, p. 61.
15 *A Survey of Buddhism*, SCW, vol. 1, p. 377.
16 *The Three Jewels*, SCW, vol. 2, p. 96,
17 *Paradox and Poetry in 'The Voice of the Silence'*, SCW, vol. 26, p. 209.
18 *Paradox and Poetry in 'The Voice of the Silence'*, SCW, vol. 26, p. 209.
19 *A Survey of Buddhism*, SCW, vol. 1, p. 170.
20 Samuel Coleridge, *Biographia Literaria*, George Bell & Sons, London, 1891, p. 145.
21 George Byron, *Don Juan*, 'Dedication', lines 15–16.
22 Aphorism in *Peace Is a Fire*, SCW, vol. 26, p. 21.
23 *Buddhism and William Blake*, SCW, vol. 26, pp. 342, 349, 350.
24 *Buddhism and William Blake*, SCW, vol. 26, p. 347.
25 *My Five Literary Heroes*, SCW, vol. 26, p. 486.
26 William Blake, in a marginal note quoted in Northrop Frye, *Fearful Symmetry: A Study of William Blake* (1947), Princeton University Press, Princeton, NJ, 1974, p. 21.
27 Frye, *Fearful Symmetry*, p. 27.
28 These phrases are from Blake's short verse 'Fourfold Vision', in *Letters*, 'To Butts' (22 November 1802).
29 'Homage to William Blake', SCW, vol. 25, p. 340.
30 *Buddhism and William Blake*, SCW, vol. 26, p. 346.
31 Plotinus, *An Essay on the Beautiful*, trans. Thomas Taylor, John Watkins, London, 1917, p. 23.
32 *Going for Refuge*, SCW, vol. 9, p. 251 ff. See also *The Launch of 'Wisdom beyond*

Words', scw, vol. 14, p. 314, which has a slightly different list, and Subhuti, *Reimagining the Buddha, Seven Papers*, p. 82.
33 *The Buddha's Noble Eightfold Path*, scw, vol. 1, p. 482.
34 William Blake, *The Marriage of Heaven and Hell*, 'Proverbs of Hell'.
35 *Buddhism and William Blake*, scw, vol. 26, pp. 349, 348.
36 William Blake, *The Marriage of Heaven and Hell*.
37 *Buddhism and William Blake*, scw, vol. 26, p. 347.
38 Harold Bloom, *The Visionary Company*, Doubleday & Co., New York, 1961, p. 18.
39 *The Religion of Art*, scw, vol. 26, pp. 170–1.
40 *Transforming Self and World*, scw, vol. 16, p. 386.
41 'The Call of the Forest' (1995), scw, vol. 25, pp. 408, 409.

Chapter Eight

1 Henry James, *Italian Hours*, William Heinemann, London, 1909. The essay on Ravenna is dated 1873.
2 *Moving against the Stream*, scw, vol. 23, p. 261.
3 *Moving against the Stream*, scw, vol. 23, p. 273.
4 *Moving against the Stream*, scw, vol. 23, p. 281.
5 *Moving against the Stream*, scw, vol. 23, p. 249.
6 *The Journey to Il Convento*, scw, vol. 26, p. 264.
7 *The Journey to Il Convento*, scw, vol. 26, p. 268. Sangharakshita had not left the Vihara at the time of his journey, so he is either confusing dates or suggesting that his time in the wilderness had already started.
8 *St Jerome Revisited*, scw, vol. 26, pp. 284, 302.
9 *The Journey to Il Convento*, scw, vol. 26, p. 268.
10 *The Journey to Il Convento*, scw, vol. 26, p. 264.
11 'St Jerome in the Desert' (1967), scw, vol. 25, p. 312.
12 Walter Pater, *The Renaissance: Studies in Art and Poetry (the 1893 Text)*, ed. Donald L. Hill, University of California Press, Berkeley, CA, 1980, p. 99.
13 *St Jerome Revisited*, scw, vol. 26, pp. 305–6.
14 *From Genesis to the Diamond Sutra*, scw, vol. 13, p. 585.
15 'Secret Wings', scw, vol. 25, p. 185.
16 *The Bodhisattva Ideal*, scw, vol. 4, p. 99.
17 *I Believe...*, scw, vol. 7, p. 38, first published in *The Middle Way*, vol. 19, no. 2 (July–August 1944).
18 'Before an Image of the Buddha' (1946), scw, vol. 25, p. 158.
19 *The Journey to Il Convento*, scw, vol. 26, pp. 269–70.
20 *From Genesis to the Diamond Sutra*, scw, vol. 13, p. 519.
21 *The Journey to Il Convento*, scw, vol. 26, pp. 270, 278.
22 *The Journey to Il Convento*, scw, vol. 26, p. 271 (original emphasis).
23 *Four Visits*, scw, vol. 26, p. 617.
24 *The Drama of Cosmic Enlightenment*, scw, vol. 16, p. 111.
25 *Milarepa and the Art of Discipleship II*, scw, vol. 19, p. 350.
26 *Precious Teachers*, scw, vol. 22, p. 463.
27 *A Survey of Buddhism*, scw, vol. 1, p. 240.
28 *Precious Teachers*, scw, vol. 22, pp. 462–3.
29 *A Survey of Buddhism*, scw, vol. 1, p. 66. See Psalm 42.7 (King James Bible): 'Deep calleth unto deep at the noise of thy waterspouts: all thy waves and thy billows are gone over me.'
30 *Precious Teachers*, scw, vol. 22, p. 463.
31 *A Reverie-cum-Reminiscence in the Form of a Letter to Paramartha* (2015), scw, vol. 26, pp. 545–6.
32 Personal communication with Subhuti.
33 *A Reverie-cum-Reminiscence in the Form of a Letter to Paramartha*, scw, vol. 26, p. 546.
34 *The Inconceivable Emancipation*, scw, vol. 16, p. 530.

35 *The Inconceivable Emancipation*, SCW, vol. 16, p. 532.
36 'Third Letter from England', SCW, vol. 24, p. 160.
37 *The Inconceivable Emancipation*, SCW, vol. 16, p. 533.
38 *The Journey to Il Convento*, SCW, vol. 26, p. 268.
39 Henry Corbin, *Alone with the Alone: Creative Imagination in the Sufism of Ibn Arabi* (1969), Princeton University Press, Princeton, NJ, 1998.
40 *The Journey to Il Convento*, SCW, vol. 26, p. 268.
41 *The Journey to Il Convento*, SCW, vol. 26, p. 271.
42 *Moving against the Stream*, SCW, vol. 23, pp. 181, 182.

Chapter Nine

1 *Facing Mount Kanchenjunga*, SCW, vol. 21, p. 245.
2 *The Meaning of Orthodoxy in Buddhism*, SCW, vol. 7, p. 529.
3 *A Survey of Buddhism*, SCW, vol. 1, pp. 16–17.
4 'The Unity of Buddhism', in *The Middle Way*, vol. 19, no. 1 (May–June 1944), SCW, vol. 7, pp. 33, 34, 35.
5 *Buddha, Dharma, Sangha*, SCW, vol. 7, pp. 69–70.
6 *My Life and Mission and the Teaching of Dr Ambedkar*, SCW, vol. 9, p. 279.
7 Letter to Clare Cameron, quoted in Kalyanaprabha's 'Introduction' to SCW, vol. 7, p. 14.
8 *Facing Mount Kanchenjunga*, SCW, vol. 21, p. 178.
9 *Facing Mount Kanchenjunga*, SCW, vol. 21, p. 246.
10 *The Parable of the Raft*, SCW, vol. 7, p. 314.
11 *The Bodhisattva Ideal*, SCW, vol. 4, pp. 40–1.
12 *Going for Refuge* (1981), SCW, vol. 2, pp. 299–300.
13 Lama Anagārika Govinda, 'Buddhism as Living Experience', in *Stepping Stones* (July 1951), p. 74.
14 Lama Govinda, 'Buddhism as Living Experience', p. 75.
15 *Facing Mount Kanchenjunga*, SCW, vol. 21, p. 244.
16 *A Survey of Buddhism*, SCW, vol. 1, p. 88.
17 *The Rainbow Road*, SCW, vol. 20, p. 302.
18 'The Coming Year', in *Maha Bodhi* (January 1956), SCW, vol. 8, p. 218.
19 *In the Sign of the Golden Wheel*, SCW, vol. 22, pp. 143, 145.
20 'Letter 9' from Lama Govinda to Sangharakshita (5 May 1957), Sangharakshita Study Centre archive.
21 The qualifications include his understanding of sangha, his attitude to sex, and the new Burmese approach to meditation.
22 Preface to *A Survey of Buddhism*, SCW, vol. 1, p. 9.
23 Preface to *A Survey of Buddhism*, SCW, vol. 1, p. 6.
24 *A Survey of Buddhism*, SCW, vol. 1, pp. 182, 392.
25 Batchelor, *The Awakening of the West*, p. 331.
26 *A Survey of Buddhism*, SCW, vol. 1, p. 398.
27 *A Survey of Buddhism*, SCW, vol. 1, p. 202.
28 Paul Williams, *Mahāyāna Buddhism*, Routledge, London, 1989, pp. 2–3.
29 *A Survey of Buddhism*, SCW, vol. 1, p. 278.
30 *A Survey of Buddhism*, SCW, vol. 1, p. 100. See Vidyaruchi, 'The Transcendental Principle and Dyads of the Understanding', available at https://apramada.org/articles/the-transcendental-principle-and-dyads-of-the-understanding, accessed on 29 January 2025.
31 *A Survey of Buddhism*, SCW, vol. 1, p. 6.
32 *The History of My Going for Refuge*, SCW, vol. 2, p. 428.
33 *A Survey of Buddhism*, SCW, vol. 1, p. 154.
34 *A Survey of Buddhism*, SCW, vol. 1, p. 202.
35 *A Survey of Buddhism*, SCW, vol. 1, p. 88.
36 *A Survey of Buddhism*, SCW, vol. 1, p. 64.

37 *The Launch of 'Wisdom beyond Words'*, SCW, vol. 14, p. 318.
38 *A Survey of Buddhism*, SCW, vol. 1, p. 265.
39 At the time Sangharakshita wrote the *Survey*, many scholars used 'Hīnayāna' as a synonym for the eighteen early Buddhist schools and regarded the Theravāda as their modern representative. More recent scholarship regards the term 'Hīnayāna' as a polemical device used by Mahāyānists to distinguish their approach. Monastic followers of the Mahāyāna belonged to the same ordination lineages as monastics who subscribed to one or other of the eighteen schools. While there are many similarities between modern Theravāda and the approach characterized as 'Hīnayāna', they are also distinct. For an account of these issues later in Sangharakshita's career see *Transforming Self and World*, SCW, vol. 16, p. 236.
40 *A Survey of Buddhism*, SCW, vol. 1, p. 238 ff. The first chapter locates these characteristics in the early sources. The third chapter illustrates the Mahāyāna outlook through a synoptic description of the major Mahāyāna schools, and the fourth chapter extends his account through an exposition of the bodhisattva ideal.
41 The formula echoes the difference between Judaism and the new Christian dispensation according to St Paul: 'for the letter kills, but the Spirit gives life', 2 Corinthians 3.6 (New English Translation).
42 *A Survey of Buddhism*, SCW, vol. 1, p. 206.
43 *The Meaning of Orthodoxy in Buddhism* (1957), SCW, vol. 7, p. 514 ff. makes this argument in full.
44 *A Survey of Buddhism*, SCW, vol. 1, p. 233.
45 *A Survey of Buddhism*, SCW, vol. 1, p. 77.
46 *A Survey of Buddhism*, SCW, vol. 1, p. 248.
47 *A Survey of Buddhism*, SCW, vol. 1, pp. 219, 189.
48 *A Survey of Buddhism*, SCW, vol. 1, p. 57.
49 *A Survey of Buddhism*, SCW, vol. 1, p. 185.
50 *A Survey of Buddhism*, SCW, vol. 1, p. 394.
51 *A Survey of Buddhism*, SCW, vol. 1, p. 277.
52 *A Survey of Buddhism*, SCW, vol. 1, p. 235.
53 *A Survey of Buddhism*, SCW, vol. 1, p. 247.
54 *A Survey of Buddhism*, SCW, vol. 1, p. 278.
55 *A Survey of Buddhism*, SCW, vol. 1, pp. 296–7.
56 *A Survey of Buddhism*, SCW, vol. 1, p. 393.
57 Rupert Gethin, *The Foundations of Buddhism*, Oxford University Press, Oxford, 1998, is a good example of such an approach.
58 Subhuti, foreword to *A Survey of Buddhism*, SCW, vol. 1, p. xi.
59 *A Survey of Buddhism*, SCW, vol. 1, p. 187.
60 *A Survey of Buddhism*, SCW, vol. 1, p. 187.
61 *Extending the Hand of Fellowship*, SCW, vol. 2, p. 548.
62 *A Survey of Buddhism*, SCW, vol. 1, p. 204.
63 Preface to *A Survey of Buddhism*, SCW, vol. 1, p. 6.
64 *A Survey of Buddhism*, SCW, vol. 1, pp. 202, 204.
65 *A Survey of Buddhism*, SCW, vol. 1, p. 20.
66 *A Survey of Buddhism*, SCW, vol. 1, p. 204.
67 Philip A. Mellor, 'Protestant Buddhism? The Cultural Translation of Buddhism in England', *Religion*, vol. 21, no. 1 (1991), pp. 73–92.
68 *The FWBO and 'Protestant Buddhism'*, SCW, vol. 13, p. 473.
69 *The FWBO and 'Protestant Buddhism'*, SCW, vol. 13, p. 473 (original emphasis).
70 Vishvapani, 'Wisdom within Words' (interview with Sangharakshita), *Dharma Life* 10 (spring 1999), SCW, vol. 11, p. 655.

71 Preface to *A Survey of Buddhism*, SCW, vol. 1, p. 8.
72 *In the Sign of the Golden Wheel*, SCW, vol. 22, p. 376.
73 *A Survey of Buddhism*, SCW, vol. 1, p. 182.
74 *The History of My Going for Refuge*, SCW, vol. 2, p. 442.
75 *Creative Symbols of Tantric Buddhism*, SCW, vol. 13, p. 200.
76 *Autumn Thoughts*, SCW, vol. 7, pp. 335–6.
77 *Creative Symbols of Tantric Buddhism*, SCW, vol. 13, p. 208.
78 *Creative Symbols of Tantric Buddhism*, SCW, vol. 13, p. 208.
79 *The History of My Going for Refuge*, SCW, vol. 2, p. 445.
80 *The History of My Going for Refuge*, SCW, vol. 2, pp. 444–5.
81 *The History of My Going for Refuge*, SCW, vol. 2, p. 428.
82 *A Survey of Buddhism*, SCW, vol. 1, p. 409.
83 *The History of My Going for Refuge*, SCW, vol. 2, p. 480.
84 *The Meaning of Conversion in Buddhism*, SCW, vol. 2, p. 242.
85 *Milarepa and the Art of Discipleship II*, SCW, vol. 19, p. 58.
86 'Preface to the Fourth Edition' (1998), *The Three Jewels*, SCW, vol. 2, p. 7.
87 *Going for Refuge* (1981), SCW, vol. 2, p. 301.
88 *The History of My Going for Refuge*, SCW, vol. 2, p. 455.
89 *A Survey of Buddhism*, SCW, vol. 1, p. 394.
90 *A Survey of Buddhism*, SCW, vol. 1, p. 397.
91 *The Bodhisattva Ideal*, SCW, vol. 4, p. 35.
92 *Precious Teachers*, SCW, vol. 22, p. 543.
93 *The History of My Going for Refuge*, SCW, vol. 2, p. 475.
94 *A Survey of Buddhism*, SCW, vol. 1, p. 229.
95 Preface to *A Survey of Buddhism*, SCW, vol. 1, p. 11.
96 *The History of My Going for Refuge*, SCW, vol. 2, p. 445.
97 *The History of My Going for Refuge*, SCW, vol. 2, p. 446.
98 *The History of My Going for Refuge*, SCW, vol. 2, p. 456.

Chapter Ten

1 *A Survey of Buddhism*, SCW, vol. 1, p. 82.
2 *A Survey of Buddhism*, SCW, vol. 1, pp. 226, 242.
3 *A Survey of Buddhism*, SCW, vol. 1, p. 226.
4 *A Survey of Buddhism*, SCW, vol. 1, p. 72.
5 *A Survey of Buddhism*, SCW, vol. 1, p. 242.
6 *A Survey of Buddhism*, SCW, vol. 1, p. 81.
7 *A Survey of Buddhism*, SCW, vol. 1, p. 242.
8 *A Survey of Buddhism*, SCW, vol. 1, p. 243.
9 *A Survey of Buddhism*, SCW, vol. 1, p. 83.
10 *A Survey of Buddhism*, SCW, vol. 1, p. 104.
11 *Philosophy and Religion in Original and Developed Buddhism*, SCW, vol. 7, p. 192.
12 *A Survey of Buddhism*, SCW, vol. 1, p. 89.
13 'The Transcendental Eightfold Path' (1994), included in *What Is the Dharma?*, SCW, vol. 3, p. 292.
14 *The Meaning of Conversion in Buddhism*, SCW, vol. 2, p. 251.
15 *A Survey of Buddhism*, SCW, vol. 1, p. 266.
16 *A Survey of Buddhism*, SCW, vol. 1, p. 114.
17 B.M. Barua, *Ceylon Lectures*, Bhāratī Mahāvidyālaya, Calcutta, 1945, p. 156.
18 Unpublished autobiographical sketch in the Sangharakshita Study Centre archive, LE26 (date unknown).
19 The *Upanisa Sutta* is found at *Saṃyutta Nikāya* 2.32. The full *nidāna* sequence, as Sangharakshita translates its constituents, is suffering, faith, joy, rapture, serenity, happiness, concentration,

knowledge and vision, repulsion, passionlessness, liberation, and knowledge of the destruction of the intoxicants. See SCW, vol. 1, p. 115. As the validity of this account of the path has been questioned, we should note the versions of the sequence at *Aṅguttara Nikāya* 11.1–11.5 (PTS 5.312–18) and elsewhere. The accompanying simile appears at *Aṅguttara Nikāya* 10.61–10.62, PTS 113–16 and 117–19). See Rupert Gethin, *The Buddhist Path to Awakening*, Oneworld, Oxford, 2001, pp. 248–9.

20 *A Survey of Buddhism*, SCW, vol. 1, p. 119.
21 *A Survey of Buddhism*, SCW, vol. 1, p. 119.
22 *Philosophy and Religion in Original and Developed Buddhism*, SCW, vol. 7, p. 200.
23 *Philosophy and Religion in Original and Developed Buddhism*, SCW, vol. 7, pp. 194, 206.
24 *A Survey of Buddhism*, SCW, vol. 1, p. 117.
25 *A Survey of Buddhism*, SCW, vol. 1, p. 119.
26 *A Survey of Buddhism*, SCW, vol. 1, p. 119.
27 *The Religion of Art*, SCW, vol. 26, p. 176.
28 Lama Anagārika Govinda, 'The Buddha as the Ideal of the Perfect Man and the Embodiment of the Dharma', in *Maha Bodhi*, vol. 62, no. 5–6 (May–June 1954), p. 155. See *A Survey of Buddhism*, SCW, vol. 1, p. 48.
29 *The Three Jewels*, SCW, vol. 2, p. 39.
30 *The Meaning of Conversion in Buddhism*, SCW, vol. 2, p. 252.
31 *The Meaning of Conversion in Buddhism*, SCW, vol. 2, p. 258.
32 *Mind Reactive and Creative*, SCW, vol. 11, p. 36.
33 *Mind Reactive and Creative*, SCW, vol. 11, p. 26.
34 'Progress shoots up in an ever-expanding spiral and never repeats itself.' *Progress and Religion* (1948), SCW, vol. 7, p. 163.
35 *Buddhism for Today – and Tomorrow*, SCW, vol. 11, p. 167.
36 *Living with Awareness*, SCW, vol. 15, p. 230.
37 Vishvapani, 'Wisdom within Words' (interview with Sangharakshita), *Dharma Life* 10 (spring 1999), pp. 28–32; SCW, vol. 11, p. 659.
38 *The Bodhisattva Ideal*, SCW, vol. 4, p. 181.
39 *The Meaning of Conversion in Buddhism*, SCW, vol. 4, p. 263.
40 *Bodhisattva Principle*, SCW, vol. 4, p. 650.
41 'Discerning the Buddha' (lecture 167), edited with some changes in *Who Is the Buddha?*, SCW, vol. 3, p. 68.
42 *The Five Pillars of the FWBO*, SCW, vol. 12, p. 467.
43 Caroline Rhys Davids, *Buddhism: A Study of the Buddhist Norm*, Williams and Norgate, London, 1913, pp. 122, 101, 240.
44 Rhys Davids, *Buddhism*, p. 118.
45 Rhys Davids, *Buddhism*, pp. 118, 119.
46 A study by Dhivan Thomas Jones concludes that Buddhaghosa uses the *niyama*s merely to indicate 'the necessity of things and events occurring in a certain order', and that the interpretations of Rhys Davids, Sangharakshita, and others represent a 'considerable conceptual expansion' from five kinds of regularity or law to 'five broad domains of nature or reality that are law-governed'. Dhivan Thomas Jones, 'The Five Niyāmas as Laws of Nature: An Assessment of Modern Western Interpretations of Theravāda Buddhist Doctrine', *Journal of Buddhist Ethics* 19 (2012), p. 565 ff.
47 *The Three Jewels*, SCW, vol. 2, p. 69.
48 *Who Is the Buddha?*, SCW, vol. 3, pp. 99–100.
49 *Wisdom before Words*, SCW, vol. 10, p. 507.
50 *Wisdom beyond Words*, SCW, vol. 14, p. 588.
51 *Revering and Relying upon the Dharma*, Seven Papers, p. 40.
52 *The Life of Service or the Life of Contemplation*, SCW, vol. 7, p. 155. *The Bodhisattva Principle*, SCW, vol. 4, p. 647 ff., repeats the arguments

of this essay, virtually point by point, adding the two modes of conditionality.
53 *The Life of Service or the Life of Contemplation*, SCW, vol. 7, p. 156.
54 *The Meaning of Buddhism and the Value of Art*, SCW, vol. 26, p. 111.
55 Letter from Sangharakshita to Subhuti (14 October 2011), quoted in *A Supra-Personal Force or Energy Working Through Me*, Seven Papers, p. 160.
56 *The Bodhisattva Ideal*, SCW, vol. 4, pp. 30, 61.
57 *The Endlessly Fascinating Cry*, SCW, vol. 4, pp. 259–60.
58 *Revering and Relying upon the Dharma*, Seven Papers, p. 52.
59 *Revering and Relying upon the Dharma*, Seven Papers, p. 59.
60 *Living Wisely*, SCW, vol. 17, p. 357.
61 *Revering and Relying upon the Dharma*, Seven Papers, p. 68.

Chapter Eleven

1 Preface to *A Survey of Buddhism*, SCW, vol. 1, p. 9.
2 *The Bodhisattva Ideal*, SCW, vol. 4, pp. 171–2.
3 *The Bodhisattva Ideal*, SCW, vol. 4, p. 172.
4 *Living with Awareness*, SCW, vol. 15, p. 225.
5 'Letter 6' from Lama Govinda to Sangharakshita (1 April 1956), Sangharakshita Study Centre archive.
6 *The Buddha's Noble Eightfold Path*, SCW, vol. 1, p. 482.
7 *The Buddha's Noble Eightfold Path*, SCW, vol. 1, p. 479.
8 *Buddhism and the Language of Myth* (1966), SCW, vol. 12, p. 107.
9 *The Buddha's Noble Eightfold Path*, SCW, vol. 1, p. 513.
10 *The Buddha's Noble Eightfold Path*, SCW, vol. 1, p. 581.
11 *The Buddha's Noble Eightfold Path*, SCW, vol. 1, p. 590.
12 *The Buddha's Noble Eightfold Path*, SCW, vol. 1, pp. 473–6.
13 *The Buddha's Noble Eightfold Path*, SCW, vol. 1, p. 481.
14 *The Meaning of Orthodoxy in Buddhism*, SCW, vol. 7, p. 522.
15 *The Bodhisattva Ideal*, SCW, vol. 4, p. 92.
16 *The Bodhisattva Ideal*, SCW, vol. 4, p. 28.
17 *The Bodhisattva Ideal*, SCW, vol. 4, pp. 31, 32
18 *The Bodhisattva Ideal*, SCW, vol. 4, pp. 33–4.
19 *The Bodhisattva Ideal*, SCW, vol. 4, pp. 32–3.
20 Plotinus, *The Enneads*, trans. Stephen MacKenna, Penguin Books, London, 1991, I.vi.9, p. 55.
21 *The Bodhisattva Ideal*, SCW, vol. 4, p. 211.
22 *A Survey of Buddhism*, SCW, vol. 1, p. 119.
23 *The Bodhisattva Ideal*, SCW, vol. 4, pp. 200–2.
24 Robert Ellis, *The Thought of Sangharakshita: A Critical Assessment*, Equinox Publishing, Sheffield, 2020, p. 75.
25 Ellis, *The Thought of Sangharakshita*, pp. 128, 131.
26 Review of *Buddhism without Beliefs* by Stephen Batchelor, SCW, vol. 8, pp. 581–2 (original emphasis).
27 *Tibetan Buddhism: An Introduction*, SCW, vol. 13, p. 84.
28 *Creative Symbols of Tantric Buddhism*, SCW, vol. 13, pp. 187–9.
29 Subhuti, 'Three Myths of the Spiritual Life', in *Madhyamavani* 10 (2005), available at http://madhyamavani.fwbo.org/10/threemyths.html, accessed on 30 January 2025.
30 *The Three Jewels*, SCW, vol. 2, p. 97.
31 See Subhuti, *Sangharakshita: A New Voice*, p. 282.
32 *The Bodhisattva Ideal*, SCW, vol. 4, p. 33.
33 *Wisdom before Words*, SCW, vol. 10, p. 440.
34 Chögyam Trungpa, *Cutting through Spiritual Materialism*, Shambhala Publications, New York, 2002, p. 3.
35 Trungpa, *Cutting through Spiritual Materialism*, p. 153.

36 *The Refuge Tree* (2009), SCW, vol. 11, p. 720.
37 *The Path of Regular and Irregular Steps*, SCW, vol. 11, p. 62.
38 Review of Irmgard Schloegl, *The Wisdom of the Zen Masters*, in *FWBO Newsletter* 27 (summer 1975), SCW, vol. 8, p. 497.
39 *The Priceless Jewel*, SCW, vol. 16, pp. 221–2.
40 *The Priceless Jewel*, SCW, vol. 16, p. 223.
41 *The Purpose and Practice of Buddhist Meditation*, SCW, vol. 5, p. 402.
42 Nagabodhi, 'Editorial', in *FWBO Newsletter* 28 (autumn 1975), p. 1.
43 'Introduction' to *The Endlessly Fascinating Cry*, SCW, vol. 4, p. 227.

Chapter Twelve

1 Sangharakshita reports giving a series of talks on 'The Myths and Parables of *The Lotus Sutra*' in Sikkim in 1961 in the *Triyana Vardhana Vihara Report, 1957–1962*. The 1971 lectures were published, with seminar extracts, as *The Drama of Cosmic Enlightenment*, and included in SCW, vol. 16.
2 *The Drama of Cosmic Enlightenment*, SCW, vol. 16, p. 117.
3 *The Drama of Cosmic Enlightenment*, SCW, vol. 16, p. 122.
4 *The Drama of Cosmic Enlightenment*, SCW, vol. 16, p. 126.
5 *The Three Jewels*, SCW, vol. 2, pp. 101–2.
6 *The Psychology of Spiritual Development*, SCW, vol. 12, p. 151.
7 *Wisdom before Words*, SCW, vol. 10, p. 567.
8 *What Is the Dharma?*, SCW, vol. 3, p. 258.
9 *New Currents in Western Buddhism*, SCW, vol. 11, p. 370.
10 *The Poetry Interviews*, SCW, vol. 25, p. 140.
11 *The Path of Regular and Irregular Steps*, SCW, vol. 11, p. 64.
12 *The Path of Regular and Irregular Steps*, SCW, vol. 11, p. 66.
13 *Enlightenment as Experience and Non-Experience*, SCW, vol. 11, p. 78. Both lectures were given under the auspices of the Buddhist Society.
14 *Enlightenment as Experience and Non-Experience*, SCW, vol. 11, p. 88.
15 *Enlightenment as Experience and Non-Experience*, SCW, vol. 11, p. 89.
16 *The Purpose and Practice of Buddhist Meditation*, SCW, vol. 5, p. 661.
17 Sangharakshita's teachings on meditation were eventually gathered into *The Purpose and Practice of Buddhist Meditation*, SCW, vol. 5.
18 *Buddhism for Today – and Tomorrow*, SCW, vol. 11, p. 147.
19 *A System of Meditation*, SCW, vol. 5, p. 29.
20 *The Rainbow Road*, SCW, vol. 20, p. 145.
21 *In the Realm of the Lotus*, SCW, vol. 26, p. 247.
22 *Auspicious Signs*, SCW, vol. 15, p. 399.
23 Many of Sangharakshita's lectures on individuality were collected in *What Is the Sangha?*, published in SCW, vol. 3. Sangharakshita lists the qualities of the individual in *The Bodhisattva Principle* (1983; SCW, vol. 4, p. 656) and 'Fidelity' (lecture 153, 1982). The edited version of 'Fidelity' in *What Is the Sangha?* (SCW, vol. 3, p. 563 ff.) omits the list.
24 *What Is the Dharma?*, SCW, vol. 3, p. 486.
25 *What Is the Sangha?*, SCW, vol. 3, p. 488.
26 *What Is the Sangha?*, SCW, vol. 3, p. 487.
27 *Living with Awareness*, SCW, vol. 15, p. 225.
28 *Archetypal Symbolism in the Biography of the Buddha*, SCW, vol. 12, p. 192.
29 *What Is the Dharma?*, SCW, vol. 3, p. 334.
30 *Buddhism for Today – and Tomorrow*, SCW, vol. 11, p. 151.
31 *The Mandala: Tantric Symbol of Integration*, SCW, vol. 12, p. 218.
32 *The Purpose and Practice of Meditation*, SCW, vol. 5, p. 10; *Tibetan Buddhism: An Introduction*, SCW, vol. 13, p. 73.
33 *The Buddha's Noble Eightfold Path*, SCW, vol. 1, p. 567 ff. Sangharakshita includes the first three *satipaṭṭhāna*s – *kāya*, *vedanā*, and *citta* – within

'awareness of self', while 'awareness of reality' equates to the fourth – *dhamma-satipaṭṭhāna*. 'Awareness of things' is an extension of *kāya-satipaṭṭhāna*, and 'awareness of others' is arguably an addition to the *satipaṭṭhāna* scheme.
34 *The Drama of Cosmic Enlightenment*, SCW, vol. 16, p. 175.
35 *A Survey of Buddhism*, SCW, vol. 1, pp. 408–9.
36 *The History of My Going for Refuge*, SCW, vol. 2, p. 481. Sangharakshita's terminology varies in different presentations, but the pattern of deepening engagement is constant.
37 *Levels of Going for Refuge* (1978), SCW, vol. 12, p. 316.
38 *Living with Awareness*, SCW, vol. 15, p. 237.
39 *Wisdom Before Words*, SCW, vol. 10, p. 432.
40 *Living with Kindness*, SCW, vol. 15, p. 328.
41 *The Poetry Interviews*, SCW, vol. 25, p. 140.
42 Lecture 135, 'The System of Meditation'. See *The Purpose and Practice of Buddhist Meditation*, SCW, vol. 5, p. 43.
43 *Living with Kindness*, SCW, vol. 15, p. 344.
44 *Living with Kindness*, SCW, vol. 15, p. 337 (original emphasis).
45 *The Purpose and Practice of Buddhist Meditation*, SCW, vol. 5, p. 453.
46 *Transforming Self and World*, SCW, vol. 16, p. 227.
47 *Transforming Self and World*, SCW, vol. 16, pp. 262–3.
48 *The Purpose and Practice of Buddhist Meditation*, SCW, vol. 5, pp. 32, 44, extracted from the 1976 seminar on Nāgārjuna's *Precious Garland*.
49 *The System of Meditation*, SCW, vol. 5, p. 33.
50 Personal communication with Subhuti.
51 *Revering and Relying upon the Dharma, Seven Papers*, pp. 59–60.
52 *Revering and Relying upon the Dharma, Seven Papers*, p. 60.
53 *Revering and Relying upon the Dharma, Seven Papers*, p. 61.
54 Subhuti (2011), *Initiation into a New Life, Seven Papers*, p. 139.

Chapter Thirteen

1 *The History of My Going for Refuge*, SCW, vol. 2, p. 473.
2 *The History of My Going for Refuge*, SCW, vol. 2, p. 478.
3 *The History of My Going for Refuge*, SCW, vol. 2, p. 474.
4 H.P. Blavatsky, *Isis Unveiled*, J.W. Bouton, New York, 1877, p. 135.
5 Blavatsky uses the term 'Higher Evolution' in passing in *Isis Unveiled* and *The Secret Doctrine*. It also appears in E. Evans Wentz, *Tibetan Yoga and Secret Doctrines*, Oxford University Press, Oxford, 1958, p. 12. See Robin Cooper, *The Evolving Mind: Buddhism, Biology and Consciousness*, Windhorse Publications, Birmingham, 1996, p. 233.
6 *Attavada and Anattavada*, SCW, vol. 7, p. 133.
7 *The Three Jewels*, SCW, vol. 2, p. 102.
8 *The Drama of Cosmic Enlightenment*, SCW, vol. 16, p. 129.
9 R.C. Zaehner, *Evolution in Religion: Study in Sri Aurobindo and Pierre Teilhard de Chardin*, Oxford University Press, Oxford, 1971.
10 *Appendix: A Letter to Dr Zaehner*, SCW, vol. 13, p. 517.
11 'The Higher Evolution' (1969) and 'Aspects of the Higher Evolution of the Individual' (1970). Many of these lectures were later included in the compilation *What Is the Sangha?*, SCW, vol. 3.
12 *What Is the Sangha?*, SCW, vol. 3, p. 9.
13 *The Bodhisattva Principle*, SCW, vol. 4, p. 654.
14 *What Is the Sangha?*, SCW, vol. 3, p. 479.
15 *What Is the Sangha?*, SCW, vol. 3, p. 481.
16 *What Is the Sangha?*, SCW, vol. 3, p. 477 (original emphasis).
17 'Meditation versus Psychotherapy', in *The Purpose and Practice of Meditation*, SCW, vol. 5, p. 664.

18 *Living with Awareness*, scw, vol. 15, p. 94.
19 *The History of My Going for Refuge*, scw, vol. 2, pp. 475–6.
20 In place of a definition, Isaiah Berlin's *Roots of Romanticism* (1965) simply lists the diverse and contradictory beliefs of Romantic thinkers and writers.
21 Sri Aurobindo and Teilhard de Chardin also influenced Sangharakshita, but he discussed their limitations in *Appendix: A Letter to Dr Zaehner*, scw, vol. 13, p. 513.
22 *What Is the Sangha?*, scw, vol. 3, p. 493, based on the lecture 'Nietzsche, Man and "The Superman"' (1969).
23 *What Is the Sangha?*, scw, vol. 3, p. 497.
24 *What Is the Sangha?*, scw, vol. 3, p. 498.
25 *What Is the Sangha?*, scw, vol. 3, pp. 498, 501.
26 'New', scw, vol. 25, p. 313.
27 *The FWBO and 'Protestant Buddhism'*, scw, vol. 13, p. 428.
28 *Breaking Through to Buddhahood*, scw, vol. 11, p. 4.
29 *Breaking Through to Buddhahood*, scw, vol. 11, pp. 6–10.
30 This passage from 'Breaking Through to Buddhahood' isn't included in scw, vol. 11, but is in the original talk and appears in *Peace Is a Fire*, scw, vol. 26, p. 20 (original emphasis).
31 *Peace Is a Fire*, scw, vol. 26, pp. 20, 18.
32 *Appendix: A Letter to Dr Zaehner*, scw, vol. 13, p. 516.
33 *Levels of Going for Refuge*, scw, vol. 12, pp. 315, 316.
34 *The Bodhisattva Ideal*, scw, vol. 4, p. 15.
35 *The Drama of Cosmic Enlightenment*, scw, vol. 16, p. 7.
36 *The History of My Going for Refuge*, scw, vol. 2, p. 478.
37 *The Bodhisattva Principle*, scw, vol. 4, p. 638.
38 *The Bodhisattva Principle*, scw, vol. 4, p. 655.
39 *Revering and Relying upon the Dharma, Seven Papers*, p. 55.
40 *Revering and Relying upon the Dharma, Seven Papers*, p. 60.
41 *Revering and Relying upon the Dharma, Seven Papers*, p. 63.
42 *The Bodhisattva Ideal*, scw, vol. 5, p. 181.

Chapter Fourteen

1 *What Might Have Been*, scw, vol. 26, pp. 590–1.
2 *Revering and Relying upon the Dharma, Seven Papers*, p. 44.
3 *In the Sign of the Golden Wheel*, scw, vol. 22, p. 463.
4 'The Buddha' (1961), scw, vol. 25, p. 296.
5 *Who Is the Buddha?*, scw, vol. 3, p. 45.
6 *Who Is the Buddha?*, scw, vol. 3, pp. 53–4.
7 *Who Is the Buddha?*, scw, vol. 3, p. 56.
8 *Wisdom before Words*, scw, vol. 10, p. 431.
9 *Wisdom before Words*, scw, vol. 10, p. 434.
10 *A Survey of Buddhism*, scw, vol. 1, p. 88.
11 *Buddhism and the Language of Myth*, scw, vol. 12, p. 106.
12 *Archetypal Symbolism in the Biography of the Buddha* (1967), scw, vol. 12, p. 187.
13 *Archetypal Symbolism in the Biography of the Buddha*, scw, vol. 12, pp. 182, 180.
14 *A Survey of Buddhism*, scw, vol. 1, pp. 55, 49.
15 *A Survey of Buddhism*, scw, vol. 1, p. 38 (original emphasis).
16 *The Three Jewels*, scw, vol. 2, p. 39.
17 *The Three Jewels*, scw, vol. 2, p. 46.
18 *The Three Jewels*, scw, vol. 2, p. 45.
19 *A Survey of Buddhism*, scw, vol. 1, p. 284.
20 *The Bodhisattva Ideal*, scw, vol. 4, pp. 204, 206.
21 *The Three Jewels*, scw, vol. 2, p. 96.
22 *The Bodhisattva Ideal*, scw, vol. 4, p. 139.
23 *Creative Symbols of Tantric Buddhism*, scw, vol. 13, p. 201.
24 *Milarepa and the Art of Discipleship I*, scw, vol. 18, p. 320.
25 *The Bodhisattva Ideal*, scw, vol. 4, p. 146.
26 *Buddhophany, Seven Papers*, p. 123.

27 *Reimagining the Buddha, Seven Papers*, p. 75.
28 *Reimagining the Buddha, Seven Papers*, p. 75.
29 From a seminar on *The Buddha* by Trevor Ling, quoted in *Peace Is a Fire*, SCW, vol. 26, p. 44.
30 *Buddhophany, Seven Papers*, p. 123.
31 *Buddhophany, Seven Papers*, p. 123.
32 *Buddhophany, Seven Papers*, p. 124.
33 *Buddhophany, Seven Papers*, p. 124.
34 *Buddhophany, Seven Papers*, p. 124.
35 *In the Sign of the Golden Wheel*, SCW, vol. 22, p. 301.
36 *The Bodhisattva Ideal*, SCW, vol. 4, p. 195.
37 *The Bodhisattva Ideal*, SCW, vol. 4, pp. 194–5.
38 *Buddhophany, Seven Papers*, pp. 124, 125.
39 *Reimagining the Buddha, Seven Papers*, p. 75.
40 Lama Govinda, 'Buddhism as Living Experience', p. 74.
41 *Reimagining the Budd.ha, Seven Papers*, p. 85.

Part Four

1 Aphorism in *A Stream of Stars*, SCW, vol. 26, p. 83.

Chapter Fifteen

1 *My Relation to the Order*, SCW, vol. 2, p. 522.
2 *The History of My Going for Refuge*, SCW, vol. 2, p. 406.
3 See the four *Triratna History* documentaries produced by Lights in the Sky, available at www.lightsinthesky.org, accessed on 3 February 2025.
4 *My Relation to the Order*, SCW, vol. 2, p. 530.
5 *What Is the Sangha?*, SCW, vol. 3, p. 555.
6 *The Inconceivable Emancipation*, SCW, vol. 16, p. 577.
7 'After Meditation', SCW, vol. 25, p. 307.
8 'A Personal Message to All Friends', SCW, vol. 11, p. 515.
9 'A Personal Message to All Friends', SCW, vol. 11, p. 517.
10 'A Personal Message to All Friends', SCW, vol. 11, p. 515.
11 'A Personal Message to All Friends', SCW, vol. 11, p. 516.
12 *My Relation to the Order*, SCW, vol. 2, pp. 530–1.
13 *Buddhism for Today – and Tomorrow*, SCW, vol. 11, p. 180.
14 *Fields of Creativity*, SCW, vol. 12, p. 639.
15 *Buddhism for Today – and Tomorrow*, SCW, vol. 11, p. 185.
16 *Buddhism for Today – and Tomorrow*, SCW, vol. 11, p. 189.
17 *The Five Pillars of the FWBO*, SCW, vol. 12, p. 462.
18 *The Five Pillars of the FWBO*, SCW, vol. 12, p. 472.
19 *The Artist's Dream*, SCW, vol. 25, p. 544 ff.
20 *The Artist's Dream*, SCW, vol. 25, p. 553.
21 *In the Realm of the Lotus*, SCW, vol. 26, p. 25: 'In my case, the artist's dream was the FWBO.'
22 *The History of My Going for Refuge*, SCW, vol. 2, p. 406.
23 *What Is the Sangha?*, SCW, vol. 3, p. 517.
24 Batchelor, *The Awakening of the West*, p. 333.
25 *The History of My Going for Refuge*, SCW, vol. 2, p. 406.
26 *Fields of Creativity*, SCW, vol. 12, p. 640.
27 *Buddhism for Today – and Tomorrow*, SCW, vol. 11, p. 181.
28 *Buddhism for Today – and Tomorrow*, SCW, vol. 11, pp. 182–3.
29 *My Relation to the Order*, SCW, vol. 2, p. 524.
30 *My Relation to the Order*, SCW, vol. 2, p. 525.
31 *Is a Guru Necessary?*, SCW, vol. 3, p. 553.
32 *My Relation to the Order*, SCW, vol. 2, p. 529.

Chapter Sixteen

1. *My Relation to the Order*, SCW, vol. 2, p. 522.
2. *The History of My Going for Refuge*, SCW, vol. 2, p. 403.
3. Vangisa, 'Ten Years in the Golden Light', in *FWBO Newsletter* 34 (spring 1977), p. 4.
4. *The Ten Pillars of Buddhism*, SCW, vol. 2, p. 323.
5. *The Ten Pillars of Buddhism*, SCW, vol. 2, p. 325.
6. *The Ten Pillars of Buddhism*, SCW, vol. 2, p. 325.
7. *The Ten Pillars of Buddhism*, SCW, vol. 2, p. 318.
8. *The Ten Pillars of Buddhism*, SCW, vol. 2, p. 362.
9. *Transforming Self and World*, SCW, vol. 16, p. 433.
10. *The Ten Pillars of Buddhism*, SCW, vol. 2, p. 396.
11. *Twenty Years on the Middle Way*, SCW, vol. 12, p. 389.
12. *The Ten Pillars of Buddhism*, SCW, vol. 2, p. 346.
13. *The Ten Pillars of Buddhism*, SCW, vol. 2, p. 347.
14. *New Currents in Western Buddhism*, SCW, vol. 11, pp. 389–90.
15. *Buddhism for Today – and Tomorrow*, SCW, vol. 11, p. 177.
16. *New Currents in Western Buddhism*, SCW, vol. 11, p. 390.
17. *Buddhism for Today – and Tomorrow*, SCW, vol. 11, p. 173.
18. *The Bodhisattva Ideal*, SCW, vol. 4, p. 30.
19. *The History of My Going for Refuge*, SCW, vol. 2, p. 474.
20. 'A Personal Message to All Friends', SCW, vol. 11, p. 517.
21. *The History of My Going for Refuge*, SCW, vol. 2, p. 502.
22. *Looking Ahead a Little Way*, SCW, vol. 12, p. 600.
23. *The History of My Going for Refuge*, SCW, vol. 2, p. 470.
24. *D.H. Lawrence and the Spiritual Community*, SCW, vol. 8, p. 547.
25. *Human Enlightenment*, SCW, vol. 11, p. 134.
26. *New Currents in Western Buddhism*, SCW, vol. 11, p. 352.
27. *D.H. Lawrence and the Spiritual Community*, SCW, vol. 8, p. 548.
28. *D.H. Lawrence and the Spiritual Community*, SCW, vol. 8, p. 547.
29. *D.H. Lawrence and the Spiritual Community*, SCW, vol. 8, p. 549.
30. From a letter to an unnamed recipient quoted in *A Stream of Stars*, SCW, vol. 26, p. 80.
31. *D.H. Lawrence and the Spiritual Community*, SCW, vol. 8, p. 547.
32. *D.H. Lawrence and the Spiritual Community*, SCW, vol. 8, p. 550.
33. *Human Enlightenment*, SCW, vol. 11, p. 138.
34. *The Meaning of Friendship in Buddhism*, SCW, vol. 11, p. 705.
35. *Fields of Creativity*, SCW, vol. 12, p. 514.
36. *Fields of Creativity*, SCW, vol. 12, p. 514.
37. *The Bodhisattva Ideal*, SCW, vol. 4, p. 172.
38. *The Inconceivable Emancipation*, SCW, vol. 16, p. 473.
39. Subhuti, *Buddhism for Today*, pp. 129–30.
40. Discussion of the Buddha's noble eightfold path, quoted in Subhuti, *Sangharakshita: A New Voice*, p. 220.
41. *Buddhism for Today – and Tomorrow*, SCW, vol. 11, p. 169 ff.
42. *Transforming Self and World*, SCW, vol. 16, p. 265.
43. *Transforming Self and World*, SCW, vol. 16, p. 229.
44. *New Currents in Western Buddhism*, SCW, vol. 11, p. 350.
45. Harold Bloom, *Ruin the Sacred Truths: Poetry and Belief from the Bible to the Present*, Harvard University Press, Cambridge, MA, 1991, p. 123.
46. 'Blake Walked among the Stones of Fire...', SCW, vol. 25, p. 360.
47. *Transforming Self and World*, SCW, vol. 16, p. 410.
48. *Transforming Self and World*, SCW, vol. 16, p. 435.
49. *Transforming Self and World*, SCW, vol. 16, p. 360.
50. *New Currents in Western Buddhism*, SCW, vol. 11, p. 377.
51. *A Survey of Buddhism*, SCW, vol. 1, p. 28.
52. *What Is the Sangha?*, SCW, vol. 3, p. 621.

53 Nagabodhi, 'Yesterday, Today and Tomorrow', in *FWBO Newsletter* 34 (spring 1977), p. 17. Interview with Sangharakshita.
54 *The Glory of the Literary World*, SCW, vol. 14, p. 287.
55 Subhuti, *Buddhism for Today*, p. 99.
56 Subhuti, 'Eros and Beauty 1a: Bhante as Daemon' (2014), available at https://www.freebuddhistaudio.com/audio/details?num=LOC2012, accessed on 3 February 2025.
57 *In the Realm of the Lotus*, SCW, vol. 26, p. 248.
58 *Some Reflections on the Garava Sutta* (2017), SCW, vol. 26, p. 628.
59 *D.H. Lawrence and the Spiritual Community*, SCW, vol. 8, p. 551.
60 *The Inconceivable Emancipation*, SCW, vol. 16, p. 466.
61 *Transforming Self and World*, SCW, vol. 16, p. 359.
62 *The Inconceivable Emancipation*, SCW, vol. 16, p. 471.
63 *FWBO Newsletter* 31 (summer 1976), p. 9.
64 Dhammadinna, 'Kalyana Mitrata: The Lifeblood of the Movement', in *FWBO Newsletter* 49 (spring 1981), pp. 3–4.
65 Padmaraja, 'Kalyana Mitrata: A Direction to the Heart', in *FWBO Newsletter* 49 (spring 1981), pp. 10–12.
66 Vishvapani, 'Learning the Harsh Way', *Dharma Life* 7 (spring 1998), p. 61.
67 Tina Fossella and John Welwood, 'Human Nature, Buddha Nature: An Interview with John Welwood', in *Tricycle: The Buddhist Review*, vol. 20, no. 3 (spring 2011), available with subscription from https://tricycle.org/magazine/human-nature-buddha-nature/, accessed on 4 February 2025.
68 Vishvapani, 'Learning the Harsh Way', p. 61.
69 *Know Your Mind*, SCW, vol. 17, p. 618.
70 *The Ten Pillars of Buddhism*, SCW, vol. 2, p. 351.
71 *The Ten Pillars of Buddhism*, SCW, vol. 2, p. 352.
72 *Buddhism for Today – and Tomorrow*, SCW, vol. 11, pp. 188–9.
73 *The Meaning of Friendship in Buddhism*, SCW, vol. 11, p. 697.
74 *D.H. Lawrence and the Spiritual Community*, SCW, vol. 8, p. 548.
75 'Second Letter from England' (1979), SCW, vol. 24, p. 95.
76 Letter to an unnamed recipient quoted in *Peace Is a Fire*, SCW, vol. 26, p. 26.
77 For example, *The Position of Women in Buddhism* (pamphlet no. 1, Poona Women's Buddhist Association, 1961), SCW, vol. 10, pp. 182–4.
78 Sinhadevi, 'Sangharakshita Talks about Women', *Dakini* 12 (December 1993), pp. 12–17, SCW, vol. 11, pp. 638–9. Interview with Sangharakshita.
79 Arthur Schopenhauer, *Parerga and Paralipomena*, vol. 2, trans. E.J. Payne, Clarendon Press, Oxford, 1974. See *The Rainbow Road*, SCW, vol. 20, p. 83.
80 *Idols of the Marketplace*, SCW, vol. 11, p. 613.
81 *The Ten Pillars of Buddhism*, SCW, vol. 2, p. 372.
82 *Peace Is a Fire*, SCW, vol. 26, p. 27.
83 *Grabbing a Firebrand*, SCW, vol. 26, p. 5.
84 Letter to an unnamed recipient quoted in *Peace Is a Fire*, SCW, vol. 26, p. 56.
85 Subhuti, '*Women, Men and Angels*: A Personal Statement by Subhuti' (March 2017), available at https://thebuddhistcentre.com/news/women-men-and-angels-apology, accessed on 3 February 2025.
86 *What Is the Western Buddhist Order?*, Seven Papers, p. 18.
87 *A Season in Hell*, SCW, vol. 26, p. 454.
88 For a fuller analysis of this period see Vajragupta, *The Triratna Story: Behind the Scenes of a New Buddhist movement*, Windhorse Publications, Cambridge, 2010, pp. 128–44, and my own essay 'Growing Pains: An Inside View of Change in the FWBO' (2006), available at https://www.freebuddhistaudio.com/texts/othertexts/Vishvapani/FBA104_Growing_Pains.pdf, accessed on 3 February 2025.

89 Subhuti, letter to Order members published in *Shabda*, the Order's private newsletter (March 2003).
90 *What Is the Western Buddhist Order?, Seven Papers*, p. 11.
91 *What Is the Western Buddhist Order?, Seven Papers*, pp. 11–12.
92 *What Is the Western Buddhist Order?, Seven Papers*, p. 12.
93 *What Is the Western Buddhist Order?, Seven Papers*, p. 9.
94 *What Is the Western Buddhist Order?, Seven Papers*, p. 14.
95 *What Is the Western Buddhist Order?, Seven Papers*, p. 20.
96 *What Is the Western Buddhist Order?, Seven Papers*, p. 18.
97 Sangharakshita, 'A Note on "Disciple": A Postscript to *What Is the Western Buddhist Order?*' (2017), available at https://thebuddhistcentre.com/adhisthana-kula/urgyen-sangharakshita-discipleship-postscript-what-western-buddhist-order, accessed on 3 February 2025.

Chapter Seventeen

1 *New Currents in Western Buddhism*, SCW, vol. 11, p. 374.
2 *New Currents in Western Buddhism*, SCW, vol. 11, p. 376.
3 Sangharakshita remarks that he was born 'a stone's throw' from where Bennett died, but the actual distance is rather greater than this suggests.
4 Colin Wilson, *Aleister Crowley: The Nature of the Beast*, Aquarian Press, London, 1987, p. 58.
5 Allan Bennett, *The Wisdom of the Aryas*, Kegan Paul, Trench, Trubner and Co., London, 1923.
6 Allan Bennett, 'Right Understanding', in *Buddhist Review* 5 (1913), pp. 85–108.
7 Allan Bennett, *The Religion of Burma and Other Papers*, Theosophical Publishing House, Adyar, 1929.
8 *Buddhism for Today – and Tomorrow*, SCW, vol. 11, p. 187.
9 *Forty-Three Years Ago*, SCW, vol. 2, p. 604.
10 *Was the Buddha a Bhikkhu?*, SCW, vol. 2, p. 628.
11 *Forty-Three Years Ago*, SCW, vol. 2, p. 589.
12 *Buddhism for Today – and Tomorrow*, SCW, vol. 11, p. 188.
13 *Was the Buddha a Bhikkhu?*, SCW, vol. 2, p. 629.
14 *Buddhism for Today – and Tomorrow*, SCW, vol. 11, p. 187.
15 *Forty-Three Years Ago*, SCW, vol. 2, p. 614.
16 As vipassanā practitioners comprise a movement rather than an organization, they are referred to in numerous ways, including the Insight Meditation movement, the vipassanā community, the vipassanā sangha, and so on.
17 *Moving against the Stream*, SCW, vol. 23, p. 367.
18 *A Survey of Buddhism*, SCW, vol. 1, p. 156.
19 Preface to *A Survey of Buddhism*, SCW, vol. 1, p. 9.
20 Barbara Gates, Jack Kornfield, and Wes Nisker, 'Possibilities of the Path: An Interview with Joseph Goldstein', in *Inquiring Mind*, vol. 6, no. 1 (1989), p. 1.
21 Joseph Goldstein, *One Dharma: The Emerging Western Buddhism*, HarperSanFrancisco, San Francisco, CA, 2002.
22 Rawlinson, *The Book of Enlightened Masters*, p. 97.
23 *Extending the Hand of Fellowship*, SCW, vol. 2, p. 561.
24 Rawlinson, *The Book of Enlightened Masters*, p. 122.
25 Gil Fronsdal, 'Insight Meditation in the United States: Life, Liberty, and the Pursuit of Happiness', in *The Faces of Buddhism in America*, ed. Charles S. Prebish and Kenneth K. Tanaka, University of California Press, Berkeley, CA, 1998, pp. 163–80.
26 'Idols of the Marketplace', in *Golden Drum* 33 (May 1994), SCW, vol. 11, p. 613.
27 Quoted in Batchelor, *The Awakening of the West*, p. 105.

28 Batchelor, *The Awakening of the West*, p. 117.
29 Chögyam Trungpa, *Crazy Wisdom*, Shambhala Publications, Boston, MA, 2001, p. 143.
30 Chögyam Trungpa, *Journey without Goal: The Tantric Wisdom of the Buddha*, Shambhala Publications, Boston, MA, 2000, p. 27.
31 Chögyam Trungpa, foreword to Dakpo Tashi Namgyal, *Mahāmudrā: The Quintessence of Mind and Meditation*, Shambhala Publications, Boston, MA, 1986, p. xv.
32 *A Complex Personality: A Note*, SCW, vol. 26, p. 640.
33 *Extending the Hand of Fellowship*, SCW, vol. 2, p. 565.
34 *What Is the Sangha?*, SCW, vol. 3, p. 561.
35 *Know Your Mind*, SCW, vol. 17, p. 627.
36 More precisely, Thich Nhat Hanh was ordained in the Lieu Quán Dharma line and the Linji lineage. Like other Vietnamese monks, he also inherited a Theravādin lineage.
37 Thich Nhat Hanh, *The Heart of Understanding: Commentaries on the Prajnaparamita Heart Sutra*, ed. Peter Levitt, Parallax Press, Berkeley, CA, 1988, pp. 3–4.
38 Thich Nhat Hanh, *No Death, No Fear*, Rider, London, 2002, p. 106.
39 David McMahon, *Buddhist Modernism*, Oxford University Press, Oxford, 2008, p. 175.
40 Thich Nhat Hanh, *Being Peace*, Parallax Press, Berkeley, CA, 1987, p. 49.
41 See Vishvapani Blomfield, obituary of Thich Nhat Hanh, *The Guardian* (23 January 2022).
42 *The Bodhisattva Ideal* (1944), SCW, vol. 7, p. 41.
43 *The Parable of the Raft* (1951), SCW, vol. 7, p. 312.
44 *The Bodhisattva Ideal*, SCW, vol. 4, p. 169.
45 *The FWBO and 'Protestant Buddhism'*, SCW, vol. 13, p. 389. See also *The Priceless Jewel*, SCW, vol. 16, p. 223. Sangharakshita probably took the term 'Rousseauism' from the American philosopher Allan Bloom in *The Closing of the American Mind*, Simon & Schuster, New York, 1987.
46 *The Path of Regular and Irregular Steps*, SCW, vol. 11, p. 56.
47 *The FWBO and 'Protestant Buddhism'*, SCW, vol. 13, p. 425.
48 *The Rainbow Road*, SCW, vol. 20, p. 379.
49 *Buddhism and the West*, SCW, vol. 11, pp. 468, 470.
50 *Extending the Hand of Fellowship*, SCW, vol. 2, pp. 550–1.

Chapter Eighteen

1 *What Is the Western Buddhist Order?*, Seven Papers, p. 18.
2 *A Survey of Buddhism*, SCW, vol. 1, p. 398.
3 *The FWBO and 'Protestant Buddhism'*, SCW, vol. 13, p. 476.
4 Preface to *A Survey of Buddhism*, SCW, vol. 1, p. 8.
5 *A Survey of Buddhism*, SCW, vol. 1, p. 301.
6 Max Weber, *Economy and Society: An Outline of Interpretive Sociology*, ed. Guenther Roth and Claus Wittich, University of California Press, Berkeley, CA, 1978, pp. 246–9.
7 'Questions and Answers with Members of the College of Public Preceptors' (April 2006), published in *Shabda* (May 2006), quoted with permission.
8 'The Sunflower's Farewell', SCW, vol. 25, p. 343.
9 'Padmaloka', SCW, vol. 25, pp. 344–5.

Bibliography

Works by Sangharakshita

Sangharakshita's works are published in a standard edition as *The Complete Works of Sangharakshita*. Most references in this book are to these volumes.

The Complete Works of Sangharakshita (scw), Windhorse Publications, Cambridge, 2018.

scw, vol. 1: *A Survey of Buddhism / The Buddha's Noble Eightfold Path*
  A Survey of Buddhism
  The Buddha's Noble Eightfold Path

scw, vol. 2: *The Three Jewels I*
  The Three Jewels
  The Meaning of Conversion in Buddhism
  Going for Refuge
  The Ten Pillars of Buddhism
  The History of My Going for Refuge
  My Relation to the Order
  Extending the Hand of Fellowship
  Forty-Three Years Ago
  Was the Buddha a Bhikkhu?

scw, vol. 3: *The Three Jewels II*
  Who Is the Buddha?
  What Is the Dharma?
  What Is the Sangha?

scw, vol. 4: *The Bodhisattva Ideal*
  The Bodhisattva Ideal
  The Endlessly Fascinating Cry (seminar)
  The Bodhisattva Principle

scw, vol. 5: *The Purpose and Practice of Buddhist Meditation*
  The Purpose and Practice of Buddhist Meditation

scw, vol. 6: *The Essential Sangharakshita*
  The Essential Sangharakshita

scw, vol. 7: *Crossing the Stream: India Writings I*
  Early Writings 1944–1954
  Crossing the Stream
  Buddhism in the Modern World: Cultural and Political Implications
  The Meaning of Orthodoxy in Buddhism
  Buddhism in India Today
  Ordination and Initiation in the Three Yānas
  A Bird's Eye View of Indian Buddhism

scw, vol. 8: *Beating the Dharma Drum: India Writings II*
  Anagārika Dharmapāla and Other 'Maha Bodhi' Writings
  Dharmapāla: The Spiritual Dimension

    Beating the Drum: 'Maha Bodhi'
        Editorials
    Alternative Traditions

scw, vol. 9: Dr Ambedkar and the Revival
    of Buddhism I
        Ambedkar and Buddhism
        Lecture Tour in India, December
            1981–March 1982

scw, vol. 10: Dr Ambedkar and the
    Revival of Buddhism II
        Remembering Ambedkar
        Buddha and the Future of His
            Religion
        The Mass Conversion and the Years
            After, 1956–1961
        Lectures in India and England 1979,
            1982–1992
        Wisdom before Words: The Udāna

scw, vol. 11: A New Buddhist Movement I
    Ritual and Devotion in Buddhism
    The Buddha's Victory
    The Taste of Freedom
    Buddha Mind
    Human Enlightenment
    New Currents in Western Buddhism
    Buddhism for Today – and
        Tomorrow
    Buddhism and the West
    Aspects of Buddhist Morality
    Buddhism and Blasphemy
    Articles and interviews

scw, vol. 12: A New Buddhist Movement
    II
        Previously unpublished talks

scw, vol. 13: Eastern and Western
    Traditions
        Tibetan Buddhism
        Creative Symbols of Tantric
            Buddhism
        The Essence of Zen
        The FWBO and 'Protestant Buddhism'
        From Genesis to the Diamond Sutra

scw, vol. 14: The Eternal Legacy / Wisdom
    beyond Words
        The Eternal Legacy
        The Glory of the Literary World
        Wisdom beyond Words

scw, vol. 15: Pāli Canon Teachings and
    Translations
        Dhammapada (translation)

    Karaṇīya Mettā Sutta (translation)
    Living with Kindness
    Living with Awareness
    Maṅgala Sutta (translation)
    Auspicious Signs (seminar)
    Salutation to the Three Jewels
        (translation)
    The Threefold Refuge (seminar)
    Further Pāli sutta commentaries

scw, vol. 16: Mahāyāna Myths and Stories
    The Drama of Cosmic
        Enlightenment
    The Priceless Jewel
    Transforming Self and World
    The Inconceivable Emancipation

scw, vol. 17: Wisdom Teachings of the
    Mahāyāna
        Know Your Mind
        Living Ethically
        Living Wisely
        The Way to Wisdom (seminar)

scw, vol. 18: Milarepa and the Art of
    Discipleship I
        The Yogi's Joy
        The Shepherd's Search for Mind
        Rechungpa's Journey to
            Enlightenment

scw, vol. 19: Milarepa and the Art of
    Discipleship II
        Rechungpa's Journey to
            Enlightenment, continued

scw, vol. 20: The Rainbow Road from
    Tooting Broadway to Kalimpong
        The Rainbow Road from Tooting
            Broadway to Kalimpong

scw, vol. 21: Facing Mount Kanchenjunga
    Facing Mount Kanchenjunga
    Dear Dinoo: Letters to a Friend

scw, vol. 22: In the Sign of the Golden
    Wheel
        In the Sign of the Golden Wheel
        Precious Teachers
        With Allen Ginsberg in Kalimpong
            (essay)

scw, vol. 23: Moving against the Stream
    Moving against the Stream
    1970 – A Retrospect

scw, vol. 24: Through Buddhist Eyes
    Travel Letters

Through Buddhist Eyes

scw, vol. 25: *Poems and Short Stories*
   Complete Poems 1941–1994
   Other Poems
   Short Stories

scw, vol. 26: *Aphorisms, the Arts, and Late Writings*
   Peace Is a Fire
   A Stream of Stars
   The Religion of Art
   In the Realm of the Lotus
   The Journey to Il Convento
   St Jerome Revisited
   A Note on 'The Burial of Count Orgaz'
   Criticism East and West
   Buddhism and William Blake
   Urthona Interviews
   Madhyamaloka Reflections
   Adhiṣṭhāna Writing

scw, vol. 27: *Concordance to the Complete Works*

Other works cited, including seminar transcripts, are in the Sangharakshita Study Centre archive, or available online as cited.

Seven Papers, Triratna InHouse Publications, 2018, is a composite work. It contains one work, *Buddhophany*, that is authored by Sangharakshita alone, and the interview *What Is the Western Buddhist Order?* The other essays are written by Subhuti on the basis of conversations with Sangharakshita. Page references are to the 2018 edition.

Secondary sources: principal works cited

Abrams, M.H., *The Mirror and the Lamp: Romantic Theory and the Critical Tradition*, Oxford University Press, Oxford, 1953.

Barua, B.M., *Ceylon Lectures*, Bhāratī Mahāvidyālaya, Calcutta, 1945.

Batchelor, Stephen, *The Awakening of the West*, Parallax Press, Berkeley, CA, 1994.

Bennett, Allan (Ananda Metteya), *The Religion of Burma and Other Papers*, Theosophical Publishing House, Adyar, 1929.

—, 'Right Understanding', in *Buddhist Review* 5 (1913), pp. 85–108.

—, *The Wisdom of the Aryas*, Kegan Paul, Trench, Trubner and Co., London, 1923.

Blavatsky, H.P., *The Secret Doctrine*, vol. 1, The Theosophical Society, London, 1888.

Bloom, Harold, *Ruin the Sacred Truths: Poetry and Belief from the Bible to the Present*, Harvard University Press, Cambridge, MA, 1991.

—, *The Visionary Company*, Doubleday & Co., New York, 1961.

Buddhadasa, *On the First Rung: Reminiscences of the Early Years of the Triratna Buddhist Order 1969–1974*, Ola Leaves, Ledbury, 2014.

Coleridge, Samuel, *Biographia Literaria*, George Bell & Sons, London, 1891.

—, *Collected Letters of Samuel Taylor Coleridge*, ed. Earl Leslie Griggs, 6 vols, Clarendon, Oxford, 1956.

Corbin, Henry, *Alone with the Alone: Creative Imagination in the Sufism of Ibn Arabi* (1969), Princeton University Press, Princeton, NJ, 1998.

Ellis, Robert, *The Thought of Sangharakshita: A Critical Assessment*, Equinox Publishing, Sheffield, 2020.

Goldstein, Joseph, *One Dharma: The Emerging Western Buddhism*, HarperSanFrancisco, San Francisco, CA, 2002.

Govinda, Lama Anagārika, 'Buddhism as Living Experience', in *Stepping Stones* (July 1951), pp. 74–5.

—, *The Way of the White Clouds*, Hutchinson, London, 1966.

Heller, Eric, *The Disinherited Mind*, Bowes & Bowes, Cambridge, 1952.

Hillman, James, *Revisioning Psychology*, Harper & Row, New York, 1975.

Humphreys, Christmas, *Both Sides of the Circle: The Autobiography of Christmas Humphreys*, Allen & Unwin, London, 1978.

James, Henry, *Italian Hours*, William Heinemann, London, 1909.

Kermode, Frank, *Romantic Image*, 2nd ed., Routledge, Abingdon, 2002.

Khantipalo, *Noble Friendship*, Windhorse Publications, Birmingham, 2002.

McGilchrist, Ian, *The Master and His Emissary*, Yale University Press, New Haven, CT, 2012.

McMahon, David, *Buddhist Modernism*, Oxford University Press, Oxford, 2008, p. 175.

Merton, Thomas, *The Asian Journal of Thomas Merton*, New Directions, London, 1975.

Midal, Fabrice, *Chögyam Trungpa: His Life and Vision*, Shambhala Publications, Boston, MA, 2004.

Miles, Barry, *Ginsberg: A Biography*, Simon & Schuster, New York, 1989.

Murry, John Middleton, *Discoveries*, Collins, London, 1924.

—, *God: An Introduction to the Science of Metabiology*, Jonathan Cape, London, 1929.

Nagabodhi, *Jai Bhim*, Windhorse Publications, Birmingham, 1996.

—, *Sangharakshita: The Boy, the Monk, the Man*, Windhorse Publications, Cambridge, 2023.

Nietzsche, Friedrich, *Thus Spake Zarathustra*, trans. R.J. Hollingdale, Penguin Books, Harmondsworth, 1961.

Oliver, Ian, *Buddhism in Britain*, Rider, London, 1979.

Pater, Walter, *The Renaissance: Studies in Art and Poetry (the 1893 Text)*, ed. Donald L. Hill, University of California Press, Berkeley, CA, 1980.

Plato, *Republic*, trans. G.M.A. Grube, Pan, London, 1974.
—, *The Symposium*, trans. W. Hamilton, Penguin Books, Harmondsworth, 1981.
Plotinus, *The Enneads*, trans. Stephen MacKenna, Penguin Books, London, 1991.
—, *An Essay on the Beautiful*, trans. Thomas Taylor, John Watkins, London, 1917.
Rawlinson, Andrew, *The Book of Enlightened Masters*, Open Court, Chicago, IL, 1997.
Rhys Davids, Caroline, *Buddhism: A Study of the Buddhist Norm*, Williams and Norgate, London, 1913.
Samuel, Geoffrey, *Civilized Shamans: Buddhism in Tibetan Societies*, Smithsonian Institute Press, Washington, DC, 1993.
Schopenhauer, Arthur, *Parerga and Paralipomena*, vol. 2, trans. E.J. Payne, Clarendon Press, Oxford, 1974.
Subhuti (Alex Kennedy), *Buddhism for Today: A Portrait of a New Buddhist Movement*, Element Books, Salisbury, 1983.
—, *Sangharakshita: A New Voice in the Buddhist Tradition*, Windhorse Publications, Birmingham, 1994.
—, 'Three Myths of the Spiritual Life', in *Madhyamavani* 10 (2005), available at http://madhyamavani.fwbo.org/10/threemyths.html, accessed on 30 January 2025.
Suvajra, *The Wheel and the Diamond: The Life of Dhardo Rimpoche*, Windhorse Publications, Glasgow, 1991.

Thich Nhat Hanh, *Being Peace*, Parallax Press, Berkeley, CA, 1987.
—, *The Heart of Understanding: Commentaries on the Prajnaparamita Heart Sutra*, ed. Peter Levitt, Parallax Press, Berkeley, CA, 1988.
—, *No Death, No Fear*, Rider, London, 2002.
Trungpa, Chögyam, *Crazy Wisdom*, Shambhala Publications, Boston, MA, 2001.
—, *Cutting through Spiritual Materialism*, Shambhala Publications, New York, 2002.
—, foreword to Dakpo Tashi Namgyal, *Mahāmudrā: The Quintessence of Mind and Meditation*, Shambhala Publications, Boston, MA, 1986.
–, *Journey without Goal: The Tantric Wisdom of the Buddha*, Shambhala Publications, Boston, MA, 2000.
Vendler, Helen, *Poets Thinking*, Harvard University Press, Cambridge, MA, 2004.
Williams, Paul, *Mahāyāna Buddhism*, Routledge, London, 1989.
Wilson, Colin, *Aleister Crowley: The Nature of the Beast*, Aquarian Press, London, 1987.
Wind, Edgar, *Pagan Mysteries in the Renaissance*, Norton, New York, 1958.
Winkler, Ken, *A Thousand Journeys: The Biography of Lama Anagārika Govinda*, Element Books, Longmead, 1990.
Zaehner, R.C., *Evolution in Religion: Study in Sri Aurobindo and Pierre Teilhard de Chardin*, Oxford University Press, Oxford, 1971.

Index

Introductory Note

References such as '178–9' indicate (not necessarily continuous) discussion of a topic across a range of pages. Wherever possible in the case of topics with many references, these have either been divided into sub-topics or only the most significant discussions are listed. Because the entire work is about 'Sangharakshita', the use of this name (and certain terms which occur constantly throughout the book) as an entry point has been minimised. Information will be found under the corresponding detailed topics.

abhiṣeka 27, 32, 37, 45–6, 48, 89, 191, 196
absolute consciousness 232, 236
absorption 105, 112, 239, 246
abstractions 8–9, 18, 153
accretions 290–1
act of going for refuge 19, 64, 249, 257, 288, 290
actions 12, 85, 87, 194, 211–12, 238, 251, 282, 331–2
  and consequences 14, 77, 79, 81, 83, 85, 87, 89, 91
adaptations 322, 333–4
Adhiṣṭhāna Kula 1–2, 47, 83, 88–9
aesthetic sensibility 246, 302
aids 45, 58, 81, 179, 181
air 14, 61, 156, 164, 234
ālaya 107
alienated awareness 52, 238, 323
alternative traditions 319–34
altruistic dimension 98, 195–7, 291
Ambedkar 30, 43, 49–50, 58, 86, 189, 297, 333
Amitābha 114–16, 125, 134, 139, 270
Amitābha's flower 114–16
anagārika 124, 321
analogy 119, 173, 183, 232, 280

ānāpāna-sati 44, 237
anatta 132, 137, 169, 205, 250
angels 157, 159–62, 311–13
  guardian 161–2
anguish 40, 66, 129, 136, 224
anicca 96, 132, 169
antiquity 144, 173–4
aphorisms 129, 255, 311–12
applications 202–3, 279
arahant 7, 133, 151, 173, 180, 195, 269
archetypal buddhas 115, 261, 266
'Archetypal Symbolism in the Biography of the Buddha' 10, 263
archetypal world 163, 165, 302
archetypes 34, 63, 119, 146, 148, 160–1, 206, 280
architect 276, 279, 284
argosies 89
arhants 7, 173, 183, 209
arms 89, 292–3
articles 28, 30–1, 36, 81, 83, 117, 125, 174
artist 63, 65–7, 158, 280–4, 295, 304
The Artist's Dream 281, 311
arūpaloka 99
ashram 43, 114, 136
Asia 11, 31, 36, 156, 319, 330, 334

asubha 132–3
atmosphere 1, 31, 46, 54, 72, 162
authority 27, 49, 64, 186–8, 276, 281, 284
   to judge 186–9
Avalokiteśvara 46, 66, 72, 113, 114, 115, 249, 270, 292, 293, 299
aversion 203, 209, 305
The Awakening of Faith in the Mahāyāna 106–8, 330–1
The Awakening of the Heart 38, 117–18, 120–1, 140
awareness 52, 55, 94–5, 207, 239–40, 251–2, 268, 328–9
   alienated 52, 238, 323
   conscious 62, 158
   constant 145, 301
   reflexive 251–2

Barua, B.M. 203, 205
basic Buddhism 176, 183
basic teachings 191, 228, 241, 288
Batchelor, Stephen 51, 176, 224, 282, 327
beauty 18, 127–41
   pure 133–4, 333
behaviour 2, 61–2, 65, 82, 103–4, 293, 328–9
   sexual 3, 82, 84–5, 87, 89, 314, 334
beings, sentient 66, 114, 138, 180, 256
Bennett, Allan 320
Bhante 4, 29, 70, 85, 315
   conversation with 82–5
bhāvanā 44, 242, 244
bhikkhu sangha 57–8, 290, 325
bhikkhus 13, 30–3, 57, 133, 157, 172, 175, 262, 320–1, 326
Bible 56, 62, 157–8, 280
biology 250, 252, 308
Blake, William 11, 73, 97, 119, 148–53, 167, 255, 299, 302
Blavatsky, Mme 7, 143, 250
blessings 46–7, 58, 101, 189, 237, 266
bliss 48, 60, 237, 242, 333
blood 47, 288
blossoms 48, 121, 174, 189, 209
Bodhicaryāvatāra 27, 214
bodhicitta 137–8, 173, 195–7, 213–14, 220–1, 228–9, 256–7, 292–3
bodhisattva figures 44, 162, 218, 245–6, 266, 270–1
Bodhisattva Ideal 195–6, 220, 222, 226, 259, 265, 271
bodhisattva path 105, 172, 190, 210, 214, 220–1, 245
Bodhisattva Principle 105, 210, 251, 257
bodhisattvas 159–61, 163–4, 195–7, 212–14, 220–2, 256–7, 266–71, 298–9
   of compassion 66, 72, 113, 115
Bombay 30, 43, 56

bonds 5, 53, 91, 111
Book of Enlightened Masters 13
branches 27, 30, 145, 174, 178, 182–3, 186, 219
breadth 121, 176, 178, 202, 235
breezes 36, 116, 138, 287
bridges 70, 314
Britain 49, 51, 72, 227, 276, 327
British Army 34, 38, 172
Buddha see also *Introductory Note*
   imagining 261–72
   meeting 261–4
   reimagining 266–72
buddha figures 27, 44, 46, 166, 240, 298
buddha land 304, 327
buddha nature 17, 94, 140, 228–9, 234, 246
   dangers 226–9
   and path of regular steps 224–30
Buddhadasa 65, 68
Buddhaghosa 205, 211
Buddhahood 34–5, 93–4, 147, 193–4, 218, 221–2, 226, 265–9
Buddha's Enlightenment 201–2, 263
Buddhism
   as living experience 174–5
   as organic whole 178–80
   perceiving unity 176–7
Buddhist community 194, 196
Buddhist history 95, 172, 174, 179, 183, 201, 232, 270
Buddhist life 8, 16, 78, 86, 169, 184, 193, 290
Buddhist movement 2, 12, 72, 75, 109, 120–1, 283, 319
Buddhist Romanticism 123–4
Buddhist schools 9, 28, 105, 181, 194, 199, 226, 314
Buddhist scriptures *see* scriptures
Buddhist Society 51–2, 57, 171
Buddhist teachings 9–10, 86, 123, 173, 190, 217, 225, 250
Buddhist traditions 4–6, 93, 95, 105, 174–6, 269–70, 319–20, 334–5
Buddhist unity 180, 189, 199
Buddhist World 172–3
Buddhophany 267, 269, 271–2
buds 117, 233–4, 239, 278
businesses, right-livelihood 278, 283, 298, 313, 321

captain 314
causality 164, 210, 232, 259, 331
caves 46, 63, 97, 114, 157–8, 277
celibacy 41, 62, 81, 137, 309, 321
Central London 4, 7, 58
central period 20, 208, 213, 216–19
ceremonies 46, 280

cessation 200, 203, 205, 245
Ceylon 124, 172
chambers 34, 97
charisma 336
Chattrul 44–5, 189
chef-d'œuvre 287, 304
Chen, Yogi 45, 49, 244–5
children 37–8, 54, 60, 159, 309, 313
The Children's Encyclopaedia 37
Chinese x, 25, 49, 124, 319
Chögyam Trungpa 60, 227, 327–9, 334
Christian theology 94, 132
Christianity 79, 131–2, 149, 152, 156, 159–60, 325
churches 55, 81, 155–6
classes 4, 53, 66, 155, 277
clouds 54, 86, 112, 280
co–operative businesses 70, 279
coherence 16, 122, 150, 185
Coleridge, Samuel 120–2, 148
colours 3, 5, 131, 149, 164, 206, 240
commentaries 17, 97, 106, 162, 215, 217, 242
commitment 86, 172, 193–4, 197, 290–1, 298, 308, 324
communication 10, 45, 61, 83, 106, 140, 209, 235, 285, 291, 307
community 279–80, 285, 294–5, 301, 306–7, 309–10, 315–16, 321–2
    Buddhist 194, 196
    challenges 305–13
    spiritual 278–9, 283, 285, 287–317
companions 2, 35, 71, 308
companionship 53, 88
compassion 66, 113, 115–16, 121, 130–1, 135, 137–40, 292
Complete Works 19, 185, 217, 311
complexity 2, 39, 199, 285, 319
conditionality 199–216, 218, 232–3, 256, 258–9, 330–1
    cyclic 203, 208
    levels of 210–11
    making accessible 206–10
    and nirvāṇa 199
    progressive 97, 204–5, 208, 210, 212, 232, 246, 268
conditioned existence 99, 108, 132–3, 175, 207, 221, 252
conditions 14, 137, 182, 202–3, 205–6, 232–5, 267, 294, 331
confidence 164, 188–9, 299–300, 306
conflicts 58, 150, 238, 240, 293, 302–3
consciousness 17–18, 63, 93–109, 214–15, 239–40, 249–50
    absolute 232, 236
    human 17, 100, 148, 228
    normal 39, 268
    ordinary 132, 238

consumerism 303
controversy 10, 21, 81, 312–13
Corbin, Henry 165
correspondence 32, 112, 125, 145–7, 150, 159–60, 221, 266
cosmic perspectives 256–8
cosmos 99–102, 183, 256
counterculture 53, 61, 81, 84, 255, 297
craving 83, 132, 203, 207, 209, 263, 308, 331
crazy wisdom 327–9
creative mind 15, 206–8, 246
Creative Symbols 10, 47, 145, 225
creativity 86, 97, 199, 208, 257, 282
creator 63, 158, 282
critical ecumenicalism 319
criticism 2–3, 15, 83, 181, 328
Criticism East and West 15
critics 56–7, 64, 82, 87, 118, 151, 171
Crowley, Aleister 320
culture 26, 118–19, 124, 160, 300–301, 305, 312, 321
    modern 119, 144, 332
    popular 128, 302
cyclic conditionality 203, 208

The Daily Telegraph 303
ḍākas 193, 209
ḍākinīs 6, 34, 74–5, 193, 209
Dalits 30
dangers 8, 11, 42, 226, 229, 337
Darjeeling 34, 124
darkness 15, 58, 117, 123, 157, 179, 187, 263
Davids, Caroline Rhys 133, 211
death 78, 157–8, 161, 199, 244–5, 329, 334, 337–8
A Defence of Poetry 304
Delamere, Terry 53–6, 66, 155
demons 26–7, 73–5
dependence 131, 232, 267, 331
    emotional 308, 312
depictions 157, 160, 271
depths 52–3, 73–4, 140–1, 156–8, 178, 197, 218, 239–40
desert 59, 158
desk 27–8, 78, 158
devotees 109, 128, 134, 265
devotion 10, 33, 35, 101–2, 134, 185, 208, 243, 269–70, 272, 322, 334
dhamma-niyama 212, 215
Dhardo Rimpoche 45, 50, 195–6
Dharma 5–6, 50–2, 120–1, 170–1, 192–4, 210–14, 233–4, 315–17
    Eye 151, 195
    practice 82, 88, 125, 133, 224, 231, 247, 268, 283, 297, 302, 307–8, 311, 314
    teacher 10–11, 139, 158, 237, 302
dharma-niyama 212–13, 215, 244, 246–7, 257–8

dharmakāya 264–5
Dharmapāla, Anagārika 30, 189, 333
dhyāna 105, 239–40, 244, 263
diamond 35–6, 93, 104
Diamond Sutra 7–8, 17, 36, 53–4, 79, 86, 111, 160, 170, 213, 228
difficulties 49, 67, 79–80, 275–6, 305, 309, 337
Diotima 135
disagreements 83, 313–17
disciples 48, 114, 116, 188, 227–8, 284–5, 295, 313–17
 female 60, 328
discipleship 2, 15, 285, 313, 317
disciplines 33, 171, 253
Discourses x, 132–3, 162, 169–70, 179–81, 200, 202–4, 261–2
disguise 58, 161
The Disinherited Mind 144
divine beings 99–100
divine vision 149–50
doctor 77–8
doctrines 7–8, 127, 132, 177–84, 186, 200, 203, 205
dreams 13, 16, 21, 43, 89, 146, 154, 281–2
drugs 59, 80, 229
Dudjom Rimpoche 48, 196
dukkha 132, 169, 202
duty 50, 56, 235, 315, 332

earth 35–6, 81, 135, 153, 156, 191, 209, 219, 253
earthly love 135, 137, 140, 147
eastern Tibet 41, 44
echo 129, 148, 263, 310
ecstasy 6, 48, 66, 162
editors 18, 30, 112
ego 17, 43, 86, 104, 226–7
ego-clinging 214, 244, 272
eightfold path 117, 151, 219, 223
Ellis, Robert 223–4
emancipation 97, 170, 192, 232
embodiment 6, 69, 160–1, 215, 259, 270, 292–3
emotional dependence 308, 312
emotional exchange 83
emotional life 32, 39
emotional positivity 230, 239, 242, 296
emotions 32, 52, 127, 136–7, 150, 152, 232, 238, 265, 268, 306
 positive 237, 242–4, 246, 296
empowerments 45, 285
emptiness 137, 330
enchantment 103, 113, 124
encouragement 125, 230, 298, 306, 312
energies 8–9, 43–4, 72–5, 87–8, 127, 212–13, 232, 267
 deep 73, 283
 unconscious 52, 62, 239

engagement 9, 21, 32, 79, 96, 257, 267, 302
England 29, 32–3, 39, 50, 69, 72, 250–1, 319
English Sangha Trust 49, 51, 56
Enlightenment 46–7, 108–9, 115–16, 121–2, 179–82, 221–5, 235–6, 262–4
 Buddha 201–2, 263
 Supreme 109, 195
equality 312, 326, 331
erotic love 130, 138
esotericists 143–4
essays 15–16, 20, 39, 96, 103, 114, 117, 135, 137, 147, 149, 151, 156–7, 203–4, 206, 214, 225
essence 46, 98, 149, 177, 186, 189, 224, 323–4
The Essence of Zen 224
The Essential Sangharakshita 18, 98
The Eternal Legacy 28, 162, 262
eternity 221–2, 237, 265
ethical observances 181, 290
ethical precepts 288, 290
ethics 81, 171, 208, 228–9, 234, 236, 243, 325, 328
evolution 250–2, 254, 256–9, 313
 lower 251, 258, 308, 310–11
existence 96–7, 130–1, 145–6, 149–52, 157–8, 205–8, 211–12, 258–9
 conditioned 99, 108, 132–3, 175, 207, 221, 252
 mundane 105, 333
 ordinary 94, 134, 208
expansion 89, 97–8, 239
expansive movement 96, 98, 214
experience
 levels of 45, 100, 220, 241–2
 ordinary 9, 93, 107, 204, 218, 221
 personal 40, 78, 99, 181, 187, 317, 336
 of reality 36, 62, 100
experiments 280
exploration 45, 159, 241, 256
Extending the Hand of Fellowship 134, 325

faces 31, 52, 72, 293, 295, 334
Facing Mount Kanchenjunga 169
faculties 11, 148–50, 161, 184, 187, 208, 272
 imaginal 165–6
faith 43, 106–9, 151, 153, 185, 264, 266, 330–1
families 37, 51, 88, 281, 294, 307–9, 313
family life 305, 308, 310
father 3, 89, 97, 308
feelings 32, 39–40, 62, 79, 84, 137, 235, 238, 270
female disciples 60, 328
feminism 81, 326
five spiritual faculties 151, 184
flames 73, 335
flesh 13, 47, 60, 70, 203, 244
flowers 12, 113, 183–5, 232–5, 239, 335–9

golden 116
followers 30, 43, 50, 58, 180–1, 194–6, 290, 297
forces 37, 57, 73–4, 87, 137–8, 214, 217, 303–4
  deep psychic 62, 86
  impersonal 44, 86, 214
  supra–personal cosmic 36, 214
forest whispers 154
forests 71, 113, 153–4, 278, 330
formalism 186, 196
formalities 193, 325
formulations 111–12, 182, 202–3, 208–10, 213, 224, 245, 263
  conceptual 182, 200
  positive 200, 204
foundations 8, 57, 147, 228, 234, 279, 288
founders 7, 12, 88, 188, 192, 275–6, 305, 319, 336
France 55, 155
freedom 4–6, 10, 44, 81, 89, 106, 154, 245, 328, 337
friends 4, 29–30, 32, 65–6, 139–40, 228–9, 277, 284–5
Friends of the Western Buddhist Order *see* FWBO
friendship 235–6, 241, 243, 285, 291, 296–7, 306–7, 309–10
  horizontal and vertical 295–7
From Genesis to the Diamond Sutra 79, 160
fruits 29, 174, 191, 233, 264, 280, 289
FWBO (Friends of the Western Buddhist Order) 2–3, 67–70, 78–9, 277–83, 291–2, 299–300, 303–5, 314–16
  centres 4, 70, 72, 81, 230, 307
FWBO Newsletter 67, 69, 73, 230, 277

garden 43, 63, 235, 277, 280, 338
gardener 276–7, 279–80, 284, 295
Gautama 264
gender 281, 308, 310–13, 334
Ginsberg, Allen 29, 328
glory 125, 265, 292, 338
goals 16–17, 58, 94, 104, 106, 135, 230, 268
goddesses 100, 163, 299
gods 73–4, 94, 100, 160, 163, 223, 253, 330
going for refuge 193
  act of 19, 64, 249, 257, 288, 290
  and lifestyle 196–7
gold 25, 60–1, 103, 129, 134, 139, 155, 209, 232, 262
golden flower 116
golden light 153, 244, 298–301, 304
goldfish 40
Goldstein, Joseph 322–7
Govinda 42, 124–5, 174–5
  Lama 32, 35, 38, 42, 124, 129, 140, 144, 174, 176, 219, 272

gravitational pull 210, 238, 311
Greece 42, 55, 156
Green Tārā 45, 134
growing plant 119, 232–3, 268, 289
growth 70, 121, 174, 184, 208, 230–47
  organic 183, 205, 232–3, 254, 258
  and the path 231–6
  spiritual 17, 121, 123, 233
Guanyin 160–1
guardian 79, 81, 193, 239
guardian angel 161–2
Guhyaloka 77, 79–80
guidance 2, 43, 45, 74, 95, 226, 256, 284
guiding principles 182, 291, 293–5
guru 73, 192–3, 285, 328
  meeting 25–50
Guru Rimpoche 34, 192
guru-yoga 47

Hampstead Buddhist Vihara 51, 57–9, 81, 157, 217, 320, 323, 334
happiness 204, 308
headship 80, 314–15
heart 36, 47, 113–14, 117–18, 120–1, 138, 140–1, 156–8
  of Buddhism 209, 245
  human 121, 140
Heart Sutra 27
heaven 36, 104, 133, 135, 149, 167, 209, 234
Heller, Eric 144
The Heritage of Buddhism 28, 30
heroic ideal 229–30
Herrick, Robert 39
hierarchy 101, 128, 151, 161, 218, 265, 292, 295, 297, 332
  of being 101, 303, 332
  spiritual 101, 292, 295
Higher Evolution 19, 64, 69, 123, 249–59, 308, 311
Himalayas 34, 42
Hīnayāna 146, 169, 173, 180–5, 190–1, 195, 203
Hindu caste system 30, 38
hippies 29, 229
historical Buddha 170, 190–1, 195, 261, 266
historical reality 164–5
history, Buddhist 95, 172, 174, 179, 183, 201, 232, 270
The History of My Going for Refuge 8–9, 11–12, 86–7, 176, 178, 193–4, 201, 213, 281–2
Hoffmann, Ernst Lothar 124
holiness 120, 156, 268
home 1, 4, 38, 41, 77, 82, 139, 163
homosexuality 39, 57, 81–2, 310
horizontal integration 151, 239
houses 37–8, 99, 103, 228, 234, 338

Index   377

human activities 158, 300, 311
human beings 98–9, 103, 118, 123, 128, 140, 251–2, 254–5
human consciousness 17, 100, 148, 228
human heart 121, 140
human nature 102, 108
humanistic psychology 123, 236, 331
humanity 31, 42, 73, 119, 150, 186, 231, 253, 277, 307, 323
Humphreys, Christmas 51, 57

idealism 131–2, 299, 305–7
ideals 195, 229, 262, 270, 280, 288, 295, 299, 305–6
  shared 295, 297
ignorance 202–3, 209, 236
Il Convento 156–7, 160, 165–6
Illumined Path 111–25, 300
illusions 213, 246, 254, 276, 330
image thinking 16, 217, 337
imagery 6, 10, 97, 133, 231, 287
  tantric 42, 45
images 4–6, 9–11, 34–5, 97–9, 143, 155–61, 165–6, 231–4
  concrete 9, 182
imaginal faculty 165–6
imagination 15–16, 143–66, 200–201, 267–8, 271–2, 280
immanence 94, 141, 224
impermanence 96, 132, 245, 267
impersonal force 44, 86, 214
IMS (Insight Meditation Society) 323
The Inconceivable Emancipation 163
indefinable motivation 213–14
India 19–20, 30–1, 39, 41, 43, 49–52, 54–5, 71
  South 107, 114
Indian Buddhists 203, 269, 297
Indians 38, 41, 48, 70, 131, 197, 231, 327
individualism 183, 326
  spiritual 173, 181, 183
individuality 213, 294–5, 313, 328, 332
individuals 69–70, 74, 249, 252, 283, 285, 291, 294–5
  committed 291, 300
Indra 107
inequality 312, 332
infinite light 115, 179, 263
infinity 111–12
inhabitants 99, 166
inimitable music 6, 106
initiations 44–6, 48, 60, 89, 314
inji gelong 172
inner life 16, 55, 122, 157
insight meditation 324–5
Insight Meditation Society (IMS) 323
insomnia 80, 314
institutions 144, 280, 283, 300, 314, 337

insubstantiality 132, 267
integration 33, 53, 62, 151, 237–8, 240, 243, 246, 263, 327
  horizontal 151, 239
  vertical 151, 239, 268
intention 11, 46, 57, 251–2, 336–7
interbeing 329–33
interconnectedness 107, 330
interpreter 29, 63, 157–8
intuition 11–13, 60, 86, 144, 174, 187, 282–3
Italy 55, 155–6, 159, 161

Jamyang Khyentse Rimpoche 45–6, 163
Jerome *see* St Jerome
jñāna 266
The Journey to Il Convento 156–7, 160, 165
joy 66, 85, 129, 136, 138, 156, 204, 242, 245, 281
judgements 186, 188
justice 14–15, 19, 102, 178, 211, 220

Kachu Rimpoche 27, 45–6, 48, 192
Kalimpong 25–7, 29–31, 34, 41–2, 44–5, 139, 191, 195–6
kalyāṇa-mitra 297, 306, 328
kāmaloka 99
karma 211–12, 256
karma-niyama 213, 215, 246, 256
Karuṇā 138
Kermode, Frank 143
Khantipalo, Bhikkhu 26–8, 31–2, 41, 50
kindness 28, 243, 311
knowledge 3, 9, 63, 68, 145, 157, 223–4, 229, 244, 276

ladder 101, 135, 209
lakes 107, 116
lamas 44, 100, 192, 328
language 9–10, 149, 152, 208–9, 211, 226, 233–4, 302
The Language of Scents 107
late papers 246–7
law 12, 39, 202, 206, 211–12, 232, 256, 289
Lawrence, D.H. 23, 119, 294, 302
layers 32, 117, 121, 241, 262
LBC (London Buddhist Centre) 70, 72–3
lectures 4–5, 69–70, 163–5, 175, 233–6, 251, 261–3, 298–303
legends 10, 34, 69, 236, 264
letters 32, 56, 102, 104, 180, 190, 246, 292
levels of experience 45, 100, 220, 241–2
levels of reality 132, 157
Li Gotami 35, 125
liberation 5, 9, 12, 37, 59, 73, 105, 140, 190, 205
lifestyle 20, 196–7, 235, 287, 290, 297, 308, 326
lifetimes 17, 281, 323, 329, 334

light 26, 31, 47–8, 115, 117, 120–1, 157, 201–2
  infinite 115, 179, 263
limitations 14, 19, 129, 223, 266, 268
lineages 192, 264, 269, 285, 330, 337
listeners 101, 104, 129, 164–5, 207, 209, 217, 226
literalism 184, 201
living beings 195, 237, 253, 289
living organisms 16, 118, 174, 179, 182, 232
logic 12, 14, 86, 177, 187, 282
Lokamitra 71–2, 305
London 5, 51, 55, 68, 74, 165
  Central 4, 7, 58
  North 51, 67
  South 4, 320
London Buddhist Centre 70–5, 230, 283, 338
lotuses 114–18, 122–3, 192, 231, 241, 245, 269–70, 277–8
  growing like a lotus 116–25
  in the mud 116–18
  thousand-petalled lotus 234, 239
  thousand-petalled rose 124–5
love 18, 40, 124, 127–41, 153, 266–7, 300, 306, 308
  earthly 135, 137, 140, 147
  erotic 130, 138
  mode 289, 292, 300
lovers 40, 84, 129–30, 135–8
loving-kindness practice 44, 52
Lower Evolution 251, 258, 308, 310–11

machines 118–19, 255, 277
Madhyamaka 184–5
Madhyamaloka 3, 82, 315
  community 2, 80
magnitudes 111
Maha Bodhi 186
The Mahabodhi Journal 30
Maharshi, Ramana 114, 135
Mahāyāna 162–6, 169–70, 177, 180–6, 189–91, 195–6, 200, 210
Mahāyānists 182, 184
mainstream society 38, 157
mandalas 18, 53, 125, 146–7, 151, 240
Mañjughoṣa 46, 225, 271
mantras 35, 68, 88, 115, 147, 246, 267
masculine qualities 208, 309, 311
meals 2, 28
meditation 133–4, 188–9, 208, 236–41, 246, 280, 288–9, 325–6
  practices 27, 182, 228, 238, 242, 323
  retreats 236–7
  system of 238, 243, 245–6
meditators 105, 144, 277
Mehta, Dr 43
Mellor, Philip 187

memoirs 7, 13, 16, 20, 26, 32, 65–6, 111–13
memories 3, 21, 79
mental states 55, 99, 105, 207, 235, 251, 293, 330
metaphors 9, 120–1, 161, 182–3, 209–10, 272, 288
  architectural 121, 280, 288
metaphysical order 144–5
mettā 44, 136, 242–4, 296
mettābhāvanā 44, 242, 244
Metteya 320–1
Midas 103
The Middle Way 159, 171
Milarepa 17, 106, 162
Mills, Laurence 26
mindfulness 27–8, 44, 184, 207–8, 237–8, 240, 243–4, 325–6
  movement 323, 331
  teachers 3, 326
The Mirror and the Lamp 119
mirrors 107, 119, 135, 244, 304
mitras 4, 89, 306
mleccha 38
modern culture 119, 144, 332
modern world 30, 70, 144, 302, 320, 325, 329
monasteries 55, 156, 281, 322, 330
monastic code 169, 196
monastic community 38, 172
monastic life 196, 321
monastic ordination 172, 270, 329
monastic sangha 49, 196
monasticism 52, 64, 196–7, 290, 320–2, 325
monastics 194, 196–7, 290, 308, 322–3, 326
monks 27, 29, 54, 60, 62, 64–5, 196–7, 321–2
  western 58, 322
Monmouth Street 58, 60, 69, 287
moon 9, 116, 129, 141, 171, 210–11, 292
moral responsibility 331–2
morality 65, 189
mosaics 155
motivations 61, 82, 85, 87, 133, 213–14, 251, 306
mountains 43, 67, 99, 107, 113–14, 223, 253
Moving against the Stream 32, 53, 58, 66
mūla-yoga 48, 192
mundane existence 105, 333
Munindra 322–3
Murry, John Middleton 12, 15–16, 122, 336
music 13, 103, 106, 109, 127, 129, 164, 302
My Relation to the Order 276, 278, 284–5, 316
mystery 14–15, 111–12, 137, 139, 259, 263
myths 10, 146, 148, 150, 164–5, 280, 283–4, 302

Nagabodhi 54, 65, 68, 82, 230
Nāgārjuna 158, 160, 215, 269

Nagpur 30, 43–4, 214
nationalism 303
natural world 39, 86, 244–5
nature 18–19, 147–8, 151–4, 212–13, 218–19, 236–7, 242–4, 289–90
  essential 174, 262
  human 102, 108
Naturphilosophie 118
Neoplatonic temperament 131–5
Neoplatonism 131–2, 136, 138, 143, 151, 265
New Society, new culture 297–303
new world 219, 254, 279, 282–3
nidāna 202–5, 232, 242, 250
Nietzsche, Friedrich 39, 253–8, 302, 311
nirmāṇakāya 264–5
nirvāṇa 9, 93–4, 104–9, 200–201, 204, 206, 210, 215, 220–2
  conceiving 199–201
  and conditionality 199
  and *saṃsāra* 205–6
nirvāṇa, scent of 106–9
niyamas 211–13, 256, 258–9, 293
Noble Friendship 26–7
noble truths 117, 175, 202, 220
non–duality 138, 225
North America 319, 323, 327
nuns 29, 322, 330

oak tree 120, 279
observance 288–9, 308, 327
ocean 5–6, 40, 106, 141, 158, 173, 233
openness 61, 95, 297, 324
Order 287–93
  members 78, 243–4, 288, 290–3, 297, 305–6, 308, 313–17
ordinations 57, 78, 89, 116, 193, 196–7, 284–5, 310, 314–16
  monastic 172, 270, 329
  private 287, 337
organic growth 183, 205, 232–3, 254, 258
organic thinking 119, 123, 148, 178, 230, 259
organic understanding 118–23
organic unity 16, 122, 182–6
organizers 72, 282
original teachings 170, 179, 181, 183–4, 190–1, 227, 323
origins 39, 170, 174, 250, 308
Oriya Encyclopaedia 28
The Outsider 37–9
outsiders 37–9, 230
outward forms 122, 178, 283, 287, 298, 334
'overman' 253–4

Padmaloka 4, 77–8, 338
Padmasambhava 21, 34–7, 45–8, 68–9, 72–5, 86, 191–3, 269
  Day 68, 70–1
Pagan Mysteries in the Renaissance 136
pain 66, 129–30, 136, 312
paints 71, 281
Pāli x, 5, 13, 27, 31, 42, 56, 68, 123–4, 133, 151, 162, 164, 169, 204, 209, 211, 219, 261
Pallis, Marco 42, 144
pansil 31
'Parable of the Raincloud' 231
'Parable of the Return Journey' 97, 114, 228
Paradox and Poetry in 'The Voice of the Silence' 147
parents 4, 38, 50, 60
particles 108
partners 62, 81–4, 309, 313
  sexual 2, 81, 308
passages 12, 28, 132, 183, 233, 299
passion 32, 129, 136, 263, 281
Pater, Walter 15, 158
path
  of beauty 132–5
  to buddhahood 93–5, 166, 194
  and conditionality 199–216
  eightfold 117, 151, 219, 223
  and growth 231–6
  in practice 217–30
  of regular steps 224–30
  spiral 210, 233, 243
  spiritual 7, 82, 101, 112, 135, 137, 204, 229, 233, 247, 291
  of transformation 48, 53, 113, 219
  versions 218–24
  of vision 53, 73, 113, 219
peace 80, 85, 130, 237, 311, 329
peaks 25, 62, 72, 107
Perfect Vision 54, 113, 123, 151, 219–20
perfection 122, 133, 158, 196, 222, 247, 266
perfume 107–8, 138, 164
personal development 230, 291, 297
personal experience 40, 78, 99, 181, 187, 317, 336
personalities 33, 73, 88, 120, 213, 268, 325, 328
petals 116, 125, 184, 239, 241, 289
phenomena 96, 107, 122, 131, 146–7, 202, 256, 292, 330–1
philosophy 13, 95, 125, 131–2, 171, 204, 223, 236, 273, 330
physical body 157, 238, 265
pigs 128, 209
pillars 280, 288–9
planes 105, 146, 157, 165
planets 11, 138

380   Index

plants 48, 120–3, 153, 178, 184, 231, 233–5, 241
   growing 119, 232–3, 268, 289
Platform Sutra 7, 17
Plato 97, 131, 135, 137, 302
Platonism 131, 143
Plotinus 131, 151
poetry 13–16, 33, 36–41, 85–6, 116–17, 129–30, 137–8
   the world as 102–6
poets 11, 15–16, 29, 86, 95, 103, 111–13, 153
politics 303–4
positive emotion 237, 242–4, 246, 296
positivity, emotional 230, 239, 242, 296
potencies 111–12
power 18, 85–6, 88, 147–8, 150, 153, 272–3, 276
   dynamics 294, 305
   imbalance 83–4
   mode 289, 292, 296, 300
practice, system of 178, 236–40, 338
practitioners 44, 185, 192–3, 214, 225, 237, 239, 265–7, 295
   spiritual 109, 214, 307
preceptors 284
   public 78, 80, 297, 314
precepts 13, 31, 193, 228, 287–90, 308
Precious Teachers 34, 79
precursors 29, 146, 250, 320
prince 114
private ordination 287, 337
progress 13, 210, 214–15, 242, 281, 287
   spiritual 45, 228, 320
progression 102, 125, 222, 258, 329
progressive conditionality 97, 204–5, 208, 210, 212, 232, 246, 268
progressive trends 205, 213, 215, 246, 256
Prometheus Unbound 36
prostration practice 47, 192, 194
'Protestant Buddhism' 79, 332
pseudo–egalitarianism 304, 332
psyche 12, 21, 33, 69, 74, 240
psychic depths 48, 52, 239, 329
psychological conditionings 35, 255
psychology 52, 99, 149, 239
   humanistic 123, 236, 331
public preceptors 78, 80, 297, 314
puja 52, 68–9, 242
Pundarika 67–9, 72
purification 46, 97, 267
purity 41, 133, 237
   original 225–6, 331

qualifications 98, 276
qualities 2, 44–5, 47, 61, 114, 200, 242, 294
   enlightened 115, 218, 245
   masculine 208, 309, 311

radiant figures 134, 209
raft 9, 173, 179–81, 280
rain 28, 121, 219, 278
The Rainbow Road 32, 112
rainbows 1, 10, 112, 164
Ratana Sutta 27
rational mind 14, 93, 96, 255
Ravenna 155
Rawlinson, Andrew 13–14, 324–5
rays 26, 48, 189
reactive mind 207–8
reactivity 97, 208
reality 99–100, 141, 146–50, 199–201, 205–6, 218–19, 257–9, 267–8
   degrees of 100–101
   historical 164–5
   levels of 132, 157
   transcendent 111, 115, 218
   ultimate 105, 108, 199, 212, 218
realization 8, 12, 187, 194, 202–3, 255, 259, 263
realms 99, 105, 159
rebirth 105, 134, 203, 244
receptivity 95, 159, 230, 302, 311
refinement 68, 163, 239, 268
reflection 15, 78–9, 88, 107, 111–12, 218, 221, 292, 299
reflexive awareness 251–2
refuge 45–7, 191–2, 194–7, 241–2, 249, 256–8, 287–8, 290–3, 324–7
   going for *see* going for refuge
   tree 191–5, 267, 269
refugees 191–2
regret 88–9, 312
regular steps, path of 224–30
relationships 96, 125, 132, 140, 185, 193, 306–7, 309
   sexual 82, 309
religion 42, 118, 121, 127–8, 131, 152, 171, 250–2
The Religion of Art 13, 103, 128, 153, 206
residential communities 70, 278, 298, 308, 310, 313
responsibilities 57–8, 78–9, 213, 238, 251, 277, 284, 293–4, 309, 312, 315, 331, 337
   moral 331–2
reticence 32, 82, 104
   metaphysical 212, 258
retreat centres 1, 70–1, 323
retreats 61, 70, 287, 298, 325
reverberations 34–5, 175
reverence 101–2, 123, 225
rhythms 4, 102–3
   deeper 15, 103, 336
right–livelihood businesses 278, 283, 298, 313, 321
rituals 5, 26, 236, 250, 280, 334

Index 381

road 39, 112, 171, 280
rocks 85, 145, 156, 158
Roerich, George 42
Romantic Image 143
Romanticism 118, 123, 253
Romantics 65, 123–4, 143, 154, 257, 282
  High 118, 143, 253
roots 42, 69, 174, 178, 182–3, 192, 219, 234, 244, 282
rumours 41, 51
rūpaloka 99

sādhana 27, 44–6, 48, 163, 225, 245, 266–8
St Jerome 62–3, 157–60, 166, 283
St Jerome Revisited 63, 78, 157–8, 160
saints 7, 16, 63, 155, 252, 262
Sakura 59, 66, 276
Śākyamuni 35, 269 *see also* historical Buddha
samādhi 44, 244
sambhogakāya 164, 264–6
sambodhi 201, 203
saṃsāra 93–4, 99, 105, 107, 121, 173, 205–8, 210, 220–1
Sangha 192–4, 239, 241, 243, 249, 285, 288, 293
  creation 293–7
  monastic 49, 196
Sangha Association 51
Sangharakshita see also *Introductory Note*
  imagination 18, 141, 155–67
  life 1, 8, 12, 17–19, 21, 62, 71, 79, 85–6, 157, 239, 338
  and modern Buddhism 333–4
  roles 275–85
  teaching 19, 58, 206, 217, 223, 225, 241, 334
  under the surface 32–4
  work 29–32
Sanskrit 27, 219
Śāntarakṣita 34
sapling 219, 280
scent of nirvāna 106–9
schools 38, 93–5, 169–70, 172, 177, 183–5, 188–9, 192
science 88, 99, 171, 211, 251
scriptures 95, 164–5, 171–2, 174, 180, 186–8, 190, 245
  Pāli 56, 163–4
A Season in Hell 80, 314
Second World War 11, 30
secret 12, 16, 46, 82, 146, 302
secret life 16, 55
sectarianism 30, 171, 173–4
seeds 118, 184, 211, 287, 335–9
self–consciousness 215
self–transcendence 127, 257–8

selfhood 103, 166, 205, 255, 299
sentient beings 66, 114, 138, 180, 256
sex 53–4, 59–60, 62, 64, 81–4, 294, 306–10, 312, 328
sexual activity/behaviour 3, 57, 79, 81–5, 89, 314, 334, 337
sexual feelings 39–46, 60
sexual partners 2, 81, 308
sexual relations 61, 84
sexuality 41, 65
shadows 39, 97, 158, 239
Shelley 11, 36, 86, 124, 131, 159, 302
shrine of Love 130
shrines 26, 29, 57, 287
Sierra de Aitana 77
silence 28, 80, 102–3, 130, 147, 162, 199–200, 287, 338
skull 78
sleep 60, 80, 111, 123
Smaller Sukhāvatī-vyūha Sūtras 169
snobbishness 303
social change 279, 298, 303–4
soil 48, 121, 153, 182–3, 234, 243, 278
Songs of Milarepa 17, 162
sotāpanna 37
soul 12, 36–7, 40, 79, 134–5, 138, 152, 154
South India 107, 114
speech 48, 193, 209, 221
spiral path 210, 233, 243
spirals 207–10, 215, 218, 232
spiritual community 278–9, 283, 285, 287–317
spiritual death 157, 237, 244–7, 338
spiritual development 98, 173, 202, 233, 244, 249, 252, 300, 304, 320
spiritual energy 6, 49, 72–3, 75, 189, 200, 214, 293, 298–9
spiritual experience 3, 88, 96, 103, 219, 233, 245, 250
spiritual friends 28, 283–5, 296, 306
spiritual friendship 121, 296–7
spiritual growth 17, 121, 123, 233
spiritual hierarchy 101, 292, 295
spiritual individualism 173, 181, 183
spiritual life 73–4, 101–2, 121–3, 184–5, 187–8, 203–4, 222–3, 230–1
spiritual path 7, 82, 101, 112, 135, 137, 204, 229, 233, 247, 291
spiritual progress 45, 228, 320
spiritual realities 13, 165, 264, 272
spiritual rebirth 194, 237, 244–7, 338
spiritual teachers 11, 276, 296
spiritual values 120, 145, 170, 301
spiritualism 43
śrāmaṇera 116, 193
standpoint 200, 223, 290
stars 20, 36, 40, 127, 129–31, 134–8, 140, 147

Stepping Stones 117, 124, 172–4
stones 29, 145, 262, 280, 289, 299
stream entry 173, 195, 210, 214, 220, 242
subha 132–3
Subhuti 82–3, 85–7, 225, 258, 267, 271, 302, 311–14
Sumedho 58, 322, 334
sun 26, 113, 115, 123, 138, 151, 156, 189–90, 209, 211, 221, 231, 265
The Sunflower's Farewell 338–9
sunshine 243, 278, 330
supporters 30, 57–9, 276, 334
supportive conditions 121, 235, 298
supra–personal force 85–91, 103
Śūraṅgamasamādhi Sūtra 163
A Survey of Buddhism 95–6, 175–82, 185–7, 189–90, 195–7, 201–2, 232, 263–5
  book with a mission 175–6
Sutra of Golden Light 153, 244, 298–9, 301
sutras/suttas x, 36, 134, 162–6, 169–70, 204, 218, 280
  world of 162–5
symbolism 9–10, 34–6, 42, 72, 143–4, 146–8, 208, 263
Symbols of Tibetan Buddhist Art 146
Symposium 131, 135, 137
System of Meditation 238, 243, 245–6
system of practice 178, 236–40, 338

Tamil Nadu 114
Tantras 36, 52, 147, 150, 184–5, 302, 328
tantric imagery 42, 45
tantric initiation 21, 29, 134, 192, 194
tantric practices 27, 47, 145–6, 328
Tārā 46, 86
  Green 45, 134
tathāgatagarbha 226
teachers 45, 47, 84, 269–70, 275–6, 284–5, 315–16, 325
teachings 9–11, 63–4, 179–81, 187–91, 223–9, 269–70, 313–17, 329–32
  original 170, 179, 181, 183–4, 190–1, 227, 323
teenagers 3, 38, 89, 103, 131, 149, 306, 310, 331
temperaments 11, 131
temples 41, 114, 280, 289, 330
tensions 13, 33, 49, 95, 109, 173, 276, 281, 285, 305, 307
tertön 73–4
testimonies 14, 81–3, 108, 189
Thailand 322
theology, Christian 94, 132
theosophy 7, 43
Theravāda 38, 57–8, 132–3, 172–4, 182–3, 185–6, 196, 319–25
Theravādin contrasts 319–20

Thich Nhat Hanh 329–34
thinkers 10–11, 148, 250
The Thought of Sangharakshita: A Critical Assessment 223–4
thousand–petalled rose 124–5
three bodies 264–6
The Three Jewels 8–9, 12, 14, 19, 72, 131–2, 192–4, 264–6
Thus Spake Zarathustra 39, 129, 253
Tibet 25, 34, 41–2, 49, 68, 100, 124, 300, 327
  eastern 41, 44
Tibetan Buddhism 27, 36, 42, 45, 48, 69, 190, 319
Tibetan Buddhists 41, 45, 192, 324
Tibetan demons 34, 48
Tibetan traditions 27, 34, 42, 44–5, 69, 172, 269, 327
totality 165, 174
town 29, 49, 191
traces 8, 14, 16, 34, 109, 154
tradition 29–30, 131, 143–4, 172, 174–5, 185–91, 319–20, 323–5
traditional accounts 118, 240
traditional formula 131, 288
traditional sense 64, 325–6
transcendence 40, 94, 112, 130–1, 136, 140–1, 152–3
transcendent 36, 94, 108, 114, 148, 221–2, 224, 288
transcendent reality 111, 115, 218
transcendental dimension 7–8
transcendental experience 8–9
transcendental qualities 19, 200, 216, 220
transformation 48, 53, 73–4, 113, 232, 280, 302
  and vision 219–20
transition 207–8, 210–11, 215, 233, 254
translations 7, 30, 63
translator 62–3, 123, 157, 281, 283–4
tree 102–3, 155–6, 178–9, 182–3, 186, 191–2, 212, 219–20
trikāya 264
Triratna x, 3, 19, 81, 88, 269–70, 312–13, 325, 335–7
Triratna Buddhist Community 2, 85, 269
Trismegistus, Hermes 145
Triyana Vardhana Vihara 25, 189
Triyāna 189–97
true nature 7, 163, 241
trunk 174, 178–9, 182–3, 191
twigs 174, 219

Übermensch 254
Udāna 5, 133, 226, 233, 242, 261–2
Uḍḍiyāna 48
ultimate reality 105, 108, 199, 212, 218
unconscious energies 52, 62, 239

Index   383

unconscious mind 53, 156, 263
unifying factors 195
unifying visions 111–14
unity, organic 16, 122, 182–6
Unity of Buddhism 169–97
Upanisa Sutta 204
Uposatha Sutta 5

vajra 35–6, 48
Vajrasattva 48, 225
Vajrayāna 36, 41–4, 124, 145–6, 150, 170, 189–91
values 120, 128, 185, 187, 273, 279–80, 297, 301
The Veil of Stars 20, 40, 127–31, 134–7, 140, 147
Vendler, Helen 15–16
veranda 26–8
verses 46, 129, 137, 190
vertical dimension 96–100, 102, 106, 157, 193, 285
vertical integration 151, 239, 268
vibration 106, 162
Vietnam War 329–30
Vihara 26, 29–30, 50–5, 57–8, 189, 191–2, 323
    Life 27–9
villages 31, 44, 77
Vimalakīrti Nirdeśa 108, 163–4, 289, 303
Vinaya x, 169, 196, 322
vipassanā 244, 324–6
    community 307, 322, 325–6
    movement 301, 325–6
    sangha 322–7
    teachers 323, 325–7
Virgin Mary 160–1
vision 53, 73, 113, 115, 150–1, 281–2, 292–3
    and transformation 219–20
visionary 14, 74, 150, 281–2, 284, 299
visitors 2–3, 29, 37, 71, 155, 161, 236, 320

vows 41, 91, 137

war 25, 38, 49, 150
warmth 48, 61, 117, 121, 156, 296–7
water 48, 107, 116–18, 153, 182, 234, 323
waves 106, 114, 169, 302
The Way of the White Clouds 42, 112
Western Buddhism 4, 11, 51–75, 301, 327, 332
Western Buddhist Order 2, 4, 56, 59, 64, 66, 68, 315–16
    Friends *see* FWBO
western culture 42, 55, 69, 149, 162, 283, 301–2, 332
western monks 58, 322
western societies 313, 323, 326–7, 333
westerners 11, 29, 42, 123, 169, 297, 322
wheel 207–8, 210, 314
White Lotus Sutra 10, 97, 114, 226, 228, 231, 257
Wilde, Oscar 15, 119
wind 23, 60, 72, 85–7, 120, 287, 299
winters 77, 245, 338–9
wisdom 113–14, 140, 148–9, 151, 153, 227–9, 288–9, 327–9
    crazy 327–9
women 4, 39, 53, 68, 70, 78, 281, 284, 305, 309–13, 317
world of the sutras 162
worldviews 160, 326, 331–2

Yeats, W.B. 11, 16
Yi-gah Cho-ling 34–5
yidam 45–6, 193, 266–7
yoga 184–5, 238
Yogācāra 53, 107
young people 55, 60, 68, 305

Zen 52, 115, 224, 228, 319, 324

WINDHORSE PUBLICATIONS

Windhorse Publications is a Buddhist charitable company based in the UK. Our books, which are distributed internationally, champion Buddhism, meditation, and mindfulness. They offer fresh interpretations of Buddhist teachings and their application to contemporary life, with subject matter and authors from across the Buddhist tradition, catering for a broad range of interest and experience. In addition to publishing titles exploring classic texts for modern audiences, we aspire to publish books that offer a Buddhist perspective on today's challenges, including social inequality, the environment and climate, gender, mental health, and more. Established in the 1970s to publish the writing of Urgyen Sangharakshita (1925–2018), the founder of the Triratna Buddhist Order, Windhorse Publications continues to be dedicated to preserving and keeping in print his impressive and influential body of work, making it accessible for future generations. As well as high-quality print and eBooks, Windhorse Publications produces accompanying audio, podcast, video, and teaching resources.

Windhorse Publications
38 Newmarket Road
Cambridge CB5 8DT
info@windhorsepublications.com

North America Distributors: Consortium Book Sales & Distribution
210 American Drive
Jackson TN 38301
USA
https://www.cbsd.com/

Australia and New Zealand Distributors: Windhorse Books
PO Box 574
Newtown NSW 2042
Australia
https://windhorse.com.au/books.html

THE TRIRATNA BUDDHIST COMMUNITY

Windhorse Publications is a part of the Triratna Buddhist Community, an international movement with centres in Europe, India, North and South America, and Australasia. At these centres, members of the Triratna Buddhist Order offer classes in meditation and Buddhism. Activities of the Triratna Community also include retreat centres, residential spiritual communities, ethical Right Livelihood businesses, and the Karuna Trust, a UK fundraising charity that supports social welfare projects in the slums and villages of India.

Through these and other activities, Triratna is developing a unique approach to Buddhism, not simply as a philosophy and a set of techniques, but as a creatively directed way of life for all people living in the conditions of the modern world.

If you would like more information about Triratna please visit thebuddhistcentre.com or write to:

London Buddhist Centre
51 Roman Road
London E2 0HU
UK
contact@lbc.org.uk

Aryaloka
14 Heartwood Circle
Newmarket NH 03857
USA
info@aryaloka.org

Sydney Buddhist Centre
24 Enmore Road
Sydney NSW 2042
Australia
info@sydneybuddhistcentre.org.au

www.ingramcontent.com/pod-product-compliance
Lightning Source LLC
Chambersburg PA
CBHW072044110526
44590CB00018B/3025